Praise for the book

'*Annihilation of Caste* has [illegible] because it is open to serious objection. Dr Ambedkar is a challenge to Hinduism… No Hindu who prizes his faith above life itself can afford to underrate the importance of this indictment' **M.K. Gandhi**

'What *Communist Manifesto* is to the capitalist world, *Annihilation of Caste* is to caste India. Arundhati Roy's introduction is expansive and excellent. S. Anand's annotations have style and perfection' **Anand Teltumbde**, author of *The Persistence of Caste: The Khairlanji Murders & India's Hidden Apartheid*

'For the 1930s, *Annihilation of Caste* was a case of marvellous writing with conceptual clarity and political understanding—something the world should know about. The annotations illumine the whole book. Roy's essay has the sharp political thrust one has come to expect from her' **Uma Chakravarti**, author of *Everyday Lives, Everyday Histories: Beyond the Kings and Brahmanas of 'Ancient' India* and *Pandita Ramabai: A Life and a Time*

'Arundhati Roy's *The Doctor and the Saint* works both at an emotive and an argumentative level. She manages to convey an intimate and deeply felt sensitivity to the history that produced *Annihilation of Caste*. Her essay is both well documented and closely argued. The annotations do an excellent job of providing supplementary information, corroboration and relevant citations… A robust edition of an under-appreciated classic' **Satish Deshpande**, Professor of Sociology, Delhi University

'S. Anand's annotations are very thorough and on the whole based on first-rate and current scholarship on South Asia and elsewhere. Their tone and style will appeal to a scholarly as well as lay audience … an important accomplishment. Arundhati

Roy's essay is punchy, eye-opening and provocative… There is very little left of the saintly stature of the Mahatma once Roy is done with him, while Ambedkar, quite rightly, is left standing as the man in full control of his senses and his very considerable intellect' **Thomas Blom Hansen**, Director, Stanford's Center for South Asia

'This annotated edition of *Annihilation of Caste* was long overdue. It makes available to all a major text of Dr Ambedkar's, where his intellectual engagement with caste is best articulated … the copious footnotes give the reader a sense of direction and all the additional information needed for making sense of the text—including the translation of the Sanskrit shlokas Ambedkar used to document his analysis. This edition is truly a remarkable achievement' **Christophe Jaffrelot**, author of *Dr Ambedkar and Untouchability: Analysing and Fighting Caste*

'This edition, with Ambedkar's words in Nietzschean aphoristic format, is extremely useful. It helps us discover new dimensions of Ambedkar's subversive power. The annotations—many times orthogonal and tangential—enhance the value of this book. Those who have read *Annihilation of Caste* many times before will still read this work for the sake of the annotations and reference-based clarifications of Ambedkar's thoughts. This edition will foster a more critical engagement among readers' **Ayyathurai Gajendran**, anthropologist

ANNIHILATION OF CASTE

SPEECH PREPARED

BY

Dr. B. R. Ambedkar

M. A., Ph. D., D. Sc., Barrister-at-Law.

FOR

The Annual Conference of the

JAT-PAT-TODAK MANDAL OF LAHORE

BUT

NOT DELIVERED

Owing to the cancellation of the Conference by the Reception Committee on the ground that the views expressed in the speech would be unbearable to the Conference.

15th May 1936 **Price As. 8/-**

Bhimrao Ramji Ambedkar was born in 1891 into an 'Untouchable' family of modest means. One of India's most radical thinkers, he transformed the social and political landscape in the struggle against British colonialism. He was a prolific writer who oversaw the drafting of the Indian Constitution and served as India's first Law Minister. In 1935, he publicly declared that though he was born a Hindu, he would not die as one. Ambedkar eventually embraced Buddhism, a few months before his death in 1956.

Arundhati Roy is the author of the novel *The God of Small Things*. Collections of her recent political writings have been published as *Listening to Grasshoppers* and *Broken Republic*.

S. Anand is the founder-publisher of Navayana. He is the co-author of *Bhimayana*, a graphic biography of Ambedkar.

Annihilation of Caste

THE ANNOTATED CRITICAL EDITION

B.R. Ambedkar

Edited and annotated by

S. ANAND

Introduced with the essay

The Doctor and the Saint by

ARUNDHATI ROY

VERSO
London • New York

This Verso paperback edition first published 2016
First published in the UK, US and Canada by Verso 2014
First published in India

Research assistance: Julia Perczel

5 7 9 10 8 6 4

Verso
UK: 6 Meard Street, London W1F 0EG
US: 20 Jay Street, Suite 1010, Brooklyn, NY 11201
www.versobooks.com

Verso is the imprint of new left books

ISBN-13: 978-1-78478-352-5 (PB)
eISBN-13: 978-1-78168-832-8 (US)
eISBN-13: 978-1-78168-830-4 (UK)

British Library Cataloguing in Publication Data
A catalogue record for this book is available from the British Library

Library of Congress Cataloging-in-Publication Data

Ambedkar, B. R. (Bhimrao Ramji), 1891—1956.
The annihilation of caste / B.R. Ambedkar ; introduced with the essay The Doctor and the Saint by Arundhati Roy. — Annotated critical edition / edited and annotated by S. Anand.
pages cm
Includes bibliographical references and index.
ISBN 978-1-78168-831-1 (hardback)
1. Caste — India. I. Title.
DS422.C3A67 2014
305.5'1220954 — dc23
2014028312

Typeset in Bembo, Frutiger and ITF Devanagari at Navayana
Printed and bound by CPI Group (UK) Ltd, Croydon, CR0 4YY

Contents

Editor's Note

Dr B.R. Ambedkar's *Annihilation of Caste* is a text in search of the audience it was written for. It survived an early assassination attempt to become what it is today—a legend. When the Hindu reformist group, the Jat-Pat Todak Mandal (Forum for Break-up of Caste) of Lahore, which had invited Ambedkar to deliver its annual lecture in 1936, asked for and received the text of the speech in advance, it found the contents "unbearable". The Mandal realised that Ambedkar intended to use its platform not merely to criticise the practice of caste, but to denounce Hinduism itself, and withdrew its invitation. In May 1936, Ambedkar printed 1,500 copies of the text of his speech at his own expense. It was soon translated into six languages. While the majority of the privileged castes are blissfully ignorant of its existence, *Annihilation of Caste* has been printed and reprinted—like most of Ambedkar's large oeuvre—by small, mostly Dalit-owned presses, and read by mostly Dalit readers over seven decades. It now has the curious distinction of being one of the most obscure as well as one of the most widely read books in India. This in itself illuminates the iron grid of the caste system.

However, *Annihilation of Caste* was a speech that Ambedkar wrote for a primarily privileged-caste audience. This audience has eluded it. This annotated, critical edition is an attempt to give his work the critical and scholarly attention it deserves.

As I read and reread the text, I realised how rich it was, and how much present-day readers would enjoy and learn from it if they could place it in a historical context: Who had founded the Jat-Pat Todak Mandal? Who was Sant Ram, the man who valiantly swam against the tide of the dominant

Arya Samaj opinion? What was the incident in Kavitha that Ambedkar mentions but does not elaborate upon? From where was he drawing the ideas of "social efficiency", "associated mode of living" or "social endosmosis"? What is the connection he suggests between the Roman Comitia Centuriata and the Communal Award of 1932? What is the connection between the American feminist anarchist Voltairine de Cleyre and Ambedkar's advocacy of direct action? To try and answer these questions, I began the task of annotating the text. In the process, I realised that by the time he published a second edition in 1937, Ambedkar had made a range of subtle and deft changes to the first edition. The second edition included his exchange with M.K. Gandhi. Ambedkar made further changes in the 1944 edition. All these are highlighted where necessary. Ambedkar's original edition tended to use long paragraphs that sometimes ran to pages. These have been divided with appropriate breaks. While the section numbers that Ambedkar provides have been retained, the new paragraphs have been numbered. Spellings and capitalisation have been standardised.

Annihilation of Caste is peppered with Sanskrit couplets. Ambedkar cites them with authority, never bothering to unpack them for his privileged audience. To translate these, I turned to the scholar Bibek Debroy, who responded with rare enthusiasm. He treated every verse as a puzzle.

Arundhati Roy's introduction "The Doctor and the Saint", is a book-length essay that familiarises the reader with caste as it plays out in contemporary India, and with the historical context of the public debate between Ambedkar and Gandhi that followed the publication of *Annihilation of Caste.* In her introduction Roy describes a little-known side of Gandhi. She shows how his disturbing views on race during his years in South Africa presaged his public pronouncements on caste. As she puts it: "Ambedkar was Gandhi's most formidable adversary.

He challenged him not just politically or intellectually, but also morally. To have excised Ambedkar from Gandhi's story, which is the story we all grew up on, is a travesty. Equally, to ignore Gandhi while writing about Ambedkar is to do Ambedkar a disservice, because Gandhi loomed over Ambedkar's world in myriad and un-wonderful ways."

The manuscript has been peer reviewed by some of the finest scholars working in this field: Christophe Jaffrelot, Thomas Blom Hansen, Ayyathurai Gajendran, Anand Teltumbde, Satish Deshpande and Uma Chakravarti. Each of them responded with empathy, diligence and care that has helped me to refine, polish and enrich the work.

S. Anand
26 January 2014
New Delhi

The Doctor and the Saint

ARUNDHATI ROY

Annihilation of Caste is the nearly eighty-year-old text of a speech that was never delivered. When I first read it I felt as though somebody had walked into a dim room and opened the windows. Reading Dr Bhimrao Ramji Ambedkar bridges the gap between what most Indians are schooled to believe in and the reality we experience every day of our lives.

My father was a Hindu, a Brahmo. I never met him until I was an adult. I grew up with my mother in a Syrian Christian family in Ayemenem, a small village in communist-ruled Kerala. And yet all around me were the fissures and cracks of caste. Ayemenem had its own separate 'Paraiyan' church where 'Paraiyan' priests preached to an 'Untouchable' congregation. Caste was implied in people's names, in the way people referred to each other, in the work they did, in the clothes they wore, in the marriages that were arranged, in the language they spoke. Even so, I never encountered the notion of caste in a single school textbook. Reading Ambedkar alerted me to a gaping hole in our pedagogical universe. Reading him also made it clear why that hole exists and why it will continue to exist until Indian society undergoes radical, revolutionary change.

Revolutions can, and often have, begun with reading.

If you have heard of Malala Yousafzai but not of Surekha Bhotmange, then do read Ambedkar.

Malala was only fifteen but had already committed several crimes. She was a girl, she lived in the Swat Valley in Pakistan, she was a BBC blogger, she was in a *New York Times* video, and she went to school. Malala wanted to be a doctor; her father wanted her to be a politician. She was a brave child. She (and her father) didn't take heed when the Taliban declared that schools were not meant for girls and threatened to kill her if she did not stop speaking out against them. On 9 October 2012, a gunman took her off her school bus and put a bullet through her head. Malala was flown to England, where, after receiving the best possible medical care, she survived. It was a miracle.

The US President and the Secretary of State sent messages of support and solidarity. Madonna dedicated a song to her. Angelina Jolie wrote an article about her. Malala was nominated for the Nobel Peace Prize; she was on the cover of *Time*. Within days of the attempted assassination, Gordon Brown, former British Prime Minister and the UN Special Envoy for Global Education, launched an 'I am Malala' petition that called on the Government of Pakistan to deliver education to every girl child. The US drone strikes in Pakistan continue with their feminist mission to 'take out' misogynist, Islamist terrorists.

Surekha Bhotmange was forty years old and had committed several crimes too. She was a woman—an 'Untouchable', Dalit woman—who lived in India, and she wasn't dirt poor. She was more educated than her husband, so she functioned as the head of her family. Dr Ambedkar was her hero. Like him, her family had renounced Hinduism and converted to Buddhism. Surekha's children were educated. Her two sons Sudhir and Roshan had been to college. Her daughter Priyanka was seventeen, and finishing high school. Surekha and her husband had bought a little plot of land in the village of Khairlanji in the state of Maharashtra. It was surrounded by farms belonging to castes that considered themselves superior to the Mahar caste that Surekha belonged to. Because she was Dalit and had no right to aspire to a good life, the village panchayat did not permit her to get an electricity connection, or turn her thatched mud hut into a brick house. The villagers would not allow her family to irrigate their fields with water from the canal, or draw water from the public well. They tried to build a public road through her land, and when she protested, they drove their bullock carts through her fields. They let their cattle loose to feed on her standing crop.

Still Surekha did not back down. She complained to the police who paid no attention to her. Over the months, the tension in the village built to fever pitch. As a warning to her, the villagers attacked a relative of hers and left him for dead. She filed another police complaint. This time, the police made some arrests, but the accused were released on bail almost immediately. At about six in the evening of the day they were released (29 September 2006), about seventy incensed villagers, men and women, arrived in tractors and surrounded the Bhotmanges' house. Her husband Bhaiyalal, who was out in the fields, heard the noise and ran home. He hid behind a bush and watched the mob attack his family. He ran to Dusala, the nearest town, and through a relative managed to call the police. (You need contacts to get the police to even pick up the phone.) They never came. The mob dragged Surekha, Priyanka and the two boys, one of them partially blind, out of the house. The boys were ordered to rape their mother and sister; when they refused, their genitals were mutilated, and eventually they were lynched. Surekha and Priyanka were gang-raped and beaten to death. The four bodies were dumped in a nearby canal, where they were found the next day.[1]

At first, the press reported it as a 'morality' murder, suggesting that the villagers were upset because Surekha was having an affair with a relative (the man who had previously been assaulted). Mass protests by Dalit organisations eventually prodded the legal system into taking cognisance of the crime. Citizens' fact-finding committees reported how evidence had been tampered with and fudged. When the lower court finally pronounced a judgement, it sentenced the main perpetrators to death but refused to invoke the Scheduled Castes and Scheduled Tribes Prevention of Atrocities Act—the judge held that the Khairlanji massacre was a crime spurred by a desire for 'revenge'. He said there was no evidence of rape and no caste angle to the killing.[2] For a judgement to weaken the legal framework in which it presents a crime, for which it then awards the death sentence, makes it easy for a higher court to eventually reduce, or even commute, the sentence. This is not uncommon practice in India.[3] For a court to sentence people to death, however heinous their crime, can hardly be called just. For a court to acknowledge that caste prejudice continues to be a horrific reality in India would have counted as a gesture towards justice. Instead, the judge simply airbrushed caste out of the picture.

Surekha Bhotmange and her children lived in a market-friendly democracy. So there were no 'I am Surekha' petitions from the United Nations to the Indian government, nor any fiats or messages of outrage from heads of state. Which was just as well, because we don't want daisy-cutters dropped on us just because we practise caste.[4]

"To the Untouchables," Ambedkar said, with the sort of nerve that present-day intellectuals in India find hard to summon, "Hinduism is a veritable chamber of horrors."[5]

For a writer to have to use terms like 'Untouchable', 'Scheduled Caste', 'Backward Class' and 'Other Backward Classes' to describe fellow human beings is like living in a chamber of horrors. Since Ambedkar used the word 'Untouchable' with a cold rage, and without flinching, so must I. Today 'Untouchable' has been substituted with the Marathi word 'Dalit' (Broken People), which is, in turn, used interchangeably with 'Scheduled Caste'. This, as the scholar Rupa Viswanath points out, is incorrect practice, because the term 'Dalit' includes

Untouchables who have converted to other religions to escape the stigma of caste (like the Paraiyans in my village who had converted to Christianity), whereas 'Scheduled Caste' does not.[6] The official nomenclature of prejudice is a maze that can make everything read like a bigoted bureaucrat's file notings. To try and avoid this, I have, mostly, though not always, used the word 'Untouchable' when I write about the past, and 'Dalit' when I write about the present. When I write about Dalits who have converted to other religions, I specifically say Dalit Sikhs, Dalit Muslims or Dalit Christians.

Let me now return to Ambedkar's point about the chamber of horrors.

According to the National Crime Records Bureau, a crime is committed against a Dalit by a non-Dalit every sixteen minutes; every day, more than four Untouchable women are raped by Touchables; every week, thirteen Dalits are murdered and six Dalits are kidnapped. In 2012 alone, the year of *the* Delhi gang-rape and murder,[7] 1,574 Dalit women were raped (the rule of thumb is that only 10 per cent of rapes or other crimes against Dalits are ever reported), and 651 Dalits were murdered.[8] That's just the rape and butchery. Not the stripping and parading naked, the forced shit-eating (literally),[9] the seizing of land, the social boycotts, the restriction of access to drinking water. These statistics wouldn't include, say, Bant Singh of Punjab, a Mazhabi Dalit Sikh,[10] who in 2005 had both his arms and a leg cleaved off for daring to file a case against the men who gang-raped his daughter. There are no separate statistics for triple amputees.

"If the fundamental rights are opposed by the community, no Law, no Parliament, no Judiciary can guarantee them in the real sense of the word," said Ambedkar. "What is the use of fundamental rights to the Negro in America, to the Jews in Germany and to the Untouchables in India? As Burke said, there is no method found for punishing the multitude."[11]

Ask any village policeman in India what his job is and he'll probably tell you it is to 'keep the peace'. That is done, most of the time, by upholding the caste system. Dalit aspirations are a breach of peace.

Annihilation of Caste is a breach of peace.

▼

Other contemporary abominations like apartheid, racism, sexism, economic imperialism and religious fundamentalism have been politically and intellectually challenged at international forums. How is it that the practice of caste in India—one of the most brutal modes of hierarchical social organisation that human society has known—has managed to escape similar scrutiny and censure? Perhaps because it has come to be so fused with Hinduism, and by extension with so much that is seen to be kind and good—mysticism, spiritualism, non-violence, tolerance, vegetarianism, Gandhi, yoga, backpackers, the Beatles—that, at least to outsiders, it seems impossible to pry it loose and try to understand it.

To compound the problem, caste, unlike say apartheid, is not colour-coded, and therefore not easy to *see*. Also, unlike apartheid, the caste system has buoyant admirers in high places. They argue, quite openly, that caste is a social glue that binds as well as separates people and communities in interesting and, on the whole, positive ways. That it has given Indian society the strength and the flexibility to withstand the many challenges it has had to face.[12] The Indian establishment blanches at the idea that discrimination and violence on the basis of caste can be compared to racism or to apartheid. It came down heavily on Dalits who tried to raise caste as an issue at the 2001 World Conference against Racism in Durban, insisting that caste was an "internal matter". It showcased theses by well-known sociologists who argued at length that the practice of caste was not the same as racial discrimination, and that caste was not the same as race.[13] Ambedkar would have agreed with them. However, in the context of the Durban conference, the point Dalit activists were making was that though caste is not the same as race, casteism and racism are indeed comparable. Both are forms of discrimination that target people because of their descent.[14] In solidarity with that sentiment, on 15 January 2014 at a public meeting on Capitol Hill in Washington D.C. commemorating Martin Luther King, Jr's 85th birth anniversary, African Americans signed "The Declaration of Empathy", which called for "an end to the oppression of Dalits in India".[15]

In the current debates about identity and justice, growth and development, for many of the best-known Indian scholars, caste is at best a topic, a subheading, and, quite often, just a footnote. By force-fitting caste into reductive Marxist class analysis, the progressive and left-leaning Indian intelligentsia has made seeing caste even harder. This erasure, this Project of Unseeing, is sometimes a conscious political act, and sometimes comes from a place of such rarefied privilege that caste has not been stumbled upon, not even in the dark, and therefore it is presumed to have been eradicated, like smallpox.

▼

The origins of caste will continue to be debated by anthropologists for years to come, but its organising principles, based on a hierarchical, sliding scale of entitlements and duties, of purity and pollution, and the ways in which they were, and still are, policed and enforced, are not all that hard to understand. The top of the caste pyramid is considered pure and has plenty of entitlements. The bottom is considered polluted and has no entitlements but plenty of duties. The pollution–purity matrix is correlated to an elaborate system of caste-based, ancestral occupation. In "Castes in India", a paper he wrote for a Columbia University seminar in 1916, Ambedkar defined a caste as an endogamous unit, an "enclosed class". On another occasion, he described the system as an "ascending scale of reverence and a descending scale of contempt."[16]

What we call the caste system today is known in Hinduism's founding texts as *varnashrama dharma* or *chaturvarna*, the system of four varnas. The approximately four thousand endogamous castes and sub-castes (*jatis*) in Hindu society, each with its own specified hereditary occupation, are divided into four varnas—Brahmins (priests), Kshatriyas (soldiers), Vaishyas (traders) and Shudras (servants). Outside of these varnas are the *avarna* castes, the Ati-Shudras, subhumans, arranged in hierarchies of their own—the Untouchables, the Unseeables, the Unapproachables—whose presence, whose touch, whose very shadow is considered to be polluting by privileged-caste Hindus. In some communities, to prevent inbreeding, each endogamous caste is divided into exogamous *gotras*. Exogamy is then policed with as much ferocity as endogamy—with beheadings and lynchings that have the approval of the community elders.[17] Each region of India has lovingly perfected its own unique version of caste-based cruelty, based on an unwritten code that is much worse than the Jim Crow laws. In addition to being forced to live in segregated settlements, Untouchables were not allowed to use the public roads that privileged castes used, they were not allowed to drink from common wells, they were not allowed into Hindu temples, they were not allowed into privileged-caste schools, they were not permitted to cover their upper bodies, they were only allowed to wear certain kinds of clothes and certain kinds of jewellery. Some castes, like the Mahars, the caste to which Ambedkar belonged, had to tie brooms to their waists to sweep away their polluted footprints, others had to hang spittoons around their necks to collect their polluted saliva. Men of the privileged castes had undisputed rights over the bodies of Untouchable women. Love is polluting. Rape is pure. In many parts of India, much of this continues to this day.[18]

What remains to be said about an imagination, human or divine, that has thought up a social arrangement such as this?

As if the dharma of varnashrama were not enough, there is also the burden of karma. Those born into the subordinated castes are supposedly being punished for the bad deeds they have done in their past lives. In effect, they are living out a prison sentence. Acts of insubordination could lead to an enhanced sentence, which would mean another cycle of rebirth as an Untouchable or as a Shudra. So it's best to behave.

"There cannot be a more degrading system of social organisation than the caste system," said Ambedkar. "It is the system that deadens, paralyses and cripples the people from helpful activity."[19]

The most famous Indian in the world, Mohandas Karamchand Gandhi, disagreed. He believed that caste represented the genius of Indian society. At a speech at a missionary conference in Madras in 1916, he said:

> The vast organisation of caste answered not only the religious wants of the community, but it answered too its political needs. The villagers managed their internal affairs through the caste system, and through it they dealt with any oppression from the ruling power or powers. It is not possible to deny the organising capability of a nation that was capable of producing the caste system its wonderful power of organisation.[20]

In 1921, in his Gujarati journal *Navajivan* he wrote:

> I believe that if Hindu Society has been able to stand, it is because it is founded on the caste system… To destroy the caste system and adopt the Western European social system means that Hindus must

> give up the principle of hereditary occupation which is the soul of the caste system. Hereditary principle is an eternal principle. To change it is to create disorder. I have no use for a Brahmin if I cannot call him a Brahmin for my life. It will be chaos if every day a Brahmin is changed into a Shudra and a Shudra is to be changed into a Brahmin.[21]

Though Gandhi was an admirer of the caste system, he believed that there should be no hierarchy between castes; that all castes should be considered equal, and that the avarna castes, the Ati-Shudras, should be brought into the varna system. Ambedkar's response to this was that "the outcaste is a bye-product of the caste system. There will be outcastes as long as there are castes. Nothing can emancipate the outcaste except the destruction of the caste system."[22]

It has been almost seventy years since the August 1947 transfer of power between the imperial British government and the Government of India. Is caste in the past? How does varnashrama dharma play out in our new 'democracy'?

▼

A lot has changed. India has had a Dalit President and even a Dalit Chief Justice. The rise of political parties dominated by Dalits and other subordinated castes is a remarkable, and in some ways a revolutionary, development. Even if the form it has taken is that a small but visible minority—the leadership—lives out the dreams of the vast majority, given our history, the aggressive assertion of Dalit pride in the political arena can only be a good thing. The complaints about corruption and callousness brought against parties like the Bahujan Samaj Party (BSP) apply to the older political parties on an even larger scale, but charges levelled against the BSP take on a shriller, more insulting tone because its leader is someone like Mayawati—a Dalit, a single woman, and unapologetic about being both. Whatever the BSP's failings may be, its contribution towards building Dalit dignity is an immense political task that ought never to be minimised. The worry is that even as subordinated castes are becoming a force to reckon with in parliamentary democracy, democracy itself is being undermined in serious and structural ways.

After the fall of the Soviet Union, India, which was once at the forefront of the Non-Aligned Movement, repositioned itself as a 'natural ally' of the United States and Israel. In the 1990s, the Indian government embarked on a process of dramatic economic reforms, opening up a previously protected market to global capital, with natural resources, essential services and national infrastructure that had been developed over fifty years with public money, now turned over to private corporations. Twenty years later, despite a spectacular GDP growth rate (which has recently slowed down), the new economic policies have led to the concentration of wealth in fewer and fewer hands. Today, India's one hundred richest people own assets equivalent to one-fourth of its celebrated GDP.[23] In a nation of 1.2 billion, more than 800 million people live on less than Rs 20 a day.[24] Giant corporations virtually own and run the country. Politicians and political parties have begun to function as subsidiary holdings of big business.

How has this affected traditional caste networks? Some argue that caste has insulated Indian society and prevented it from fragmenting and atomising like Western society did after the Industrial Revolution.[25] Others argue the opposite; they say that the unprecedented levels of urbanisation and the creation of a new work environment have shaken up the old order and rendered caste hierarchies irrelevant if not obsolete. Both claims deserve serious attention. Pardon the somewhat unliterary interlude that follows, but generalisations cannot replace facts.

A recent list of dollar billionaires published by *Forbes*

magazine features fifty-five Indians.[26] The figures, naturally, are based on revealed wealth. Even among these dollar billionaires the distribution of wealth is a steep pyramid in which the cumulative wealth of the top ten outstrips the forty-five below them. Seven out of those top ten are Vaishyas, all of them CEOs of major corporations with business interests all over the world. Between them they own and operate ports, mines, oilfields, gas fields, shipping companies, pharmaceutical companies, telephone networks, petrochemical plants, aluminium plants, cellphone networks, television channels, fresh food outlets, high schools, film production companies, stem cell storage systems, electricity supply networks and Special Economic Zones. They are: Mukesh Ambani (Reliance Industries Ltd), Lakshmi Mittal (Arcelor Mittal), Dilip Shanghvi (Sun Pharmaceuticals), the Ruia brothers (Ruia Group), K.M. Birla (Aditya Birla Group), Savitri Devi Jindal (O.P. Jindal Group), Gautam Adani (Adani Group) and Sunil Mittal (Bharti Airtel). Of the remaining forty-five, nineteen are Vaishyas too. The rest are for the most part Parsis, Bohras and Khattris (all mercantile castes) and Brahmins. There are no Dalits or Adivasis in this list.

Apart from big business, Banias (Vaishyas) continue to have a firm hold on small trade in cities and on traditional rural moneylending across the country, which has millions of impoverished peasants and Adivasis, including those who live deep in the forests of Central India, caught in a spiralling debt trap. The tribal-dominated states in India's North East—Arunachal Pradesh, Manipur, Mizoram, Tripura, Meghalaya, Nagaland and Assam—have, since 'independence', witnessed decades of insurgency, militarisation and bloodshed. Through all this, Marwari and Bania traders have settled there, kept a low profile, and consolidated their businesses. They now control almost all the economic activity in the region.

In the 1931 Census, which was the last to include caste as

an aspect of the survey, Vaishyas accounted for 2.7 per cent of the population (while the Untouchables accounted for 12.5 per cent).[27] Given their access to better health care and more secure futures for their children, the figure for Vaishyas is likely to have decreased rather than increased. Either way, their economic clout in the new economy is extraordinary. In big business and small, in agriculture as well as industry, caste and capitalism have blended into a disquieting, uniquely Indian alloy. Cronyism is built into the caste system.

Vaishyas are only doing their divinely ordained duty. The *Arthashastra* (circa 350 BCE) says usury is the Vaishya's right. The *Manusmriti* (circa 150 CE) goes further and suggests a sliding scale of interest rates: 2 per cent per month for Brahmins, 3 per cent for Kshatriyas, 4 per cent for Vaishyas and 5 per cent for Shudras.[28] On an annual basis, the Brahmin was to pay 24 per cent interest and the Shudra and Dalit, 60 per cent. Even today, for moneylenders to charge a desperate farmer or landless labourer an annual interest of 60 per cent (or more) for a loan is quite normal. If they cannot pay in cash, they have to pay what is known as 'bodily interest', which means they are expected to toil for the moneylender from generation to generation to repay impossible debts. It goes without saying that according to the *Manusmriti* no one can be forced into the service of anyone belonging to a 'lower' caste.

Vaishyas control Indian business. What do the Brahmins—the *bhudevas* (gods on earth)—do? The 1931 Census puts their population at 6.4 per cent, but, like the Vaishyas and for similar reasons, that percentage too has probably declined. According to a survey by the Centre for the Study of Developing Societies (CSDS), from having a disproportionately high number of representatives in Parliament, Brahmins have seen their numbers drop dramatically.[29] Does this mean Brahmins have become less influential?

According to Ambedkar, Brahmins, who were 3 per cent of the population in the Madras Presidency in 1948, held 37 per cent of the gazetted posts and 43 per cent of the non-gazetted posts in government jobs.[30] There is no longer a reliable way to keep track of these trends because after 1931 the Project of Unseeing set in. In the absence of information that ought to be available, we have to make do with what we can find. In a 1990 piece called "Brahmin Power", the writer Khushwant Singh said:

> Brahmins form no more than 3.5 per cent of the population of our country... today they hold as much as 70 per cent of government jobs. I presume the figure refers only to gazetted posts. In the senior echelons of the civil service from the rank of deputy secretaries upward, out of 500 there are 310 Brahmins, i.e. 63 per cent; of the 26 state chief secretaries, 19 are Brahmins; of the 27 Governors and Lt Governors, 13 are Brahmins; of the 16 Supreme Court Judges, 9 are Brahmins; of the 330 judges of High Courts, 166 are Brahmins; of 140 ambassadors, 58 are Brahmins; of the total 3,300 IAS officers, 2,376 are Brahmins. They do equally well in electoral posts; of the 508 Lok Sabha members, 190 were Brahmins; of 244 in the Rajya Sabha, 89 are Brahmins. These statistics clearly prove that this 3.5 per cent of Brahmin community of India holds between 36 per cent to 63 per cent of all the plum jobs available in the country. How this has come about I do not know. But I can scarcely believe that it is entirely due to the Brahmin's higher IQ.[31]

The statistics Khushwant Singh cites may be flawed, but are unlikely to be drastically flawed. They are a quarter of a century old now. Some new census-based information would help, but is unlikely to be forthcoming.

According to the CSDS study, 47 per cent of all Supreme Court Chief Justices between 1950 and 2000 were Brahmins. During the same period, 40 per cent of the Associate Justices in the High Courts and lower courts were Brahmin. The Backward Classes Commission, in a 2007 report, said that 37.17 per cent of the Indian bureaucracy was made up of Brahmins. Most of them occupied the top posts.

Brahmins have also traditionally dominated the media. Here too, what Ambedkar said in 1945 still has resonance:

> The Untouchables have no Press. The Congress Press is closed to them and is determined not to give them the slightest publicity. They cannot have their own Press and for obvious reasons. No paper can survive without advertisement revenue. Advertisement revenue can come only from business and in India all business, both high and small, is attached to the Congress and will not favour any Non-Congress organisation. The staff of the Associated Press in India, which is the main news distributing agency in India, is entirely drawn from the Madras Brahmins—indeed the whole of the Press in India is in their hands—and they, for well-known reasons, are entirely pro-Congress and will not allow any news hostile to the Congress to get publicity. These are reasons beyond the control of the Untouchables.[32]

In 2006, the CSDS did a survey on the social profile of New Delhi's media elite. Of the 315 key decision-makers surveyed from thirty-seven Delhi-based Hindi and English publications and television channels, almost 90 per cent of the decision-makers in the English language print media and 79 per cent in television were found to be 'upper caste'. Of them, 49 per cent were Brahmins. Not one of the 315 was a Dalit or an Adivasi; only 4 per cent belonged to castes designated as Shudra, and 3 per cent were Muslim (who make up 13.4 per cent of the population).

That's the journalists and the 'media personalities'. Who owns the big media houses that they work for? Of the four most important English national dailies, three are owned by Vaishyas and one by a Brahmin family concern. The Times

Group (Bennett, Coleman Company Ltd), the largest mass media company in India, whose holdings include *The Times of India* and the 24-hour news channel Times Now, is owned by the Jain family (Banias). The *Hindustan Times* is owned by the Bhartiyas, who are Marwari Banias; *The Indian Express* by the Goenkas, also Marwari Banias; *The Hindu* is owned by a Brahmin family concern; the *Dainik Jagran* Hindi daily, which is the largest selling newspaper in India with a circulation of fifty-five million, is owned by the Gupta family, Banias from Kanpur. *Dainik Bhaskar*, among the most influential Hindi dailies with a circulation of 17.5 million, is owned by Agarwals, Banias again. Reliance Industries Ltd (owned by Mukesh Ambani, a Gujarati Bania) has controlling shares in twenty-seven major national and regional TV channels. The Zee TV network, one of the largest national TV news and entertainment networks, is owned by Subhash Chandra, also a Bania. (In southern India, caste manifests itself somewhat differently. For example, the Eenadu Group—which owns newspapers, the largest film city in the world and a dozen TV channels, among other things—is headed by Ramoji Rao of the Kamma peasant caste of Andhra Pradesh, which bucks the trend of Brahmin–Bania ownership of Big Media. Another major media house, the Sun TV group, is owned by the Marans, who are designated as a 'backward' caste, but are politically powerful today.)

After independence, in an effort to right a historic wrong, the Indian government implemented a policy of reservation (positive discrimination) in universities and for jobs in state-run bodies for those who belong to Scheduled Castes and Scheduled Tribes.[33] Reservation is the only opportunity the Scheduled Castes have to break into the mainstream. (Of course, the policy does not apply to Dalits who have converted to other religions but continue to face discrimination.) To be eligible for the reservation policy, a Dalit needs to have completed high school.

According to government data, 71.3 per cent of Scheduled Caste students drop out before they matriculate, which means that even for low-end government jobs, the reservation policy only applies to one in every four Dalits.[34] The minimum qualification for a white-collar job is a graduate degree. According to the 2001 Census, only 2.24 per cent of the Dalit population are graduates.[35] The policy of reservation, however minuscule the percentage of the Dalit population it applies to, has nevertheless given Dalits an opportunity to find their way into public services, to become doctors, scholars, writers, judges, policemen and officers of the civil services. Their numbers are small, but the fact that there is some Dalit representation in the echelons of power alters old social equations. It creates situations that were unimaginable even a few decades ago in which, say, a Brahmin clerk may have to serve under a Dalit civil servant.[36] Even this tiny opportunity that Dalits have won for themselves washes up against a wall of privileged-caste hostility.

The National Commission for Scheduled Castes and Scheduled Tribes, for example, reports that in Central Public Sector Enterprises, only 8.4 per cent of the A-Grade officers (pardon the horrible term) belong to the Scheduled Castes, when the figure should be 15 per cent.

The same report has some disturbing statistics about the representation of Dalits and Adivasis in India's judicial services: among Delhi's twenty High Court judges, not one belonged to the Scheduled Castes, and in all other judicial posts, the figure was 1.2 per cent; similar figures were reported from Rajasthan; Gujarat had no Dalit or Adivasi judges; in Tamil Nadu, with its legacy of social justice movements, only four out of thirty-eight High Court judges were Dalit; Kerala, with its Marxist legacy, had one Dalit High Court judge among twenty-five.[37] A study of the prison population would probably reveal an inverse ratio.

Former President K.R. Narayanan, a Dalit himself, was

mocked by the judicial fraternity when he suggested that Scheduled Castes and Tribes, who according to the 2011 Census make up 25 per cent of India's 1.2 billion population, should find proportionate representation as judges in the Supreme Court. "Eligible persons from these categories are available and their under-representation or non-representation would not be justifiable," he said in 1999. "Any reservation in judiciary is a threat to its independence and the rule of law," was the response of a senior Supreme Court advocate. Another high-profile legal luminary said: "Job quotas are a vexed subject now. I believe the primacy of merit must be maintained."[38]

'Merit' is the weapon of choice for an Indian elite that has dominated a system by allegedly divine authorisation, and denied knowledge—of certain kinds—to the subordinated castes for thousands of years. Now that it is being challenged, there have been passionate privileged-caste protests against the policy of reservation in government jobs and student quotas in universities. The presumption is that 'merit' exists in an ahistorical social vacuum and that the advantages that come from privileged-caste social networking and the establishment's entrenched hostility towards the subordinated castes are not factors that deserve consideration. In truth, 'merit' has become a euphemism for nepotism.

In Jawaharlal Nehru University (JNU)—which is regarded as a bastion of progressive social scientists and historians—only 3.29 per cent of the faculty is Dalit and 1.44 per cent Adivasi,[39] while the quotas are meant to be 15 per cent and 7.5 per cent respectively. This, despite having supposedly implemented reservation for twenty-seven years. In 2010, when the subject was raised, some of its Professors Emeritus said that implementing the constitutionally mandated reservation policy would "prevent JNU from remaining one of the premier centres of excellence".[40] They argued that if reservation was implemented in faculty positions at JNU, "the well-to-do will move to foreign and private universities, and the disadvantaged will no longer be able to get world class education which JNU has been so proud to offer them so far".[41] B.N. Mallick, a professor of life sciences, was less shy: "Some castes are genetically malnourished and so very little can be achieved in raising them up; and if they are, it would be undoing excellence and merit."[42] Year after year, privileged-caste students have staged mass protests against reservation across India.

That's the news from the top. At the other end of New India, the Sachar Committee Report tells us that Dalits and Adivasis still remain at the bottom of the economic pyramid where they always were, below the Muslim community.[43] We know that Dalits and Adivasis make up the majority of the millions of people displaced by mines, dams and other major infrastructure projects. They are the pitifully low-paid farm workers and the contract labourers who work in the urban construction industry. Seventy per cent of Dalits are by and large landless. In states like Punjab, Bihar, Haryana and Kerala, the figure is as high as 90 per cent.[44]

There is one government department in which Dalits are over-represented by a factor of six. Almost 90 per cent of those designated as sweepers—who clean streets, who go down manholes and service the sewage system, who clean toilets and do menial jobs—and employed by the Government of India are Dalits.[45] (Even this sector is up for privatisation now, which means private companies will be able to subcontract jobs on a temporary basis to Dalits for less pay and with no guarantee of job security.)

While janitors' jobs in malls and in corporate offices with swanky toilets that do not involve 'manual scavenging' go to non-Dalits, there are (officially) 1.3 million people,[46] mostly women, who continue to earn their living by carrying baskets of human shit on their heads as they clean out traditional-style toilets that use no water. Though it is against the law, the Indian Railways is one of the biggest employers of manual scavengers. Its 14,300 trains transport twenty-five million passengers across 65,000 kilometres every day. Their shit is funnelled straight onto the railway tracks through 172,000 open-discharge toilets. This shit, which must amount to several tonnes a day, is cleaned by hand, without gloves or any protective equipment, exclusively by Dalits.[47] While the Prohibition of Employment as Manual Scavengers and their Rehabilitation Bill, 2012, was cleared by the Cabinet and by the Rajya Sabha in September 2013, the Indian Railways has ignored it. With deepening poverty and the steady evaporation of government jobs, a section of Dalits has to fiercely guard its 'permanent' state employment as hereditary shit-cleaners against predatory interlopers.

A few Dalits have managed to overcome these odds. Their personal stories are extraordinary and inspirational. Some Dalit businessmen and women have come together to form their own institution, the Dalit Indian Chamber of Commerce and Industry (DICCI), which is praised and patronised by big business and given plenty of play on television and big media because it helps to give the impression that as long as you work hard, capitalism is intrinsically egalitarian.[48]

Time was when a caste Hindu crossing the oceans was said to have lost caste and become polluted. Now, the caste system is up for export. Wherever Hindus go, they take it with them. It exists among the brutalised Tamils in Sri Lanka; it exists among upwardly mobile Indian immigrants in the 'Free World', in Europe as well as in the United States. For about ten years, Dalit-led groups in the UK have been lobbying to have caste discrimination recognised by British law as a form of racial discrimination. Caste-Hindu lobbies have managed to scuttle it for the moment.[49]

Democracy hasn't eradicated caste. It has entrenched and modernised it. This is why it's time to read Ambedkar.

▼

Ambedkar was a prolific writer. Unfortunately his work, unlike the writings of Gandhi, Nehru or Vivekananda, does not shine out at you from the shelves of libraries and bookshops.

Of his many volumes, *Annihilation of Caste* is his most radical text. It is not an argument directed at Hindu fundamentalists or extremists, but at those who considered themselves moderate, those whom Ambedkar called "the best of Hindus"—and some academics call "left-wing Hindus".[50] Ambedkar's point is that to believe in the Hindu shastras and to simultaneously think of oneself as liberal or moderate is a contradiction in terms. When the text of *Annihilation of Caste* was published, the man who is often called the 'Greatest of Hindus'—Mahatma Gandhi—responded to Ambedkar's provocation.

Their debate was not a new one. Both men were their generation's emissaries of a profound social, political and philosophical conflict that had begun long ago and has still by no means ended. Ambedkar, the Untouchable, was heir to the anticaste intellectual tradition that goes back to 200–100 BCE. The practice of caste, which is believed to have its genesis in the Purusha Sukta hymn[51] in the *Rig Veda* (1200–900 BCE), faced its first challenge only a thousand years later, when the Buddhists broke with caste by creating sanghas that admitted everybody, regardless of which caste they belonged to. Yet caste endured and evolved. In the mid-twelfth century, the Veerashaivas led by Basava challenged caste in South India, and were crushed. From the fourteenth century onwards, the beloved Bhakti poet-saints—Cokhamela, Ravidas, Kabir, Tukaram, Mira, Janabai—became, and still remain, the poets of the anticaste tradition. In the nineteenth and early twentieth centuries came Jotiba Phule and his Satyashodhak Samaj in western India; Pandita Ramabai, perhaps India's first feminist, a Marathi Brahmin who rejected Hinduism and converted to Christianity (and challenged that too); Swami Achhutanand Harihar, who led the Adi Hindu movement, started the Bharatiya Achhut Mahasabha (Parliament of Indian Untouchables), and edited *Achhut*, the first Dalit journal; Ayyankali and Sree Narayana Guru who shook up the old order in Malabar and Travancore; the iconoclast Iyothee Thass and his Sakya Buddhists who ridiculed Brahmin supremacy in the Tamil world. Among Ambedkar's contemporaries in the anticaste tradition were E.V. Ramasamy Naicker, known as 'Periyar' in the Madras Presidency, Jogendranath Mandal of Bengal, and Babu Mangoo Ram, who founded the Ad Dharm movement in the Punjab that rejected both Sikhism and Hinduism. These were Ambedkar's people.

Gandhi, a Vaishya, born into a Gujarati Bania family, was the latest in a long tradition of privileged-caste Hindu reformers and their organisations—Raja Ram Mohan Roy who founded the Brahmo Samaj in 1828; Swami Dayananda Saraswati who founded the Arya Samaj in 1875; Swami Vivekananda who established the Ramakrishna Mission in 1897 and a host of other, more contemporary reformist organisations.[52]

Putting the Ambedkar–Gandhi debate into context for those unfamiliar with its history and its protagonists will require detours into their very different political trajectories. For this was by no means just a theoretical debate between two men who held different opinions. Each represented very separate interest groups, and their battle unfolded in the heart of India's national movement. What they said and did continues to have an immense bearing on contemporary politics. Their differences were (and remain) irreconcilable. Both are deeply loved and often deified by their followers. It pleases neither constituency to have the other's story told, though the two are inextricably linked. Ambedkar was Gandhi's most formidable adversary. He challenged him not just politically or intellectually, but also morally. To have excised Ambedkar from Gandhi's story, which is the story we all grew up on, is a travesty. Equally, to ignore Gandhi while writing about Ambedkar is to do Ambedkar a disservice, because Gandhi loomed over Ambedkar's world in myriad and un-wonderful ways.

▼

The Indian national movement, as we know, had a stellar cast. It has even been the subject of a Hollywood blockbuster that won eight Oscars. In India, we have made a pastime of holding opinion polls and publishing books and magazines in which our constellation of founding fathers (mothers don't make the cut) are arranged and rearranged in various hierarchies and formations. Mahatma Gandhi does have his bitter critics, but he still tops the charts. For others to even get a look-in, the Father of the Nation has to be segregated, put into a separate category: Who, after Mahatma Gandhi, is the greatest Indian?[53]

Dr Ambedkar (who, incidentally, did not even have a walk-on part in Richard Attenborough's *Gandhi*, though the film was co-funded by the Indian government) almost always makes it into the final heat. He is chosen more for the part he played in drafting the Indian Constitution than for the politics and the passion that were at the core of his life and thinking. You definitely get the sense that his presence on the lists is the result of positive discrimination, a desire to be politically correct. The caveats continue to be murmured: 'opportunist' (because he served as Labour Member of the British Viceroy's Executive Council, 1942–46), 'British stooge' (because he accepted an invitation from the British government to the First Round Table

Conference in 1930 when Congressmen were being imprisoned for breaking the salt laws), 'separatist' (because he wanted separate electorates for Untouchables), 'anti-national' (because he endorsed the Muslim League's case for Pakistan, and because he suggested that Jammu and Kashmir be trifurcated).[54]

Notwithstanding the name-calling, the fact, as we shall see, is that neither Ambedkar nor Gandhi allows us to pin easy labels on them that say 'pro-imperialist' or 'anti-imperialist'. Their conflict complicates and perhaps enriches our understanding of imperialism as well as the struggle against it.

History has been kind to Gandhi. He was deified by millions of people in his own lifetime. Gandhi's godliness has become a universal and, so it seems, an eternal phenomenon. It's not just that the metaphor has outstripped the man. It has entirely reinvented him. (Which is why a critique of Gandhi need not automatically be taken to be a critique of all Gandhians.) Gandhi has become all things to all people: Obama loves him and so does the Occupy Movement. Anarchists love him and so does the Establishment. Narendra Modi loves him and so does Rahul Gandhi. The poor love him and so do the rich.

He is the Saint of the Status Quo.

Gandhi's life and his writing—48,000 pages bound into ninety-eight volumes of collected works—have been disaggregated and carried off, event by event, sentence by sentence, until no coherent narrative remains, if indeed there ever was one. The trouble is that Gandhi actually said everything and its opposite. To cherry pickers, he offers such a bewildering variety of cherries that you have to wonder if there was something the matter with the tree.

For example, there's his well-known description of an arcadian paradise in "The Pyramid vs. the Oceanic Circle", written in 1946:

> Independence begins at the bottom. Thus every village will be a republic or panchayat having full powers. It follows, therefore, that every village has to be self-sustained and capable of managing its affairs even to the extent of defending itself against the whole world... In this structure composed of innumerable villages there will be ever-widening, never-ascending circles. Life will not be a pyramid with the apex sustained by the bottom. But it will be an oceanic circle whose centre will be the individual always ready to perish for the village... Therefore the outermost circumference will not wield power to crush the inner circle but will give strength to all within and derive its own strength from it.[55]

Then there is his endorsement of the caste system in 1921 in *Navajivan*. It is translated from Gujarati by Ambedkar (who suggested more than once that Gandhi "deceived" people, and that his writings in English and Gujarati could be productively compared):[56]

> Caste is another name for control. Caste puts a limit on enjoyment. Caste does not allow a person to transgress caste limits in pursuit of his enjoyment. That is the meaning of such caste restrictions as inter-dining and inter-marriage... These being my views I am opposed to all those who are out to destroy the Caste System.[57]

Is this not the very antithesis of "ever-widening and never ascending circles"?

It's true that these statements were made twenty-five years apart. Does that mean that Gandhi reformed? That he changed his views on caste? He did, at a glacial pace. From believing in the caste system in all its minutiae, he moved to saying that the four thousand separate castes should 'fuse' themselves into the four varnas (what Ambedkar called the 'parent' of the caste system). Towards the end of Gandhi's life (when his views were just views and did not run the risk of translating into political action), he said that he no longer objected to inter-dining and intermarriage between castes. Sometimes he said that though he believed in the varna system, a person's varna ought to be decided by their worth and not their birth (which was also the Arya Samaj position). Ambedkar pointed out the absurdity of this idea: "How are you going to compel people who have acquired a higher status based on birth, without reference to their worth, to vacate that status? How are you going to compel people to recognise the status due to a man, in accordance to his worth, who is occupying a lower status based on his birth?"[58] He went on to ask what would happen to women, whether their status would be decided upon their own worth or their husbands' worth.

Notwithstanding stories and anecdotes from Gandhi's followers about Gandhi's love for Untouchables and the inter-caste weddings he attended, in the ninety-eight volumes of his writing, Gandhi never decisively and categorically renounced his belief in chaturvarna, the system of four varnas. Though he was given to apologising and agonising publicly and privately over things like the occasional lapses in his control over his sexual desire,[59] he never agonised over the extremely damaging things he had said and done on caste.

Still, why not eschew the negative and concentrate instead on what was good about Gandhi, use it to bring out the best in people? It is a valid question, and one that those who have built shrines to Gandhi have probably answered for themselves. After all, it is possible to admire the work of great composers, writers, architects, sportspersons and musicians whose views are inimical to our own. The difference is that Gandhi was not a composer or writer or musician or a sportsman. He offered himself to us as a visionary, a mystic, a moralist, a great humanitarian, the man who brought down a mighty empire armed only with Truth and Righteousness. How do we reconcile the idea of the non-violent Gandhi, the Gandhi who spoke Truth to Power, Gandhi the Nemesis of Injustice, the Gentle Gandhi, the Androgynous

Gandhi, Gandhi the Mother, the Gandhi who (allegedly) feminised politics and created space for women to enter the political arena, the eco-Gandhi, the Gandhi of the ready wit and some great one-liners—how do we reconcile all this with Gandhi's views (and deeds) on caste? What do we do with this structure of moral righteousness that rests so comfortably on a foundation of utterly brutal, institutionalised injustice? Is it enough to say Gandhi was complicated, and let it go at that? There is no doubt that Gandhi was an extraordinary and fascinating man, but during India's struggle for freedom, did he really speak Truth to Power? Did he really ally himself with the poorest of the poor, the most vulnerable of his people?

"It is foolish to take solace in the fact that because the Congress is fighting for the freedom of India, it is, therefore, fighting for the freedom of the people of India and of the lowest of the low," Ambedkar said. "The question whether the Congress is fighting for freedom has very little importance as compared to the question for whose freedom is the Congress fighting."[60]

In 1931, when Ambedkar met Gandhi for the first time, Gandhi questioned him about his sharp criticism of the Congress (which, it was assumed, was tantamount to criticising the struggle for the Homeland). "Gandhiji, I have no Homeland," was Ambedkar's famous reply. "No Untouchable worth the name will be proud of this land."[61]

History has been unkind to Ambedkar. First it contained him, and then it glorified him. It has made him India's Leader of the Untouchables, the King of the Ghetto. It has hidden away his writings. It has stripped away the radical intellect and the searing insolence.

All the same, Ambedkar's followers have kept his legacy alive in creative ways. One of those ways is to turn him into a million mass-produced statues. The Ambedkar statue is a radical and animate object.[62] It has been sent forth into the world to claim the space—both physical and virtual, public and private—that is the Dalit's due. Dalits have used Ambedkar's statue to assert their civil rights—to claim land that is owed them, water that is theirs, commons they are denied access to. The Ambedkar statue that is planted on the commons and rallied around always holds a book in its hand. Significantly, that book is not *Annihilation of Caste* with its liberating, revolutionary rage. It is a copy of the Indian Constitution that Ambedkar played a vital role in conceptualising—the document that now, for better or for worse, governs the life of every single Indian citizen.

Using the Constitution as a subversive object is one thing. Being limited by it is quite another. Ambedkar's circumstances forced him to be a revolutionary and to simultaneously put his foot in the door of the establishment whenever he got a chance to. His genius lay in his ability to use both these aspects of himself nimbly, and to great effect. Viewed through the prism of the present, however, it has meant that he left behind a dual and sometimes confusing legacy: Ambedkar the Radical, and Ambedkar the Father of the Indian Constitution. Constitutionalism can come in the way of revolution. And the Dalit revolution has not happened yet. We still await it. Before that there cannot be any other, not in India.

This is not to suggest that writing a constitution cannot be a radical act. It can be, it could have been, and Ambedkar tried his best to make it one. However, by his own admission, he did not entirely succeed.

As India hurtled towards independence, both Ambedkar and Gandhi were seriously concerned about the fate of minorities, particularly Muslims and Untouchables, but they responded to the approaching birth of the new nation in very different ways. Gandhi distanced himself more and more from the business of nation building. For him, the Congress party's work was done. He wanted the party dissolved. He believed (quite rightly) that the state represented violence in a concentrated and organised form, that because it was not a human entity, because it was soulless, it owed its very existence to violence.[63] In Gandhi's understanding swaraj (self-rule) lived in the moral heart of his people, though he made it clear that by 'his people' he did not mean the majority community alone:

> It has been said that Indian swaraj will be the rule of the majority community, i.e., the Hindus. There could not be a greater mistake than that. If it were to be true, I for one would refuse to call it swaraj and would fight it with all the strength at my command, for to me *Hind Swaraj* is the rule of all the people, is the rule of justice.[64]

For Ambedkar, "the people" was not a homogeneous category that glowed with the rosy hue of innate righteousness. He knew that, regardless of what Gandhi said, it would inevitably be the majority community that decided what form swaraj would take. The prospect of India's Untouchables being ruled by nothing other than the moral heart of India's predominantly Hindu people filled him with foreboding. Ambedkar became anxious, even desperate, to manoeuvre himself into becoming a member of the Constituent Assembly, a position that would enable him to influence the shape and the spirit of the Constitution for the emerging nation in real and practical ways. For this he was even prepared to set aside his pride, and his misgivings about his old foe, the Congress party.

Ambedkar's main concern was to privilege and legalise "constitutional morality" over the traditional, social morality of the caste system. Speaking in the Constituent Assembly on 4 November 1948, he said, "Constitutional morality is not a natural sentiment. It has to be cultivated. We must realise that our people have yet to learn it. Democracy in India is only a top-dressing on an Indian soil which is essentially undemocratic."[65]

Ambedkar was seriously disappointed with the final draft of the Constitution. Still, he did succeed in putting in place certain rights and safeguards that would, as far as the subordinated castes were concerned, make it a document that was more enlightened than the society it was drafted for. (For others, however, like India's Adivasis, the Constitution turned out to be just an extension of colonial practice. We'll come to that later.) Ambedkar thought of the Constitution as a work in progress. Like Thomas Jefferson, he believed that unless every generation had the right to create a new constitution for itself, the earth would belong to "the dead and not the living".[66] The trouble is that the living are not necessarily more progressive or enlightened than the dead. There are a number of forces today, political as well as commercial, that are lobbying to rewrite the Constitution in utterly regressive ways.

Though Ambedkar was a lawyer, he had no illusions about law-making. As Law Minister in post-independence India, he worked for months on a draft of the Hindu Code Bill. He believed that the caste system advanced itself by controlling women, and one of his major concerns was to make Hindu personal law more equitable for women.[67] The Bill he proposed sanctioned divorce and expanded the property rights of widows and daughters. The Constituent Assembly dragged its feet over it for four years (from 1947 to 1951) and then blocked it.[68] The President, Rajendra Prasad, threatened to stall the Bill's passage into law. Hindu sadhus laid siege to Parliament. Industrialists and zamindars warned they would withdraw their support in the coming elections.[69] Eventually Ambedkar resigned as Law Minister. In his resignation speech he said: "To leave inequality between class and class, between sex and sex, which is the soul of Hindu society, and to go on passing legislation relating to economic problems is to make a farce of our Constitution and to build a palace on a dung heap."[70]

More than anything else, what Ambedkar brought to a complicated, multifaceted political struggle, with more than its fair share of sectarianism, obscurantism and skulduggery, was intelligence.

▼

Annihilation of Caste is often called (even by some Ambedkarites) Ambedkar's utopia—his impracticable, unfeasible dream. He was rolling a boulder up a cliff, they say. How can a society so steeped in faith and superstition be expected to be open to such a ferocious attack on its most deeply held beliefs? After all, for millions of Hindus of all castes, including Untouchables, Hinduism in its practice is a way of life that pervades everything—birth, death, war, marriage, food, music, poetry, dance. It is their culture, their very identity. How can Hinduism be renounced only because the practice of caste is sanctioned in its foundational texts, which most people have never read?

Ambedkar's point is—how can it not be? How can such institutionalised injustice, even if it is divinely ordained, be acceptable to anyone?

> It is no use seeking refuge in quibbles. It is no use telling people that the shastras do not say what they are believed to say, if they are grammatically read or logically interpreted. What matters is how the shastras have been understood by people. You must take the stand that Buddha took... You must not only discard the shastras, you must deny their authority as did Buddha and Nanak. You must have the courage to tell the Hindus that what is wrong with them is their religion—the religion which has produced in them this notion of the sacredness of caste. Will you show that courage?[71]

Gandhi believed that Ambedkar was throwing the baby out with the bathwater. Ambedkar believed the baby and the bathwater were a single, fused organism.

Let us concede—but never accept—that *Annihilation of Caste* is indeed a piece of utopian thinking. If it is, then let us concede and accept how reduced, how depleted and how pitiable we would be as a people if even this—this rage, this audacious denunciation—did not exist in our midst. Ambedkar's anger gives us all a little shelter, a little dignity.

The utopianism that Ambedkar is charged with was very much part of the tradition of the anticaste movement. The poetry of the Bhakti movement is replete with it. Unlike the nostalgia-ridden, mythical village republics in Gandhi's 'Ram Rajya' (the reign of Lord Ram), the subaltern Bhakti sants sang of towns.[72] They sang of towns in timeless places, where Untouchables would be liberated from ubiquitous fear, from unimaginable indignity and endless toil on other peoples' land. For Ravidas (also known as Raidas, Ruhidas, Rohidas), that place was Be-gham-pura, the City without Sorrow, the city without segregation, where people were free to go wherever they wanted:

Where there is no affliction or suffering
Neither anxiety nor fear, taxes nor capital
No menace, no terror, no humiliation…
Says Raidas the emancipated Chamar:
One who shares with me that city is my friend.[73]

For Tukaram, the city was Pandharpur, where everybody was equal, where the headman had to work as hard as everyone else, where people danced and sang and mingled freely. For Kabir, it was Premnagar, the City of Love.

Ambedkar's utopia was a pretty hard-nosed one. It was, so to speak, the City of Justice—worldly justice. He imagined an enlightened India, Prabuddha Bharat, that fused the best ideas of the European Enlightenment with Buddhist thought. *Prabuddha Bharat* was, in fact, the name he gave to the last of the four newspapers he edited in his lifetime.

If Gandhi's radical critique of Western modernity came from a nostalgic evocation of a uniquely Indian pastoral bliss, Ambedkar's critique of that nostalgia came from an embrace of pragmatic Western liberalism and its definitions of progress and happiness. (Which, at this moment, is experiencing a crisis from which it may not recover.)

Gandhi called modern cities an "excrescence" that "served at the present moment the evil purpose of draining the life-blood of the villages".[74] To Ambedkar, and to most Dalits, Gandhi's ideal village was, understandably, "a sink of localism, a den of ignorance, narrow-mindedness and communalism".[75] The impetus towards justice turned Ambedkar's gaze away from the village towards the city, towards urbanism, modernism and industrialisation—big cities, big dams, big irrigation projects. Ironically, this is the very model of 'development' that hundreds of thousands of people today associate with injustice, a model that lays the environment to waste and involves the forcible displacement of millions of people from their villages and homes by mines, dams and other major infrastructural projects. Meanwhile, Gandhi—whose mythical village is so blind to appalling, inherent injustice—has, as ironically, become the talisman for these struggles for justice.

While Gandhi promoted his village republic, his pragmatism, or what some might call his duality, allowed him to support and be supported by big industry and big dams as well.[76]

The rival utopias of Gandhi and Ambedkar represented the classic battle between tradition and modernity. If utopias can be said to be 'right' and 'wrong', then both were right, and both were also grievously wrong. Gandhi was prescient enough to recognise the seed of cataclysm that was implanted in the project of Western modernity:

> God forbid that India should ever take to industrialism after the

> manner of the West. The economic imperialism of a single tiny island kingdom is today keeping the world in chains. If an entire nation of 300 millions took to similar economic exploitation it would strip the world bare like locusts.[77]

As the earth warms up, as glaciers melt and forests disappear, Gandhi's words have turned out to be prophetic. But his horror of modern civilisation led him to eulogise a mythical Indian past that was, in his telling, just and beautiful. Ambedkar, on his part, was painfully aware of the iniquity of that past, but in his urgency to move away from it, he failed to recognise the catastrophic dangers of Western modernity.

Ambedkar's and Gandhi's very different utopias ought not to be appraised or assessed by the 'end product' alone—the village or the city. Equally important is the impetus that drove those utopias. For Ambedkarites to call mass struggles against contemporary models of development 'eco-romantic' and for Gandhians to hold Gandhi out as a symbol of justice and moral virtue are shallow interpretations of the very different passions that drove the two men.

The towns the Bhakti poet-saints dreamed of—Beghampura, Pandharpur, Premnagar—had one thing in common. They all existed in a time and space that was liberated from the bonds of Brahminism. Brahminism was the term that the anticaste movement preferred over 'Hinduism'. By Brahminism, they didn't mean Brahmins as a caste or a community. They meant the domino effect, what Ambedkar called the "infection of imitation", that the caste that first "enclosed" itself—the Brahmins—set off. "Some closed the door," he wrote, "others found it closed against them."[78]

The "infection of imitation", like the half-life of a radioactive atom, decays exponentially as it moves down the caste ladder, but never quite disappears. It has created what Ambedkar describes as a system of "graded inequality" in which "there is no such class as a completely unprivileged class except the one which is at the base of the social pyramid. The privileges of the rest are graded. Even the low is privileged as compared with lower. Each class being privileged, every class is interested in maintaining the system."[79]

The exponential decay of the radioactive atom of caste means that Brahminism is practised not just by the Brahmin against the Kshatriya or the Vaishya against the Shudra, or the Shudra against the Untouchable, but also by the Untouchable against the Unapproachable, the Unapproachable against the Unseeable. It means there is a quotient of Brahminism in everybody, regardless of which caste they belong to. It is the ultimate means of control in which the concept of pollution and purity and the perpetration of social as well as physical violence—an inevitable part of administering an oppressive hierarchy—is not just outsourced, but implanted in everybody's imagination, including those at the bottom of the hierarchy. It's like an elaborate enforcement network in which everybody polices everybody else. The Unapproachable polices the Unseeable, the Malas resent the Madigas, the Madigas turn upon the Dakkalis who sit on the Rellis; the Vanniyars quarrel with the Paraiyars who in turn could beat up the Arundhatiyars.

Brahminism makes it impossible to draw a clear line between victims and oppressors, even though the hierarchy of caste makes it more than clear that there are victims and oppressors. (The line between Touchables and Untouchables, for example, is dead clear.) Brahminism precludes the possibility of social or political solidarity across caste lines. As an administrative system, it is pure genius. "A single spark can light a prairie fire" was Mao Zedong's famous message to his guerrilla army. Perhaps. But Brahminism has given us in India a labyrinth instead of a prairie. And the poor little single spark wanders, lost in a warren of firewalls. Brahminism, Ambedkar said, "is the very negation of the spirit of Liberty, Equality and Fraternity".[80]

▼

Annihilation of Caste is the text of a speech Ambedkar was supposed to deliver in Lahore in 1936 to an audience of privileged-caste Hindus. The organisation that had been bold enough to invite him to deliver its presidential address was the Jat-Pat Todak Mandal (Forum for Break-up of Caste) of Lahore, a 'radical' offshoot of the Arya Samaj. Most of its members were privileged-caste Hindu reformers. They asked to be provided the text of the speech in advance, so that they could print and distribute it. When they read it and realised that Ambedkar was going to launch an intellectual assault on the Vedas and shastras, on Hinduism itself, they wrote to him:

> [T]hose of us who would like to see the conference terminate without any untoward incident would prefer that at least the word 'Veda' be left out for the time being. I leave this to your good sense. I hope, however, in your concluding paragraphs you will make it clear that the views expressed in the address are your own and that the responsibility does not lie on the Mandal.[81]

Ambedkar refused to alter his speech, and so the event was cancelled. His text ought not to have come as such a surprise to the Mandal. Just a few months previously, on 13 October 1935, at the Depressed Classes Conference in Yeola in the Bombay Presidency (now in the state of Maharashtra), Ambedkar had told an audience of more than ten thousand people:

> Because we have the misfortune of calling ourselves Hindus, we are treated thus. If we were members of another faith none would treat us so. Choose any religion which gives you equality of status and treatment. We shall repair our mistake now. I had the misfortune of being born with the stigma of an Untouchable. However, it is not my fault; but I will not die a Hindu, for this is in my power.[82]

At that particular moment in time, the threat of religious conversion by an Untouchable leader of Ambedkar's standing came as the worst possible news to Hindu reformers.

Conversion was by no means new. Seeking to escape the stigma of caste, Untouchable and other degraded labouring castes had begun to convert to other religions centuries ago. Millions had converted to Islam during the years of Muslim rule. Later, millions more had taken to Sikhism and Christianity. (Sadly, caste prejudice in the subcontinent trumps religious belief. Though their scriptures do not sanction it, elite Indian Muslims, Sikhs and Christians all practise caste discrimination.[83] Pakistan, Bangladesh and Nepal all have their own communities of Untouchable sweepers. So does Kashmir. But that's another story.)

The mass conversion of oppressed-caste Hindus, particularly to Islam, continues to sit uncomfortably with Hindu supremacist history writing, which dwells on a golden age of Hinduism that was brought to naught by the cruelty and vandalism of Muslim rule.[84] Vandalism and cruelty there certainly was. Yet it meant different things to different people. Here is Jotiba Phule (1827 –90), the earliest of the modern anticaste intellectuals, on the subject of the Muslim rule and of the so-called golden age of the Arya Bhats (Brahmins):

> The Muslims, destroying the carved stone images of the cunning Arya Bhats, forcibly enslaved them and brought the Shudras and Ati-Shudras in great numbers out of their clutches and made them Muslims, including them in the Muslim Religion. Not only this, but they established inter-dining and intermarriage with them and gave them all equal rights. They made them all as happy as themselves and forced the Arya Bhats to see all this.[85]

By the turn of the century, however, religious conversion came to have completely different implications in India. A new set of unfamiliar considerations entered the mix. Opposing an unpopular regime was no longer just a question of a conquering army riding into the capital, overthrowing the monarch and taking the throne. The old idea of empire was metamorphosing into the new idea of the nation state. Modern governance now involved addressing the volatile question of the right to representation: who had the right to represent the Indian people? The Hindus, the Muslims, the Sikhs, the Christians, the privileged castes, the oppressed castes, the farmers, the workers? How would the 'self' in self-rule—the 'swa' in swaraj—be constituted? Who would decide? Suddenly, a people who belonged to an impossibly diverse range of races, castes, tribes and religions—who, between them, spoke more than one thousand languages—had to be transformed into modern citizens of a modern nation. The process of synthetic homogenisation began to have the opposite effect. Even as the modern Indian nation constituted itself, it began to fracture.

Under the new dispensation, demography became vitally important. The empirical taxonomy of the British census had solidified and freeze-dried the rigid but not entirely inflexible hierarchy of caste, adding its own prejudices and value judgements to the mix, classifying entire communities as 'criminals' and 'warriors' and so on. The Untouchable castes were entered under the accounting head 'Hindu'. (In 1930, according to Ambedkar, the Untouchables numbered about 44.5 million.[86] The population of African Americans in the US around the same time was 8.8 million.) The large-scale exodus of Untouchables from the 'Hindu fold' would have been catastrophic for the 'Hindu' majority. In pre-partition, undivided Punjab, for example, between 1881 and 1941, the Hindu population dropped from 43.8 per cent to 29.1 per cent, due largely to the conversion of the subordinated castes to Islam, Sikhism and Christianity.[87]

Hindu reformers hurried to stem this migration. The Arya Samaj, founded in 1875 in Lahore by Dayananda Saraswati (born Mool Shankar, a Gujarati Brahmin from Kathiawar), was one of the earliest. It preached against the practice of untouchability and banned idol worship. Dayananda Saraswati initiated the Shuddhi programme in 1877, to 'purify the impure', and, in the early twentieth century, his disciples took this up on a mass scale in North India.

In 1899, Swami Vivekananda of the Ramakrishna Math—the man who became famous in 1893 when he addressed the Parliament of the World's Religions in Chicago in his sadhu's robes—said, "Every man going out of the Hindu pale is not only a man less, but an enemy the more."[88] A raft of new reformist outfits appeared in Punjab, committed to saving Hinduism by winning the 'hearts and minds' of Untouchables: the Shradhananda Dalituddhar Sabha, the All-India Achhutodhar Committee, the Punjab Achhut Udhar Mandal[89] and the Jat-Pat Todak Mandal which was part of the Arya Samaj.

The reformers' use of the words 'Hindu' and 'Hinduism' was new. Until then, they had been used by the British as well as the Mughals, but it was not the way people who were described as Hindus chose to describe themselves. Until the panic over demography began, they had always foregrounded their jati, their caste identity. "The first and foremost thing that must be recognised is that Hindu society is a myth. The name Hindu is itself a foreign name," said Ambedkar.

> It was given by the Mohammedans to the natives [who lived east of the river Indus] for the purpose of distinguishing themselves. It does not occur in any Sanskrit work prior to the Mohammedan invasion. They did not feel the necessity of a common name, because they had no conception of their having constituted a community. Hindu society as such does not exist. It is only a collection of castes.[90]

When reformers began to use the word 'Hindu' to describe themselves and their organisations, it had less to do with religion than with trying to forge a unified political constitution out of a divided people. This explains the reformers' constant references to the 'Hindu nation' or the 'Hindu race'.[91] This political Hinduism later came to be called Hindutva.[92]

The issue of demography was addressed openly, and head-on. "In this country, the government is based on numbers," wrote the editor of *Pratap*, a Kanpur newspaper, on 10 January 1921.

> Shuddhi has become a matter of life and death for Hindus. The Muslims have grown from negative quantity into 70 million. The Christians number four million. 220 million Hindus are finding it hard to live because of 70 million Muslims. If their numbers increase only God knows what will happen. It is true that Shuddhi should be for religious purposes alone, but the Hindus have been obliged by other considerations as well to embrace their other brothers. If the Hindus do not wake up now, they will be finished.[93]

Conservative Hindu organisations like the Hindu Mahasabha took the task beyond rhetoric, and against their own deeply held beliefs and practice began to proselytise energetically against untouchability. Untouchables had to be prevented from defecting. They had to be assimilated, their proteins broken down. They had to be brought into the Big House, but kept in the servants' quarters. Here is Ambedkar on the subject:

> It is true that Hinduism can absorb many things. The beef-eating Hinduism (or strictly speaking Brahminism which is the proper name of Hinduism in its earlier stage) absorbed the non-violence theory of Buddhism and became a religion of vegetarianism. But there is one thing which Hinduism has never been able to do—namely to adjust itself to absorb the Untouchables or to remove the bar of untouchability.[94]

While the Hindu reformers went about their business, anticaste movements led by Untouchables began to organise themselves too. Swami Achhutanand Harihar presented the Prince of Wales with a charter of seventeen demands including land reform, separate schools for Untouchable children and separate electorates. Another well-known figure was Babu Mangoo Ram. He was a member of the revolutionary, anti-imperialist Ghadar Party established in 1913, predominantly by Punjabi migrants in the United States and Canada. Ghadar (Revolt) was an international movement of Punjabi Indians who had been inspired by the 1857 Mutiny, also called the First War of Independence. Its aim was to overthrow the British by means of armed struggle. (It was, in some ways, India's first communist party. Unlike the Congress, which had an urban, privileged-caste leadership, the Ghadar Party was closely linked to the Punjab peasantry. Though it has ceased to exist, its memory continues to be a rallying point for several left-wing revolutionary parties in Punjab.) However, when Babu Mangoo Ram returned to India after a decade in the United States, the caste system was waiting for him. He found he was Untouchable again.[95] In 1926, he founded the Ad Dharm movement, with Ravidas, the Bhakti sant, as its spiritual hero. Ad Dharmis declared that they were neither Sikh nor Hindu. Many Untouchables left the Arya Samaj to join the Ad Dharm movement.[96] Babu Mangoo Ram went on to become a comrade of Ambedkar's.

The anxiety over demography made for turbulent politics. There were other lethal games afoot. The British government had given itself the right to rule India by imperial fiat and had consolidated its power by working closely with the Indian elite, taking care never to upset the status quo.[97] It had drained the wealth of a once-wealthy subcontinent—or, shall we say, drained the wealth of the elite in a once-wealthy subcontinent. It had caused famines in which millions had died while the British government exported food to England.[98] None of that stopped it from also lighting sly fires that ignited caste and communal tension. In 1905, it partitioned Bengal along communal lines. In 1909, it passed the Morley–Minto reforms, granting Muslims a separate electorate in the Central as well as Provincial Legislative Councils. It began to question the moral and political legitimacy of anybody who opposed it. How could a people who practised something as primitive as untouchability talk of self-rule? How could the Congress party, run by elite, privileged-caste Hindus, claim to represent the Muslims? Or the Untouchables? Coming from the British government, it was surely wicked, but even wicked questions need answers.

The person who stepped into the widening breach was perhaps the most consummate politician the modern world has ever known—Mohandas Karamchand Gandhi. If the British had their imperial mandate to raise them above the fray, Gandhi had his Mahatmahood.

▼

Gandhi returned to India in 1915 after twenty years of political activity in South Africa, and plunged into the national movement. His first concern, as any politician's would be, was to stitch together the various constituencies that would allow the Indian National Congress to claim it was the legitimate and sole representative of the emerging nation. It was a formidable task. The temptations and contradictions of attempting to represent everybody—Hindus, Muslims, Christians, Sikhs, privileged castes, subordinated castes, peasants, farmers, serfs, zamindars, workers and industrialists—were all absorbed into the other-worldly provenance of Gandhi's Mahatmahood.

Like Shiva in the myth, who swallowed poison to save the world in the story of the Samudra Manthan—the churning of the Ocean of Milk—Gandhi stood foremost among his peers and fellow-churners, and tried to swallow the poison that rose up from the depths as he helped to roil the new nation into existence. Unfortunately, Gandhi was not Shiva, and the poison eventually overwhelmed him. The greater the Congress party's impulse to hegemony, the more violently things blew apart.

The three main constituencies it had to win over were the conservative, privileged-caste Hindus, the Untouchables and the Muslims.

For the conservative Hindus, the Congress party's natural constituency, Gandhi held aloft the utopia of Ram Rajya and the *Bhagvad Gita*, his "spiritual dictionary". (It's the book most Gandhi statues hold.) He called himself a "Sanatani Hindu". Sanatan dharma, by virtue of being 'eternal law', positions itself as the origin of all things, the 'container' of everything. Spiritually, it is a generous and beautiful idea, the very epitome of tolerance and pluralism. Politically, it is used in the opposite way, for the very narrow purpose of assimilation and domination, in which all religions—Islam, Buddhism, Jainism, Sikhism, Christianity—are sought to be absorbed. They're expected to function like small concerns under the umbrella of a larger holding company.

To woo its second major constituency, the Untouchables, the Indian National Congress passed a resolution in 1917 abolishing untouchability. Annie Besant of the Theosophical Society, a founding member of the Congress, presided over the meeting. Ambedkar called it "a strange event".[99] He republished Besant's essay published in the *Indian Review* in 1909, in which she had made a case for segregating Untouchable children from the children of 'purer' castes in schools:

> Their bodies at present are ill-odorous and foul with the liquor and strong-smelling food out of which for generations they have been built up; it will need some generations of purer food and

> living to make their bodies fit to sit in the close neighbourhood of a school room with children who have received bodies trained in habits of exquisite personal cleanliness and fed on pure food stuffs. We have to raise the Depressed Classes to a similar level of purity, not drag the clean to the level of the dirty, and until that is done, close association is undesirable.[100]

The third big constituency the Congress party needed to address was the Muslims (who, for caste Hindus, counted on the purity–pollution scale as *mleccha*—impure; sharing food and water with them was forbidden). In 1920, the Congress decided to ally with conservative Indian Muslims who were leading the pan-Islamist agitation against the partitioning of the Ottoman territories by the Allies after the First World War. The Sultan of the defeated Ottomans was the Caliph, the spiritual head of Sunni Islam. Sunni Muslims equated the partition of the Ottoman Empire with a threat to the Islamic Caliphate itself. Led by Gandhi, the Congress party leapt into the fray and included the Khilafat (Caliphate) agitation in its first national satyagraha. The satyagraha had been planned to protest the Rowlatt Act passed in 1919 to extend the British government's wartime emergency powers.

Whether or not Gandhi's support for the Khilafat Movement was just ordinary political opportunism is a subject that has been debated endlessly. The historian Faisal Devji argues convincingly that at this point Gandhi was acting with a certain internationalism; as a responsible 'imperial subject' (which was how he saw himself in his years in South Africa), he was attempting to morally transform Empire and hold it accountable to all its subjects.[101] Gandhi called Khilafat an "ideal" and asked that the struggle of "Non-cooperation be recognised as a struggle of 'religion against irreligion'".[102] By this he meant that Hinduism and Islam should join forces to transform a Christianity that, as Gandhi saw it, was losing its moral core. It was during the first

Non-Cooperation Movement that Gandhi made religion and religious symbolism the central tenet of his politics. Perhaps he thought he was lighting a wayside fire for pilgrims to warm their souls. But it ended in a blaze that has still not been put out.

By expressing solidarity with a pan-Islamic movement, Gandhi was throwing his turban into a much larger ring. Though he went to great lengths to underline his 'Hinduness', he was staking his claim to be more than just a Hindu or even an Indian leader—he was aspiring to be the leader of all the subjects of the British Empire. Gandhi's support for Khilafat, however, played straight into the hands of Hindu extremists, who had by then begun to claim that Muslims were not 'true' Indians because the centre of gravity of Muslim fealty lay outside of India. The Congress party's alliance with conservative Muslims angered conservative Hindus as well as moderate Muslims.

In 1922, when the Non-Cooperation Movement was at its peak, things went out of control. A mob killed twenty-two policemen and burnt down a police station in Chauri Chaura in the United Provinces (today's Uttar Pradesh). Gandhi saw this violence as a sign that people had not yet evolved into true satyagrahis, that they were not ready for non-violence and non-cooperation. Without consulting any other leaders, Gandhi unilaterally called off the satyagraha. Since the Non-Cooperation Movement and the Khilafat Movement were conjoined, it meant an end to the Khilafat Movement too. Infuriated by this arbitrariness, the leaders of the Khilafat Movement parted ways with the Congress. Things began to unravel.

By 1925, Dr K.B. Hedgewar had founded the Rashtriya Swayamsevak Sangh (RSS), a Hindu nationalist organisation. B.S. Moonje, one of the early ideologues of the RSS, travelled to Italy in 1931 and met Mussolini. Inspired by European fascism, the RSS began to create its own squads of storm troopers. (Today they number in the millions. RSS members include former

Prime Minister Atal Bihari Vajpayee, former Home Minister L.K. Advani, and four-time Chief Minister of Gujarat Narendra Modi.) By the time the Second World War broke out, Hitler and Mussolini were the RSS's spiritual and political leaders (and so they still remain). The RSS subsequently declared that India was a Hindu nation and that Muslims in India were the equivalent of the Jews in Germany. In 1939, M.S. Golwalkar, who succeeded Hedgewar as the head of the RSS, wrote in what is regarded as the RSS bible, *We, or Our Nationhood Defined*:

> To keep up the purity of its race and culture, Germany shocked the world by purging the country of the semitic races—the Jews. Race pride at its highest has been manifested here … a good lesson for us in Hindustan to learn and profit by.[103]

By 1940, the Muslim League, led by M.A. Jinnah, had passed the Pakistan Resolution.

In 1947, in what must surely count as one of the most callous, iniquitous acts in history, the British government drew a hurried border through the country that cut through communities and people, villages and homes, with less care than it might have taken to slice up a leg of lamb.

Gandhi, the Apostle of Peace and Non-violence, lived to see the movement he thought he led dissolve into a paroxysm of genocidal violence in which half a million people (a million, according to Stanley Wolpert in *A New History of India*) lost their lives and almost twelve million lost their homes, their past and everything they had ever known. Through the horror of partition, Gandhi did all he could to still the madness and bloodlust. He travelled deep into the very heart of the violence. He prayed, he pleaded, he fasted, but the incubus had been unleashed and could not be recalled. The hatred spilled over and consumed everything that came in its path. It continues to branch out, over-ground and underground. It has bequeathed the subcontinent a dangerous, deeply wounded psyche.

Amidst the frenzy of killing, ethnic cleansing and chest-thumping religious fundamentalism on both sides, the Government of Pakistan kept its head about one thing: it declared that Untouchable municipal sweepers were part of the country's 'essential services' and impounded them, refusing them permission to move to India. (Who else was going to clean people's shit in the Land of the Pure?) Ambedkar raised the matter with Prime Minister Jawaharlal Nehru in a letter in December 1947.[104] With great difficulty Ambedkar managed to help at least a section of the 'essential services' get across the border. Even today in Pakistan, while various Islamist sects slaughter each other over who is the better, more correct, more faithful Muslim, there does not seem to be much heartache over the very un-Islamic practice of untouchability.

Five months after partition, in January 1948, Gandhi was shot dead at a prayer meeting on the lawns of Birla House, where he usually lived when he visited Delhi. His assassin was Nathuram Godse, a Brahmin, and a former activist of the Hindu Mahasabha and the RSS. Godse was, if such a thing is possible, a most respectful assassin. First he saluted Gandhi for the work he had done to 'awaken' people, and then he shot him. After pulling the trigger, he stood his ground. He made no attempt to escape or to kill himself. In his book, *Why I Assassinated Mahatma Gandhi*, he said:

> [But] in India communal franchise, separate electorates and the like had already undermined the solidarity of the nation, more of such were in the offing and the sinister policy of communal favouritism was being pursued by the British with the utmost tenacity and without any scruple. Gandhiji therefore found it most difficult to obtain the unquestioned leadership of the Hindus and Muslims as in South Africa. But he had been accustomed to be the leader of all Indians. And quite frankly he could not understand

> the leadership of a divided country. It was absurd for his honest mind to think of accepting the generalship of any army divided against itself.[105]

Gandhi's assassin seemed to feel that he was saving the Mahatma from himself. Godse and his accomplice, Narayan Apte, climbed the gallows carrying a saffron flag, a map of undivided India and, ironically, a copy of the *Bhagvad Gita*, Gandhi's "spiritual dictionary".

The *Gita*, essentially Krishna's counsel to Arjuna during the battle of the Mahabharata (in which brothers fought brothers), is a philosophical and theological treatise on devotion and ethical practice on a battlefield. Ambedkar wasn't enamoured of the *Bhagvad Gita*. His view was that the *Gita* contained "an unheard of defence of murder". He called it a book that "offers a philosophic basis to the theory of Chaturvarna by linking it to the theory of innate, inborn qualities in men".[106]

Mahatma Gandhi died a sad and defeated man. Ambedkar was devastated. He wanted his adversary exposed, not killed. The country went into shock.

All that came later. We're getting ahead of the story.

▼

For more than thirty-five years before that, Gandhi's Mahatmahood had billowed like a sail in the winds of the national movement. He captured the world's imagination. He roused hundreds of thousands of people into direct political action. He was the cynosure of all eyes, the voice of the nation. In 1931, at the Second Round Table Conference in London, Gandhi claimed—with complete equanimity—that he represented all of India. In his first public confrontation with Ambedkar (over Ambedkar's proposal for a separate electorate for Untouchables),

Gandhi felt able to say, "I claim myself in my own person to represent the vast mass of Untouchables."[107]

How could a privileged-caste Bania claim that he, in his own person, represented forty-five million Indian Untouchables unless he believed he actually was a Mahatma? Mahatmahood provided Gandhi with an amplitude that was not available to ordinary mortals. It allowed him to use his 'inner voice' affectively, effectively, and often. It allowed him the bandwidth to make daily broadcasts on the state of his hygiene, his diet, his bowel movements, his enemas and his sex life, and to draw the public into a net of prurient intimacy that he could then use and manipulate when he embarked on his fasts and other public acts of self-punishment. It permitted him to contradict himself constantly and then say: "My aim is not to be consistent with my previous statements on a given question, but to be consistent with the truth as it may present itself to me in a given moment. The result has been that I have grown from truth to truth."[108]

Ordinary politicians oscillate from political expediency to political expediency. A Mahatma can grow from truth to truth.

How did Gandhi come to be called a Mahatma? Did he begin with the compassion and egalitarian instincts of a saint? Did they come to him along the way?

In his recent biography of Gandhi, the historian Ramachandra Guha argues that it was the two decades he spent working in South Africa that made Gandhi a Mahatma.[109] His canonisation—the first time he was publicly called Mahatma—was in 1915, soon after he returned from South Africa to begin work in India, at a meeting in Gondal, close to his hometown, Porbandar, in Gujarat.[110] At the time, few in India knew more than some very sketchy, rather inaccurate accounts of the struggles he had been engaged in. These need to be examined in some detail because whether or not they made him a Mahatma, they certainly shaped and defined his views on caste, race and imperialism. His views on race presaged his views on caste. What happened in South Africa continues to have serious implications for the Indian community there. Fortunately, we have the Mahatma's own words (and inconsistencies) to give us the detail and texture of those years.[111] To generations who have been raised on a diet of Gandhi hagiographies (including myself), to learn of what happened in South Africa is not just disturbing, it is almost stupefying.

THE SHINING PATH

Gandhi, twenty-four years old and trained as a lawyer in London's Inner Temple, arrived in South Africa in May 1893. He had a job as legal adviser to a wealthy Gujarati Muslim merchant. Imperial Britain was tightening its grip on the African continent. Gandhi was unkindly jolted into political awakening a few months after he arrived. Half the story is legendary: Gandhi was thrown out of a 'Whites only' first-class coach of a train in Pietermaritzburg. The other half of the story is less known: Gandhi was not offended by racial segregation. He was offended that 'passenger Indians'—Indian merchants who were predominantly Muslim but also privileged-caste Hindus—who had come to South Africa to do business, were being treated on a par with native Black Africans. Gandhi's argument was that passenger Indians came to Natal as British subjects and were entitled to equal treatment on the basis of Queen Victoria's 1858 proclamation, which asserted the equality of all imperial subjects.

In 1894, he became secretary of the Natal Indian Congress founded and funded by rich Indian merchants and traders. The membership fee, of three pounds,was a princely sum that meant the NIC would remain an elite club. (For a sense of proportion—twelve years later, the Zulus would rise in rebellion against the British for imposing an unaffordable one-pound poll tax on them.)

One of the earliest political victories for the NIC came in 1895 with a 'solution' to what was known as the Durban Post Office problem. The Post Office had only two entrances: one for Blacks and one for Whites. Gandhi petitioned the authorities and had a third entrance opened so that Indians did not need to use the same entrance as the 'Kaffirs'.[113] In an open letter to the Natal Legislative Assembly dated 19 December 1894, he says that both the English and the Indians "spring from common stock, called the Indo-Aryan", and cites Max Müller, Arthur Schopenhauer and William Jones to buttress his argument. He complains that the "Indian is being dragged down to the position of a raw Kaffir".[114] As spokesman for the Indian community, Gandhi was always careful to distinguish—and distance—passenger Indians from indentured (bonded) workers:

> Whether they are Hindus or Mahommedans, they are absolutely without any moral or religious instruction worthy of the name. They have not learned enough to educate themselves without any outside help. Placed thus, they are apt to yield to the slightest temptation to tell a lie. After some time, lying with them becomes a habit and a disease. They would lie without any reason, without any prospect of bettering themselves materially, indeed, without knowing what they are doing. They reach a stage in life when their moral faculties have completely collapsed owing to neglect.[115]

The Indian indentured labour whose "moral faculties" were in such a state of collapse were largely from the subordinated castes and lived and worked in conditions of virtual slavery, incarcerated on sugar cane farms. They were flogged, starved, imprisoned, often sexually abused, and died in great numbers.[116]

Gandhi soon became the most prominent spokesperson for the cause of the passenger Indians. In 1896, he travelled to India where he addressed packed—and increasingly indignant—meetings about the racism that Indians were being subjected to in South Africa. At the time, the White regime was getting increasingly anxious about the rapidly expanding Indian population. For them Gandhi was the leader of the 'coolies'—their name for all Indians.[117] In a perverse sense, their racism was inclusive. It didn't notice the distinctions that Gandhi went to such great lengths to make.

When Gandhi returned to Durban in January 1897, the news of his campaign had preceded him. His ship was met by thousands of hostile White demonstrators, who refused to let it dock. It took several days of negotiation before Gandhi was allowed to disembark. On his way home, on 12 January 1897, he was attacked and beaten. He bore the attack with fortitude and dignity.[118] Two days later, in an interview to *The Natal Advertiser*, Gandhi once again distanced himself from the 'coolies':

> I have said most emphatically, in the pamphlets and elsewhere, that the treatment of the indentured Indians is no worse or better in Natal than they receive in any other parts of the world. I have never endeavoured to show that the indentured Indians have been receiving cruel treatment.[119]

In 1899, the British went to war with Dutch settlers over the spoils of South Africa. Diamonds had been discovered in Kimberley in 1870, and gold on the Witwatersrand in 1886. The Anglo-Boer War, as it was called then, is known more properly today as the South African War or the White Man's War. Thousands of Black Africans and indentured Indian labourers were dragooned into the armies on either side. The Indians were not given arms, so they worked as menials and stretcher-bearers. Gandhi and a band of passenger Indians, who felt it was their responsibility as imperial subjects, volunteered their services to the British. Gandhi was enlisted in the Ambulance Corps.

It was a brutal war in which British troops fought Boer guerrillas. The British burnt down thousands of Boer farms, slaughtering people and cattle as they swept through the land.

Tens of thousands of Boer civilians, mostly women and children, were moved into concentration camps, in which almost thirty thousand people died. Many simply starved to death.[120] These concentration camps were the first of their kind, the progenitors of Hitler's extermination camps for Jews. Several years later, after he returned to India, when Gandhi wrote about the South African war in his memoirs, he suggested that the prisoners in the camps were practising a cheerful form of satyagraha (which was the course of action he prescribed to the Jews of Germany too):[121]

> Boer women understood that their religion required them to suffer in order to preserve their independence, and therefore, patiently and cheerfully endured all hardships... They starved, they suffered biting cold and scorching heat. Sometimes a soldier intoxicated by liquor or maddened by passion might even assault these unprotected women. Still the brave women did not flinch.[122]

After the war, the British announced that their troops would be given a slab each of "Queen's Chocolate" as a reward for their bravery. Gandhi wrote a letter to the Colonial Secretary to ask for the largesse to be extended to the Ambulance Corps leaders, who had volunteered without pay: "It will be greatly appreciated by them and prized as a treasure if the terms under which the gift has been graciously made by Her Majesty would allow of its distribution among the Indian leaders."[123] The Colonial Secretary replied curtly to say that the chocolate was only for non-commissioned officers.

In 1901, with the Boer War now behind him, Gandhi spoke of how the objective of the Natal Indian Congress was to achieve a better understanding between the English and the Indians. He said he was looking forward to an "Imperial Brotherhood", towards which "everyone who was the friend of the Empire should aim".[124]

This was not to be. The Boers managed to outmanoeuvre and out-brotherhood Gandhi. In 1902, they signed the Treaty of Vereeniging with the British. According to the treaty, the Boer republics of the Transvaal and the Orange Free State became colonies of the British Empire under the sovereignty of the British Crown. In return, the British government agreed to give the colonies self-rule. The Boers became the British government's brutal lieutenants. Jan Smuts, once a dreaded Boer 'terrorist', switched sides and eventually led the British Army of South Africa in the First World War. The White folks made peace. They divided the diamonds, the gold and the land between themselves. Blacks, Indians and 'coloureds' were left out of the equation.

Gandhi was not deterred. A few years after the South African War, he once again volunteered for active service.

In 1906, the Zulu chief Bambatha kaMancinza led his people in an uprising against the British government's newly imposed one-pound poll tax. The Zulus and the British were old enemies and had fought each other before. In 1879, the Zulus had routed the British Army when it attacked the Zulu kingdom, a victory that put the Zulu on the world map. Eventually, over the years, because they could not match the firepower of British troops, they were conquered and driven off their land. Still, they refused to work on the White man's farms; which is why bonded, indentured labour was shipped in from India. Time and again, the Zulus had risen up. During the Bambatha Rebellion, the rebels, armed only with spears and cowhide shields, fought British troops equipped with modern artillery.

As the news of the rebellion came in, Gandhi published a series of letters in *Indian Opinion*, a Gujarati–English newspaper he had started in 1903. (One of its chief benefactors was Sir Ratanji Jamsetji Tata of the Tata industrial empire.) In a letter dated 18 November 1905, Gandhi said:

> At the time of the Boer War, it will be remembered, the Indians volunteered to do any work that might be entrusted to them, and it was with great difficulty that they could get their services accepted even for ambulance work. General Butler has certified as to what kind of work the Natal Indian Volunteer Ambulance Corps did. If the Government only realised what reserve force is being wasted, they would make use of it and would give Indians a thorough training for actual warfare.[125]

On 14 April 1906, Gandhi wrote again in *Indian Opinion* (translated from Gujarati):

> What is our duty during these calamitous times in the Colony? It is not for us to say whether the revolt of the Kaffirs [Zulus] is justified or not. We are in Natal by virtue of British Power. Our very existence depends on it. It is therefore our duty to render whatever help we can. There was a discussion in the Press as to what part the Indian community would play in the event of an actual war. We have already declared in the English columns of this journal that the Indian community is prepared to play its part; and we believe what we did during the Boer War should also be done now.[126]

The rebellion was eventually contained. Chief Bambatha was captured and beheaded. Four thousand Zulus were killed, thousands more flogged and imprisoned. Even Winston Churchill, Master of War, at the time Under Secretary of State, was disturbed by the violence. He said: "It is my duty to warn the Secretary of State that this further disgusting butchery will excite in all probability great disapproval in the House of Commons… The score between black and white stands at present at about 3500 to 8."[127]

Gandhi, on his part, never regretted the role he played in the White Man's War and in the Bambatha uprising. He just reimagined it. Years later, in 1928, in *Satyagraha in South Africa*,[128] the memoirs he wrote in Yerawada Central Jail, both stories had, shall we say, evolved. By then the chessmen on the board had moved around. Gandhi had turned against the British. In his new account, the 'Truth' about the stretcher-bearer corps in the Bambatha Rebellion had 'grown' into another 'Truth':

> The Zulu 'rebellion' broke out just while attempts were being made to impose further disabilities upon Indians in the Transvaal … therefore I made an offer to the Government to raise a Stretcher-bearer Corps for service with the troops… The corps was on active service for a month… We had to cleanse the wounds of several Zulus which had not been attended to for as many as five or six days and were therefore stinking horribly. We liked the work. The Zulus could not talk to us, but from their gestures and the expression in their eyes they seemed to feel as if God had sent them our succour.[129]

The retrospectively constructed image of the flogged, defeated Zulu—a dumb animal conveying his gratitude to God's missionaries of peace—is completely at odds, as we shall see, with his views about Zulus that were published in the pages of his newspapers during those years. In Gandhi's reimagining of the story of the Bambatha Rebellion, the broken Zulu becomes the inspiration for another of his causes: celibacy.

> While I was working with the Corps, two ideas which had long been floating in my mind became firmly fixed. First, an aspirant after a life exclusively devoted to service must lead a life of celibacy. Second, he must accept poverty as a constant companion through life. He may not take up any occupation which would prevent him or make him shrink from undertaking the lowliest of duties or largest risks.[130]

Gandhi's experiments with poverty and celibacy began in the Phoenix Settlement, a commune he had set up in 1904. It was built on a hundred-acre plot of land in the heart of Natal amidst the sugar fields that were worked by Indian indentured labour. The members of the commune included a few Europeans and (non-indentured) Indians, but no Black Africans.

In September 1906, only months after the Bambatha Rebellion, despite his offers of friendship and his demonstrations of loyalty, Gandhi was let down once again. The British government passed the Transvaal Asiatic Law Amendment Act. Its purpose was to control Indian merchants (who were regarded as competition to White traders) from entering the Transvaal.[131] Every male Asian had to register himself and produce on demand a thumbprinted certificate of identity. Unregistered people were liable to be deported. There was no right of appeal. Suddenly, a community whose leader had been dreaming of an "Imperial Brotherhood" had been once again reduced "to a status lower than that of the aboriginal races of South Africa and the Coloured People".[132]

Gandhi led the struggle of the passenger Indians bravely, and from the front. Two thousand people burned their passes in a public bonfire; Gandhi was assaulted mercilessly, arrested and imprisoned. And then his worst nightmares became a reality. The man who could not bear to even share the entrance to a post office with 'Kaffirs' now had to share a prison cell with them:

> We were all prepared for hardships, but not quite for this experience. We could understand not being classed with the Whites, but to be placed on the same level with the Natives seemed to be too much to put up with. I then felt that Indians had not launched our passive resistance too soon. Here was further proof that the obnoxious law was meant to emasculate the Indians... Apart from whether or not this implies degradation, I must say it is rather dangerous. Kaffirs as a rule are uncivilised—the convicts even more so. They are troublesome, very dirty and live almost like animals.[133]

A year later, the sixteenth of the twenty years he would spend in South Africa, he wrote "My Second Experience in Gaol" in *Indian Opinion* (16 January 1909):

> I was given a bed in a cell where there were mostly Kaffir prisoners who had been lying ill. I spent the night in this cell in great misery and fear... I read the *Bhagvad Gita* which I had carried

> with me. I read the verses which had a bearing on my situation and meditating on them, managed to compose myself. The reason why I felt so uneasy was that the Kaffir and Chinese prisoners appeared to be wild, murderous and given to immoral ways... He [the Chinese] appeared to be worse. He came near the bed and looked closely at me. I kept still. Then he went to a Kaffir lying in bed. The two exchanged obscene jokes, uncovering each other's genitals... I have resolved in my mind on an agitation to ensure that Indian prisoners are not lodged with Kaffirs or others. We cannot ignore the fact that there is no common ground between them and us. Moreover those who wish to sleep in the same room as them have ulterior motives for doing so.[134]

From inside jail Gandhi began to petition the White authorities for separate wards in prisons. He led battles demanding segregation on many counts: he wanted separate blankets because he worried that "a blanket that has been used by the dirtiest of Kaffirs may later fall to an Indian's lot".[135] He wanted prison meals specially suited to Indians—rice served with ghee[136]—and refused to eat the "mealie pap" that the 'Kaffirs' seemed to relish. He also agitated for separate lavatories for Indian prisoners.[137]

Twenty years later, in 1928, the 'Truth' about all this had transmogrified into another story altogether. Responding to a proposal for segregated education for Indians and Africans in South Africa, Gandhi wrote:

> Indians have too much in common with the Africans to think of isolating themselves from them. They cannot exist in South Africa for any length of time without the active sympathy and friendship of the Africans. I am not aware of the general body of the Indians having ever adopted an air of superiority towards their African brethren, and it would be a tragedy if any such movement were to gain ground among the Indian settlers of South Africa.[138]

Then, in 1939, disagreeing with Jawaharlal Nehru, who believed that Black Africans and Indians should stand together against the White regime in South Africa, Gandhi contradicted himself once more: "However much one may sympathise with the Bantus, Indians cannot make common cause with them."[139]

Gandhi was an educated, well-travelled man. He would have been aware of the winds that were blowing in other parts of the world. His disgraceful words about Africans were written around the same time W.E.B. Du Bois wrote *The Souls of Black Folk*: "One ever feels this two-ness—an American, a Negro; two souls, two thoughts, two un-reconciled strivings; two warring ideals in one dark body, whose dogged strength alone keeps it from being torn asunder."[140]

Gandhi's attempts to collaborate with a colonial regime were taking place at the same time that the anarchist Emma Goldman was saying:

> The centralisation of power has brought into being an international feeling of solidarity among the oppressed nations of the world; a solidarity which represents a greater harmony of interests between the working man of America and his brothers abroad than between the American miner and his exploiting compatriot; a solidarity which fears not foreign invasion, because it is bringing all the workers to the point when they will say to their masters, 'Go and do your own killing. We have done it long enough for you.'[141]

Pandita Ramabai (1858–1922), Gandhi's contemporary from India, did not have his unfortunate instincts. Though she was born a Brahmin, she renounced Hinduism for its patriarchy and its practice of caste, became a Christian, and quarrelled with the Anglican Church too, earning a place of pride in India's anticaste tradition. She travelled to the US in 1886 where she met Harriet Tubman, who had once been a slave, whom she admired more than anybody she had ever met. Contrast Gandhi's attitude towards the African people to Pandita Ramabai's description of her meeting with Harriet Tubman:

> Harriet still works. She has a little house of her own, where she and her husband live and work together for their own people… Harriet is very large and strong. She hugged me like a bear and shook me by the hand till my poor little hand ached![142]

In 1873, Jotiba Phule dedicated his *Gulamgiri* (Slavery) to

> The good people of the United States as a token of admiration for their sublime disinterested and self sacrificing devotion in the cause of Negro Slavery; and with an earnest desire, that my countrymen may take their noble example as their guide in the emancipation of their Shudra Brothers from the trammels of Brahmin thraldom.[143]

Phule—who, among other things, campaigned for widow remarriage, girls' education, and started a school for Untouchables—described how "the owners of slaves treated the slaves as beasts of burden, raining kicks and blows on them all the time and starving them", and how they would "harness the slaves as bullocks and make them plough the fields in the blazing sun". Phule believed that the Shudra and Ati-Shudra would understand slavery better than anyone else because "they have a direct experience of slavery as compared to the others who have never experienced it so; the Shudras were conquered and enslaved by the Brahmins".[144]

The connection between racism and casteism was made more than a century before the 2001 Durban conference. Empathy sometimes achieves what scholarship cannot.

▼

Despite all of Gandhi's suffering in unsegregated South African prisons, the satyagraha against the Pass Laws did not gain much traction. After leading a number of protests against registering and fingerprinting, Gandhi suddenly announced that Indians would agree to be fingerprinted as long as it was voluntary. It would not be the first time that he would make a deal that contradicted what the struggle was about in the first place.

Around this time, his wealthy architect friend Hermann Kallenbach gifted him 1,100 acres of farmland just outside Johannesburg. Here he set up his second commune, Tolstoy Farm, with one thousand fruit trees on it. On Tolstoy Farm he began his experiments in purity and spirituality, and developed his home-grown protocol for the practice of satyagraha.

Given Gandhi's proposals to partner with the British in their colonisation of South Africa—and British reluctance to accept that partnership—satyagraha, appealing to your opponent with the force of Truth and Love, was the perfect political tool. Gandhi was not trying to overwhelm or destroy a ruling structure; he simply wanted to be friends with it. The intensity of his distaste for the "raw Kaffir" was matched by his affection and admiration for the British. Satyagraha seemed to be a way of reassuring them, a way of saying: "You can trust us. Look at us. We would rather harm ourselves than harm you." (This is not to suggest that satyagraha is not, and cannot, in certain situations, be an effective means of political resistance. I am merely describing the circumstances in which Gandhi began his experiments with satyagraha.)

Essentially, his idea of satyagraha revolved around a regimen of renunciation and purification. Renunciation naturally segued into a missionary approach to politics. The emphasis on purity and purification obviously derived from the caste system, though Gandhi inverted the goalposts and called his later ministrations to Untouchables a process of 'self-purification'. On the whole, it was a brand of hair-shirt Christianity combined with his own version of Hinduism and esoteric vegetarianism (which ended up underlining the 'impurity' of Dalits, Muslims and all the rest of us meat-eaters—in other words, the majority of the Indian population). The other attraction was *brahmacharya*—celibacy. The practice of semen retention and complete sexual abstinence became the minimum qualification for a 'pure' satyagrahi. Crucifixion of the flesh, denial of pleasure and desire—and eventually almost every normal human instinct—became a major theme. Even eating came in for some serious stick: "Taking food is as dirty an act as answering the call of nature."[145]

Would a person who was starving think of eating as a 'dirty act'?

Gandhi always said that he wanted to live like the poorest of the poor. The question is, can poverty be simulated? Poverty, after all, is not just a question of having no money or no possessions. Poverty is about having no power. As a politician, it was Gandhi's business to accumulate power, which he did effectively. Satyagraha wouldn't have worked, even as much as it did, if it wasn't for his star power. If you are powerful, you can live simply, but you cannot be poor. In South Africa, it took a lot of farmland and organic fruit trees to keep Gandhi in poverty.

The battle of the poor and the powerless is one of reclamation, not renunciation. But Gandhi, like many successful godmen, was an astute politician. He understood that the act of renunciation by someone who has plenty to renounce has always appealed to the popular imagination. (Gandhi would eventually discard his Western suit and put on a dhoti in order to dress like the poorest of the poor. Ambedkar, on the other hand, born unmoneyed, Untouchable, and denied the right to wear clothes that privileged-caste people wore, would show his defiance by wearing a three-piece suit.)

The irony is that while Gandhi was performing the rituals of poverty in Tolstoy Farm, he was not questioning the accumulation of capital or the unequal distribution of wealth. He was not holding out for improved working conditions for the indentured, or for the return of land to those it had been stolen from. He was fighting for Indian merchants' right to expand their businesses to the Transvaal and to compete with British merchants.

For centuries before Gandhi and for years after him, Hindu rishis and yogis have practised feats of renunciation far more arduous than Gandhi's. However, they have usually done it alone, on a snowy mountainside or in a cave set in a windblown cliff. Gandhi's genius was that he yoked his other-worldly search for moksha to a very worldly, political cause and performed both, like a fusion dance, for a live audience, in a live-in theatre. Over the years, he expanded his strange experiments to include his wife as well as other people, some of them too young to know what they were being subjected to. Towards the end of his life, as an old man in his seventies, he took to sleeping with two young girls, Manu, his seventeen-year-old grand-niece, and Abha (who were known as his "walking sticks").[146] He did this, he said, in order to gauge the degree of success or failure of his conquest over sexual desire. Leaving aside the very contentious, disturbing issues of consent and propriety, leaving aside the effect it had on the girls, the 'experiment' raises another distressing, almost horrifying question. For Gandhi to extrapolate from the 'results' of sleeping with two (or three, or four) women that he had, or had not, conquered heterosexual desire suggests that he viewed women not as individuals, but as a category. That, for him, a very small sample of a few physical specimens, including his own grand-niece, could stand in for the whole species.

Gandhi wrote at length about the experiments he conducted at Tolstoy Farm. On one occasion, he describes how he slept with young boys and girls spread around him, "taking care to arrange the order of the beds", but knowing full well that "any amount of such care would have been futile in case of a wicked mind". Then:

> I sent the boys reputed to be mischievous and the innocent

> young girls to bathe in the same spot at the same time. I had fully explained the duty of self-restraint to the children, who were all familiar with my Satyagraha doctrine. I knew, and so did the children, that I loved them with a mother's love... Was it a folly to let the children meet there for bath and yet to expect them to be innocent?

The 'trouble' that Gandhi had been anticipating—spoiling for, actually—with a mother's prescience, took place:

> One day, one of the young men made fun of two girls, and the girls themselves or some child brought me the information. The news made me tremble. I made inquiries and found that the report was true. I remonstrated with the young men, but that was not enough. I wished the two girls to have some sign on their person as a warning to every young man that no evil eye might be cast upon them, and as a lesson to every girl that no one dare assail their purity. The passionate Ravana could not so much as touch Sita with evil intent while Rama was thousands of miles away. What mark should the girls bear so as to give them a sense of security and at the same time to sterilise the sinner's eye? This question kept me awake for the night.

By morning, Gandhi had made his decision. He "gently suggested to the girls that they might let him cut off their fine long hair". At first they were reluctant. He kept the pressure up and managed to win the elderly women of the farm over to his side. The girls came around after all, "and at once the very hand that is narrating this incident set to cut off their hair. And afterwards analysed and explained my procedure before my class, with excellent results. I never heard of a joke again."[147]

There is no mention of what punishment the same mind that had thought up the idea of cutting the girls' hair had thought up for the boys.

Gandhi did indeed make the space for women to participate in the national movement. But those women had to be virtuous;

they had to, so to speak, bear "marks" upon their person that would "sterilise the sinner's eye". They had to be obedient women who never challenged the traditional structures of patriarchy.

Gandhi may have enjoyed and learned a great deal from his 'experiments'. But he's gone now, and left his followers with a legacy of a joyless, joke-free world: no desire, no sex—which he described as a poison worse than snakebite[148]—no food, no beads, no nice clothes, no dance, no poetry. And very little music. It is true that Gandhi fired the imagination of millions of people. It's also true that he has debilitated the political imagination of millions with his impossible standards of 'purity' and righteousness as a minimum qualification for political engagement:

> Chastity is one of the greatest disciplines without which the mind cannot attain the requisite firmness. A man who loses stamina becomes emasculated and cowardly… Several questions arise: How is one to carry one's wife with one? Yet those who wish to take part in great work are bound to solve these puzzles.[149]

No questions seem to have arisen as to how one was to carry one's *husband* with one. Nor any thoughts on whether satyagraha would be effective, for example, against the hoary tradition of marital rape.

▼

In 1909, Gandhi published his first and most famous political tract, *Hind Swaraj*. It was written in Gujarati and translated into English by Gandhi himself. It is considered to be a piece of genuinely original thinking, a classic. Gandhi himself remained pleased with it to the end of his days. *Hind Swaraj* defines Gandhi in the way *Annihilation of Caste* defines Ambedkar. Soon after it was published, copies of it were seized in Bombay, and it was banned for being seditious. The ban was lifted only in 1938.[150]

It was conceived of as Gandhi's response to Indian socialists, impatient young nihilists and nationalists he had met in London. Like the *Bhagvad Gita* (and Jotiba Phule's *Gulamgiri*), *Hind Swaraj* is written as a conversation between two people. Its best and most grounded passages are those in which he writes about how Hindus and Muslims would have to learn to accommodate each other after swaraj. This message of tolerance and inclusiveness between Hindus and Muslims continues to be Gandhi's real, lasting and most important contribution to the idea of India.

Nevertheless, in *Hind Swaraj*, Gandhi (like many right-wing Hindu nationalists would do in the future)[151] superimposes Hinduism's spiritual map—the map of its holy places—on the territorial map of India, and uses that to define the boundaries of the country. By doing so, consciously or unconsciously, Gandhi presents the Homeland as unmistakably Hindu. But he goes on, in the manner of a good host, to say that "a country must have a faculty for assimilation" and that "the Hindus, the Mohammedans, the Parsees and the Christians who have made India their country, are fellow countrymen".[152] The time Gandhi spent in South Africa—where the majority of his clients, and later his political constituency, were wealthy Muslim businessmen—seems to have made him more attentive to the Muslim question than he might have otherwise been. For the sin of this attentiveness, this obviously unforgivable complexity, he paid with his life.

The rest of *Hind Swaraj* is a trenchant (some say lyrical) denunciation of modernity. Like the Luddites, but with no calls for machine smashing, it indicts the industrial revolution and modern machinery. It calls the British Parliament a "sterile woman" and a "prostitute". It condemns doctors, lawyers and the railways, and dismisses Western civilisation as "satanic". It might not have been a crude or even excessive adjective to use from the point of view of the genocide of tens of millions of people in the Americas, in Australia, the Congo and West Africa that was an inalienable part of the colonial project. But it was a little odd, considering Gandhi's proposals for an "Imperial Brotherhood". And even odder, considering his respect for the British and his disdain for the uncivilised "raw Kaffir".

"What then is civilisation?" the 'Reader' eventually asks the 'Editor'. The Editor then launches into an embarrassing, chauvinistic reverie of a mythical India: "I believe that the civilisation India has evolved is not to be beaten in the world."[153] It's tempting to reproduce the whole chapter, but since that isn't possible, here are some key passages:

> A man is not necessarily happy because he is rich or unhappy because he is poor. The rich are often seen to be unhappy, the poor to be happy. Millions will always remain poor... Observing all this our ancestors dissuaded us from luxuries and pleasures. We have managed with the same kind of plough as it existed thousands of years ago. We have retained the same kind of cottages we had in former times and our indigenous education remains the same as before. We have had no system of life-corroding competition. Each followed his own occupation or trade. And charged a regulation wage. It was not that we did not know how to invent machinery, but our forefathers knew that, if we set our hearts after such things we would become slaves and lose our moral fibre... A nation with a constitution like this is fitter to teach others than to learn from others. This nation had courts, lawyers and doctors, but they were all within bounds... Justice was tolerably fair.[154]

Gandhi's valorisation of the mythic village came at a point in his life when he does not seem to have even visited an Indian village.[155] And yet his faith in it is free of doubt or caveats.

> The common people lived independently, and followed their agricultural occupation. They enjoyed true Home Rule. And

> where this cursed modern civilisation has not reached, India remains as it was before... I would certainly advise you and those like you who love the motherland to go into the interior that has yet not been polluted by the railways, and to live there for at least six months; you might be patriotic and speak of Home Rule. Now you see what I consider to be real civilisation. Those who want to change conditions such as I have described are enemies of the country and are sinners.[156]

Other than the vague allusion to the idea of people following an ancestral occupation or trade that was rewarded by a "regulation wage", caste is absent in Gandhi's reverie. Though Gandhi later insisted that untouchability had troubled him since he was a boy,[157] in *Hind Swaraj* he makes absolutely no mention of it.

Around the time *Hind Swaraj* was published, the first biographies of Gandhi were also published: *M.K. Gandhi: An Indian Patriot in South Africa* by Reverend Joseph Doke (a minister of the Johannesburg Baptist Church) in 1909, and *M.K. Gandhi: A Sketch of His Life and Work* in 1910 by Henry S.L. Polak, one of Gandhi's closest friends and most admiring of disciples. These contained the first intimations of coming Mahatmahood.

In 1910, the separate British colonies of Natal, the Cape, the Transvaal and the Orange Free State united to become the Union of South Africa, a self-governing Dominion under the British crown, with Louis Botha as its first Prime Minister. Segregation began to harden.

Around then, only three years before he was to leave South Africa, Gandhi condescendingly began to admit that Africans were the original inhabitants of the land:

> The negroes alone are the original inhabitants of this land. We have not seized the land from them by force; we live here with their goodwill. The whites, on the other hand, have occupied the country forcibly and appropriated it to themselves.[158]

By now he seems to have forgotten that he had actively collaborated with the Whites in their wars to forcibly occupy the country, appropriate the land and enslave Africans. Gandhi chose to ignore the scale and extent of the brutality that was taking place around him. Did he really believe that it was the "negroes' goodwill" that allowed Indian merchants to ply their trade in South Africa, and not, despite its racist laws, British colonialism? In 1906, during the Zulu rebellion, he had been less woolly about things like "goodwill" when he said, "We are in Natal by virtue of British Power. Our very existence depends on it."

By 1911, the anxiety of the White folks about the burgeoning Indian population led to legislation that stopped the import of labour from India.[159] Then came 1913—the year the first volume of Marcel Proust's *À la recherche du temps perdu* was first published, the year Rabindranath Tagore won the Nobel Prize for literature—South Africa's year of blood. It was the year the foundations for apartheid were laid, the year of the Land Act, legislation that created a system of tenure that deprived the majority of South Africa's inhabitants of the right to own land. It was the year African women marched against the Pass Laws that herded them into townships and restricted inter-province movement, the year White mine workers and railway workers, and then African mine workers, went on strike. It was the year Indian workers rose against a new three-pound tax and against a new marriage law that made their existing marriages illegal and their children illegitimate. The year the three-pound tax was imposed on those who had worked off their indenture and wanted to live on in South Africa as free citizens. Being unaffordable, the tax would have forced workers to re-indenture and lock themselves into a cycle of servitude.

For the first time in twenty years, Gandhi aligned himself politically with the people he had previously taken care to distance himself from. He stepped in to 'lead' the Indian workers' strike. In fact, they did not need 'leading'. For years before, during and after Gandhi, they had waged their own heroic resistance. It could be argued that they were fortunate to have escaped Gandhi's attentions, because they did not just wage a resistance, they also broke caste in the only way it can be broken—they transgressed caste barriers, got married to each other, made love and had babies.

Gandhi travelled from town to town, addressing coal miners and plantation workers. The strike spread from the collieries to the sugar plantations. Non-violent satyagraha failed. There was rioting, arson and bloodshed. Thousands were arrested as they defied the new immigration bill and crossed the border into the Transvaal. Gandhi was arrested too. He lost control of the strike. Eventually, he signed a settlement with Jan Smuts. The settlement upset many in the Indian community, who saw it as a pyrrhic victory. One of its most controversial clauses was the one in which the government undertook to provide free passage to Indians who wished to return permanently to India. It reinforced and formalised the idea that Indians were sojourners who could be repatriated. (In their 1948 election manifesto the apartheid National Party called for the repatriation of all Indians. Indians finally became full-fledged citizens only in 1960, when South Africa became a republic.)

P.S. Aiyar, an old adversary of Gandhi's, had accused him of being primarily concerned with the rights of the passenger Indians. (During the struggle against the first proposal of the draft Immigration Bill in 1911, while some Indians, including Aiyar, were agitating for the free movement of all Indians to all provinces, Gandhi and Henry Polak were petitioning for six new entrants a year to be allowed into the Transvaal.)[160] Aiyar was editor of the *African Chronicle*, a newspaper with a predominantly Tamil readership that reported the terrible conditions in which indentured labourers worked and lived. About the Gandhi–

Smuts settlement, Aiyar said that Gandhi's "ephemeral fame and popularity in India rest on no glorious achievement for his countrymen, but on a series of failures, which has resulted in causing endless misery, loss of wealth, and deprivation of existing rights". He added that Gandhi's leadership over the previous two decades had "resulted in no tangible good to anyone". On the contrary, Gandhi and his band of passive resisters had made themselves "an object of ridicule and hatred among all sections of the community in South Africa".[161] (A joke among some Blacks and Indians goes like this: Things were good then, back in 1893. Gandhi only got thrown *off* a train. By 1920, we couldn't even get on one.[162])

Though it was not put down in writing, part of the Gandhi–Smuts settlement seems to have been that Gandhi would have to leave South Africa.[163]

In all his years in South Africa, Gandhi maintained that Indians deserved better treatment than Africans. The jury is still out on whether or not Gandhi's political activity helped or harmed the Indian community in the long run. But his consistent attempts to collaborate with the British government certainly made the Indian community vulnerable during the rise of African nationalism. When Indian political activists joined the liberation movement under African leadership in the 1950s and saw their freedom as being linked to the freedom of African people, they were breaking with Gandhi's politics, not carrying on his legacy. When Indians joined the Black Consciousness Movement in the 1970s seeking to build a broader Black identity, they were actually upending Gandhian politics. It is these people, many of whom did their time in Robben Island with Nelson Mandela and other African comrades, who have saved the South African Indian community from being painted as a race of collaborators and from being isolated, even expelled, like the Indians in Uganda were in 1972.

That Gandhi is a hero in South Africa is as undeniable as it is baffling. One possible explanation is that after he left South Africa, Gandhi was *reimported*, this time as the shining star of the freedom struggle in India. The Indian community in South Africa, already cut adrift from its roots, was, after Gandhi left, further isolated and brutalised by the apartheid regime. Gandhi's cult status in India and his connection to South Africa would have provided South African Indians with a link to their history and their motherland.

In order for Gandhi to be a South African hero, it became necessary to rescue him from his past, and rewrite it. Gandhi himself began that project. Some writers of history completed it. Towards the end of Gandhi's stay in South Africa, the first few biographies had spread the news, and things were moving fast on the messiah front. The young Reverend Charles Freer Andrews travelled to South Africa and fell on his knees when he met Gandhi at the Durban dock.[164] Andrews, who became a lifelong devotee, went on to suggest that Gandhi, the leader of the "humblest, the lowliest and lost", was a living avatar of Christ's spirit. Europeans and Americans vied with each other to honour him.

In 1915, Gandhi returned to India via London where he was awarded something far better than the Queen's chocolate. For his services to the British Empire, he was honoured with the Kaiser-e-Hind Gold Medal for Public Service, presented to him by Lord Hardinge of Penshurst. (He returned it in 1920 before the first national Non-Cooperation Movement.) Honoured thus, he arrived in India fitted out as the Mahatma—Great Soul—who had fought racism and imperialism and had stood up for the rights of Indian workers in South Africa. He was forty-six years old.

To honour the returning hero, G.D. Birla, a leading Indian industrialist (and a fellow Bania), organised a grand reception in Calcutta. The Birlas ran an export–import business based in Calcutta and Bombay. They traded in cotton, wheat and silver. G.D. Birla was a wealthy man who was chafing at the bit, offended by the racism he had personally encountered at the hands of the British. He had had several run-ins with the colonial government. He became Gandhi's chief patron and sponsor and paid him a generous monthly retainer to cover the costs of running his ashrams and for his Congress party work. There were other industrialist sponsors as well, but Gandhi's arrangement with G.D. Birla lasted for the rest of his days.[165] In addition to mills and other businesses, G.D. Birla owned a newspaper, *Hindustan Times*, where Gandhi's son, Devdas, eventually worked as managing editor.

So the Mahatma who promoted homespun khadi and the wooden charkha was sponsored by a mill-owner. The man who raged against the machine was kept afloat by industrialists. This arrangement was the precursor to the phenomenon of the corporate-sponsored NGO.

Once the finances were in place and the ashrams were up and running, Gandhi set off on his mission of rallying people against the British government, yet never harming the old hierarchies that he (and his sponsors) intrinsically believed in. He travelled the length and breadth of the country to get to know it. His first satyagraha was in Champaran, Bihar, in 1917. Three years prior to his arrival there, landless peasants living on the verge of famine, labouring on British-owned indigo plantations, had risen in revolt against a new regime of British taxes. Gandhi travelled to Champaran and set up an ashram from where he backed their struggle. The people were not sure exactly who he was. Jacques Pouchepadass, who studied the Champaran Satyagraha, writes: "Rumours ... reported that Gandhi had been sent into Champaran by the Viceroy, or even the King, to redress all the grievances of the raiyats [farmers] and that his mandate overruled all the local officials and the courts."[166] Gandhi stayed in Champaran for a year and then left. Says Pouchepadass, "It is a fact that from 1918 onwards, after Gandhi had left and the planters' influence had begun to fade away, the hold of the rural oligarchy grew stronger than ever."

To rouse people against injustice and yet control them and persuade them to *his* view of injustice, Gandhi had to make some complicated manoeuvres. In 1921, when peasants (kisans) rose against their Indian landlords (zamindars) in the United Provinces, Gandhi sent them a message:

> Whilst we will not hesitate to advise kisans when the moment comes to suspend payment of taxes to Government, it is not contemplated that at any stage of non-cooperation we would seek to deprive the zamindars of their rent. The kisan movement must be confined to the improvement of the status of the kisans and the betterment of the relations between the zamindars and them. The kisans must be advised scrupulously to abide by the terms of their agreement with the zamindars, whether such agreement is written or inferred from custom.[167]

Inferred from custom. We needn't guess what that means. It's the whole ball of wax.

Though Gandhi spoke of inequality and poverty, though he sometimes even sounded like a socialist, at no point in his political career did he ever seriously criticise or confront an Indian industrialist or the landed aristocracy. This was of a piece with his doctrine of trusteeship or what today goes by the term Corporate Social Responsibility (CSR). Expanding on this in an essay called "Equal Distribution", Gandhi said: "The rich man will be left in possession of his wealth, of which he will use what he reasonably requires for his personal needs and will act as a trustee for the remainder to be used for society. In this argument, honesty on the part of the trustee is assumed."[168] To justify the idea of the rich becoming the "guardians of the poor", he argued that "the rich cannot accumulate wealth without the co-operation of the poor in society".[169] And then, to empower the poor wards of the rich guardians: "If this knowledge were to penetrate to and spread amongst the poor, they would become strong and would learn how to free themselves by means of non-violence from the crushing inequalities which have brought them to the verge of starvation."[170] Gandhi's ideas of trusteeship echo almost verbatim what American capitalists—the Robber Barons—like J.D. Rockefeller and Andrew Carnegie were saying at the time. Carnegie writes in *The Gospel of Wealth* (1889):

> This, then, is held to be the duty of the man of Wealth: First, to set an example of modest, unostentatious living, shunning display or extravagance; to provide moderately for the legitimate wants of those dependent upon him; and after doing so to consider all surplus revenues which come to him simply as trust funds, which he is called upon to administer, and strictly bound as a matter of duty to administer, in the manner which, in his judgement, is best calculated to produce the most beneficial results for the community—the man of wealth thus becoming the mere agent and trustee for his poorer brethren, bringing to their service his superior wisdom, experience and ability to administer, doing for them better than they would or could do for themselves.[171]

The contradictions mattered little, because by then, Gandhi was far beyond all that. He was a sanatani Hindu (which is how he described himself), and an avatar of Christ (which is how he allowed himself to be described). The trains he travelled in were mobbed by devotees seeking 'darshan' (a sighting). The biographer D.G. Tendulkar, who travelled with him, describes the phenomenon as "mass conversions to the new creed".

> This simple faith moved India's millions who greeted him everywhere with cries of 'Mahatma Gandhi ki Jai'. Prostitutes of Barisal, the Marwari merchants of Calcutta, Oriya coolies, railway strikers, Santhals eager to present khadi chaadars, all

> claimed his attention ... wherever he went he had to endure the tyranny of love.[172]

In his classic essay, "Gandhi as Mahatma", the historian Shahid Amin describes how the combination of cleverly planted rumours by local Congress leaders, adulatory—and sometimes hallucinatory—newspaper reporting, a gullible people and Gandhi's extraordinary charisma built up mass hysteria which culminated in the deification of Mahatma Gandhi. Even back then, not everyone was convinced. An editorial in *The Pioneer* of 23 April 1921 said, "The very simple people in the east and south of the United Provinces afford a fertile soil in which a belief in the power of the 'mahatmaji', who is after all little more than a name of power to them, may grow." The editorial was criticising an article that had appeared in *Swadesh*, a Gorakhpur newspaper, that had published rumours about the miracles that surrounded Gandhi: he had made fragrant smoke waft up from a well, a copy of the Holy Quran had appeared in a locked room, a buffalo that belonged to an Ahir who refused money to a sadhu begging in the Mahatma's name had perished in a fire, and a Brahmin who had defied Gandhi's authority had gone mad.[173]

The taproot of Gandhi's Mahatmahood had found its way into a fecund rill, where feudalism met the future, where miracles met modernity. From there it drew sustenance and prospered.

The sceptics were few and did not count for much. Gandhi was by now addressing rallies of up to two hundred thousand people. The hysteria spread abroad. In 1921, the Unitarian minister John Haynes Holmes of the Community Church in New York in a sermon called "Who is the Greatest Man in the World?" introduced Gandhi to his congregation as "The Suffering Christ of the twentieth century".[174] Years later, in 1958, Martin Luther King, Jr would do the same: "Christ furnished the spirit and motivation, while Gandhi furnished the method."[175]

They presented Gandhi with a whole new constituency: a paradoxical gift for a man who so feared and despised Africans.

Perhaps because the Western Christian world was apprehensive about the spreading influence of the Russian Revolution, and was traumatised by the horror of the First World War, Europeans and Americans vied to honour the living avatar of Christ. It didn't seem to matter that unlike Gandhi, who was from a well-to-do family (his father was the prime minister of the princely state of Porbandar), Jesus was a carpenter from the slums of Jerusalem who stood up against the Roman Empire instead of trying to make friends with it. And he wasn't sponsored by big business.

The most influential of Gandhi's admirers was the French dramatist Romain Rolland, who won the Nobel Prize for literature in 1915. He had not met Gandhi when in 1924 he published *Mahatma Gandhi: The Man Who Became One with the Universal Being*. It sold more than a hundred thousand copies and was translated into several European languages.[176] It opens with Tagore's invocation from the Upanishads:

> He is the One Luminous, Creator of All, Mahatma,
> Always in the hearts of the people enshrined,
> Revealed through Love, Intuition and Thought,
> Whoever knows him, Immortal becomes

Gandhi said he found a "real vision of truth" in the book. He called Rolland his "self-chosen advertiser" in Europe.[177] By 1924, on the list of executives of his own organisation, All-India Spinners Association, his name appeared as Mahatma Gandhi.[178] Sad then, for him to say in the first paragraph of his response to *Annihilation of Caste*: "Whatever label he wears in the future, Dr Ambedkar is not the man to allow himself to be forgotten." As though pointing to the profound horrors of the caste system was just a form of self-promotion for Ambedkar.

This is the man, or, if you are so inclined, the Saint, that

Doctor Bhimrao Ramji Ambedkar, born in 1891 into an Untouchable Mahar family, presumed to argue with.

THE CACTUS GROVE

Ambedkar's father Ramji Sakpal and both his grandfathers were soldiers in the British Army. They were Mahars from the Konkan, then a part of the Bombay Presidency and, at the time, a hotbed of nationalist politics. The two famous Congressmen, Bal Gangadhar Tilak of the 'garam dal' (militant faction) and Gandhi's mentor, Gopal Krishna Gokhale, of the 'naram dal' (moderate faction), were both Chitpavan Brahmins from the Konkan. (It was Tilak who famously said, "Swaraj is my birthright, and I shall have it.")

The Konkan coast was also home to Ambedkar's political forebear, Jotiba Phule, who called himself Joti Mali, the Gardener. Phule was from Satara, the town where Ambedkar spent his early childhood. The Mahars were considered Untouchables and, though they were landless agricultural labourers, they were comparatively better off than the other Untouchable castes. In the seventeenth century, they served in the army of Shivaji, the Maratha king of western India. After Shivaji's death, they served the Peshwas, an oppressive Brahminical regime that treated them horribly. (It was the Peshwas who forced Mahars to hang pots around their necks and tie brooms to their hips.) Unwilling to enter into a 'trusteeship' of this sort, the Mahars shifted their loyalty to the British. In 1818, in the Battle of Koregaon, a small British regiment of Mahar soldiers defeated the massive army of the last Peshwa ruler, Bajirao II.[179] The British subsequently raised a Mahar Regiment, which is still part of the Indian Army.

Over time, a section of the Mahar population left their villages and moved to the city. They worked in the Bombay mills and as casual, unorganised labour in the city. The move widened their horizons and perhaps accounts for why the Mahars were politicised quicker than other Untouchable communities in the region.

Ambedkar was born on 14 April 1891 in the cantonment town of Mhow near Indore in Central India. He was the fourteenth and last child of Ramji Sakpal and Bhimabai Murbadkar Sakpal. His mother died when he was two years old, the same year that his father retired from the army. The family was brought up in the Bhakti tradition of Kabir and Tukaram, but Ramji Sakpal also educated his children in the Hindu epics. As a young boy, Ambedkar was sceptical about the Ramayana and the Mahabharata, and their capricious lessons in morality. He was particularly distressed by the story of the killing and dismembering of the 'low-born' Karna. (Karna was born of Surya, the Sun God, and the unmarried Kunti. Abandoned by his mother, he was brought up by a lowly charioteer. Karna was killed while he was repairing his chariot wheel on the battlefield by his half-brother Arjun on the advice of Krishna.) Ambedkar argued with his father: "Krishna believed in fraud. His life is nothing but a series of frauds. Equal dislike I have for Rama."[180] Later, in a series of essays called *Riddles in Hinduism*, published posthumously, he would expand on the themes of what he saw as inexcusable misogyny in Rama's and Krishna's slippery ethics.[181]

Ambedkar's encounters with humiliation and injustice began from his early childhood. When Gandhi was serving in the South African War, Ambedkar was ten years old, living with his aunt and going to a local government school in Satara. Thanks to a new British legislation,[182] he was *allowed* to go to a Touchable school, but he was made to sit apart from his classmates, on a scrap of gunnysack, so that he would not pollute the classroom floor. He remained thirsty all day because he was not allowed to drink from the Touchables' tap. Satara's barbers would not cut his hair, not even the barbers who sheared goats and buffaloes. This cruelty continued in school after school. His older brothers were not allowed to learn Sanskrit because it was the language of the Vedas, and the colonisation of knowledge was a central tenet of the caste system. (If a Shudra listens intentionally to the Vedas, the *Gautama Dharma Sutra* says, his ears must be filled with molten tin or lac.) Much later, in the 1920s, Ambedkar studied Sanskrit (and in the 1940s also studied Pali), and became familiar with Brahminical texts—and when he wrote *Annihilation of Caste*, he deployed this knowledge explosively.

Eventually, in 1897, the family moved to a chawl in Bombay. In 1907, Ambedkar matriculated, the only Untouchable student in Elphinstone High School. It was an exceptional achievement for a Mahar boy. Soon after, he was married to nine-year-old Ramabai (not to be confused with Pandita Ramabai) in a ceremony that took place in a shed built over a city drain. While he was doing his bachelor's degree at Elphinstone College, a well-wisher introduced him to Sayajirao Gaekwad, the progressive Maharaja of Baroda. The Maharaja gave him a scholarship of Rs 25 a month to complete his graduation. The Maharaja was one of a number of unusual, privileged-caste Hindu individuals who helped or allied with Ambedkar in times of adversity and in his political confrontations.

The times were turbulent. The Morley–Minto reforms, which advocated a separate electorate for Muslims, had been passed. Nationalists were infuriated and saw the reforms as a British ploy to undermine the unity of the growing national movement. Tilak was convicted of sedition and deported to Mandalay. In 1910, Vinayak Damodar Savarkar, a young follower of Tilak, was arrested for organising an armed revolt against the Morley–Minto reforms. (In prison Savarkar turned towards political Hinduism and in 1923 wrote *Hindutva: Who is a Hindu?*)

When Ambedkar graduated, he became one of three students who was given a scholarship by Sayajirao Gaekwad to travel abroad to continue his studies. In 1913 (Gandhi's last year in South Africa), the boy who had to sit on a gunnysack on his classroom floor was admitted to Columbia University in New York. It was while he was there, under the tutelage of John Dewey (of 'Deweyan liberalism' fame), Edwin Seligman, James Shotwell, James Harvey Robinson and A.A. Goldenweiser, that he wrote his original, path-breaking paper on caste, "Castes in India: Their Mechanism, Genesis and Development",[183] in which he argued that caste could not be equated with either race or class, but was a unique social category in itself—an enclosed, endogamous class. When he wrote it, Ambedkar was only twenty-five years old. He returned briefly to India and then went to London to study economics at the London School of Economics and simultaneously take a degree in law at Gray's Inn in London—a degree he had to abandon halfway, but completed later.

Ambedkar returned to Baroda in 1917. To repay his scholarship, he was expected to serve as military secretary to the Maharaja. He came back to a very different reception from the one Gandhi received. There were no glittering ceremonies, no wealthy sponsors. On the contrary, from spending hours reading in the university library with its endless books, and eating at dining tables with napkins and cutlery, Ambedkar returned to the thorny embrace of the caste system. Afraid of even accidentally touching Ambedkar, clerks and peons in his office would fling files at him. Carpets were rolled up when he walked in and out of office so that they would not be polluted by him. He found no accommodation in the city: his Hindu, Muslim and Christian friends, even those he had known in Columbia, turned him down. Eventually, by masquerading as a Parsi, he got a room at a Parsi inn. When the owners discovered he was an Untouchable, he was thrown onto the street by armed men. "I can even now vividly recall it and never recall it without tears in my eyes," Ambedkar wrote. "It was then for the first time I learnt that a person who is Untouchable to a Hindu is also Untouchable to a Parsi."[184]

Unable to find accommodation in Baroda, Ambedkar returned to Bombay, where, after initially teaching private tutorials, he got a job as a professor at Sydenham College.

In 1917, Hindu reformers were wooing Untouchables with an edge of desperation. The Congress had passed its resolution against untouchability. Both Gandhi and Tilak called untouchability a 'disease' that was antithetical to Hinduism. The first All-India Depressed Classes Conference was held in Bombay, presided over by Ambedkar's patron and mentor, Maharaja Sayajirao Gaekwad, and attended by several luminaries of the time, including Tilak. They passed the All-India Anti-Untouchability Manifesto, which was signed by all of them (except Tilak, who managed to find a way around it).[185]

Ambedkar stayed away from these meetings. He had begun to grow sceptical about these very public but completely out-of-character displays of solicitude for Untouchables. He saw that these were ways in which, in the changing times, the privileged castes were manoeuvring to consolidate their control over the Untouchable community. While his audience, his constituency and his chief concern were the Untouchables, Ambedkar believed that it was not just the stigma, the pollution–purity issues around untouchability, but caste itself that had to be dismantled. The practice of untouchability, cruel as it was—the broom tied to the waist, the pot hung around the neck—was the performative, ritualistic end of the practice of caste. The real violence of caste was the denial of *entitlement*: to land, to wealth, to knowledge, to equal opportunity. (The caste system is the feudal version of the doctrine of trusteeship: the entitled must be left in possession of their entitlement, and be trusted to use it for the public good.)

How can a system of such immutable hierarchy be maintained if not by the threat of egregious, ubiquitous violence? How do landlords force labourers, generation after generation, to toil night and day on subsistence wages? Why would an Untouchable labourer, who is not allowed to even dream of being a landowner one day, put his or her life at the landlord's disposal, to plough the land, to sow seed and harvest the crop, if it were not out of sheer terror of the punishment that awaits the wayward? (Farmers, unlike industrialists, cannot afford strikes. Seed must be sown when it must be sown, the crop must be harvested when it must be harvested. The farmworker must be terrorised into abject submission, into being available when he must be available.) How were African slaves forced to work on American cotton fields? By being flogged, by being lynched, and if that did not work, by being hung from a tree for others to see and be afraid. Why are the murders of insubordinate Dalits even today never simply murders but ritual slaughter? Why are they always burnt alive, raped, dismembered and paraded naked? Why did Surekha Bhotmange and her children have to die the way they did?

Ambedkar tried to provide an answer:

> Why have the mass of people tolerated the social evils to which they have been subjected? There have been social revolutions in other countries of the world. Why have there not been social revolutions in India, is a question that has incessantly troubled me. There is only one answer which I can give and it is that the lower classes of Hindus have been completely disabled for direct action on account of this wretched caste system. They could not bear arms, and without arms they could not rebel. They were all ploughmen—or rather condemned to be ploughmen—and they were never allowed to convert their ploughshares into swords. They had no bayonets, and therefore everyone who chose, could and did sit upon them. On

> account of the caste system, they could receive no education. They could not think out or know the way to their salvation. They were condemned to be lowly; and not knowing the way of escape, and not having the means of escape, they became reconciled to eternal servitude, which they accepted as their inescapable fate.[186]

In rural areas, the threat of actual physical violence sometimes paled before the spectre of the 'social boycott' that orthodox Hindus would proclaim against any Untouchable who dared to defy the system. (This could mean anything from daring to buy a piece of land, wearing nice clothes, smoking a bidi in the presence of a caste Hindu, or having the temerity to wear shoes, or ride a mare in a wedding procession. The crime could even be an attitude, a posture that was less craven than an Untouchable's is meant to be.) It's the opposite of the boycott that the Civil Rights Movement in the US used as a campaign tool; the American Blacks at least had a modicum of economic clout to boycott buses and businesses that held them in contempt. Among privileged castes, the social boycott in rural India traditionally means 'hukka-pani bandh'—no hukka (tobacco) and no pani (water) for a person who has annoyed the community. Though it's called a 'social boycott', it is an *economic* as well as social boycott. For Dalits, that is lethal. The 'sinners' are denied employment in the neighbourhood, denied the right to food and water, denied the right to buy provisions in the village Bania's shop. They are hounded out and left to starve. The social boycott continues to be used as a weapon against Dalits in Indian villages. It is non-cooperation by the powerful against the powerless—non-cooperation, as we know it, turned on its head.

In order to detach caste from the political economy, from conditions of enslavement in which most Dalits lived and worked, in order to elide the questions of entitlement, land reforms and the redistribution of wealth, Hindu reformers cleverly narrowed the question of caste to the issue of untouchability. They framed it as an erroneous religious and cultural practice that needed to be reformed.

Gandhi narrowed it even further to the issue of 'Bhangis'—scavengers, a mostly urban and therefore somewhat politicised community. From his childhood, he resurrected the memory of Uka, the boy scavenger who used to service the household's lavatory, and often spoke of how the Gandhi family's treatment of Uka had always troubled him.[187] Rural Untouchables—ploughmen, potters, tanners and their families—lived in scattered, small communities, in hutments on the edges of villages (beyond polluting distance). Urban Untouchables—Bhangis, Chuhras and Mehtars—scavengers, as Gandhi liked to call them, lived together in numbers and actually formed a political constituency. In order to discourage them from converting to Christianity, Lala Mulk Raj Bhalla, a Hindu reformer of the Punjabi Khatri caste, re-baptised them in 1910, and they came to collectively be called Balmikis. Gandhi seized upon the Balmikis and made them his show window for untouchability. Upon them he performed his missionary acts of goodness and charity. He preached to them how to love and hold on to their heritage, and how to never aspire towards anything more than the joys of their hereditary occupation. All through his life, Gandhi wrote a great deal about the importance of 'scavenging' as a religious duty. It did not seem to matter that people in the rest of the world were dealing with their shit without making such a fuss about it.

Delivering the presidential address at the Kathiawar Political Conference in Bhavnagar on 8 January 1925, Gandhi said:

> If at all I seek any position it is that of a Bhangi. Cleansing of dirt is sacred work which can be done by a Brahmin as well as a Bhangi, the former doing it with and the latter without the knowledge of its holiness. I respect and honour both of them. In the absence of

either of the two, Hinduism is bound to face extinction. I like the path of service; therefore, I like the Bhangi. I have personally no objection to sharing my meal with him, but I am not asking you to inter-dine with or inter-marry him. How can I advise you?[188]

Gandhi's attentiveness towards the Balmikis, his greatly publicised visits to 'Bhangi colonies', paid dividends, despite the fact that he treated them with condescension and contempt. When he stayed in one such colony in 1946:

half the residents were moved out before his visit and the shacks of the residents torn down and neat little huts constructed in their place. The entrances and windows of the huts were screened with matting, and during the length of Gandhi's visit, were kept sprinkled with water to provide a cooling effect. The local temple was white-washed and new brick paths were laid. In an interview with Margaret Bourke-White, a photo-journalist for *Life* magazine, one of the men in charge of Gandhi's visit, Dinanath Tiang of the Birla Company, explained the improvements in the untouchable colony, "We have cared for Gandhiji's comfort for the last twenty years."[189]

In his history of the Balmiki workers of Delhi, the scholar Vijay Prashad says when Gandhi staged his visits to the Balmiki Colony on Mandir Marg (formerly Reading Road) in 1946, he refused to eat with the community:

'You can offer me goat's milk,' he said, 'but I will pay for it. If you are keen that I should take food prepared by you, you can come here and cook my food for me'... Balmiki elders recount tales of Gandhi's hypocrisy, but only with a sense of uneasiness. When a dalit gave Gandhi nuts, he fed them to his goat, saying that he would eat them later, in the goat's milk. Most of Gandhi's food, nuts and grains, came from Birla House; he did not take these from the dalits. Radical Balmikis took refuge in Ambedkarism which openly confronted Gandhi on these issues.[190]

Ambedkar realised that the problem of caste would only be

further entrenched unless Untouchables were able to organise, mobilise and become a political constituency with their own representatives. He believed that reserved seats for Untouchables within the Hindu fold, or within the Congress, would just produce pliable candidates—servants who knew how to please their masters. He began to develop the idea of a separate electorate for Untouchables. In 1919, he submitted a written testimony to the Southborough Committee on electoral reforms. The committee's brief was to propose a scheme of territorial constituencies based on existing land revenue districts, and separate communal representation for Muslims, Christians and Sikhs, for a new constitution that was to be drafted to prepare for Home Rule. The Congress boycotted the committee. To his critics, who called him a collaborator and a traitor, Ambedkar said that Home Rule was as much the right of the Untouchable as it was of the Brahmin, and it was the duty of privileged castes to do what they could to put everybody on an equal plane. In his testimony, Ambedkar argued that Untouchables were as separate a social group from Touchable Hindus as Muslims, Christians and Sikhs:

> The right of representation and the right to hold office under the State are the two most important rights that make up citizenship. But the untouchability of the untouchables puts these rights far beyond their reach. In a few places they do not even possess such insignificant rights as personal liberty and personal security, and equality before law is not always assured to them. These are the interests of the Untouchables. And as can be easily seen they can be represented by the Untouchables alone. They are distinctively their own interests and none else can truly voice them... Hence it is evident that we must find the Untouchables to represent their grievances which are their interests and, secondly, we must find them in such numbers as will constitute a force sufficient to claim redress.[191]

The British government did not, at that point, pay much attention to his testimony, though his presentation did perhaps provide the basis for Ambedkar being invited to the First Round Table Conference ten years later, in 1930.

Around this time, Ambedkar started his first journal, *Mook Nayak* (Leader of the Voiceless). Tilak's newspaper, *Kesari*, refused to carry even a paid advertisement announcing the publication of *Mook Nayak*.[192] The editor of *Mook Nayak* was P.N. Bhatkar, the first Mahar to matriculate and go to college.[193] Ambedkar wrote the first thirteen editorials himself. In the first one, he described Hindu society in a chilling metaphor—as a multi-storeyed tower with no staircase and no entrance. Everybody had to die in the storey they were born in.

In May 1920, backed by Chhatrapati Shahu, the Maharaja of Kolhapur, known for his anti-Brahmin views and for pioneering the policy of reservation in education and jobs as far back as 1902, Ambedkar and his colleagues organised the first All-India Depressed Classes Conference in Nagpur. It was agreed that no Untouchable representative chosen by a caste-Hindu majority could (or would) genuinely work against chaturvarna.

The 1920s marked the beginning of an era of direct action by Untouchables for the right to use wells, schools, courts, offices and public transport. In 1924, in what came to be known as the Vaikom Satyagraha, the Ezhavas, a community designated Shudra, and the Pulayas, who were Untouchables, agitated to use the public roads that skirted the Mahadeva temple in Vaikom, twenty miles from Kottayam in Travancore (now in the state of Kerala). One of the leaders of the Vaikom Satyagraha was George Joseph, a Syrian Christian, and an admirer of Gandhi. Gandhi, on his part, disapproved of a "non-Hindu" intervening in what he believed to be an "internal matter" of the Hindus.[194] (The same logic had not applied three years before, when he 'led' the Khilafat Movement.) He was also reluctant to support a full-blown satyagraha in an "Indian-ruled" state. During the course of the Vaikom Satyagraha, George Joseph was imprisoned. He became deeply disillusioned by what he saw as Gandhi's inexcusable ambivalence on the issue of caste. As the tension in Vaikom rose, C. Rajagopalachari,[195] Congress leader and Gandhi's chief lieutenant, travelled to Vaikom to oversee matters. On 27 May 1924, he reassured the worried privileged-caste Hindus of Vaikom in a public speech:

> Let not the people of Vykom or any other place fear that Mahatmaji wants caste abolished. Mahatmaji does not want the caste system abolished but holds that untouchability should be abolished... Mahatmaji does not want you to dine with Thiyas or Pulayas. What he wants is that we must be prepared to touch or go near other human beings as you go near a cow or a horse... Mahatmaji wants you to look upon so-called untouchables as you do at the cow and the dog and other harmless creatures.[196]

Gandhi himself arrived in Vaikom in March 1925 to arbitrate. He consulted with the Brahmin priests of the temple—who did not allow him, a non-Brahmin, to enter the sanctum—and the Queen of Travancore, and negotiated a compromise: the roads were realigned so that they were no longer within 'polluting' distance from the temple. The contentious portion of the road remained closed to Christians and Muslims as well as avarnas (Untouchables) who continued to have no right to enter the temple. Saying he was "unable to satisfy the orthodox friends" Gandhi advised the "withdrawal of satyagraha",[197] but the local satyagrahis continued with their struggle. Twelve years later, in November 1936, the Maharaja of Travancore issued the first Temple Entry Proclamation in India.[198]

▼

If one of Gandhi's first major political actions was the 'solution' to the problem of the Durban Post Office, Ambedkar's was the Mahad Satyagraha of 1927.

In 1923, the Legislative Council of Bombay (whose elections had been boycotted by the Congress) passed a resolution, the Bole Resolution, that allowed Untouchables to use public tanks, wells, schools, courts and dispensaries. In the town of Mahad, the municipality declared that it had no objection if Untouchables used the Chavadar Tank in the town. Passing a resolution was one thing, acting on it quite another. After four years of mobilisation, the Untouchables gathered courage and, in March 1927, held a two-day conference in Mahad. Money for the conference was raised by public contribution. In an unpublished manuscript, the scholar Anand Teltumbde quotes Anant Vinayak Chitre, one of the organisers of the Mahad Satyagraha, saying that forty villages contributed Rs 3 each, and a play about Tukaram was staged in Bombay that made Rs 23, making the total collection Rs 143. Contrast this with Gandhi's troubles. Just a few months before the Mahad Satyagraha, on 10 January 1927, Gandhi wrote to his industrialist-patron, G.D. Birla:

> My thirst for money is simply unquenchable. I need at least Rs 200,000—for Khadi, Untouchability and education. The dairy work makes another 50,000. Then there is the Ashram expenditure. No work remains unfinished for want of funds, but God gives after severe trials. This also satisfies me. You can give as you like for whatever work you have faith in.[199]

The Mahad conference was attended by about three thousand Untouchables, and a handful of progressive members of the privileged castes. (V.D. Savarkar, out of jail by now, was one of the supporters of the Mahad Satyagraha.) Ambedkar presided over the meeting. On the morning of the second day people decided to march to the Chavadar Tank and drink water. The privileged castes watched in horror as a procession of Untouchables walked through the town, four abreast, and drank water from the tank. After the shock subsided came the violent counter-attack, with clubs and sticks. Twenty Untouchables were injured. Ambedkar urged his people to stay firm and not to strike back. A rumour was deliberately spread that the Untouchables planned to enter the Veereshwar temple, which added a hysterical edge to the violence. The Untouchables scattered. Some found shelter in Muslim homes. For his own safety, Ambedkar spent the night in the police station. Once calm returned, the Brahmins 'purified' the tank with prayers, and with 108 pots of cow dung, cow urine, milk, curd and ghee.[200] The symbolic exercise of their rights did not satisfy the Mahad satyagrahis. In June 1927, an advertisement appeared in *Bahishkrit Bharat* (Excluded India), a fortnightly Ambedkar had founded, asking those members of the Depressed Classes who wished to take the agitation further to enlist themselves. The orthodox Hindus of Mahad approached the sub-judge of the town and got a temporary legal injunction against the Untouchables using the tank. Still, the Untouchables decided to hold another conference and regrouped in Mahad in December. Ambedkar's disenchantment with Gandhi was still some years away. Gandhi had, in fact, spoken approvingly of the Untouchables' composure in the face of the attacks from the orthodoxy, so his portrait was put up on stage.[201]

Ten thousand people attended the second Mahad conference. On this occasion Ambedkar and his followers publicly burnt a copy of the *Manusmriti*,[202] and Ambedkar gave a stirring speech:

> Gentlemen, you have gathered here today in response to the invitation of the Satyagraha Committee. As the Chairman of that Committee, I gratefully welcome you all... This lake at Mahad is public property. The caste Hindus of Mahad are so reasonable that they not only draw water from the lake themselves but freely permit people of any religion to draw water from it, and

> accordingly people of other religions, such as Islam, do make use of this permission. Nor do the caste Hindus prevent members of species considered lower than the human, such as birds and beasts, from drinking at the lake. Moreover, they freely permit beasts kept by untouchables to drink at the lake.
>
> The caste Hindus of Mahad prevent the untouchables from drinking the water of the Chavadar Lake not because they suppose that the touch of the Untouchables will pollute the water or that it will evaporate and vanish. Their reason for preventing the Untouchables from drinking it is that they do not wish to acknowledge by such permission that castes declared inferior by sacred tradition are in fact their equals.
>
> It is not as if drinking the water of the Chavadar Lake will make us immortal. We have survived well enough all these days without drinking it. We are not going to the Chavadar Lake merely to drink its water. We are going to the Lake to assert that we too are human beings like others. It must be clear that this meeting has been called to set up the norm of equality…

Time and again Ambedkar returned to the theme of equality. Men may not all be equal, he said, but equality was the only possible governing principle because the classification and assortment of human society was impossible.

> To sum up, untouchability is not a simple matter; it is the mother of all our poverty and lowliness and it has brought us to the abject state we are in today. If we want to raise ourselves out of it, we must undertake this task. We cannot be saved in any other way. It is a task not for our benefit alone; it is also for the benefit of the nation.
>
> Even this will not be enough. The inequality inherent in the four-castes system must be rooted out… Our work has been begun to bring about a real social revolution. Let no one deceive himself by supposing that it is a diversion to quieten minds entranced with sweet words. The work is sustained by strong feeling, which is the power that drives the movement. No one can now arrest it. I pray to god that the social revolution that begins here today may fulfil

> itself by peaceful means. We say to our opponents too: please do not oppose us. Put away the orthodox scriptures. Follow justice. And we assure you that we shall carry out our programme peacefully.[203]

The thousands attending the conference were in a militant mood, and wanted to defy the court injunction and march to the tank. Ambedkar decided against it, hoping that after hearing the matter, the courts would declare that Untouchables had the right to use public wells. He thought that a judicial order would be a substantial step forward from just a municipal resolution. Although the High Court did eventually lift the injunction, it found a technical way around making a legal declaration in favour of the Untouchables.[204] (Like the judge who, almost eighty years later, wrote the Khairlanji verdict.)

That same month (December 1927), Gandhi spoke at the All-India Suppressed Classes Conference in Lahore, where he preached a gospel opposite to Ambedkar's. He urged Untouchables to fight for their rights by "sweet persuasion and not by Satyagraha which becomes Duragraha when it is intended to give rude shock to the deep-rooted prejudices of the people".[205] Duragraha, he defined as "devilish force", which was the polar opposite of Satyagraha, "soul force".[206]

Ambedkar never forgot Gandhi's response to the Mahad Satyagraha. Writing in 1945, in *What Congress and Gandhi Have Done to the Untouchables* he said:

> The Untouchables were not without hope of getting the moral support of Mr Gandhi. Indeed they had very good ground for getting it. For the weapon of satyagraha—the essence of which is to melt the heart of the opponent by suffering—was the weapon which was forged by Mr Gandhi, and who had led the Congress to practise it against the British Government for winning swaraj. Naturally the Untouchables expected full support from Mr Gandhi to their satyagraha against the Hindus the object of which was to establish their right to take water from public wells and to

> enter public Hindu temples. Mr Gandhi however did not give his support to the satyagraha. Not only did he not give his support, he condemned it in strong terms.[207]

▼

Logically, the direction in which Ambedkar was moving ought to have made him a natural ally of the Communist Party of India, founded in 1925, two years before the Mahad Satyagraha. Bolshevism was in the air. The Russian Revolution had inspired communists around the world. In the Bombay Presidency, the trade union leader S.A. Dange, a Maharashtrian Brahmin, organised a large section of the Bombay textile workers into a breakaway union—India's first communist trade union—the Girni Kamgar Union, with seventy thousand members. At the time a large section of the workforce in the mills were Untouchables, many of them Mahars, who were employed only in the much lower paid spinning department, because in the weaving department workers had to hold thread in their mouths, and the Untouchables' saliva was believed to be polluting to the product. In 1928, Dange led the Girni Kamgar Union's first major strike. Ambedkar suggested that one of the issues that ought to be raised was equality and equal entitlement *within* the ranks of workers. Dange did not agree, and this led to a long and bitter falling out.[208]

Years later, in 1949, Dange, who is still a revered figure in the communist pantheon, wrote a book, *Marxism and Ancient Indian Culture: India from Primitive Communism to Slavery*, in which he argued that ancient Hindu culture was a form of primitive communism in which "Brahman is the commune of Aryan man and yagnya [ritual fire sacrifice] is its means of production, the primitive commune with the collective mode of production."

D.D. Kosambi, the mathematician and Marxist historian, said in a review: "This is so wildly improbable as to plunge into the ridiculous."[209]

The Bombay mills have since closed down, though the Girni Kamgar Union still exists. Mill workers are fighting for compensation and housing and resisting the takeover of mill lands for the construction of malls. The Communist Party has lost its influence, and the union has been taken over by the Shiv Sena, a party of militant Maharashtrian Hindu chauvinists.

Years before Ambedkar and Dange were disagreeing about the internal inequalities between labourers, Gandhi was already an established labour organiser. What were his views on workers and strikes?

Gandhi returned from South Africa at a time of continuous labour unrest.[210] The textile industry had done well for itself during the First World War, but the prosperity was not reflected in workers' wages. In February 1918, millworkers in Ahmedabad went on strike. To mediate the dispute, Ambalal Sarabhai, president of the Ahmedabad Mill Owners' Association, turned to Gandhi, who had set up his ashram in Sabarmati, just outside Ahmedabad. It was the beginning of Gandhi's lifelong career as a labour union organiser in India. By 1920, he had managed to set up a labour union called the Majoor Mahajan Sangh—which translates as the Workers and Mill-Owners Association. The English name was the Textile Labour Union. Anusuyaben, Ambalal Sarabhai's sister, a labour organiser, was elected president for life, and Gandhi became a pivotal member of the advisory committee, also for life. The union did work at improving the hygiene and living conditions of workers, but no worker was ever elected to the union leadership. No worker was permitted to be present at closed-door arbitrations between the management and the union. The union was divided up into a federation of smaller, occupation-based unions whose members worked in the different stages of the production process. In other words, the structure of the union institutionalised caste divisions. According to a worker interviewed by the scholar Jan Breman, Untouchables were not allowed into the common canteen, they had separate drinking water tanks and segregated housing.[211]

In the union, Gandhi was the prime organiser, negotiator and decision-maker. In 1921, when workers did not turn up for work for three days, Gandhi was infuriated:

> Hindu and Muslim workers have dishonoured and humiliated themselves by abstaining from mills. Labour cannot discount me. I believe no one in India can do so. I am trying to free India from bondage and I refuse to be enslaved by workers.[212]

Here is a 1925 entry from a report of the Textile Labour Union. We don't know who wrote it, but its content and its literary cadence are unmistakably similar to what Gandhi had said about indentured labour in South Africa more than thirty years before:

> They are not as a rule armed with sufficient intelligence and moral development to resist the degrading influences which surround them on all sides in a city like this. So many of them sink in one way or another. A large number of them lose their moral balance and become slaves to liquor habits, many go down as physical wrecks and waste away from tuberculosis.[213]

Since Gandhi's main sponsor was a mill-owner and his main constituency was supposed to be the labouring class, Gandhi developed a convoluted thesis on capitalists and the working class:

> The mill-owner may be wholly in the wrong. In the struggle between capital and labour, it may be generally said that more often than not capitalists are in the wrong box. But when labour comes fully to realise its strength, I know it can become more tyrannical than capital. The mill-owners will have to work on

> the terms dictated by labour, if the latter could command the intelligence of the former. It is clear, however, that labour will never attain to that intelligence... It would be suicidal if the labourers rely upon their numbers or brute-force, i.e., violence. By doing so they would do harm to industries in the country. If on the other hand they take their stand on pure justice and suffer in their person to secure it, not only will they always succeed but they will reform their masters, develop industries, and both masters and men will be as members of one and the same family.[214]

Gandhi took a dim view of strikes. But his views on sweepers' strikes, which he published in 1946, were even more stringent than those on other workers' strikes:

> There are certain matters on which strikes would be wrong. Sweepers' grievances come in this category. My opinion against sweepers' strikes dates back to about 1897 when I was in Durban. A general strike was mooted there, and the question arose as to whether scavengers should join it. My vote was registered against the proposal. Just as a man cannot live without air, so too he cannot exist for long if his home and surroundings are not clean. One or the other epidemic is bound to break out, especially when modern drainage is put out of action... A Bhangi [scavengers] may not give up his work even for a day. And there are many other ways open to him for securing justice.[215]

It's not clear what the "other" ways were for securing justice: Untouchables on satyagraha were committing duragraha. Sweepers on strike were sinning. Everything other than 'sweet persuasion' was unacceptable.

While workers could not strike for fair wages, it was perfectly correct for Gandhi to be generously sponsored by big industrialists. (It was with this same sense of exceptionalism that in his reply to *Annihilation of Caste* he wrote, as point number one, "He [Ambedkar] has priced it at 8 annas, I would have advised 2 or at least 4 annas.")

▼

The differences between Ambedkar and the new Communist Party of India were not superficial. They went back to first principles. Communists were people of The Book, and The Book was written by a German Jew who had heard of, but had not actually encountered, Brahminism. This left Indian communists without theoretical tools to deal with caste. Since they were people of The Book, and since the caste system had denied Shudra and Untouchable castes the opportunity of learning, by default the leaders of the Communist Party of India and its subsequent offshoots belonged to (and by and large continue to belong to) the privileged castes, mostly Brahmin. Despite intentions that may have been genuinely revolutionary, it was not just theoretical tools they lacked, but also a ground-level understanding and empathy with 'the masses' who belonged to the subordinated castes. While Ambedkar believed that class was an important—and even primary—prism through which to view and understand society, he did not believe it was the only one. Ambedkar believed that the two enemies of the Indian working class were capitalism (in the liberal sense of the word) *and* Brahminism. Reflecting perhaps on his experience in the 1928 textile workers' strike, in *Annihilation of Caste* he asks:

> That seizure of power must be by a proletariat. The first question I ask is: Will the proletariat of India combine to bring about this revolution?... Can it be said that the proletariat of India, poor as it is, recognises no distinctions except that of the rich and poor? Can it be said that the poor in India recognise no such distinctions of caste or creed, high or low?[216]

To Indian communists, who treated caste as a sort of folk dialect derived from the classical language of class analysis, rather than as a unique, fully developed language of its own,

Ambedkar said, "[T]he caste system is not merely a division of labour. *It is also a division of labourers.*"[217]

Unable to reconcile his differences with the communists, and still looking for a political home for his ideas, Ambedkar decided to try and build one himself. In 1938, he founded his own political party, the Independent Labour Party (ILP). As its name suggests, the programme of the ILP was broad-based, overtly socialist and was not limited to issues of caste. Its manifesto announced "the principle of State management and State ownership of industry whenever it may become necessary in the interests of the people". It promised a separation between the judiciary and the executive. It said it would set up land mortgage banks, agriculturist producers' cooperatives and marketing societies.[218] Though it was a young party, the ILP did extremely well in the 1937 elections, winning sixteen of the eighteen seats it contested in the Bombay Presidency and the Central Provinces and Berar. In 1939, the British government, without consulting any Indians, declared that India was at war with Germany. In protest, the Congress party resigned from all provincial ministries and the provincial assemblies were dissolved. The brief but vigorous political life of the ILP came to an abrupt end.

Angered by Ambedkar's display of independence, the communists denounced him as an 'opportunist' and an 'imperial stooge'. In his book *History of the Indian Freedom Struggle*, E.M.S. Namboodiripad, the (Brahmin) former Chief Minister of Kerala and head of the first ever democratically elected communist government in the world, wrote about the conflict between Ambedkar and the left: "However, this was a great blow to the freedom movement. For this led to the diversion of the peoples' attention from the objective of full independence to the *mundane cause* of the uplift of Harijans [Untouchables]."[219]

The rift has not mended and has harmed both sides

mortally. For a brief period in the 1970s, the Dalit Panthers in Maharashtra tried to bridge the gap. They were the progeny of Ambedkar the radical (as opposed to Ambedkar the writer of the Constitution). They gave the Marathi word 'Dalit'—oppressed, broken—an all-India currency, and used it to refer not just to Untouchable communities, but to "the working people, the landless and poor peasants, women and all those who are being exploited politically and economically and in the name of religion".[220] This was a phenomenal and politically confident act of solidarity on their part. They saw Dalits as a Nation of the Oppressed. They identified their friends as "revolutionary parties set to break down the caste system and class rule" and "Left parties that are left in the true sense"; and their enemies as "Landlords, Capitalists, moneylenders and their lackeys". Their manifesto, essential reading for students of radical politics, fused the thinking of Ambedkar, Phule and Marx. The founders of the Dalit Panthers—Namdeo Dhasal, Arun Kamble and Raja Dhale—were writers and poets, and their work created a renaissance in Marathi literature.

It could have been the beginning of the revolution that India needed and is still waiting for, but the Dalit Panthers swiftly lost their bearings and disintegrated.

The caste–class question is not an easy one for political parties to address. The Communist Party's theoretical obtuseness to caste has lost it what ought to have been its natural constituency. The Communist Party of India and its offshoot, the Communist Party of India (Marxist), have more or less become bourgeois parties enmeshed in parliamentary politics. Those that split away from them in the late 1960s and independent Marxist-Leninist parties in other states (collectively known as the 'Naxalites', named after the first uprising in the village of Naxalbari in West Bengal) have tried to address the issue of caste and to make common cause with Dalits, but with little success. The few efforts they made to seize land from big zamindars and redistribute it to labourers failed because they did not have the mass support or the military firepower to see it through. Their sidelong nod to caste as opposed to a direct engagement with it has meant that even radical communist parties have lost the support of what could have been a truly militant and revolutionary constituency.

Dalits have been fragmented and pitted against each other. Many have had to move either into mainstream parliamentary politics or—with the public sector being hollowed out, and job opportunities in the private sector being denied to them—into the world of NGOs, with grants from the European Union, the Ford Foundation and other funding agencies with a long, self-serving history of defusing radical movements and harnessing them to 'market forces'.[221] There is no doubt that this funding has given a few Dalits an opportunity to be educated in what are thought to be the world's best universities. (This, after all, is what made Ambedkar the man he was.) However, even here, the Dalits' share in the massive NGO money-pie is minuscule. And within these institutions (some of which are generously funded by big corporations to work on issues of caste discrimination,[222] like Gandhi was), Dalits can be treated in unfair and ugly ways.

▼

In his search for primitive communism, S.A. Dange would have been better advised to look towards indigenous Adivasi communities rather than towards the ancient Vedic Brahmins and their yagnyas. Gandhi too could have done the same. If anybody was even remotely living out his ideal of frugal village life, of stepping lightly on the earth, it was not the Vedic Hindus, it was the Adivasis. For them, however, Gandhi showed the same level of disdain that he did for Black Africans. Speaking in 1896 at a public meeting in Bombay, he said: "The Santhals of Assam will be as useless in South Africa as the natives of that country."[223]

On the Adivasi question, Ambedkar too stumbles. So quick to react to slights against his own people, Ambedkar, in a passage in *Annihilation of Caste*, echoes the thinking of colonial missionaries and liberal ideologues, and adds his own touch of Brahminism:

> Thirteen million people living in the midst of civilisation are still in a savage state, and are leading the life of hereditary criminals... The Hindus will probably seek to account for this savage state of the aborigines by attributing to them congenital stupidity. They will probably not admit that the aborigines have remained savages because they made no effort to civilise them, to give them medical aid, to reform them, to make them good citizens... Civilising the aborigines means adopting them as your own, living in their midst, and cultivating fellow-feeling—in short, loving them...
>
> The Hindu has not realised that these aborigines are a source of potential danger. If these savages remain savages, they may not do any harm to the Hindus. But if they are reclaimed by non-Hindus and converted to their faiths, they will swell the ranks of the enemies of the Hindus.[224]

Today, Adivasis are the barricade against the pitiless march of modern capitalism. Their very existence poses the most radical questions about modernity and 'progress'—the ideas that Ambedkar embraced as one of the ways out of the caste system. Unfortunately, by viewing the Adivasi community through the lens of Western liberalism, Ambedkar's writing, which is otherwise so relevant in today's context, suddenly becomes dated.

Ambedkar's opinions about Adivasis betrayed a lack of information and understanding. First of all, Hindu evangelists like the Hindu Mahasabha had been working to 'assimilate' the

Adivasis since the 1920s (just like they were Balmiki-ising castes that were forced into cleaning and scavenging work). Tribes like the Ho, the Oraon, the Kols, the Santhals, the Mundas and the Gonds did not wish to be 'civilised' or 'assimilated'. They had rebelled time and again against the British as well as against zamindars and Bania moneylenders, and had fought fiercely to protect their land, culture and heritage. Thousands had been killed in these uprisings, but unlike the rest of India, they were never conquered. They still have not been. Today, they are the armed, militant end of a spectrum of struggles. They are waging nothing short of a civil war against the Indian state which has signed over Adivasi homelands to infrastructure and mining corporations. They are the backbone of the decades-long struggle against big dams in the Narmada Valley. They make up the ranks of the People's Liberation Guerilla Army of the Communist Party of India (Maoist) that is fighting tens of thousands of paramilitary forces that have been deployed by the government in the forests of Central India.

In a 1945 address in Bombay ("The Communal Deadlock and a Way to Solve It"), discussing the issue of proportionate representation, Ambedkar brought up the issue of Adivasi rights once again. He said:

> My proposals do not cover the Aboriginal Tribes although they are larger in number than the Sikhs, Anglo-Indians, Indian Christians and Parsis... The Aboriginal Tribes have not as yet developed any political sense to make the best use of their political opportunities and they may easily become mere instruments in the hands either of a majority or a minority and thereby disturb the balance without doing any good to themselves.[225]

This unfortunate way of describing a community was sometimes aimed at non-Adivasis too, in an equally troubling manner. At one point in *Annihilation of Caste* Ambedkar resorts to using the language of eugenics, a subject that was popular with European fascists: "Physically speaking the Hindus are a C3 people. They are a race of pygmies and dwarfs, stunted in stature and wanting in stamina."[226]

His views on Adivasis had serious consequences. In 1950, the Indian Constitution made the state the custodian of Adivasi homelands, thereby ratifying British colonial policy. The Adivasi population became squatters on their own land. By denying them their traditional rights to forest produce, it criminalised a whole way of life. It gave them the right to vote, but snatched away their livelihood and dignity.[227]

How different are Ambedkar's words on Adivasis from Gandhi's words on Untouchables when he said:

> Muslims and Sikhs are all well organised. The 'Untouchables' are not. There is very little political consciousness among them, and they are so horribly treated that I want to save them against themselves. If they had separate electorates, their lives would be miserable in villages which are the strongholds of Hindu orthodoxy. It is the superior class of Hindus who have to do penance for having neglected the 'Untouchables' for ages. That penance can be done by active social reform and by making the lot of the 'Untouchables' more bearable by acts of service, but not by asking for separate electorates for them.[228]

Gandhi said this at the Second Round Table Conference in London in 1931. It was the first public face-to-face encounter between Ambedkar and Gandhi.

THE CONFRONTATION

The Congress had boycotted the First Round Table Conference in 1930, but nominated Gandhi as its representative in the second. The aim of the conference was to frame a new constitution for self-rule. The princely states and representatives of various minority communities—Muslims, Sikhs, Christians, Parsis and Untouchables—were present. Adivasis went unrepresented. For Untouchables, it was a historic occasion. It was the first time that they had been invited as a separately represented constituency. One of the several committees that made up the conference was the Minority Committee, charged with the task of finding a workable solution to the growing communal question. It was potentially the most inflammable and, perhaps for that reason, was chaired by the British Prime Minister, Ramsay MacDonald.

It was to this committee that Ambedkar submitted his memorandum, which he described as *A Scheme of Political Safeguards for the Protection of the Depressed Classes in the Future Constitution of a Self-Governing India*. It was, for its time, within the framework of liberal debates on rights and citizenship, a revolutionary document. In it, Ambedkar tried to do in law what he dreamt of achieving socially and politically. This document was an early draft of some of the ideas that Ambedkar eventually managed to put into the Constitution of post-1947 India.

Under "Condition No. 1: Equal Citizenship", it says:

> The Depressed Classes cannot consent to subject themselves to majority rule in their present state of hereditary bondsmen. Before majority rule is established, their emancipation from the system of untouchability must be an accomplished fact. It must not be left to the will of the majority. The Depressed Classes must be made free citizens entitled to all the rights of citizenship in common with other citizens of the State.[229]

The memorandum went on to delineate what would constitute Fundamental Rights and how they were to be protected. It gave Untouchables the right to access all public places. It dwelt at length on social boycotts and suggested they be declared a criminal offence. It prescribed a series of measures by which Untouchables would be protected from social boycotts and caste Hindus punished for instigating and promoting them. Condition No. 5 asked that a Public Service Commission be set up to ensure Untouchables "Adequate Representation in the Services". This is what has eventually evolved into the system of reservation in educational institutions and government jobs, against which privileged castes in recent times have militantly agitated.[230]

The most unique aspect of Ambedkar's memorandum was his proposal for a system of positive discrimination within the electoral system. Ambedkar did not believe that universal adult franchise alone could secure equal rights for Untouchables. Since the Untouchable population was scattered across the country in little settlements on the outskirts of Hindu villages, Ambedkar realised that within the geographical demarcation of a political constituency, they would always be a minority and would never be in a position to elect a candidate of their own choice. He suggested that Untouchables, who had been despised and devalued for so many centuries, be given a separate electorate so that they could, without interference from the Hindu orthodoxy, develop into a political constituency with a leadership of its own. In addition to this, and in order that they retain their connection with mainstream politics, he suggested that they be given the right to vote for general candidates too. Both the separate electorate and the double vote were to last for a period of only ten years. Though the details were not agreed upon, when the conference concluded, all the delegates unanimously agreed that the Untouchables should, like the other minorities, have a separate electorate.[231]

While the First Round Table Conference was in session in London, India was in turmoil. In January 1930, the Congress had declared its demand for Poorna Swaraj—complete independence. Gandhi showcased his genius as a political organiser and launched his most imaginative political action yet—the Salt Satyagraha. He called on Indians to march to the sea and break the British salt tax laws. Hundreds of thousands of Indians rallied to his call. Jails filled to overflowing. Ninety thousand people were arrested. Between salt and water, between the Touchables' satyagraha and the Untouchables' 'duragraha' lay a sharply divided universe—of politics, of philosophy and of morality.

At its Karachi Session in March 1931, the Congress passed a Resolution of Fundamental Rights for a free India.[232] It was a valuable, enlightened document, and it included some of the rights Ambedkar had been campaigning for. It laid the foundation for a modern, secular and largely socialist state. The rights included the freedoms of speech, press, assembly and association, equality before law, universal adult franchise, free and compulsory primary education, a guaranteed living wage for every citizen and limited hours of work. It underlined the protection of women and peasants, and state ownership or control of key industries, mines and transport. Most important, it created a firewall between religion and the state.

Notwithstanding the admirable principles of the Resolution of Fundamental Rights that had been passed, the view from the bottom was slightly different. The 1930 elections to the provincial legislatures coincided with the Salt Satyagraha. The Congress had boycotted the elections. In order to embarrass 'respectable' Hindus who did not heed the boycott and stood as independent candidates, the Congress fielded mock candidates who were Untouchables—two cobblers, a barber, a milkman and a sweeper. The idea was that no self-respecting, privileged-caste Hindu would want to be part of an institution where he or she was put on a par with Untouchables.[233] Putting up Untouchables as mock candidates was a Congress party tactic that had begun with the 1920 elections and went on right up to 1943. Ambedkar says:

> What were the means adopted by the Congress to prevent Hindus from standing on an independent ticket? The means were to make the legislatures objects of contempt. Accordingly, the Congress, in various provinces, started processions carrying placards saying, 'Who will go to the Legislatures? Only barbers, cobblers, potters and sweepers.' In the processions, one man would utter the question as part of the slogan and the whole crowd would repeat as answer the second part of the slogan.[234]

At the Round Table Conference, Gandhi and Ambedkar clashed, both claiming that they were the real representatives of the Untouchables. The conference went on for weeks. Gandhi eventually agreed to separate electorates for Muslims and Sikhs, but would not countenance Ambedkar's argument for a separate electorate for Untouchables. He resorted to his usual rhetoric: "I would far rather that Hinduism died than that Untouchability lived."[235]

Gandhi refused to acknowledge that Ambedkar had the right to represent Untouchables. Ambedkar would not back down either. Nor was there a call for him to. Untouchable groups from across India, including Mangoo Ram of the Ad Dharm movement, sent telegrams in support of Ambedkar. Eventually Gandhi said, "Those who speak of the political rights of Untouchables do not know their India, do not know how Indian society is today constructed, and therefore I want to say with all the emphasis that I can command that if I was the only person to resist this thing I would resist it with my life."[236] Having delivered his threat, Gandhi took the boat back to India. On the way, he dropped in on Mussolini in Rome and was extremely impressed by him and his "care of the poor, his opposition to super-urbanisation, his efforts to bring about co-ordination between capital and labour".[237]

A year later, Ramsay MacDonald announced the British government's decision on the Communal Question. It awarded the Untouchables a separate electorate for a period of twenty years. At the time, Gandhi was serving a sentence in Yerawada Central Jail in Poona. From prison, he announced that unless the provision of separate electorates for Untouchables was revoked, he would fast to death.

He waited for a month. When he did not get his way, Gandhi began his fast from prison. This fast was completely against his own maxims of satyagraha. It was barefaced blackmail, nothing less manipulative than the threat of committing public suicide. The British government said it would revoke the provision only if the Untouchables agreed. The country spun like a top. Public statements were issued, petitions signed, prayers offered, meetings held, appeals made. It was a preposterous situation: privileged-caste Hindus, who segregated themselves from Untouchables in every possible way, who deemed them unworthy of human association, who shunned their very touch, who wanted separate food, water, schools, roads, temples and wells, now said that India would be balkanised if Untouchables had a separate electorate. And Gandhi, who believed so fervently and so vocally in the system that upheld that separation was starving himself to death to deny Untouchables a separate electorate.

The gist of it was that the caste Hindus wanted the power to close the door on Untouchables, but on no account could Untouchables be given the power to close the door on themselves. The masters knew that choice was power.

As the frenzy mounted, Ambedkar became the villain, the traitor, the man who wanted to dissever India, the man who was trying to kill Gandhi. Political heavyweights of the garam dal (militants) as well as the naram dal (moderates), including Tagore, Nehru and C. Rajagopalachari, weighed in on Gandhi's side. To placate Gandhi, privileged-caste Hindus made a show of sharing food on the streets with Untouchables, and many Hindu temples were thrown open to them, albeit temporarily. Behind those gestures of accommodation, a wall of tension built up too. Several Untouchable leaders feared that Ambedkar would be held responsible if Gandhi succumbed to his fast, and this in turn, could put the lives of ordinary Untouchables in danger. One of them was M.C. Rajah, the Untouchable leader from Madras, who, according to an eyewitness account of the events, said:

> For thousands of years we had been treated as Untouchables, downtrodden, insulted, despised. The Mahatma is staking his life for our sake, and if he dies, for the next thousands of years we shall be where we have been, if not worse. There will be such a strong feeling against us that we brought about his death, that the mind of the whole Hindu community and the whole civilised community will kick us downstairs further still. I am not going to stand by you any longer. I will join the conference and find a solution and I will part company from you.[238]

What could Ambedkar do? He tried to hold out with his usual arsenal of logic and reason, but the situation was way beyond all that. He didn't stand a chance. After four days of the fast, on 24 September 1932, Ambedkar visited Gandhi in Yerawada prison and signed the Poona Pact. The next day in Bombay he made a public speech in which he was uncharacteristically gracious about Gandhi: "I was astounded to see that the man who held such divergent views from mine at the Round Table Conference came immediately to my rescue and not to the rescue of the other side."[239]

Later, though, having recovered from the trauma, Ambedkar wrote:

> There was nothing noble in the fast. It was a foul and filthy act... [I]t was the worst form of coercion against a helpless people to give up the constitutional safeguards of which they had become possessed under the Prime Minister's Award and agree to live on the mercy of the Hindus. It was a vile and wicked act. How can

the Untouchables regard such a man as honest and sincere?[240]

According to the Pact, instead of separate electorates, the Untouchables would have reserved seats in general constituencies. The number of seats they were allotted in the provincial legislatures increased (from seventy-eight to 148), but the candidates, because they would now have to be acceptable to their privileged-caste–dominated constituencies, lost their teeth.[241] Uncle Tom won the day. Gandhi saw to it that leadership remained in the hands of the privileged castes.

In *The New Jim Crow*, Michelle Alexander[242] describes how, in the United States, criminalisation and mass incarceration has led to the disenfranchisement of an extraordinary percentage of the African American population. In India, in a far slyer way, an apparently generous form of enfranchisement has ensured the virtual disenfranchisement of the Dalit population.

Nevertheless, what to Ambedkar was a foul and filthy act appeared to others as nothing less than a divine miracle. Louis Fischer, author of perhaps the most widely read biography of Gandhi ever written, said:

> The fast could not kill the curse of untouchability which was more than three thousand years old … but after the fast, untouchability forfeited its public approval; the belief in it was destroyed… Gandhi's 'Epic Fast' snapped a long chain that stretched back into antiquity and had enslaved tens of millions. Some links of the chain remained. Many wounds from the chain remained. But nobody would forge new links, nobody would link the links together again… It [the Poona Pact] marked a religious reformation, a psychological revolution. Hinduism was purging itself of a millennial sickness. The mass purified itself in practice… If Gandhi had done nothing else in his life but shatter the structure of untouchability he would have been a great social reformer… Gandhi's agony gave vicarious pain to his adorers who knew they must not kill God's messenger on earth. It was evil to prolong his

> suffering. It was blessed to save him by being good to those whom he had called 'The Children of God'.[243]

On the great occasion of the Poona Pact, contradicting the stand he took at the Round Table Conference, Gandhi was quite willing to accept Ambedkar's signature on the pact as the representative of the Untouchables. Gandhi himself did not sign the pact, but the list of the other signatories is interesting: G.D. Birla, Gandhi's industrialist-patron; Pandit Madan Mohan Malaviya, a conservative Brahmin leader and founder of the right-wing Hindu Mahasabha (of which Gandhi's future assassin, Nathuram Godse, was a member); V.D. Savarkar, accused of conspiracy in Gandhi's assassination, who also served as president of the Mahasabha; Palwankar Baloo, an Untouchable cricketer of the Chambhar caste, who was celebrated earlier as a sporting idol by Ambedkar, and whom the Congress and the Hindu Mahasabha propped up as an opponent of Ambedkar;[244] and, of course, M.C. Rajah (who would, much later, regret his collusion with Gandhi, the Hindu Mahasabha and the Congress).[245]

Among the (many) reasons that criticism of Gandhi is not just frowned upon, but often censored in India, 'secularists' tell us, is that Hindu nationalists (from whose midst Gandhi's assassins arose, and whose star is on the ascendant in India these days) will seize upon such criticism and turn it to their advantage. The fact is there was never much daylight between Gandhi's views on caste and those of the Hindu right. From a Dalit point of view, Gandhi's assassination could appear to be more a fratricidal killing than an assassination by an ideological opponent. Even today, Narendra Modi, Hindu nationalism's most aggressive proponent, and a possible future prime minister, is able to invoke Gandhi in his public speeches without the slightest discomfort. (Modi invoked Gandhi to justify the introduction of two anti-minority legislations in Gujarat—the anti-conversion law of

2003, called the Gujarat Freedom of Religion Act, and the amendment to the old cow-slaughter law in 2011.[246]) Many of Modi's pronouncements are delivered from the Mahatma Mandir in Gandhinagar, a spanking new convention hall whose foundation contains sand brought in special urns from each of Gujarat's 18,000 villages, many of which continue to practise egregious forms of untouchability.[247]

After the Poona Pact, Gandhi directed all his energy and passion towards the eradication of untouchability. For a start, he rebaptised Untouchables and gave them a patronising name: Harijans. 'Hari' is the name for a male deity in Hinduism, 'jan' is people. So Harijans are People of God, though in order to infantilise them even further, in translation they are referred to as 'Children of God'. In this way, Gandhi anchored Untouchables firmly to the Hindu faith.[248] He founded a new newspaper called *Harijan*. He started the Harijan Sevak Sangh (Harijan Service Society), which he insisted would be manned only by privileged-caste Hindus who had to do penance for their past sins against Untouchables. Ambedkar saw all this as the Congress's plan to "kill Untouchables by kindness".[249]

Gandhi toured the country, preaching against untouchability. He was heckled and attacked by Hindus even more conservative than himself, but he did not swerve from his purpose. Everything that happened was harnessed to the cause of eradicating caste. In January 1934, there was a major earthquake in Bihar. Almost twenty thousand people lost their lives. Writing in the *Harijan* on 24 February, Gandhi shocked even his colleagues in the Congress when he said it was god's punishment to the people for the sin of practising untouchability. None of this stopped the Congress party from continuing with a tradition it had invented: it once again fielded mock Untouchable candidates in the 1934 elections to the Central Legislature.[250]

Gandhi could not, it appears, conceive of a role for

Untouchables other than as victims in need of ministration. That they had also been psychologically hardwired into the caste system, that they too might need to be roused out of thousands of years of being conditioned to think of themselves as subhuman, was an antithetical, intimidating idea to Gandhi. The Poona Pact was meant to defuse or at least delay the political awakening of Untouchables.

What Gandhi's campaign against untouchability did, and did effectively, was to rub balm on injuries that were centuries old. To a vast mass of Untouchables, accustomed only to being terrorised, shunned and brutalised, this missionary activity would have induced feelings of gratitude and even worship. Gandhi knew that. He was a politician. Ambedkar was not. Or, at any rate, not a very good one. Gandhi knew how to make charity an event, a piece of theatre, a spectacular display of fireworks. So, while the Doctor was searching for a more lasting cure, the Saint journeyed across India distributing a placebo.

The chief concern of the Harijan Sevak Sangh was to persuade privileged castes to open up temples to Untouchables—ironic, because Gandhi was no temple-goer himself. Nor was his sponsor G.D. Birla, who, in an interview to Margaret Bourke-White, said, "Frankly speaking, we build temples but we don't believe in temples. We build temples to spread a kind of religious mentality."[251] The opening of temples had already begun during the days of Gandhi's epic fast. Under pressure from the Harijan Sevak Sangh, hundreds of temples were thrown open to Untouchables. (Some, like the Guruvayur temple in Kerala, refused point-blank. Gandhi contemplated a fast but soon changed his mind.[252]) Others announced that they were open to Untouchables but found ways of humiliating them and making it impossible for them to enter with any sort of dignity.

A Temple Entry Bill was tabled in the Central Legislature in 1933. Gandhi and the Congress supported it enthusiastically.

But when it became apparent that the privileged castes were seriously opposed to it, they backed out.[253]

Ambedkar was sceptical about the temple entry programme. He saw that it had a tremendous psychological impact on Untouchables, but he recognised temple entry as the beginning of 'assimilation'—of Hinduising and Brahminising Untouchables, drawing them further into being partners in their own humiliation. If the "infection of imitation" of Brahminism had been implanted in Untouchables even when they had been denied entry into temples for centuries, what would temple entry do for them? On 14 February 1933, Ambedkar issued a statement on temple entry:

> What the Depressed Classes want is a religion that will give them equality of social status ... nothing can be more odious and vile than that admitted social evils should be sought to be justified on the ground of religion. The Depressed Classes may not be able to overthrow inequities to which they are subjected. But they have made up their mind not to tolerate a religion that will lend its support to the continuance of these inequities.[254]

Ambedkar was only echoing what a fourteen-year-old Untouchable Mang girl, Muktabai Salve, had said long ago. She was a student in the school for Untouchable children that Jotiba and Savitri Phule ran in Poona. In 1855, she said, "Let that religion, where only one person is privileged and the rest are deprived, perish from the earth and let it never enter our minds to be proud of such a religion."[255]

Ambedkar had learned from experience that Christianity, Sikhism, Islam and Zoroastrianism were not impervious to caste discrimination. In 1934, he had a reprise of his old experiences. He was visiting the Daulatabad fort, in the princely state of Hyderabad, with a group of friends and co-workers. It was the month of Ramzan. Dusty and tired from their journey,

Ambedkar and his friends stopped to drink water and wash their faces from a public tank. They were surrounded by a mob of angry Muslims calling them 'Dheds' (a derogatory term for Untouchables). They were abused, nearly assaulted and prevented from touching the water. "This will show," Ambedkar writes in his *Autobiographical Notes*, "that a person who is Untouchable to a Hindu, is also Untouchable to a Mohammedan."[256]

A new spiritual home was nowhere in sight.

Still, at the 1935 Yeola conference, Ambedkar renounced Hinduism. In 1936, he published the incendiary (and overpriced, as Gandhi patronisingly commented) text of *Annihilation of Caste* that set out the reasons for why he had done so.

That same year, Gandhiji too made a memorable contribution to literature. He was by now sixty-eight years old. He wrote a classic essay called "The Ideal Bhangi":

> The Brahmin's duty is to look after the sanitation of the soul, the Bhangi's that of the body of society ... and yet our woebegone Indian society has branded the Bhangi as a social pariah, set him down at the bottom of the scale, held him fit only to receive kicks and abuse, a creature who must subsist on the leavings of the caste people and dwell on the dung heap.
>
> If only we had given due recognition to the status of the Bhangi as equal to that of the Brahmin, our villages, no less their inhabitants would have looked a picture of cleanliness and order. I therefore make bold to state without any manner of hesitation or doubt that not till the invidious distinction between Brahmin and Bhangi is removed will our society enjoy health, prosperity and peace and be happy.

He then outlined the educational requirements, practical skills and etiquette an ideal Bhangi should possess:

> What qualities therefore should such an honoured servant of society exemplify in his person? In my opinion an ideal Bhangi

> should have a thorough knowledge of the principles of sanitation. He should know how a right kind of latrine is constructed and the correct way of cleaning it. He should know how to overcome and destroy the odour of excreta and the various disinfectants to render them innocuous. He should likewise know the process of converting urine and night soil into manure. But that is not all. My ideal Bhangi would know the quality of night soil and urine. He would keep a close watch on these and give timely warning to the individual concerned...

The *Manusmriti* says a Shudra should not amass wealth even if he has the ability, for a Shudra who amasses wealth annoys the Brahmin.[257] Gandhi, a Bania, for whom the *Manusmriti* prescribes usury as a divine calling, says: "Such an ideal Bhangi, while deriving his livelihood from his occupation, would approach it only as a sacred duty. In other words, he would not dream of amassing wealth out of it."[258]

Seventy years later, in his book *Karmayogi* (which he withdrew after the Balmiki community protested), Narendra Modi proved he was a diligent disciple of the Mahatma:

> I do not believe they have been doing this job just to sustain their livelihood. Had this been so, they would not have continued with this kind of job generation after generation... At some point of time somebody must have got the enlightenment that it is their (Balmikis') duty to work for the happiness of the entire society and the Gods; that they have to do this job bestowed upon them by Gods; and this job should continue as internal spiritual activity for centuries.[259]

The naram dal and the garam dal may be separate political parties today, but ideologically they are not as far apart from each other as we think they are.

Like all the other Hindu reformers, Gandhi too was alarmed by Ambedkar's talk of renouncing Hinduism. He adamantly opposed the religious conversion of Untouchables. In November

1936, in a now-famous conversation with John Mott—an American evangelist and chairman of the International Missionary Council—Gandhi said:

> It hurt me to find Christian bodies vying with the Muslims and Sikhs in trying to add to the numbers of their fold. It seemed to me an ugly performance and a travesty of religion. They even proceeded to enter into secret conclaves with Dr Ambedkar. I should have understood and appreciated your prayers for the Harijans, but instead you made an appeal to those who had not even the mind and intelligence to understand what you talked; they have certainly not the intelligence to distinguish between Jesus and Mohammed and Nanak and so on… If Christians want to associate themselves with this reform movement they should do so without any idea of conversion.
> J.M.: Apart from this unseemly competition, should they not preach the Gospel with reference to its acceptance?
> G: Would you, Dr Mott, preach the Gospel to a cow? Well, some of the untouchables are worse than cows in understanding. I mean they can no more distinguish between the relative merits of Islam and Hinduism and Christianity than a cow. You can only preach through your life. The rose does not say: 'Come and smell me.'[260]

It's true that Gandhi often contradicted himself. It's also true that he was capable of being remarkably consistent. For more than half a century—throughout his adult life—his pronouncements on the inherent qualities of Black Africans, Untouchables and the labouring classes remained consistently insulting. His refusal to allow working-class people and Untouchables to create their own political organisations and elect their own representatives (which Ambedkar considered to be fundamental to the notion of citizenship) remained consistent too.[261]

Gandhi's political instincts served the Congress party extremely well. His campaign of temple entry drew the Untouchable population in great numbers to the Congress.

Though Ambedkar had a formidable intellect, he didn't have the sense of timing, the duplicity, the craftiness and the ability to be unscrupulous—qualities that a good politician needs. His constituency was made up of the poorest, most oppressed sections of the population. He had no financial backing. In 1942, Ambedkar reconfigured the Independent Labour Party into the much more self-limiting Scheduled Castes Federation. The timing was wrong. By then, the national movement was reigniting. Gandhi had announced the Quit India Movement. The Muslim League's demand for Pakistan was gaining traction, and for a while caste identity became less important that the Hindu–Muslim issue.

By the mid-1940s, as the prospect of partition loomed, the subordinated castes in several states had been 'assimilated' into Hinduism. They began to participate in militant Hindu rallies; in Noakhali in Bengal, for instance, they functioned as an outlying vigilante army in the run-up to the bloodbath of partition.[262]

In 1947 Pakistan became the world's first Islamic republic. More than six decades later, as the War on Terror continues in its many avatars, political Islam is turning inwards, narrowing and hardening its precincts. Meanwhile, political Hinduism is expanding and broadening. Today, even the Bhakti movement has been 'assimilated' as a form of popular, folk Hinduism.[263] The naram dal, often dressed up as 'secular nationalism', has recruited Jotiba Phule, Pandita Ramabai and even Ambedkar, all of whom denounced Hinduism, back into the 'Hindu fold' as people Hindus can be 'proud' of.[264] Ambedkar is being assimilated in another way too—as Gandhi's junior partner in their joint fight against untouchability.

The anxiety around demography has by no means abated. Hindu supremacist organisations like the Rashtriya Swayamsevak Sangh and the Shiv Sena are working hard (and successfully) at luring Dalits and Adivasis into the 'Hindu fold'. In the forests of Central India, where a corporate war for minerals is raging, the Vishwa Hindu Parishad (VHP) and the Bajrang Dal (both organisations that are loosely linked to the RSS) run mass conversion programmes called 'ghar wapsi'—the return home—in which Adivasi people are 'reconverted' to Hinduism. Privileged-caste Hindus, who pride themselves on being descendants of Aryan invaders, are busy persuading people who belong to indigenous, autochthonous tribes to return 'home'. It makes you feel that irony is no longer a literary option in this part of the world.

Dalits who have been harnessed to the 'Hindu fold' serve another purpose: even if they have not been part of the outlying army, they can be used as scapegoats for the crimes the privileged castes commit.

In 2002, in the Godhra railway station in Gujarat, a train compartment was mysteriously burned down, and fifty-eight Hindu pilgrims were charred to death. With not much evidence to prove their guilt, some Muslims were arrested as the perpetrators. The Muslim community as a whole was collectively blamed for the crime. Over the next few days, the VHP and the Bajrang Dal led a pogrom in which more than two thousand Muslims were murdered, women were mob-raped and burnt alive in broad daylight and a hundred and fifty thousand people were driven from their homes.[265] After the pogrom, 287 people were arrested under the Prevention of Terrorism Act (POTA). Of them, 286 were Muslim and one was a Sikh.[266] Most of them are still in prison.

If Muslims were the 'terrorists', who were the 'rioters'? In his essay "Blood Under Saffron: The Myth of Dalit–Muslim Confrontation", Raju Solanki, a Gujarati Dalit writer who studied the pattern of arrests, says that of the 1,577 'Hindus' who were arrested (not under POTA of course), 747 were Dalits and 797 belonged to 'Other Backward Classes'. Nineteen were Patels, two were Banias and two were Brahmins. The massacres of Muslims occurred in several cities and villages in Gujarat. However, Solanki points out that not a single massacre took place in *bastis* where Dalits and Muslims lived together.[267]

Narendra Modi, the Chief Minister of Gujarat who presided over the pogrom, has since won the state elections three times in a row. Despite being a Shudra, he has endeared himself to the Hindu right by being more blatantly and ruthlessly anti-Muslim than any other Indian politician. When he was asked in a recent interview whether he regretted what happened in 2002, he said, "[I]f we are driving a car, we are a driver, and someone else is driving a car and we're sitting behind, even then if a puppy comes under the wheel, will it be painful or not? Of course it is. If I'm a Chief Minister or not, I'm a human being. If something bad happens anywhere, it is natural to be sad."[268]

As blatantly casteist and communal as the Hindu right is, in their search for a foothold in mainstream politics, even radical Dalits have made common cause with it. In the mid-1990s, the remarkable Dalit poet Namdeo Dhasal, one of the founders of the Dalit Panthers, joined the Shiv Sena. In 2006, Dhasal shared the dais with RSS chief K.S. Sudarshan at a book launch and praised the RSS's efforts at equality.[269]

It is easy to dismiss what Dhasal did as an unforgivable compromise with fascists. However, in parliamentary politics, after the Poona Pact—rather *because* of the Poona Pact—Dalits as a political constituency have had to make alliances with those whose interests are hostile to their own. For Dalits, as we have seen, the distance between the Hindu 'right' and the Hindu 'left' is not as great as it might appear to be to others.

Despite the debacle of the Poona Pact, Ambedkar didn't entirely give up the idea of separate electorates. Unfortunately, his second party, the Scheduled Castes Federation, was defeated in the 1946 elections to the Provincial Legislature. The defeat meant that Ambedkar lost his place on the Executive Council in the Interim Ministry that was formed in August 1946. It was a serious blow, because Ambedkar desperately wanted to use his position on the Executive Council to become part of the committee that would draft the Indian Constitution. Worried that this was not going to be possible, and in order to put external pressure on the Drafting Committee, Ambedkar, in March 1947, published a document called *States and Minorities*—his proposed constitution for a 'United States of India' (an idea whose time has perhaps come). Fortunately for him, the Muslim League chose Jogendranath Mandal, a colleague of Ambedkar's and a Scheduled Castes Federation leader from Bengal, as one of its candidates on the Executive Council. Mandal made sure that Ambedkar was elected to the Constituent Assembly from the Bengal province. But disaster struck again. After partition, East Bengal went to Pakistan and Ambedkar lost his position once more. In a gesture of goodwill, and perhaps because there was no one as equal to the task as he was, the Congress appointed Ambedkar to the Constituent Assembly. In August 1947, Ambedkar was appointed India's first Law Minister and Chairman of the Drafting Committee for the Constitution. Across the new border, Jogendranath Mandal became Pakistan's first Law Minister.[270] It was extraordinary that, through all the chaos and prejudice, the first law ministers of both India and Pakistan were Dalits. Mandal was eventually disillusioned with Pakistan and returned to India. Ambedkar was disillusioned too, but he really had nowhere to go.

The Indian Constitution was drafted by a committee, and reflected the views of its privileged-caste members more than Ambedkar's. Still, several of the safeguards for Untouchables that he had outlined in *States and Minorities* did find their way in. Some of Ambedkar's more radical suggestions, such as nationalising agriculture and key industries, were summarily dropped. The drafting process left Ambedkar more than a little unhappy. In March 1955, he said in the Rajya Sabha (India's Upper House of Parliament): "The Constitution was a wonderful temple we built for the gods, but before they could be installed, the devils have taken possession."[271] In 1954, Ambedkar contested his last election as a Scheduled Castes Federation candidate and lost.

▼

Ambedkar was disillusioned with Hinduism, with its high priests, its saints and its politicians. Yet, the response to temple entry probably taught him how much people long to belong to a spiritual community, and how inadequate a charter of civil rights or a constitution is to address those needs.

After twenty years of contemplation, during which he studied Islam as well as Christianity, Ambedkar turned to Buddhism. This, too, he entered in his own, distinct, angular way. He was wary of classical Buddhism, of the ways in which Buddhist philosophy could, had and continues to be used to justify war and unimaginable cruelty. (The most recent example is the Sri Lankan government's version of state Buddhism, which culminated in the genocidal killing of at least 40,000 ethnic Tamils and the internal displacement of 300,000 people in 2009.[272]) Ambedkar's Buddhism, called 'Navayana Buddhism'[273] or the Fourth Way, distinguished between religion and dhamma. "The purpose of Religion is to explain the origin of the world," Ambedkar said, sounding very much like Karl Marx, "the purpose of Dhamma is to reconstruct the world."[274] On 14 October 1956, in Nagpur, only months before his death, Ambedkar, Sharda Kabir, his (Brahmin) second wife, and half a million supporters took the vow of the Three Jewels and Five Precepts and converted to Buddhism. It was his most radical act.

It marked his departure from Western liberalism and its purely materialistic vision of a society based on 'rights', a vision whose origin coincided with the rise of modern capitalism.

Ambedkar did not have enough money to print his major work on Buddhism, *The Buddha and His Dhamma*, before he died.[275]

He wore suits, yes. But he died in debt.

▼

Where does that leave the rest of us?

Though they call the age we are living through the Kali Yuga,[276] Ram Rajya could be just around the corner. The fourteenth-century Babri Masjid, supposedly built on the birthplace of Lord Ram in Ayodhya, was demolished by Hindu storm troopers on 6 December 1992, Ambedkar's death anniversary. We await with apprehension the construction of a grand Ram temple in its place. As Mahatma Gandhi desired, the rich man has been left in possession of his (as well as everybody else's) wealth. Chaturvarna reigns unchallenged: the Brahmin largely controls knowledge; the Vaishya dominates trade. The Kshatriyas have seen better days, but they are still, for the most part, rural landowners. The Shudras live in the basement of the Big House and keep intruders at bay. The Adivasis are fighting for their very survival. And the Dalits—well, we've been through all that.

Can caste be annihilated?

Not unless we show the courage to rearrange the stars in our firmament. Not unless those who call themselves revolutionary develop a radical critique of Brahminism. Not unless those who understand Brahminism sharpen their critique of capitalism.

And not unless we read Babasaheb Ambedkar. If not inside our classrooms, then outside them. Until then we will remain what he called the "sick men" and women of Hindustan, who seem to have no desire to get well.

NOTES

1 For this account of Khairlanji, I have drawn on Anand Teltumbde (2010a). For one of the first comprehensive news reports on the incident, see Sabrina Buckwalter (2006).

2 For an analysis of the lower court judgement, see S. Anand (2008b).

3 On 11 July 1996, the Ranveer Sena, a privileged-caste, feudal militia murdered twenty-one landless labourers in Bathani Tola village in the state of Bihar. In 2012, the Patna High Court acquitted all the accused. On 1 December 1997, the Ranveer Sena massacred fifty-eight Dalits in Laxmanpur Bathe village, also in Bihar. In April 2010, the trial court convicted all the twenty-six accused. It sentenced ten of them to life imprisonment and sixteen to death. In October 2013, the Patna High Court suspended the conviction of all twenty-six accused, saying the prosecution had not produced any evidence to guarantee any punishment at all.

4 These are some of the major crimes against Dalits and subordinated castes that have taken place in recent times: in 1968, in Keezhvenmani in the state of Tamil Nadu, forty-four Dalits were burnt alive; in 1977, in Belchi village of Bihar, fourteen Dalits were burnt alive; in 1978, in Marichjhapi, an island in the Sundarbans mangrove forest of West Bengal, hundreds of Dalit refugees from Bangladesh were massacred during a left-led government's eviction drive; in 1984, in Karamchedu in the state of Andhra Pradesh, six Dalits were murdered, three Dalit women raped and many more wounded; in 1991, in Chunduru, also in Andhra Pradesh, nine Dalits were slaughtered and their bodies dumped in a canal; in 1997, in Melavalavu in Tamil Nadu, an elected Dalit panchayat leader and five Dalits were murdered; in 2000, in Kambalapalli in the state of Karnataka, six Dalits were burnt alive; in 2002, in Jhajjar in the state of Haryana, five Dalits were lynched outside a police station. See also the documentation by Human Rights Watch (1999) and the Navsarjan report (2009).

5 BAWS 9, 296. All references to B.R. Ambedkar's writings, except

from *Annihilation of Caste*, are from the *Babasaheb Ambedkar: Writings and Speeches* (BAWS) series published by the Education Department, Government of Maharashtra. All references to *Annihilation of Caste* (henceforth AoC) are from the Navayana edition.

6 Rupa Viswanath (2012) writes, "Where 'Dalit' refers to all those Indians, past and present, traditionally regarded as outcastes and untouchable, 'SC' is a modern governmental category that explicitly excludes Christian and Muslim Dalits. For the current version of the President's Constitution (Scheduled Castes) Order, which tells us who will count as SC for the purposes of constitutional and legal protections, is entirely unambiguous: 'No person who professes a religion different from the Hindu, the Sikh or the Buddhist religion shall be deemed to be a member of a Scheduled Caste.'" She goes on to say, "It was only under Congress rule, in 1950, that the President's Order explicitly defined SC on the basis of religious criteria, although Christian Dalits were excluded from SC for electoral purposes by the Government of India Act 1935. From that point onwards, Dalits who had converted out of Hinduism lost not only reservations, but also, after 1989, protection under the Prevention of Atrocities Act. Later, SC was expanded to include Sikh and Buddhist Dalits, but official discrimination against Muslim and Christian Dalits remains." If Christians as well as Muslims who face the stigma of caste were to be included in the number of those who can be counted as Dalit, their share in the Indian population would far exceed the official 2011 Census figure of 17 per cent. See also Note 2 to the Preface of the 1937 edition of AoC (184).

7 On 16 December 2012, a woman was brutally tortured and gang-raped in a bus in New Delhi. She died on 29 December. The atrocity led to mass protests for days together. Unusually, a large number of middle-class people participated in them. In the wake of the protests the law against rape was made more stringent. See Jason Burke's reports in *The Guardian*, especially "Delhi Rape: How India's Other Half Lives" (10 September 2013). http://www.theguardian.com/world/2013/sep/10/delhi-gang-rape-india-women. Accessed 12 September 2013.

8 National Crime Records Bureau (NCRB) 2012, 423–4.

9 Privileged castes punish Dalits by forcing them to eat human excreta though this often goes unreported. In Thinniyam village in Tamil Nadu's Tiruchi district, on 22 May 2002, two Dalits, Murugesan and Ramasami, were forced to feed each other human excreta and branded with hot iron rods for publicly declaring that they had been cheated by the village chief. See Viswanathan (2005). In fact, "The Statement of Objects and Reasons of the Scheduled Castes and Scheduled Tribes (Prevention of Atrocities) Act, 1989" states this as one of the crimes it seeks to redress: "Of late, there has been an increase in the disturbing trend of commission of certain atrocities like making the Scheduled Caste person eat inedible substances like human excreta and attacks on and mass killings of helpless Scheduled Castes and Scheduled Tribes and rape of women belonging to the Scheduled Castes and Scheduled Tribes."

10 According to the tenets of their faith, Sikhs are not supposed to practise caste. However, those from the Untouchable castes who converted to Sikhism continue to be treated as Untouchable. For an account of how caste affects Sikhism, see Mark Juergensmeyer (1982/2009).

11 BAWS 1, 222.

12 See, for example, Madhu Kishwar (*Tehelka*, 11 February 2006) who says "the much reviled caste system has played a very significant role in making Indian democracy vibrant by making it possible for people to offer a good measure of resistance to centralised, authoritarian power structures that came to be imposed during colonial rule and were preserved even after Independence."

13 See Béteille (2001) and Gupta (2001, 2007). Dipankar Gupta, formerly professor of sociology at Jawaharlal Nehru University, was part of the official Indian delegation that in 2007 opposed the Dalit caucus's demand to treat caste discrimination as being akin to racial discrimination. In an essay in 2007, Gupta argued that "the allegation that caste is a form of racial discrimination is not just an academic misjudgement but has unfortunate policy consequences as well". For a cross-section of views on the caste–race debate at the United Nations Committee on Elimination of Racial Discrimination, see Thorat and Umakant (ed., 2004), which features counter-arguments by a range of scholars

including Gail Omvedt and Kancha Ilaiah. Also see Natarajan and Greenough (ed., 2009).

14 For a response to Béteille and Gupta, see Gerald D. Berreman in Natarajan and Greenough (2009). Berreman says: "What is 'scientifically nonsensical' is Professor Béteille's misunderstanding of 'race'. What is 'mischievous' is his insistence that India's system of ascribed social inequality should be exempted from the provisions of a UN Convention whose sole purpose is the extension of human rights to include freedom from all forms of discrimination and intolerance—and to which India, along with most other nations, has committed itself" (54–5).

15 See www.declarationofempathy.org. Accessed 16 January 2014.

16 Das 2010, 25.

17 Inter-caste and intra-gotra marriages are resisted in the name of 'honour'; in extreme cases, the couple, or one of the partners, is killed. For an account of the case of Ilavarasan and Divya from Tamil Nadu, see Meena Kandasamy (2013). For an account of the consequences of violating 'gotra laws' in Haryana, see Chander Suta Dogra's recent *Manoj and Babli: A Hate Story* (2013). Also see "Day after their killing, village goes quiet", *Indian Express*, 20 September 2013, and Chowdhry (2007).

18 In 2009, Ahmedabad-based Navsarjan Trust and the Robert F. Kennedy Center for Justice and Human Rights, published a joint report, "Understanding Untouchability". It listed ninety-nine forms of untouchability in 1,589 villages of Gujarat. It looked at the prevalence of untouchability under eight broad heads: 1. Water for Drinking; 2. Food and Beverage; 3. Religion; 4. Caste-based Occupations; 5. Touch; 6. Access to Public Facilities and Institutions; 7. Prohibitions and Social Sanctions; 8. Private Sector Discrimination. The findings were shocking. In 98.4 per cent of villages surveyed, inter-caste marriage was prohibited; in 97.6 per cent of villages, Dalits were forbidden to touch water pots or utensils that belonged to non-Dalits; in 98.1 per cent of villages, a Dalit could not rent a house in a non-Dalit area; in 97.2 per cent of villages, Dalit religious leaders were not allowed to celebrate a religious ceremony in a non-Dalit area; in 67 per cent of villages, Dalit panchayat members were either not offered tea or were served in separate cups called 'Dalit' cups.

19 AoC 17.7.

20 CWMG 15, 160–1. All references to Gandhi's works, unless otherwise stated, are from *The Collected Works of Mahatma Gandhi* (CWMG) (1999). Wherever possible, first publication details are also provided since scholars sometimes refer to an earlier edition of the CWMG.

21 Cited in BAWS 9, 276.

22 Cited in CWMG 59, 227.

23 See the 20 November 2009 UNI report, "India's 100 richest are 25 pc of GDP". http://ibnlive.in.com/news/indias-100-richest-are-25-pc-of-gdp-forbes/105548-7.html?utm_source=ref_article. Accessed 8 September 2013.

24 A Reuters report (10 August 2007) based on "Conditions of Work and Promotions of Livelihoods in the Unorganised Sector" by the National Commission for Enterprises in the Unorganised Sector said: "Seventy-seven per cent of Indians—about 836 million people—live on less than half a dollar a day in one of the world's hottest economies." http://in.reuters.com/article/2007/08/10/idIN India-28923020070810. Accessed 26 August 2013.

25 S. Gurumurthy, co-convenor of the Hindu right-wing Swadeshi Jagaran Manch, talks of how caste and capitalism can coexist: "Caste is a very strong bond. While individuals are related by families, castes link the families. Castes transcended the local limits and networked the people across [sic]. This has prevented the disturbance that industrialism caused to neighbourhood societies in the West, resulting in unbridled individualism and acute atomization." He goes on to argue that the caste system "has in modern times engaged the market in economics and democracy in politics to reinvent itself. It has become a great source of entrepreneurship". See "Is Caste an Economic Development Vehicle?", *The Hindu*, 19 January 2009. http://www.hindu.com/2009/01/19/stories/2009011955440900.htm. Accessed 26 August 2013.

26 See "Forbes: India's billionaire wealth much above country's fiscal deficit", *The Indian Express*, 5 March 2013. http://www.indianexpress.com/news/forbes-indias-billionaire-wealth-much-above-countrys-fiscal-deficit/1083500/#sthash.KabcY8BJ.dpuf. Accessed 26 August 2013.

27 Hutton 1935.

28 Hardiman 1996, 15.

29 See "Brahmins in India", *Outlook*, 4 June 2007. http://www.outlookindia.com/article.aspx?234783. Accessed 5 September 2013. Despite the decline, the Lok Sabha in 2007 had fifty Brahmin Members of Parliament—9.17 per cent of the total strength of the House. The data given by *Outlook* is based on four surveys conducted by the Centre for the Study of Developing Societies, Delhi, between 2004 and 2007.

30 BAWS 9, 207.

31 See Singh 1990. Singh's figures are based on information provided by one of his readers.

32 BAWS 9, 200.

33 Reservation was first introduced in India during the colonial period. For a history of the policy of reservation, see Bhagwan Das (2000).

34 *Selected Educational Statistics 2004–05*, p.xxii, Ministry of Human Resource Development. Available at http://www.education-forallinindia.com/SES2004-05.pdf. Accessed 11 November 2013.

35 Under the new economic regime, education, health care, essential services and other public institutions are rapidly being privatised. It has led to a haemorrhage of government jobs. For a population of 1.2 billion people, the total number of organised sector jobs is 29 million (as of 2011). Of these, the private sector accounts for only 11.4 million. See the *Economic Survey 2010–11*, p.A52. http://indiabudget.nic.in/budget2011-2012/es2010-11/estat1.pdf. Accessed 10 November 2013.

36 See Ajay Navaria's story "Yes Sir" in *Unclaimed Terrain* (2013).

37 National Commission for Scheduled Castes and Scheduled Tribes (NCSCST) 1998, 180–1.

38 Prabhu Chawla, "Courting Controversy", *India Today* (29 January 1999). The lawyers quoted are Anil Divan and Fali S. Nariman. Later, India did get a Dalit Supreme Court Chief Justice in K.G. Balakrishnan (2007–10).

39 Santhosh and Abraham 2010, 28.

40 Ibid., 27.

41 The note submitted to the JNU vice-chancellor was signed by, among others, Yoginder K. Alagh, T.K. Oommen and Bipan

Chandra. Alagh is an economist and a former Member of Parliament (Rajya Sabha), a former union minister and regular newspaper columnist. Oomen was president of the International Sociological Association (1990–4), and published an edited volume called *Classes, Citizenship and Inequality: Emerging Perspectives*. Chandra is a Marxist historian, former president of the Indian History Congress, and was chairperson of the Centre for Historical Studies, JNU.

42 Raman 2010.

43 The Justice Rajinder Sachar Committee was appointed by Prime Minister Manmohan Singh on 9 March 2005 to assess the social, economic and educational status of the Muslim community of India; its 403-page report was tabled in Parliament on 30 November 2006. The report establishes that caste oppression affects India's Muslims too. According to Teltumbde (2010a, 16), "working from the Sachar Committee data, the SC and ST components of India's population can be estimated at 19.7 and 8.5 per cent respectively".

44 According to economist Sukhadeo Thorat (2009, 56), "Nearly 70 per cent of SC households either do not own land or have very small landholdings of less than 0.4 ha [hectare]. A very small proportion (less than 6 per cent) consists of medium and large farmers. The scenario of landownership among SCs is even grimmer in Bihar, Haryana, Kerala and Punjab, where more than 90 per cent of SC households possess negligible or no land." Citing Planning Commission data, another research paper states that the majority of the Scheduled Castes (77 per cent) are landless, without any productive assets and sustainable employment opportunities. According to the Agricultural Census of 1990–1, the essay says, "Around 87 per cent of the landholders of scheduled castes and 65 per cent of scheduled tribes in the country belong to the category of small and marginal farmers" (Mohanty 2001, 3857).

45 NCSCST 1998, 176.

46 "13 lakh Dalits still engaged in manual scavenging: Thorat", *The New Indian Express*, 8 October 2013. See http://www.newindianexpress.com/cities/hyderabad/13-lakh-Dalits-still-engaged-in-manual-scavenging-Thorat/2013/10/08/article1824760.ece. Accessed

10 October 2013. See also the status papers on the website of the International Dalit Solidarity Network, http://idsn.org/caste-discrimination/key-issues/manual-scavenging/. Accessed 10 October 2013.

47 Data from http://www.indianrailways.gov.in/railwayboard/uploads/directorate/stat_econ/pdf/Summarypercent20Sheet_Eng.pdf accessed 26 August 2013, and Bhasin (2013).

48 See the interview of Milind Kamble, chairman of DICCI, and Chandra Bhan Prasad, mentor to DICCI, in *The Indian Express*, 11 June 2013: "Capitalism is changing caste much faster than any human being. Dalits should look at capitalism as a crusader against caste." Available at http://m.indianexpress.com/news/capitalism-is-changing-caste-much-faster-than-any-human-being.-dalits-should-look-at-capitalism-as-a-crusader-against-caste/1127570/. Accessed 20 August 2013. For an analysis of how India's policies of liberalisation and globalisation since 1990 have actually benefited rural Dalits of Uttar Pradesh's Azamgarh and Bulandshahar districts, see Kapur, et al. (2010). See also Milind Khandekar's *Dalit Millionaires: 15 Inspiring Stories* (2013). For a critique of the "low-intensity spectacle of Dalit millionaires", see Gopal Guru (2012).

49 "Anti-caste discrimination reforms blocked, say critics", *The Guardian*, 29 July 2013. See http://www.theguardian.com/uk-news/2013/jul/29/anticaste-discrimination-reforms. Accessed 5 August 2013.

50 Vanita 2002.

51 Sukta 90 in Book X of the *Rig Veda* tells the story of the myth of creation. It describes the sacrifice of the Purusha (primeval man), from whose body the four varnas and the entire universe emerged. When (the gods) divided the Purusha, his mouth became Brahmin, his arms Kshatriya, his thighs Vaishya and Shudra sprang from his feet. See Doniger (translation, 2005). Some scholars believe that Sukta is a latter-day interpolation into the Rig Veda.

52 Susan Bayly (1998) shows how Gandhi's caste politics are completely in keeping with the views of modern, privileged-caste Hindu 'reformers'.

53 In 2012, the newsmagazine *Outlook* published the result of just

such a poll conducted on the eve of independence day. The question was: "Who, after the Mahatma, is the greatest Indian to have walked our soil?" Ambedkar topped the poll and *Outlook* devoted an entire issue (20 August 2012) to him. See http://www.outlookindia.com/content10894.asp. Accessed 10 August 2013.

54 See Ambedkar's *Pakistan or the Partition of India* (1945), first published as *Thoughts on Pakistan* (1940), and featured now in BAWS 8.

55 Parel 1997, 188–9.

56 In a 1955 interview to BBC radio, Ambedkar says: "A comparative study of Gandhi's Gujarati and English writings will reveal how Mr Gandhi was deceiving people." See http://www.youtube.com/watch?v=ZJs-BjoSzbo. Accessed 12 August 2013.

57 Cited in BAWS 9, 276.

58 AoC 16.2.

59 See Tidrick 2006, 281, 283–4. On 2 May 1938, after Gandhi had a seminal discharge at the age of sixty-four, in a letter to Amritlal Nanavati he said: "Where is my place, and how can a person subject to passion represent non-violence and truth?" (CWMG 73, 139).

60 BAWS 9, 202.

61 Keer 1954/1990, 167.

62 For an analysis of the radicalism inherent in the Ambedkar statue, in the context of Uttar Pradesh, see Nicolas Jaoul (2006). "To Dalit villagers, whose rights and dignity have been regularly violated, setting up the statue of a Dalit statesman wearing a red tie and carrying the Constitution involves dignity, pride in emancipated citizenship and a practical acknowledgement of the extent to which the enforcement of laws could positively change their lives" (204).

63 "The State represents violence in a concentrated and organised form. The individual has a soul, but as the State is a soulless machine, it can never be weaned from violence to which it owes its very existence. Hence I prefer the doctrine of trusteeship." *Hindustan Times*, 17 October 1935; CWMG 65, 318.

64 *Young India*, 16 April 1931; CWMG 51, 354.

65 Das 2010, 175.

66 Jefferson says this in his letter of 6 September 1789 to James

Madison. Available at http://press-pubs.uchicago.edu/founders/documents/v1ch2s23.html. Accessed 21 November 2013.

67 Ambedkar argues in "Castes in India", his 1916 essay, that women are the gateways of the caste system and that control over them through child marriages, enforced widowhood and sati (being burnt on a dead husband's pyre) are methods to keep a check on women's sexuality. For an analysis of Ambedkar's writings on this issue, see Sharmila Rege (2013).

68 For a discussion of the Hindu Code Bill, its ramifications and how it was sabotaged, see Sharmila Rege (2013, 191–244). Rege shows how from 11 April 1947, when it was introduced in the Constituent Assembly, till September 1951, the Bill was never taken seriously. Ambedkar finally resigned on 10 October 1951. The Hindu Marriage Act was finally enacted in 1955, granting divorce rights to Hindu women. The Special Marriage Act, passed in 1954 allows inter-caste and inter-religious marriage.

69 Rege 2013, 200.

70 Rege 2013, 241. Ambedkar's disillusionment with the new legal regime in India went further. On 2 September 1953, Ambedkar declared in the Rajya Sabha, "Sir, my friends tell me that I made the Constitution. But I am quite prepared to say that I shall be the first person to burn it out. I do not want it. It does not suit anybody. But whatever that may be, if our people want to carry on, they must remember that there are majorities and there are minorities; and they simply cannot ignore the minorities by saying: 'Oh, no, to recognise you is to harm democracy'" (Keer 1990, 499).

71 AoC 20.12.

72 Omvedt 2008, 19.

73 Unpublished translation by Joel Lee, made available through personal communication.

74 *Young India*, 17 March 1927; CWMG 38, 210.

75 Ambedkar said this during his speech delivered as Chairman of the Constitution Drafting Committee in the Constituent Assembly on 4 November 1948. See Das 2010, 176.

76 For an analysis of Gandhi's relationship with Indian capitalists, see Leah Renold (1994). Gandhi's approach to big dams is revealed in a letter dated 5 April 1924, in which he advised villagers who faced displacement by the Mulshi Dam, being built by the Tatas

to generate electricity for their Bombay mills, to give up their protest (CWMG 27, 168):

1. I understand that the vast majority of the men affected have accepted compensation and that the few who have not cannot perhaps even be traced.

2. The dam is nearly half-finished and its progress cannot be permanently stopped. There seems to me to be no ideal behind the movement.

3. The leader of the movement is not a believer out and out in non-violence. This defect is fatal to success.

Seventy-five years later, in 2000, the Supreme Court of India used very similar logic in its infamous judgement on the World Bank-funded Sardar Sarovar Dam on the Narmada river, when it ruled against tens of thousands of local people protesting their displacement, and ordered the construction of the dam to continue.

77 *Young India*, 20 December 1928; CWMG 43, 412. Also see Gandhi's *Hind Swaraj* (1909) in Anthony Parel (1997).

78 Rege 2013, 100.

79 BAWS 5, 102.

80 In Das 2010, 51.

81 AoC, Preface to 1937 edition.

82 Cited in Zelliot 2013, 147.

83 Here, for example, is Ismat Chugtai, a Muslim writer celebrated for her progressive, feminist views, describing an Untouchable sweeper in her short story, "A Pair of Hands": "Gori was her name, the feckless one, and she was dark, dark like a glistening pan on which a roti had been fried but which a careless cook had forgotten to clean. She had a bulbous nose, a wide jaw, and it seemed she came from a family where brushing one's teeth was a habit long forgotten. The squint in her left eye was noticeable despite the fact that her eyes were heavily kohled; it was difficult to imagine how, with a squinted eye, she was able to throw darts that never failed to hit their mark. Her waist was not slim; it had thickened, rapidly increasing in diameter from all those handouts she consumed. There was also nothing delicate about her feet which reminded one of a cow's hoofs, and she left a coarse smell of mustard oil in her wake. Her voice however, was sweet" (2003, 164).

84 In 1981, all the Dalits of the village of Meenakshipuram—renamed Rahmat Nagar—in Tamil Nadu's Tirunelveli district converted to Islam. Worried by this, Hindu supremacist groups such as the Vishwa Hindu Parishad and the Rashtriya Swayamsevak Sangh together with the Sankaracharya of Kanchipuram began to work proactively to 'integrate' Dalits into Hinduism. A new 'Tamil Hindu' chauvinist group called the Hindu Munnani was formed. Eighteen years later, P. Sainath revisited Meenakshipuram and filed two reports (1999a, 1999b). For a similar case from Koothirambakkam, another village in Tamil Nadu, see S. Anand (2002).

85 Cited in Omvedt 2008, 177.

86 The figure Ambedkar cites is drawn from the Simon Commission report of 1930. When the Lothian Committee came to India in 1932 Ambedkar said, "The Hindus adopted a challenging mood and refused to accept the figures given by the Simon Commission as a true figure for the Untouchables of India." He then argues that, "this is due to the fact that the Hindus had by now realised the danger of admitting the existence of the Untouchables. For it meant that a part of the representation enjoyed by the Hindus will have to be given up by them to the Untouchables" (BAWS 5, 7–8).

87 See Note 69 at 9.4 of this AoC edition.

88 He says this in the April 1899 issue of the journal *Prabuddha Bharata*, in an interview to its editor. In the same interview, when asked specifically what would be the caste of those who "re-converted" to Hinduism, Vivekananda says: "Returning converts ... will gain their own castes, of course. And new people will make theirs. You will remember ... that this has already been done in the case of Vaishnavism. Converts from different castes and aliens were all able to combine under that flag and form a caste by themselves—and a very respectable one too. From Ramanuja down to Chaitanya of Bengal, all great Vaishnava Teachers have done the same." Available at http://www.ramakrishnavivekananda.info/vivekananda/volume_5/interviews/on_the_bounds_of_hinduism.htm. Accessed 20 August 2013.

89 The names of these organisations translate as: Forum for Dalit

Uplift; the All-India Committee for the Uplift of Untouchables; the Punjab Society for Untouchable Uplift.

90 AoC 6.2.

91 Bayly 1998.

92 The term was coined by V.D. Savarkar (1883–1966), one of the principal proponents of modern, right-wing Hindu nationalism, in his 1923 pamphlet *Essentials of Hindutva* (later retitled *Hindutva: Who Is a Hindu?*). The first edition (1923) of this work carried the pseudonymous "A Maratha" as author. For a critical introduction to Hindutva, see Jyotirmaya Sharma (2006).

93 Cited in Prashad 1996, 554–5.

94 BAWS 9, 195.

95 A few privileged-caste Hindu members of the Ghadar Party later turned towards Hindu nationalism and became Vedic missionaries. On Bhai Parmanand, a founder-member of the Ghadar Party who later became a Hindutva ideologue, see Note 11 in the Prologue to AoC.

96 For a monograph on the Ad Dharm movement, see Juergensmeyer (1982/2009).

97 Rupa Viswanath (forthcoming 2014) details the history of the colonial state's alliance with the landed castes against landless Dalits in the context of the Madras Presidency.

98 Davis 2002, 7.

99 BAWS 9, 1.

100 Ibid., 3.

101 See Devji 2012, chapter 3, "In Praise of Prejudice", especially 47–8.

102 Cited from *Young India*, 23 March 1921, in Devji 2012, 81.

103 Golwalkar 1945, 55–6.

104 BAWS 17, Part 1, 369–75.

105 Godse 1998, 43.

106 BAWS 3, 360.

107 Cited in BAWS 9, 68.

108 *Harijan*, 30 September 1939; CWMG 76, 356.

109 See Guha 2013b.

110 Tidrick 2006, 106.

111 For an archive of Gandhi's writings about his years in South Africa (1893 to 1914), see G.B. Singh (2004).

112 Swan 1985, 52.

113 Kaffir is an Arabic term that originally meant 'one who hides or covers'—a description of farmers burying seeds in the ground. After the advent of Islam, it came to mean 'non-believers' or 'heretics', those 'who covered the truth (Islam)'. It was first applied to non-Muslim Black people encountered by Arab traders along the Swahili coast. Portuguese explorers adopted the term and passed it on to the British, French and Dutch. In South Africa, it became a racial slur the Whites and Afrikaners (and Indians like Gandhi) used to describe native Africans. Today, to call someone a Kaffir in South Africa is an actionable offence.

114 CWMG 1, 192–3.

115 CWMG 1, 200.

116 For a history of indentured labour in South Africa, see Ashwin Desai and Goolam Vahed (2010).

117 Between the early 1890s and 1913, the Indian population in South Africa tripled, from 40,000 to 135,000 (Guha 2013b, 463).

118 Guha 2013b, 115.

119 CWMG 2, 6.

120 Hochschild 2011, 33–4.

121 During the Second World War, he advised the Jews to "summon to their aid the soul-power that comes only from non-violence" and assured them that Herr Hitler would "bow before their courage" (*Harijan*, 17 December 1938; CWMG 74, 298). He urged the British to "fight Nazism without arms" (*Harijan*, 6 July 1940; CWMG 78, 387).

122 CWMG 34, 18.

123 CWMG 2, 339–40.

124 *The Natal Advertiser*, 16 October 1901; CWMG 2, 421.

125 CWMG 5, 11.

126 Ibid., 179.

127 Guy 2005, 212.

128 According to a note on the first page of volume 34 of CWMG, "Gandhiji started writing in Gujarati the history of Satyagraha in South Africa on November 26, 1923, when he was in the Yeravada Central Jail; vide Jail Diary, 1923. By the time he was released, on February 5, 1924, he had completed 30 chapters... The English translation by Valji G. Desai, which was seen and approved by

Gandhiji, was published by S. Ganesan, Madras, in 1928."

129 CWMG 34, 82–3.

130 Ibid., 84.

131 Of a total population of 135,000 Indians, only 10,000, who were mostly traders, lived in the Transvaal. The rest were based in Natal (Guha 2013b, 463).

132 CWMG 5, 337. This is from Clause 3 from Resolution 2 of the Five Resolutions passed by the British Indian Association in Johannesburg, following the 'Mass Meeting' of 11 September 1906.

133 *Indian Opinion*, 7 March 1908; CWMG 8, 198–9.

134 CWMG 9, 256–7.

135 *Indian Opinion*, 23 January 1909; CWMG 9, 274.

136 In a letter dated 18 May 1899 to the Colonial Secretary, Gandhi wrote: "An Indian may fancy that he has a wrong to be redressed in that he does not get ghee instead of oil" (CWMG 2, 266). On another occasion: "The regulations here do not provide for any ghee or fat to Indians. A complaint has therefore been made to the physician, and he has promised to look into it. So there is reason to hope that the inclusion of ghee will be ordered" (*Indian Opinion*, 17 October 1908; CWMG 9, 197).

137 *Indian Opinion*, 23 January 1909; CWMG 9, 270.

138 *Young India*, 5 April 1928; CWMG 41, 365.

139 Lelyveld 2011, 74.

140 Cited in Zinn and Arnove 2004, 265.

141 Ibid., 270.

142 Cited in Omvedt 2008, 219.

143 In Deshpande 2002, 25.

144 Ibid., 38–40.

145 Cited in Ambedkar 1945; BAWS 9, 276.

146 See Adams 2011, 263–5. Also see Rita Banerji 2008, especially 265–81.

147 CWMG 34, 201–2.

148 *Hind Swaraj* in Parel 1997, 106.

149 Ibid., 97

150 See Gandhi's Preface to the English translation of *Hind Swaraj*, in Parel (1997, 5).

151 Savarkar, the militant Hindutva ideologue, said a true Indian is one whose *pitrabhoomi* (fatherland) as well as *punyabhoomi* (holy

land) is India—not some foreign land. See his *Hindutva* (1923, 105).

152 Parel 1997, 47–51.

153 Ibid., 66.

154 Ibid., 68–9.

155 Ramachandra Guha (2013b, 383) says: "Gandhi wrote *Hind Swaraj* in 1909 at a time he scarcely knew India at all. By 1888, when he departed for London, at the age of nineteen, he had lived only in towns in his native Kathiawar. There is no evidence that he had travelled in the countryside, and he knew no other part of India."

156 Parel 1997, 69–70.

157 Gandhi says this in 1932, in connection with the debate around separate electorates for Untouchables, in a letter to Sir Samuel Hoare, Secretary of State for India. Cited in BAWS 9, 78.

158 *Indian Opinion*, 22 October 1910; CWMG 11, 143–4. Cited also in Guha 2013b, 395.

159 Guha 2013b, 463.

160 Ibid., 406.

161 Aiyar quoted in Lelyveld 2011, 21.

162 Personal communication, Ashwin Desai, professor of sociology at University of Johannesburg.

163 Lelyveld 2011, 130.

164 Tidrick 2006, 188.

165 See Renold 1994. Also see Louis Fischer, *A Week with Gandhi* (1942), quoted by Ambedkar: "'I said I had several questions to ask him about the Congress Party. Very highly placed Britishers, I recalled, had told me that Congress was in the hands of big business and that Gandhi was supported by the Bombay Mill-owners who gave him as much money as he wanted. 'What Truth is there in these assertions', I asked. 'Unfortunately, they are true,' he declared simply … 'What portion of the Congress budget,' I asked, 'is covered by rich Indians?' 'Practically all of it,' he stated. 'In this ashram, for instance, we could live much more poorly than we do and spend less money. But we do not and the money comes from our rich friends.'" Cited in BAWS 9, 208.

166 Cited in Amin 1998, 293.

167 *Young India*, 18 August 1921; CWMG 23, 158.

168 *Harijan*, 25 August 1940; CWMG 79, 133–4.

169 Ibid., 135.

170 Ibid., 135.

171 *The Gospel of Wealth* (1889). Available at http://www.swarthmore.edu/SocSci/rbannis1/AIH19th/Carnegie.html. Accessed 26 August 2013.

172 Cited in Amin 1998, 290–1.

173 Amin 291–2.

174 Tidrick 2006, 191.

175 Cited in Singh 2004, 124.

176 Tidrick 2006, 192.

177 Ibid., 194.

178 Ibid., 195.

179 Zelliot 2013, 48.

180 This is from the unpublished preface to Ambedkar's *The Buddha and His Dhamma* (1956). It first appeared as part of a book of Ambedkar's prefaces, published by Bhagwan Das and entitled *Rare Prefaces* (1980). Eleanor Zelliot later published it on the Columbia University website dedicated to Ambedkar's life and selected works. http://www.columbia.edu/itc/mealac/pritchett/00ambedkar/ambedkar_buddha/00_pref_unpub.html. Accessed 10 September 2013.

181 BAWS 4, 1986.

182 On 20 May 1857, the Education Department issued a directive that "no boy be refused admission to a government college or school merely on the ground of caste" (Nambissan 2002, 81).

183 For an annotated edition of this essay, see Sharmila Rege (2013). It also appears in BAWS 1.

184 In *Autobiographical Notes* 2003, 19.

185 Keer 1990, 36–7.

186 AoC 17.5.

187 Prashad 1996, 552. In his speech at the Suppressed Classes Conference in Ahmedabad on 13 April 1921, reported in *Young India* on 27 April 1921 and 4 May 1921 (reproduced in CWMG 23, 41–7), Gandhi discussed Uka at length for the first time (42). Bakha, the main protagonist in Mulk Raj Anand's iconic novel *Untouchable* (1935), is said to be inspired by Uka. According to the researcher Lingaraja Gandhi (2004), Anand showed his

manuscript to Gandhi, who suggested changes. Anand says: "I read my novel to Gandhiji, and he suggested that I should cut down more than a hundred pages, especially those passages in which Bakha seemed to be thinking and dreaming and brooding like a Bloomsbury intellectual." Lingaraja Gandhi further says: "Anand had provided long and flowery speeches to Bakha in his draft. Gandhi instructed Anand that untouchables don't speak that way: in fact, they hardly speak. The novel underwent metamorphosis under the tutelage of Gandhi."

188 *Navajivan*, 18 January 1925; CWMG 30, 71. In the account of Gandhi's secretary, Mahadev Desai, this speech from Gujarati is rendered differently: "The position that I really long for is that of the Bhangi. How sacred is this work of cleanliness! That work can be done only by a Brahmin or by a Bhangi. The Brahmin may do it in his wisdom, the Bhangi in ignorance. I respect, I adore both of them. If either of the two disappears from Hinduism, Hinduism itself would disappear. And it is because seva-dharma (self-service) is dear to my heart that the Bhangi is dear to me. I may even sit at my meals with a Bhangi by my side, but I do not ask you to align yourselves with them by inter-caste dinners and marriages." Cited in Ramaswamy 2005, 86.

189 Renold 1994, 19–20. Highly publicised symbolic visits to Dalit homes has become a Congress party tradition. In January 2009, in the glare of a media circus, the Congress party's vice-president and prime ministerial candidate, Rahul Gandhi, along with David Milliband, the British foreign secretary, spent a night in the hut of a Dalit family in Simra village of Uttar Pradesh. For an account of this, see Anand Teltumbde (2013).

190 Prashad 2001, 139.

191 BAWS 1, 256.

192 Keer 1990, 41.

193 Zelliot 2013, 91.

194 See Joseph 2003, 166. Objecting to Sikhs running a langar (free, common kitchen) for the satyagrahis of Vaikom, Gandhi wrote in *Young India* (8 May 1924), "The Vaikom satyagraha is, I fear, crossing the limits. I do hope that the Sikh free kitchen will be withdrawn and that the movement will be confined to Hindus only" (CWMG 27, 362).

195 Chakravarti Rajagopalachari, a Tamil Brahmin, known affectionately as Rajaji, was a close friend and confidant of Gandhi. In 1933, his daughter Leela married Gandhi's son Devdas. Rajagopalachari later served as the acting Governor General of India. In 1947, he became the first Governor of West Bengal, and in 1955 received the Bharat Ratna, India's highest civilian award.

196 Cited in Joseph 2003, 168.

197 *Young India*, 14 August 1924; CWMG 28, 486.

198 Joseph 2003, 169.

199 Birla 1953, 43.

200 Keer 1990, 79.

201 Speaking at a Depressed Classes Conference in 1925, Ambedkar said: "When one is spurned by everyone, even the sympathy shown by Mahatma Gandhi is of no little importance." Cited in Jaffrelot 2005, 63. Gandhi visited Mahad on 3 March 1927, a fortnight before the first satyagraha, but unlike at Vaikom he did not interfere. For an account of the second Mahad Satyagraha when a copy of the *Manusmriti* was burnt, see K. Jamnadas (2010).

202 According to Anand Teltumbde's unpublished manuscript on the two Mahad conferences, Resolution No. 2 seeking a 'ceremonial cremation' of the *Manusmriti* was proposed by G.N. Sahasrabuddhe, a Brahmin, who played an important role in the March events as well; it was seconded by P.N. Rajbhoj, a Chambhar leader. According to Teltumbde, "There was a deliberate attempt to get some progressive people from non-untouchable communities to the conference, but eventually only two names materialised. One was Gangadhar Nilkanth Sahasrabuddhe, an activist of the Social Service League and a leader of the cooperative movement belonging to Agarkari Brahman caste, and the other was Vinayak alias Bhai Chitre, a Chandraseniya Kayastha Prabhu." In the 1940s, Sahasrabuddhe became the editor of *Janata*—another of Ambedkar's newspapers.

203 Dangle, ed., 1992, 231–3.

204 Keer 1990, 170.

205 Cited in Prashad 1996, 555.

206 Gandhi outlined the difference between satyagraha and duragraha in a speech on 3 November 1917: "There are two

methods of attaining one's goal: Satyagraha and Duragraha. In our scriptures, they have been described, respectively, as divine and devilish modes of action." He went on to give an example of duragraha: "the terrible War going on in Europe". Also, "The man who follows the path of Duragraha becomes impatient and wants to kill the so-called enemy. There can be but one result of this. Hatred increases" (CWMG 16, 126–8).

207 BAWS 9, 247.

208 On the fallout with the Girni Kamgar Union, see Teltumbde (2012). For how Dange and the Communist Party worked towards ensuring Ambedkar's defeat in the Bombay City North constituency in the 1952 general election, see S. Anand (2012a), and Rajnarayan Chandavarkar (2009, 161), where he says: "The decision by the socialists and the communists not to forge an electoral pact, let alone join together to combine with Ambedkar's Scheduled Castes Federation, against the Congress lost them the Central Bombay seat. Dange, for the CPI, Asoka Mehta for the socialists and Ambedkar each stood separately and fell together. Significantly, Dange instructed his supporters to spoil their ballots in the reserved constituency for Central Bombay rather than vote for Ambedkar. Indeed, Ambedkar duly lost and attributed his defeat to the communist campaign. Although the communists could not win the Central Bombay seat, their influence in Girangaon, including its dalit voters, was sufficient to decisively influence the outcome. The election campaign created a lasting bitterness. As Dinoo Ranadive recalls, 'the differences between the dalits and the communists became so sharp that even today it has become difficult for the communists to appeal to the Republicans' or at any rate to some sections of dalit voters." Republicans here refers to the Republican Party of India (RPI) that Ambedkar had conceived of a short while before his death in December 1956. It came to be established only in September 1957 by his followers, but today there are over a dozen splintered factions of the RPI.

209 Kosambi 1948, 274.

210 For an account of this, see Jan Breman's *The Making and Unmaking of an Industrial Working Class* (2004), especially chapter 2, "The Formalization of Collective Action: Mahatma Gandhi as a Union Leader" (40–68).

211 Breman 2004, 57.

212 Shankerlal Banker cited in Breman (2004, 47).

213 Annual Report of the Textile Labour Union, 1925, cited in Breman (2004, 51).

214 *Navajivan*, 8 February 1920; cited in BAWS 9, 280.

215 *Harijan*, 21 April 1946; CWMG 90, 255–6.

216 AoC 3.10 and 3.11.

217 AoC 4.1, emphasis original.

218 Zelliot 2013, 178.

219 Namboodiripad 1986, 492, emphasis added.

220 The text of the manifesto is reproduced in Satyanarayana and Tharu (2013, 62).

221 For a critical piece on the NGO–Dalit movement interface that traces it to the history of colonial and missionary activity in India, see Teltumbde (2010b), where he argues: "Unsurprisingly, most Dalits in Indian NGOs are active at the field level. Dalit boys and girls appear to be doing social services for their communities, which is what Ambedkar expected educated Dalits to do, and Dalit communities therefore perceive such workers quite favourably—more favourably, certainly, than Dalit politicians, who are often seen as engaged in mere rhetoric. The NGO sector has thus become a significant employer for many Dalits studying for their humanities degree, typically capped with a postgraduate degree in social work. Further, as the prospects of public-sector jobs have decreased since the government's neoliberal reforms of the mid-1980s and later, the promise of NGOs as employers assumed great importance."

222 For instance, see the list of NGOs that work with the multinational mining corporation Vedanta, under fire for land-grab and several violations against the environment and Adivasi rights, at http://www.vedantaaluminium.com/ngos-govt-bodies.htm. Accessed 20 November 2013.

223 Speech on 26 September 1896 at a public meeting in Bombay where he said he was representing the "100,000 British Indians at present residing in South Africa". See CWMG 1, 407.

224 AoC 8.2–4.

225 BAWS 1, 375.

226 AoC 5.8.

227 There are different aspects of the Constitution that govern the Adivasis of the heartland (the Fifth Schedule) and those of the Northeast of India (the Sixth Schedule). As the political scientist Uday Chandra points out in a recent paper (2013, 155), "The Fifth and Sixth Schedules of the Constitution perpetuate the languages and logics of the Partially and Wholly Excluded Areas defined in the Government of India Act (1935) and the Typically and Really Backward Tracts defined by the Government of India (1918)... In the Schedule V areas, dispersed across eastern, western, and central Indian states, state governors wield special powers to prohibit or modify central or state laws, to prohibit or regulate the transfer of land by or among tribals, to regulate commercial activities, particularly by non-tribals, and to constitute tribal advisory councils to supplement state legislatures. In principle, New Delhi also reserves the right to intervene directly in the administration of these Scheduled Areas by bypassing elected state and local governments. In the Schedule VI areas, dispersed across the seven northeastern states formed out of the colonial province of Assam, state governors preside over District and Regional Councils in Autonomous Districts and Regions to ensure that state and central laws do not impinge on these administrative zones of exception."

228 Cited in BAWS 9, 70.

229 BAWS 9, 42.

230 As prime minister of a non-Congress, Janata Dal–led coalition government from December 1989 to November 1990, Vishwanath Pratap Singh (1931–2008) took the decision to implement the recommendations of the Mandal Commission, which fixed a quota for members of the Backward Classes in jobs in the public sector to redress caste discrimination. The Commission, named after B.P. Mandal, a parliamentarian who headed it, had been established in 1979 by another non-Congress (Janata Party) government, headed by Morarji Desai, but the recommendations of its 1980 report—which extended the scope of reservation in public sector employment beyond Dalits and Adivasis, and allocated 27 per cent to Other Backward Classes (OBCs)—had not been implemented for ten years. When it was implemented, the privileged castes took to the streets.

They symbolically swept the streets, pretended to shine shoes and performed other 'polluting' tasks to suggest that instead of becoming doctors, engineers, lawyers or economists, the policy of reservation was now going to reduce privileged castes to doing menial tasks. A few people attempted to publicly immolate themselves, the most well-known being a Delhi University student, Rajiv Goswami, in 1990. Similar protests were repeated in 2006 when the Congress-led United Progressive Alliance tried to extend reservation to the OBCs in institutes of higher education.

231 BAWS 9, 40.

232 See Menon 2003, 52–3.

233 In his 1945 indictment of the Congress and Gandhi, Ambedkar lists the names of these mock candidates in his footnotes: Guru Gosain Agamdas and Babraj Jaiwar were the two cobblers; Chunnu was the milkman; Arjun Lal the barber; Bansi Lal Chaudhari the sweeper (BAWS 9, 210).

234 BAWS 9, 210.

235 Ibid., 68.

236 Ibid., 69.

237 Tidrick 2006, 255.

238 Servants of India Society member Kodanda Rao's account cited in Jaffrelot (2005, 66).

239 In Pyarelal 1932, 188.

240 BAWS 9, 259.

241 As Ambedkar saw it, "The increase in the number of seats for the Untouchables is no increase at all and was no recompense for the loss of separate electorates and the double vote" (BAWS 9, 90). Ambedkar himself lost twice in the polls in post-1947 India. It took more than half a century for Kanshi Ram, the founder of a predominantly Dalit party, the Bahujan Samaj Party, and his protégé Mayawati to succeed in a first-past-the-post parliamentary democracy. This happened *despite* the Poona Pact. Kanshi Ram worked for years, painstakingly making alliances with other subordinated castes to achieve this victory. To succeed in the elections, the BSP needed the peculiar demography of Uttar Pradesh and the support of many OBCs. For a Dalit candidate to win an election from an open seat—

even in Uttar Pradesh—continues to be almost impossible.

242 See Alexander 2010.

243 Fischer 1951, 400–03.

244 Eleanor Zelliot writes, "Ambedkar had written the *manpatra* (welcome address, or literally, letter of honor) for Baloo Babaji Palwankar, known as P. Baloo, upon his return from a cricket tour in England nearly twenty years earlier, and had had some part in P. Balu's selection as a Depressed Class nominee on the Bombay Municipal Corporation in the early 1920s" (2013, 254). Baloo supported Gandhi during the Round Table Conferences and supported the Hindu Mahasabha position. Soon after the Poona Pact, in October 1933, Baloo contested as a Hindu Mahasabha candidate for the Bombay Municipality, but lost. In 1937, the Congress, in an effort to split the Untouchable vote, pitted Baloo, a Chambhar, against Ambedkar, a Mahar, who contested on the Independent Labour Party ticket, for a Bombay (East) 'reserved' seat in the Bombay Legislative Assembly. Ambedkar won narrowly.

245 For an outline of Rajah's career and how he came around to supporting Ambedkar in 1938 and 1942, see Note 5 at 1.5 of "A Vindication of Caste by Mahatma Gandhi" in AoC.

246 The Gujarat Freedom of Religion Act, 2003, makes it mandatory for a person who wants to convert into another religion to seek prior permission from a district magistrate. The text of the Act is available at http://www.lawsofindia.org/statelaw/2224/TheGujaratFreedomofReligionAct2003.html. An amendment bill to the Act was sent back to the Legislative Assembly by the then Gujarat Governor, Nawal Kishore Sharma, for reconsideration. It was subsequently dropped by the state government. One of the provisions in the amendment bill sought to clarify that Jains and Buddhists were to be construed as denominations of Hinduism. The Governor said that the amendment would be in violation of Article 25 of the Indian Constitution. See http://www.indianexpress.com/news/gujarat-withdraws-freedom-of-religion-amendment-bill/282818/1. To watch a video of Modi invoking M.K. Gandhi against conversion, see http://ibnlive.in.com/news/modi-quotes-mahatma-flays-religious-conversion/75119-3.html.

Also see http://www.youtube.com/watch?v=wr6q1drP558. The Gujarat Animal Preservation (Amendment) Act, 2011, makes "transport of animals for slaughter" a punishable offence, widening the ambit of the original Act, which bans cow-slaughter. The Amendment Act has also augmented the punishment to seven years' rigorous imprisonment from the earlier six months. In 2012, Narendra Modi greeted Indians on Janmashtami (observed as Krishna's birthday) with the following words: "Mahatma Gandhi and Acharya Vinoba Bhave worked tirelessly for the protection of mother cow, but this Government abandoned their teachings." See http://ibnlive.in.com/news/narendra-modi-rakes-up-cow-slaughter-issue-in-election-year-targets-congress/280876-37-64.html?utm_source=ref_article. (All internet links cited here were accessed 10 September 2013.) Gandhi said, "Anyone who is not ready to give his life to save the cow is not a Hindu" (interview to *Goseva* on 8 September 1933; CWMG 61, 372). Earlier, in 1924, he said, "When I see a cow, it is not an animal to eat, it is a poem of pity for me and I worship it and I shall defend its worship against the whole world" (reported in *Bombay Chronicle*, 30 December 1924; CWMG 29, 476).

247 See for instance, http://articles.timesofindia.indiatimes.com/keyword/mahatma-mandir. Accessed 20 December 2013.

248 For a history of the terms Harijan, Dalit and Scheduled Caste, see Note 8 to the Prologue of AoC.

249 BAWS 9, 126.

250 Ibid., 210.

251 Renold 1994, 25.

252 Tidrick 2006, 261.

253 BAWS 9, 125.

254 Ibid., 111.

255 Tharu and Lalita 1997, 215.

256 Ambedkar 2003, 25.

257 *Manusmriti* X: 123. See Doniger 1991.

258 *Harijan*, 28 November 1936; CWMG 70, 126–8.

259 Reported by the columnist Rajiv Shah in his *Times of India* blog of 1 December 2012, http://blogs.timesofindia.indiatimes.com/true-lies/entry/modi-s-spiritual-potion-to-woo-karmayogis. Shah says 5,000 copies of *Karmayogi* were printed with

funding from the public sector unit, Gujarat State Petroleum Corporation, and that later he was told, by the Gujarat Information Department that it had, on instructions from Modi, withdrawn the book from circulation. Two years later, addressing 9,000-odd Safai Karmacharis (sanitation workers), Modi said, "A priest cleans a temple every day before prayers, you also clean the city like a temple. You and the temple priest work alike." See Shah's blog of 23 January 2013, http://blogs.timesofindia.indiatimes.com/true-lies/entry/modi-s-postal-ballot-confusion?sortBy=AGREE&th=1. Both accessed 12 November 2013.

260 CWMG 70, 76–7.

261 See "A Note on the Poona Pact" in this book (357–76).

262 Menon 2006, 20.

263 This assimilation finds its way into the Constitution. Explanation II of Article 25(2)(b) of the Constitution was the first time in independent India when the law categorised Buddhists, Sikhs and Jains as 'Hindu', even if 'only' for the purpose of "providing social welfare and reform or the throwing open of Hindu religious institutions of a public character to all classes and sections of Hindus". Later, codified Hindu personal law, like the Hindu Marriage Act, 1955, the Hindu Succession Act, 1956, etc., reinforced this position, as these statutes were applied to Buddhists, Sikhs and Jains. Pertinently, under Indian law an atheist is automatically classified as a Hindu. The judiciary has been sending out mixed signals, sometimes recognising the 'independent character' of these religions, and at other times, asserting that the "Sikhs and Jains, in fact, have throughout been treated as part of the wider Hindu community which has different sects, sub-sects, faiths, modes of worship and religious philosophies" (*Bal Patil & Anr* vs *Union Of India & Ors*, 8 August 2005). For Buddhists, Sikhs and Jains the struggle for recognition continues. There has been some success; for example, the Anand Marriage (Amendment) Act, 2012, freed Sikhs from the Hindu Marriage Act. On 20 January 2014, the Union Cabinet approved the notification of Jains as a minority community at the national level. Also see Note 246 on the Gujarat Freedom of Religion Act.

264 See Guha 2013a.

265 While NGOs and news reports suggest a toll of two thousand persons (see "A Decade of Shame" by Anupama Katakam, *Frontline*, 9 March 2012), then Union Minister of State for Home, Shriprakash Jaiswal (of the Congress party), told Parliament on 11 May 2005 that 790 Muslims and 254 Hindus were killed in the riots; 2,548 were injured and 223 persons were missing. See "Gujarat riot death toll revealed", http://news.bbc.co.uk/2/hi/south_asia/4536199.stm. Accessed 10 November 2013.

266 "Peoples Tribunal Highlights Misuse of POTA", *The Hindu*, 18 March 2004. See also "Human Rights Watch asks Centre to Repeal POTA", Press Trust of India, 8 September 2002.

267 See "Blood Under Saffron: The Myth of Dalit-Muslim Confrontation," *Round Table India*, 23 July 2013. http://goo.gl/7DU9uH. Accessed 10 September 2013.

268 See http://blogs.reuters.com/india/2013/07/12/interview-with-bjp-leader-narendra-modi/. Accessed 8 September 2013

269 See "Dalit Leader Buries the Hatchet with RSS", *Times of India*, 31 August 2006. http://articles.timesofindia.indiatimes.com/2006-08-31/india/27792531_1_rss-chief-k-sudarshan-rashtriya-swayamsevak-sangh-dalit-leader. Accessed 10 August 2013.

270 See Zelliot 2013, especially chapter 5, "Political Development, 1935–56". For an account of Jogendranath Mandal's life and work, see Dwaipayan Sen (2010).

271 PTI News Service, 20 March 1955, cited in Zelliot (2013, 193).

272 See Weiss, 2011.

273 For an account of how Ambedkar's Buddhism is an attempt to reconstruct the world, see Jondhale and Beltz (2004). For an alternative history of Buddhism in India, see Omvedt (2003).

274 BAWS 11, 322.

275 BAWS 17, Part 2, 444–5. On 14 September 1956, Ambedkar wrote a letter to Prime Minister Nehru. "The cost of printing is very heavy and will come to about Rs 20,000. This is beyond my capacity, and I am, therefore, canvassing help from all quarters. I wonder if the Government of India could purchase 500 copies for distribution among the various libraries and among the many scholars whom it is inviting during the course of this year for the

celebration of Buddha's 2,500 years' anniversary." Nehru did not help him. The book was published posthumously.

276 Brahminic Hinduism believes in cosmic time that has neither beginning nor end, and alternates between cycles of creation and cessation. Each Mahayuga consists of four yuga—Krta or Satya Yuga (the golden age), followed by Treta, Dwapara and Kali. Each era, shorter than the previous one, is said to be more degenerate and depraved than the preceding one. In Kali Yuga, there is disregard for varnashrama dharma—the Shudras and Untouchables wrest power—and chaos reigns, leading to complete destruction. About Kali Yuga, the *Bhagvad Gita* says (IX: 32): "Even those who are of evil birth, women, Vaishyas and Shudras, having sought refuge in me will attain supreme liberation" (Debroy 2005, 137).

BIBLIOGRAPHY

Adams, Jad. 2011. *Gandhi: Naked Ambition*. London: Quercus.

Alexander, Michelle. 2010. *The New Jim Crow: Mass Incarceration in the Age of Colorblindness*. New York: The New Press.

Aloysius, G. 1997. *Nationalism Without a Nation in India*. New Delhi: Oxford University Press.

Ambedkar, B.R. 2003. *Ambedkar: Autobiographical Notes*. Ed. Ravikumar. Pondicherry: Navayana.

——. 1979–2003. *Dr Babasaheb Ambedkar: Writings and Speeches* (BAWS). Volumes 1–17. Mumbai: Education Department, Government of Maharashtra.

——. 1992. "Dr Ambedkar's Speech at Mahad." In *Poisoned Bread: Translations from Modern Marathi Dalit Literature*. Ed. Arjun Dangle. Hyderabad: Orient Longman.

Amin, Shahid. 1998. "Gandhi as Mahatma: Gorakhpur District, Eastern UP, 1921–2." In *Selected Subaltern Studies*. Ed. Ranajit Guha and Gayatri Spivak, 288–348. New Delhi: Oxford University Press.

Anand, S. 2002. "Meenakshipuram Redux." *Outlook*, 21 October. http://www.outlookindia.com/article.aspx?217605. Accessed 1 August 2013.

——. 2008a. "Despite Parliamentary Democracy." *Himal*, August. http://www.himalmag.com/component/content/article/838-despite-parliamentary-democracy.html. Accessed 20 July 2013.

——. 2008b. "Understanding the Khairlanji Verdict." *The Hindu*, 5 October.

——. 2009. "Resurrecting the Radical Ambedkar." *Seminar*, September.

——. 2012a. "Between Red And Blue." 16 April. http://www.outlookindia.com/article.aspx?280573. Accessed 10 August 2013.

——. 2012b. "A Case for Bhim Rajya." *Outlook*, 20 August.

Anderson, Perry. 2012. *The Indian Ideology*. New Delhi: Three Essays Collective.

Banerji, Rita. 2008. *Sex and Power: Defining History, Shaping Societies*. New Delhi: Penguin.

——. 2013. "Gandhi used His Position to Sexually Exploit Young

Women." 15 October. http://www.youthkiawaaz.com/2013/10/gandhi-used-power-position-exploit-young-women-way-react-matters-even-today/. Accessed 20 October 2013.

Bayly, Susan. 1998. "Hindu Modernisers and the 'Public' Arena. Indigenous Critiques of Caste in Colonial India." In *Vivekananda and the Modernisation of Hinduism*. Ed. William Radice, 93–137. New Delhi: Oxford University Press.

Béteille, André. 2001. "Race and Caste." *The Hindu*, 10 March.

Bhasin, Agrima. 2013. "The Railways in Denial." Infochange News and Features, February. http://infochangeindia.org/human-rights/struggle-for-human-dignity/the-railways-in-denial.html. Accessed 5 August 2013.

Birla, G.D. 1953. *In the Shadow of the Mahatma: A Personal Memoir*. Calcutta: Orient Longman.

Breman, Jan. 2004. *The Making and Unmaking of an Industrial Working Class: Sliding Down the Labour Hierarchy in Ahmedabad, India*. New Delhi: Oxford University Press.

Buckwalter, Sabrina. 2006. "Just Another Rape Story." *Sunday Times of India*, 29 October.

Carnegie, Andrew. 1889. *The Gospel of Wealth*. http://www.swarthmore.edu/SocSci/rbannis1/AIH19th/Carnegie.html. Accessed 26 August 2013.

Chandavarkar, Rajnarayan. 2009. *History, Culture and the Indian City: Essays*. Cambridge: Cambridge University Press.

Chandra, Uday. 2013. "Liberalism and Its Other: The Politics of Primitivism in Colonial and Postcolonial Indian Law." *Law & Society Review* 47 (1): 135–68.

Chawla, Prabhu. 1999. "Courting Controversy." *India Today*, 29 January.

Chitre, Dilip. 2003. *Says Tuka: Selected Poems of Tukaram*. Pune: Sontheimer Cultural Association.

Chowdhry, Prem. 2007. *Contentious Marriages, Eloping Couples: Gender, Caste and Patriarchy in Northern India*. New Delhi: Oxford University Press.

Chugtai, Ismat. 2003. *A Chugtai Collection*. Tr. Tahira Naqvi and Syeda S. Hameed. New Delhi: Women Unlimited.

Damodaran, Harish. 2008. *India's New Capitalists: Caste, Business, and Industry in a Modern Nation*. New Delhi: Permanent Black.

Dangle, Arjun, ed. 1992. *Poisoned Bread: Translations from Modern Marathi Dalit Literature*. Hyderabad: Orient Longman.

Das, Bhagwan, ed., 1980. *Rare Prefaces* [of B.R. Ambedkar]. Jullundur: Bheem Patrika.

——. 2000. "Moments in a History of Reservations". *Economic & Political Weekly*, 28 October: 3381–4.

——. 2010. *Thus Spoke Ambedkar, Vol. 1: A Stake in the Nation*. New Delhi: Navayana.

Davis, Mike. 2002. *The Great Victorian Holocausts: El Nino Famines and the Making of the Third World*. New York: Verso.

Debroy, Bibek, tr. 2005. *The Bhagavad Gita*. New Delhi: Penguin.

Desai, Ashwin and Goolam Vahed. 2010. *Inside Indian Indenture: A South African Story, 1860–1914*. Cape Town: HSRC Press.

Deshpande, G.P., ed. 2002. *Selected Writings of Jotirao Phule*. New Delhi: LeftWord.

Devji, Faisal. 2012. *The Impossible Indian: Gandhi and the Temptation of Violence*. Cambridge, Massachusetts: Harvard University Press.

Dogra, Chander Suta. 2013. *Manoj and Babli: A Hate Story*. New Delhi: Penguin.

Doniger, Wendy. 2005. *The Rig Veda*. New Delhi: Penguin.

——. and Brian K. Smith. Tr. 1991. *The Laws of Manu*. New Delhi: Penguin Books.

Fischer, Louis. 1951. *The Life of Mahatma Gandhi*. New Delhi: HarperCollins. (Rpr. 1997.)

Gajvee, Premanand. 2013. "Gandhi–Ambedkar." In *The Strength of Our Wrists: Three Plays*. Tr. from Marathi by Shanta Gokhale and M.D. Hatkanangalekar, 91–150. New Delhi: Navayana.

Gandhi, Leela. 1996–97. "Concerning Violence: The Limits and Circulations of Gandhian Ahimsa or Passive Resistance." *Cultural Critique*, 35. 105–47.

Gandhi, Lingaraja. 2004. "Mulk Raj Anand: Quest for So Many Freedoms." *Deccan Herald*, 3 October. http://archive.deccanherald.

com/deccanherald/oct032004/sh1.asp. Accessed 5 October 2013.

Gandhi, M.K. 1999. *The Collected Works of Mahatma Gandhi* (Electronic Book). 98 volumes. New Delhi: Publications Division, Government of India.

Ghosh, Suniti Kumar. 2007. *India and the Raj, 1919–1947: Glory, Shame, and Bondage*. Calcutta: Sahitya Samsad.

Godse, Nathuram. 1998. *Why I Assassinated Mahatma Gandhi*. New Delhi: Surya Bharti Prakashan.

Golwalkar, M.S. 1945. *We, or Our Nationhood Defined*. Nagpur: Bharat Prakashan. Fourth ed.

Guha, Ramachandra. 2013a. "What Hindus Can and Should be Proud Of." *The Hindu*, 23 July. http://www.thehindu.com/opinion/lead/what-hindus-can-and-should-be-proud-of/article4941930.ece. Accessed 24 July 2013.

——. 2013b. *India Before Gandhi*. New Delhi: Penguin.

Gupta, Dipankar. 2001. "Caste, Race and Politics." *Seminar*, December.

——. 2007. "Why Caste Discrimination is not Racial Discrimination." *Seminar*, April.

Guru, Gopal. 2012. "Rise of the 'Dalit Millionaire': A Low Intensity Spectacle." *Economic & Political Weekly*, 15 December: 41–49.

Guy, Jeff. 1994. *The Destruction of the Zulu Kingdom: The Civil War in Zululand, 1879–1884*. Pietermaritzburg: University of Natal Press.

——. 2005. *The Maphumulo Uprising: War, Law and Ritual in the Zulu Rebellion*. Scotsville, South Africa: University of KwaZulu-Natal Press.

Hardiman, David. 1996. *Feeding the Baniya: Peasants and Usurers in Western India*. New Delhi: Oxford University Press.

——. 2006. "A Forgotten Massacre: Motilal Tejawat and His Movement amongst the Bhils, 1921–2." In *Histories for the Subordinated*, 29–56. Calcutta: Seagull.

——. 2004. *Gandhi: In His Time and Ours: The Global Legacy of His Ideas*. New York: Columbia University Press.

Hickok, Elonnai. 2012. "Rethinking DNA Profiling in India." *Economic & Political Weekly*, 27 October. Web exclusive piece: http://www.epw.in/web-exclusives/rethinking-dna-profiling-india.

html#sdfootnote20anc. Accessed 10 September 2013.

Hochschild, Adam. 2011. *To End All Wars: A Story of Loyalty and Rebellion, 1914–1918*. London: Houghton Mifflin Harcourt.

Human Rights Watch. 1999. *Broken People: Caste Violence against India's "Untouchables"*. New York: Human Rights Watch.

Hutton, J.H. 1935. *Census of India 1931*. Delhi: Government of India.

Ilaiah, Kancha. 1996. *Why I Am Not a Hindu: A Sudra Critique of Hindutva Philosophy, Culture and Political Economy*. Calcutta: Samya.

Jaffrelot, Christophe. 2005. *Dr Ambedkar and Untouchability: Analysing and Fighting Caste*. New Delhi: Permanent Black.

Jamnadas, K. 2010. "*Manusmriti* Dahan Din" [*Manusmriti* burning day]. 14 July. *Round Table India* (roundtableindia.co.in). Accessed 6 September 2013.

Janyala, Sreenivas. 2005. "Tsunami Can't Wash this Away: Hatred for Dalits." *The Indian Express*, 7 January.

Jaoul, Nicolas. 2006. "Learning the Use of Symbolic Means: Dalits, Ambedkar Statues and the State in Uttar Pradesh." *Contributions to Indian Sociology* 40 (2): 175–207.

Jondhale, Surendra and Johannes Beltz. 2004. *Reconstructing the World: B.R. Ambedkar and Buddhism in India*. New Delhi: Oxford University Press.

Joseph, George Gheverghese. 2003. *George Joseph: The Life and Times of a Kerala Christian Nationalist*. Hyderabad: Orient Longman.

Jose, Vinod K. 2010. "Counting Castes." *Caravan*, June.

Josh, Sohan Singh. 2007. *Hindustan Gadar Party: A Short History*. Jalandhar: Desh Bhagat Yadgar Committee. (Orig. publ. 1977.)

Juergensmeyer, Mark. 2009. *Religious Rebels in the Punjab: The Ad Dharm Challenge to Caste*. New Delhi: Navayana. (Orig. publ. 1982.)

Kael, Pauline. 1982. "Tootsie, Gandhi, and Sophie." *The New Yorker*, 27 December.

Kandasamy, Meena. 2013. "How Real-Life Tamil Love Stories End." *Outlook*, 22 July.

Kapur, Devesh, Chandra Bhan Prasad, Lant Pritchett and D. Shyam Babu. 2010. "Rethinking Inequality: Dalits in Uttar Pradesh in the Market Reform Era." *Economic & Political Weekly*. 28 August: 39–49.

Keer, Dhananjay. 1990. *Dr Ambedkar: Life and Mission*. Mumbai: Popular Prakashan. (Orig. publ. 1954.)

Khandekar, Milind. 2013. *Dalit Millionaires: 15 Inspiring Stories*. Tr. from Hindi by Vandana R. Singh and Reenu Talwar. New Delhi: Penguin.

Kishwar, Madhu. 2006. "Caste System: Society's Bold Mould." *Tehelka*, 11 February http://archive.tehelka.com/story_main16.asp?filename=In021106Societys_12.asp. Accessed 10 October 2013.

Kosambi, D.D. 1948. "Marxism and Ancient Indian Culture." *Annals of the Bhandarkar Oriental Research Institute*. Vol. 26, 271–7.

Krishna, Raj. 1979. "The Nehru Gandhi Polarity and Economic Policy." Ed. B.R. Nanda, P.C. Joshi and Raj Krishna, 51–64. In *Gandhi and Nehru*. New Delhi: Oxford University Press.

Kumar, Vinoj P.C. 2009. "Bringing Out the Dead." *Tehelka*, 4 July. http://www.tehelka.com/bringing-out-the-dead/#. Accessed 10 August 2013.

——. 2009b. "Numbness of Death." *Tehelka*, 4 July. http://www.tehelka.com/numbness-of-death/. Accessed 10 August 2013.

Lal, Vinay. 2008. "The Gandhi Everyone Loves to Hate." *Economic & Political Weekly*, 4 October: 55–64.

Lelyveld, Joseph. 2011. *Great Soul: Mahatma Gandhi and His Struggle With India*. New York: Alfred A. Knopf.

Mani, Braj Ranjan. 2005. *Debrahmanising History: Dominance and Resistance in Indian Society*. New Delhi: Manohar.

——. 2012. "Amartya Sen's Imagined India." 4 June. http://www.countercurrents.org/mani040612.htm. Accessed 15 July 2013.

Mendelsohn, Oliver and Marika Vicziany. 1998. *The Untouchables: Subordination, Poverty and the State in Modern India*. Cambridge: Cambridge University Press.

Menon, Dilip. 2006. *The Blindness of Insight: Essays on Caste in Modern India*. Pondicherry: Navayana.

Menon, Meena and Neera Adarkar. 2005. *One Hundred Years, One Hundred Voices: The Millworkers of Girangaon: An Oral History*. Calcutta: Seagull.

Menon, Visalakshi. 2003. *From Movement to Government: The Congress in the United Provinces, 1937–42*. New Delhi: Sage.

Mishra, Sheokesh. 2007. "Holy Word." *India Today*, 20 December. http://

indiatoday.intoday.in/story/Holy+word/1/2736.html. Accessed 26 August 2013.

Mohanty, B.B. 2001. "Land Distribution among Scheduled Castes and Tribes." *Economic & Political Weekly*, 6 October: 1357–68.

Mukherjee, Aditya, Mridula Mukherjee and Sucheta Mahajan. 2008. *RSS School Texts and the Murder of Mahatma Gandhi: The Hindu Communal Project*. New Delhi: Sage.

Muktabai (Salve). 1855/1991. "Mang Maharachya Dukhavisayi." Tr. Maya Pandit, "About the Griefs of the Mangs and Mahars." In *Women Writing in India: 600 B.C. to the Present*. Ed. Susie Tharu and K. Lalita, 214–16. New Delhi: Oxford University Press.

Murthy, Srinivasa. 1987. *Mahatma Gandhi and Leo Tolstoy: Letters*. Long Beach: Long Beach Publications.

Nagaraj. D.R. 2010. *The Flaming Feet and Other Essays: The Dalit Movement in India*. Ranikhet: Permanent Black.

Nambissan, Geetha B. 2002. "Equality in Education: The Schooling of Dalit Children in India." In *Dalits and the State*. Ed. Ghanshyam Shah, 79–128. New Delhi: Concept.

Namboodiripad, E.M.S. 1986. *History of the Indian Freedom Struggle*. Trivandrum: Social Scientist Press.

Nandy, Ashis. 1983. *Intimate Enemy: Loss and Recovery of Self under Colonialism*. New Delhi: Oxford University Press.

Natarajan, Balmurli. 2007. "Misrepresenting Caste and Race." *Seminar*, April.

——. and Paul Greenough, ed. 2009. *Against Stigma: Studies in Caste, Race and Justice Since Durban*. Hyderabad: Orient Blackswan.

National Commission for Scheduled Castes and Scheduled Tribes. 1998. *Fourth Report*. New Delhi: NCSCST.

National Crime Records Bureau. 2012. *Crime in India 2011: Statistics*. New Delhi: NCRB, Ministry of Home Affairs.

Nauriya, Anil. 2006. "Gandhi's Little-Known Critique of Varna." *Economic & Political Weekly*, 13 May: 1835–8.

Navaria, Ajay. 2013. *Unclaimed Terrain*. Tr. Laura Brueck. New Delhi: Navayana.

Navsarjan Trust and Robert F. Kennedy Center for Justice & Human

Rights. N.d. *Understanding Untouchability: A Comprehensive Study of Practices and Conditions in 1589 Villages*. http://navsarjan.org/Documents/Untouchability_Report_FINAL_Complete.pdf. Accessed 12 September 2013.

Omvedt, Gail. 1994. *Dalits and the Democratic Revolution: Dr Ambedkar and the Dalit Movement in Colonial India*. New Delhi: Sage.

——. 2003. *Buddhism in India: Challenging Brahmanism and Caste*. New Delhi: Sage.

——. 2004. *Ambedkar: Towards an Enlightened India*. New Delhi: Penguin.

——. 2008. *Seeking Begumpura: The Social Vision of Anticaste Intellectuals*. New Delhi: Navayana.

Parel, Anthony, ed. 1997. *'Hind Swaraj' and Other Writings*. Cambridge: Cambridge University Press.

Patel, Sujata. 1988. "Construction and Reconstruction of Women in Gandhi." *Economic & Political Weekly*, 20 February: 377–87.

Patwardhan, Anand. 2011. *Jai Bhim Comrade*. DVD, documentary film.

Phadke, Y.D. 1993. *Senapati Bapat: Portrait of a Revolutionary*. New Delhi: National Book Trust.

Prashad, Vijay. 1996. "The Untouchable Question." *Economic & Political Weekly*, 2 March: 551–9.

——. 2001. *Untouchable Freedom: A Social History of a Dalit Community*. New Delhi: Oxford University Press.

Pyarelal. 1932. *The Epic Fast*. Ahmedabad: Navajivan.

Raman, Anuradha. 2010. "Standard Deviation." *Outlook*, 26 April.

Ramaswamy, Gita. 2005. *India Stinking: Manual Scavengers in Andhra Pradesh and Their Work*. Chennai: Navayana.

Ravikumar. 2009. *Venomous Touch: Notes on Caste, Culture and Politics*. Calcutta: Samya.

Rege, Sharmila. 2013. *Against the Madness of Manu: B.R. Ambedkar's Writings on Brahmanical Patriarchy*. New Delhi: Navayana.

Renold, Leah. 1994. "Gandhi: Patron Saint of the Industrialist." *Sagar: South Asia Graduate Research Journal* 1 (1): 16–38.

Sainath, P. 2013a. "Over 2,000 Fewer Farmers Every Day." *The Hindu*, 2 May.

——. 2013b. "Farmers' Suicide Rates Soar Above the Rest." *The Hindu*, 18 May.

——. 1999a. "One People, Many Identities." *The Hindu*, 31 January.

——. 1999b. "After Meenakshipuram: Caste, Not Cash, Led to Conversions." *The Hindu*, 7 February.

Santhosh S. and Joshil K. Abraham. 2010. "Caste Injustice in Jawaharlal Nehru University." *Economic & Political Weekly*, 26 June: 27–9.

Satyanarayana, K. and Susie Tharu, ed. 2013. *The Exercise of Freedom: An Introduction to Dalit Writing*. New Delhi: Navayana.

Savarkar, V.D. 1923. *Hindutva*. Nagpur: V.V. Kelkar.

Sen, Dwaipayan. 2010. "A Politics Subsumed." *Himal*, April.

Singh, G.B. 2004. *Gandhi: Behind the Mask of Divinity*. New York: Prometheus Books.

Singh, Khushwant. 1990. "Brahmin Power." *Sunday*, 29 December.

Singh, Patwant. 1999. *The Sikhs*. London: John Murray/New Delhi: Rupa.

Skaria, Ajay. 2006. "Only One Word, Properly Altered: Gandhi and the Question of the Prostitute." *Economic & Political Weekly*, 9 December: 5065–72.

Swan, Maureen. 1984. "The 1913 Natal Indian Strike." *Journal of Southern African Studies* 10 (2): 239–58.

——. 1985. *Gandhi: The South African Experience*. Johannesburg: Ravan Press.

Tagore, Rabindranath. 2007. *The English Writings of Rabindranath Tagore, Vol 2: Poems*. New Delhi: Atlantic.

Teltumbde, Anand. 2005. *Anti-Imperialism and Annihilation of Castes*. Thane: Ramai Prakashan.

——. 2010a. *The Persistence of Caste: The Khairlanji Murders and India's Hidden Apartheid*. New Delhi: Navayana/London: Zed Books.

——. 2010b. "Dangerous Sedative". *Himal*, April. http://www.himalmag.com/component/content/article/132-.html. Accessed 20 August 2013.

——. 2012. "It's Not Red vs. Blue." *Outlook*, 20 August. http://www.outlookindia.com/article.aspx?281944. Accessed 22 August 2013.

—— and Shoma Sen, ed. 2012a. *Scripting the Change: Selected Writings of Anuradha Ghandy*. New Delhi: Danish Books.

——. 2013. "*Aerocasteics* of Rahul Gandhi." *Economic & Political Weekly*: 2 November: 10–11.

Tharu, Susie and K. Lalita, ed. 1997. *Women Writing in India, Vol. 1: 600 B.C. to the Early Twentieth Century*. New Delhi: Oxford University Press. (Orig. publ. 1991.)

Thorat, S.K. and Umakant, ed. 2004. *Caste, Race, and Discrimination: Discourses in International Context*. New Delhi: Rawat.

——. 2009. *Dalits in India: Search for a Common Destiny*. New Delhi: Sage.

Tidrick, Kathryn. 2006. *Gandhi: A Political and Spiritual Life*. London: I.B. Tauris.

Valmiki, Omprakash. 2003. *Joothan: A Dalit's Life*. Calcutta: Samya.

Vanita, Ruth. 2002. "Whatever Happened to the Hindu Left?" *Seminar*, April.

Viswanathan, S. 2005. *Dalits in Dravidian Land: Frontline Reports on Anti-Dalit Violence in Tamil Nadu (1995–2004)*. Chennai: Navayana.

Viswanath, Rupa. 2012. "A Textbook Case of Exclusion." *The Indian Express*, 20 July.

——. 2014 (forthcoming). *The Pariah Problem: Caste, Religion, and the Social in Modern India*. New York: Columbia University Press/New Delhi: Navayana.

Vyam, Durgabai, Subhash Vyam, Srividya Natarajan and S. Anand. 2011. *Bhimayana: Experiences of Untouchability*. New Delhi: Navayana.

Weiss, Gordon. 2011. *The Cage: The Fight for Sri Lanka and the Last Days of the Tamil Tigers*. London: The Bodley Head.

Wolpert, Stanley. 1993. *A New History of India*. New York: Oxford University Press. (Orig. Publ. 1973.)

Zelliot, Eleanor. 2013. *Ambedkar's World: The Making of Babasaheb and the Dalit Movement*. New Delhi: Navayana.

Zinn, Howard and Anthony Arnove. 2004. *Voices of a People's History of the United States*. New York: Seven Stories Press.

Annihilation of Caste

Know truth as truth and untruth as untruth.—Buddha

He that will not reason is a bigot. He that cannot reason is a fool. He that dare not reason is a slave—H. Drummond*

* These epigraphs were added by Ambedkar to the title page of the 1937 edition. The quote from Buddha is from Verse 12 of *The Dhammapada and Sutta Nipata* (p.3), part of *Sacred Books of the East*, Vol. 10 by Max Müller and Max Fausböll (1881). Drummond's words are derived from the last lines from his preface to *Academical Questions*, Vol. 1 (1805, xv). Sir William Drummond (not H. Drummond as erroneously printed in the 1937 edition) was a Scottish diplomat and Member of Parliament, poet and philosopher. Ambedkar amends the punctuation and wording of Drummond's words which read: "He, who will not reason, is a bigot; he, who cannot, is a fool; he, who dares not, is a slave."

Preface to the Second Edition, 1937

The speech prepared by me for the Jat-Pat Todak Mandal[1] of Lahore has had an astonishingly warm reception from the Hindu public for whom it was primarily intended. The English edition of one thousand five hundred copies was exhausted within two months of its publication. It has been translated into Gujarati and Tamil. It is being translated into Marathi, Hindi, Punjabi and Malayalam. The demand for the English text still continues unabated. To satisfy this demand it has become necessary to issue a second edition. Considerations of history and effectiveness of

1 The Jat-Pat Todak Mandal (Forum for the Break-up of Caste) was a radical faction of the Arya Samaj, a Hindu reformist organisation that was founded in Lahore on 10 April 1875 by Swami Dayananda Saraswati (1824–83). According to Sant Ram (see Note 3), in November 1922, about twenty-two men and women, at the behest of Arya Samaj leader Bhai Parmanand, met at his Lahore residence with the objective of forming a separate outfit to fight caste. In his autobiography *Mere jivan ke anubhav* (Experiences of my life, 1963/2008), Sant Ram says he suggested the name Jat-Pat Todak Mandal. The eighteen founding members of the Mandal listed by Sant Ram are: Bhai Parmanand (president); Pandit Bhoomanand, Pandit Paramanand, B.A.; Chowdhary Kanhaiyalal; Babu Teertharam, cotton factory owner; Chak Jhumra; Pandit Brahmadatt Vidyalankar of Delhi; Shri Sudarshan, short-story writer; Pandit Dharmadev; Deewanchand, office-bearer of Arya Samaj, Jalandhar; Pandit Sant Ram, priest and Arya Samaj worker of Nau Shehra; Paramanand Arya, coal company, Lahore; Pandit Chetram, teacher, Girls School, Jalandhar; Devnath of Gurudutt Bhavan, Lahore; Devamitra, M.Sc., of Gurudutt Bhavan, Lahore; Dharmendra Nath, M.A., of Meerut; Sant Ram, B.A.; Mrs Parvati, wife of Pandit Bhoomanand; Mrs Subhadra Devi, wife of Pandit Paramanand. From the names, it appears that 'Untouchables' were not part of this distinctly caste-Hindu initiative, a point that Ambedkar draws our attention to in the Prologue of this address (p.189). The Mandal insisted on inter-dining and intermarriage. Membership, on paying two rupees as annual subscription, was meant for Hindus who took a vow to marry themselves or their children out of their caste.

appeal have led me to retain the original form of the essay—namely, the speech form—although I was asked to recast it in the form of a direct narrative.

To this edition I have added two appendices. I have collected in Appendix I the two articles written by Mr Gandhi by way of review of my speech in the *Harijan*,[2] and his letter to Mr Sant Ram,[3] a member of the Jat-Pat Todak Mandal.[4]

---

2 Following his fallout with Ambedkar over the Communal Award of 1932 and the signing of the Poona Pact (see "A Note on the Poona Pact", in this book, 357–76), M.K. Gandhi launched the Harijan Sevak Sangh in 1932 and an English weekly named *Harijan* in 1933. Ambedkar preferred the term Untouchable, with capitals, or the official term, Depressed Classes. He also preferred to address those within the varna fold as "caste Hindus" or *savarnas*, and sometimes as Touchables.

3 Sant Ram B.A., one of the founder-members of the Jat-Pat Todak Mandal, was born on 14 February 1887 in Puranibassi, Hoshiarpur district, Punjab. In his autobiography, he (1963/2008, 12) says the Gohil surname his father carried was found among Rajputs (warriors), Banias (traders) and Kumhars (potters). Sant Ram always used his graduation degree—B.A.—as initials to disavow caste-related surnames, though he identifies himself as a Kumhar. However, one source says he was born into the Megh caste, listed as a Scheduled Caste in today's Punjab (Kshirsagar 1994, 323). Sant Ram says that Kumhars in his village did not make pots but practised trade. Sant Ram's father, Ramdas Gohil, the first person in the village to educate his children, acquired wealth and influence through trade which took him as far away as Central Asia. Sant Ram was married at the age of twelve to an unlettered girl whom he taught to read and write and brought out of purdah. Five years after his first wife died, in 1929, according to the journal *The Indian Rationalist* (1952), he married "Sundar Bai Proothan, a Maharashtrian virgin widow. The marriage was notable for three reasons: it was a widow marriage, an inter-caste marriage, and an inter-provincial marriage." Sundar Bai had been rendered a child widow at the age of eight. Sant Ram recounts two instances of caste discrimination, the first when studying in fourth grade in Ambala and the second when at college in Lahore at the hands of Banias, the merchant caste. In 1930, he published *Phansi ke pujari* (Priests of the noose) in Urdu, featuring biographies of nationalists, entitled *Inquilab ke parvane* (Moths to the flame of revolution) on the inside title page. A 1947 partition refugee, Sant Ram died in New Delhi in 1998 at the age of 101. In one of his exchanges with the Mandal featured in the Prologue, Ambedkar describes Sant Ram as the "moving spirit and the leading light" of the Mandal (p.199).

4 In 1931, the Mandal campaigned against the declaration of caste in the census. Mark Juergensmeyer (1982/2009, 39) writes that the Mandal relied heavily on the support of privileged-caste Arya Samajis in this regard. This may have caused the Mandal to refuse the address prepared by Ambedkar. Bhai Parmanand was the first president and he continued to support the Mandal despite the rift in 1924 when its permission to use the Arya Samaj pandal was revoked.

In Appendix II, I have printed my views in reply to the articles of Mr Gandhi collected in Appendix I. Besides Mr Gandhi, many others have adversely criticised my views as expressed in my speech. But I have felt that in taking notice of such adverse comments, I should limit myself to Mr Gandhi. This I have done not because what he has said is so weighty as to deserve a reply, but because to many a Hindu he is an oracle, so great that when he opens his lips it is expected that the argument must close and no dog must bark.

But the world owes much to rebels who would dare to argue in the face of the pontiff and insist that he is not infallible. I do not care for the credit which every progressive society must give to its rebels. I shall be satisfied if I make the Hindus realise that they are the sick men of India, and that their sickness is causing danger to the health and happiness of other Indians.

B.R. Ambedkar

Preface to the Third Edition, 1944

The second edition of this essay appeared in 1937, and was exhausted within a very short period. A new edition has been in demand for a long time. It was my intention to recast the essay so as to incorporate into it another essay of mine called "Castes in India: Their Mechanism, Genesis and Development," which appeared in the issue of the *Indian Antiquary* journal for May 1917.[5] But as I could not find time, and as there is very little prospect of my being able to do so, and as the demand for it from the public is very insistent, I am content to let this be a mere reprint of the second edition.

I am glad to find that this essay has become so popular, and I hope that it will serve the purpose for which it was intended.

B.R. Ambedkar
22, Prithviraj Road
New Delhi
1 December 1944

5 For an annotated edition of "Castes in India", see Rege (2013). *Indian Antiquary* was an Orientalist monthly founded in 1872 by Dr James Burgess. It provided a platform for scholarly articles by both European and Indian scholars. In full, it was called *The Indian Antiquary: A Journal of Oriental Research in Archaeology, Epigraphy, Ethnology, Geography, History, Folklore, Languages, Literature, Numismatics, Philosophy, Religion, Etc.*

Prologue

On 12 December 1935,[6] I received the following letter from Mr Sant Ram, the secretary of the Jat-Pat Todak Mandal:

> My dear Doctor Saheb,
>
> Many thanks for your kind letter of the 5th December. I have released it for press without your permission for which I beg your pardon, as I saw no harm in giving it publicity. You are a great thinker, and it is my well-considered opinion that none else has studied the problem of caste so deeply as you have. I have always benefited myself and our Mandal from your ideas. I have explained and preached it in the *Kranti*[7] many times and

6 The portion of the Prologue from here till the end of Sant Ram's letter has been added in the 1937 edition.

7 *Kranti* (Revolution), edited by Sant Ram, was an Urdu monthly published from Lahore. After the founding of the Jat-Pat Todak Mandal, Sant Ram (1963/2008, 116) says the forum tried publishing a monthly magazine in Hindi. A monthly eight-page broadsheet called *Jat-Pat Todak*, priced at Rs 1.50, was published from December 1922 to September 1924, but it failed owing to the lack of Hindi readers. The Mandal produced, for free distribution, many books in Hindi, Urdu and English on the question of caste. In January 1927, *Jat-Pat Todak* was revived, this time as an Urdu publication. In January 1928, this was renamed *Kranti*, with Sant Ram as chief editor. "This became a very popular magazine," according to Sant Ram. "Produced in Royal Octavo size, it had 64 pages. The magazine's Health Special, Children's Special, Women's Special, and Men's Special were extremely popular... Since the Mandal's key assets were stuck in Pakistan, *Kranti* folded up after its last issue in August 1947... After a gap, we revived it for two or three issues in India. Since the conditions were not right, we lost about Rs 2,000 and shut down *Kranti* for good" (117). According to Bhagwan Das (2010a, 21–2), *Kranti* was the only Urdu magazine that reported on the speeches of Ambedkar. Das also mentions the Mandal's strong aversion to the conversion of Untouchables due to its proximity to the Arya Samaj.

I have even lectured on it in many conferences. I am now very anxious to read the exposition of your new formula—"It is not possible to break caste without annihilating the religious notions on which it, the caste system, is founded." Please do explain it at length at your earliest convenience, so that we may take up the idea and emphasise it from press and platform. At present, it is not fully clear to me.

Our executive committee persists in having you as our president for our annual conference. We can change our dates to accommodate your convenience. Independent Harijans[8] of

8 Harijan, 'children of god', was the epithet used by M.K. Gandhi, beginning 1932, to paternalistically refer to 'Untouchables'. The term figures in the bhajan "Vaishnava jana to" by Narsinh Mehta (1414?–1481?), a Gujarati Brahmin Vaishnavite poet-saint, which was popularised by Gandhi. The scholar Aishwary Kumar (2014) draws our attention to Gandhi citing Tulsidas's sixteenth-century Ramayana, one of his favourite books on this term: "You know the word 'Harijan' occurs in Tulsidas's Ramayana? There Lakshmana describes to Parashurama the characteristic of a true Kshatriya. He says: सुर महिसुर हरिजन अरु गाई। हमरें कुल इन्ह पर न सुराई॥ (It is the trait of our clan never to use force towards a god, a Brahmin, a Harijan or a cow)" (CWMG 68, 327). The British government, from 1916 onwards, deployed the bureaucratic term Depressed Classes (used first in the volumes of the *Bombay Gazetteer* in 1877), which was replaced by Scheduled Castes in 1935 by the Government of India Act—a term that continues to be used in official parlance till date. 'Harijan' has been steadfastly rejected by the Ambedkarite and Dalit movements. Though the founding of the militant organisation Dalit Panther in Bombay in 1972 gave an all-India currency to Dalit (broken, crushed people), the term has been used in western India in this sense at least since Jotiba Phule's (1827–90) time. Phule is supposed to have used Dalit in terms of *dalittuthan* (uplift of the downtrodden), but the evidence is anecdotal (Louis 2003, 144). Phule used the term Ati-Shudra for Untouchables in his writings. Etymologically, the origins of the term Dalit can be traced to the Buddha's usage of the Pali *dalidda* in the *Dalidda Sutta*, said to have been preached at the Kalandakanivapa in Rajagaha (*Samyutta Nikaya*: XI.14). In Pali Buddhist literature, the term dalidda (*daridra* in Sanskrit) is used for the property-less poor in contrast to the *gahapati* class of the rich. Nalin Swaris (2011, 99), citing *Anguttara Nikaya*: III.84, says: "The *dalidda-kula*, the pauper-lineage, is described as people without enough to eat and drink, without even a covering for their back." More recently, the Dalit leader P.N. Rajbhoj founded the journal *Dalit Bandhu* (Friend of Dalits) in Pune in 1928. For an account of the nascent histories of the terms Untouchable, Depressed Classes, Harijan, Scheduled Caste, etc., see Simon Charsley (1996). Sant Ram's use of the term Harijan here shows how within three years of Gandhi coining the term it had entrenched itself among reformers and intellectuals. As Ambedkar says in the very opening paragraph of AoC, "I have questioned the authority of the Mahatma whom they [the Mandal] revere".

> Punjab are very much desirous to meet you and discuss with you their plans. So if you kindly accept our request and come to Lahore to preside over the conference it will serve double purpose. We will invite Harijan leaders of all shades of opinion and you will get an opportunity of giving your ideas to them.
>
> The Mandal has deputed our assistant secretary, Mr Indra Singh, to meet you at Bombay in Xmas and discuss with you the whole situation with a view to persuade you to please accept our request.

▼

The Jat-Pat Todak Mandal is, I was given to understand, an organisation of caste-Hindu social reformers, with the one and only aim, namely, to eradicate the caste system from amongst the Hindus. As a rule, I do not like to take any part in a movement which is carried on by caste Hindus. Their attitude towards social reform is so different from mine that I have found it difficult to pull on with them. Indeed, I find their company quite uncongenial to me on account of our differences of opinion. Therefore when the Mandal first approached me, I declined their invitation to preside. The Mandal, however, would not take a refusal from me, and sent down one of its members to Bombay to press me to accept the invitation. In the end I agreed to preside. The annual conference was to be held at Lahore, the headquarters of the Mandal. The conference was to meet at Easter, but was subsequently postponed to the middle of May 1936.[9]

The reception committee of the Mandal has now cancelled the conference. The notice of cancellation came long after my presidential address had been printed. The copies of this address

9 In the process of opening with Sant Ram's letter in the 1937 edition, Ambedkar rearranges the contents of this paragraph without affecting its import.

are now lying with me. As I did not get an opportunity to deliver the address from the presidential chair, the public has not had an opportunity to know my views on the problems created by the caste system. To let the public know them, and also to dispose of the printed copies which are lying on my hand, I have decided to put the printed copies of the address in the market. The accompanying pages contain the text of that address.

The public will be curious to know what led to the cancellation of my appointment as the president of the conference. At the start, a dispute arose over the printing of the address. I desired that the address should be printed in Bombay. The Mandal wished that it should be printed in Lahore, on the grounds of economy. I did not agree, and insisted upon having it printed in Bombay. Instead of their agreeing to my proposition, I received a letter signed by several members of the Mandal, from which I give the following extract:

> 27 March 1936
>
> Revered Doctor ji,
>
> Your letter of the 24th instant addressed to Sjt. Sant Ram[10] has been shown to us. We were a little disappointed to read it. Perhaps you are not fully aware of the situation that has arisen here. Almost all the Hindus in the Punjab are against your being invited to this province. The Jat-Pat Todak Mandal has been subjected to the bitterest criticism and has received censorious rebuke from all quarters. All the Hindu leaders among whom being Bhai Parmanand, MLA (ex-president, Hindu Mahasabha),[11] Mahatma

10 Sjt. here is short for the respectful prefix 'Srijut', commonly used during this period. For instance, in Gandhi's autobiography the prefix Sjt. is often used (such as Sjt. Vitthalbhai Patel). The 1931 Macmillan edition of *Mahatma Gandhi: His Own Story* edited by C.F. Andrews has a glossary page that explains Srijut as "a common title the equivalent to 'Esquire'".

11 Bhai Parmanand (1876–1947) wore many hats. Born in Lahore, he started as an Arya Samaji under the influence of Lala Lajpat Rai and Lala Har Dayal, and moved to the far right as a Vedic missionary of the Samaj, travelling the world (South Africa,

Hans Raj, Dr Gokal Chand Narang, minister for local self-government, Raja Narendra Nath,[12] MLC etc., have dissociated themselves from this step of the Mandal.

Despite all this the runners of the Jat-Pat Todak Mandal (the leading figure being Sjt. Sant Ram) are determined to wade through thick and thin but would not give up the idea of your presidentship. The Mandal has earned a bad name.

Under the circumstances it becomes your duty to co-operate with the Mandal. On the one hand, they are being put to so much trouble and hardship by the Hindus, and if on the other hand you too augment their difficulties it will be a most sad coincidence of bad luck for them.

We hope you will think over the matter and do what is good for us all.

Guyana, Martinique, the US, South America) preaching, and became a founder-member of the Ghadar Party that sought to overthrow British rule. Remembered today for his leadership of the Hindu Mahasabha and for being a proponent of Hindutva, he was sentenced in 1915 to imprisonment on the Andamans in the First Lahore Conspiracy Case. Parmanand is also regarded as the first advocate of an Islamic state divided out of the subcontinent. Following the British announcement of the partition of Bengal in 1905, he suggested that "the territory beyond Sindh should be united with Afghanistan and North-West Frontier Province into a great Musulman Kingdom. The Hindus of the region should come away, while at the same time the Musulmans in the rest of the country should go and settle in this territory" (cited in Yadav and Arya 1988, 196). Also see Parmanand's autobiography translated into English, *The Story of My Life* (1934/2003). Jaffrelot (2010, 139) cites Parmanand's 1936 work, *Hindu Sangathan*, where he excoriates the Buddha for attacking the varnashrama system: "The abolition of castes and ashrams cut at the very root of social duties. How could a nation hope to live after having lost sight of this aspect of Dharma? 'Equality for all' is an appealing abstraction; but the nation could not long survive the rejection or destruction of Dharma." Parmanand espouses such views in the year of inviting Ambedkar, and even as he is the founder-president of the Jat-Pat Todak Mandal.

12 Mahatma Hans Raj was among the first wave of a young, new generation of educated Hindus joining the Arya Samaj. Later he became the principal of the Dayanand Anglo-Vedic College, Lahore, over which he presided from 1888 to 1911. Gokal Chand Narang belonged to the DAV (College) faction of the Arya Samaj and acquired influence alongside the rich landowner, Raja Narendra Nath, in the Legislative Assembly opposed to the encroachment of the Congress in the Punjab. For a history of the Arya Samaj and its leaders, see Kenneth W. Jones (1976).

▼

This letter puzzled me greatly. I could not understand why the Mandal should displease me, for the sake of a few rupees, in the matter of printing the address. Secondly, I could not believe that men like Sir Gokal Chand Narang had really resigned as a protest against my selection as president, because I had received the following letter from Sir Gokal Chand himself:

> 5 Montgomery Road, Lahore
> 7 February 1936
> Dear Doctor Ambedkar,
> I am glad to learn from the workers of the Jat-Pat Todak Mandal that you have agreed to preside at their next anniversary to be held at Lahore during the Easter holidays. It will give me much pleasure if you stay with me while you are at Lahore.
> More when we meet.
> Yours sincerely,
> G.C. Narang

▼

Whatever be the truth, I did not yield to this pressure. But even when the Mandal found that I was insisting upon having my address printed in Bombay, instead of agreeing to my proposal the Mandal sent me a wire that they were sending Mr Har Bhagwan[13] to Bombay to "talk over matters

13 Har Bhagwan's full name, according to the journal *The Atheist* (March–April 1974), was Har Bhagwan Sethi. He may have given up his (Bania) caste surname owing to his membership of the Jat-Pat Todak Mandal; he served as its secretary at one time. As an associate of Sant Ram, he was "closely associated with the abolition of caste distinctions". He died in 1976 at the age of eight-one in Delhi, having emigrated after partition from

personally". Mr Har Bhagwan came to Bombay on the 9th of April. When I met Mr Har Bhagwan, I found that he had nothing to say regarding the issue. Indeed he was so unconcerned regarding the printing of the address—whether it should be printed in Bombay or in Lahore—that he did not even mention it in the course of our conversation.

All that he was anxious for was to know the contents of the address. I was then convinced that in getting the address printed in Lahore, the main object of the Mandal was not to save money but to get at the contents of the address. I gave him a copy. He did not feel very happy with some parts of it. He returned to Lahore. From Lahore, he wrote to me the following letter:

> Lahore, 14 April 1936
> My dear Doctor Saheb,
> Since my arrival from Bombay, on the 12th, I have been indisposed owing to my having not slept continuously for five or six nights, which were spent in the train. Reaching

---

Lahore like Sant Ram. Notably, Har Bhagwan was the publisher of Swami Dharmateertha's *The Menace of Hindu Imperialism* (1941). Dharmateertha, born Parameswara Menon, a Nair from Kerala, came under the influence of Sree Narayana Guru (1856–1928), the pioneering anticaste social reformer who preached the message of "one caste, one religion, one god". In 1937, Dharmateertha led "the life of a wandering sannyasin and spread the Guru's social message of castelessness and social egalitarianism across the sub-continent" (Aloysius 2004, 19). Aloysius cites Ambedkar's words on this work in the blurb of the new edition: "This book is written from a point of view which I appreciate very much. I am myself writing a book in which I have touched many of the points which I find are dealt with in this book. The book therefore was a very welcome thing to me." After touring much of North India, Dharmateertha settled down in Lahore for five years (1941–6) at Har Bhagwan's house, and as a member of the Indian Social Congress met and held discussions with Jinnah, Ambedkar and the Sikh leader Master Tara Singh. In a short account in *The Atheist* (1974), Har Bhagwan says that after moving to Delhi he founded the Jat-Pat Todak Samata Sangh (Association for Equality Without Caste) which was soon renamed Avarnodaya Samata Sangh (Association for the Advancement of Casteless People).

here I came to know that you had come to Amritsar.[14] I would have seen you there if I were well enough to go about. I have made over your address to Mr Sant Ram for translation and he has liked it very much, but he is not sure whether it could be translated by him for printing before the 25th. In any case, it would have a wide publicity and we are sure it would wake the Hindus up from their slumber.

The passage I pointed out to you at Bombay has been read by some of our friends with a little misgiving, and those of us who would like to see the conference terminate without any untoward incident would prefer that at least the word "Veda" be left out for the time being. I leave this to your good sense. I hope, however, in your concluding paragraphs you will make it clear that the views expressed in the address are your own and that the responsibility does not lie on the Mandal. I hope you will not mind this statement of mine and would let us have 1,000 copies of the address, for which we shall, of course, pay. To this effect I have sent you a telegram today. A cheque of Rs 100 is enclosed herewith which kindly acknowledge, and send us your bills in due time.

I have called a meeting of the reception committee and shall communicate their decision to you immediately.

---

14 On 13–14 April 1936, Ambedkar attended the Sikh Prachar Conference in Amritsar (50 km from Lahore). In his address he extolled the principle of equality within the Sikh community and alluded to the possibility of converting to Sikhism. Zelliot (2013, 162) writes: "There is an unverified story that Ambedkar spoke to a Sikh group at this time, asking them if they were willing to allow inter-marriage between Sikhs and new converts, and the Sikhs responded in the affirmative." For an analysis of why Ambedkar gave up on Sikhism, see Puri (2003, 2698), who says: "After participating in the Sikh Missionary Conference at Amritsar in April, Ambedkar sent his son, Yashwant Rao, and nephew to the Golden Temple in May, where they stayed for one month and a half, to observe the situation and meet with leaders of the community." Puri argues that perhaps the Shiromani Gurdwara Parbandhak Committee (SGPC) feared that "after six crore (60 million) untouchables became Sikhs" the clout of dominant-caste Jats in the SGPC and the gurdwaras would be undermined.

In the meantime kindly accept my heartfelt thanks for the kindness shown to me and the great pains taken by you in the preparation of your address. You have really put us under a heavy debt of gratitude.

Yours sincerely,

Har Bhagwan

P.S.: Kindly send the copies of the address by passenger train as soon as it is printed, so that copies may be sent to the press for publication.

Accordingly I handed over my manuscript to the printer with an order to print thousand copies. Eight days later, I received another letter from Mr Har Bhagwan which I reproduce below:

Lahore, 22 April 1936

Dear Dr Ambedkar,

We are in receipt of your telegram and letter, for which kindly accept our thanks. In accordance with your desire, we have again postponed our conference, but feel that it would have been much better to have it on the 25th and 26th, as the weather is growing warmer and warmer every day in the Punjab. In the middle of May it would be fairly hot, and the sittings in the daytime would not be very pleasant and comfortable. However, we shall try our best to do all we can to make things as comfortable as possible, if it is held in the middle of May.

There is, however, one thing that we have been compelled to bring to your kind attention. You will remember that when I pointed out to you the misgivings entertained by some of our people regarding your declaration on the subject of change of religion,[15] you

15 This must be seen in the light of the statement Ambedkar had made on 13 October 1935 at the Yeola Depressed Classes conference: "I had the misfortune of being born with the stigma of an Untouchable. However, it is not my fault; but I will not die a Hindu, for this is in my power" (Zelliot

told me that it was undoubtedly outside the scope of the Mandal and that you had no intention to say anything from our platform in that connection. At the same time when the manuscript of your address was handed to me you assured me that that was the main portion of your address and that there were only two or three concluding paragraphs that you wanted to add. On receipt of the second instalment of your address we have been taken by surprise, as that would make it so lengthy, that we are afraid very few people would read the whole of it. Besides that you have more than once stated in your address that you had decided to walk out of the fold of the Hindus and that that was your last address as a Hindu. You have also unnecessarily attacked the morality and reasonableness of the Vedas and other religious books of the Hindus, and have at length dwelt upon the technical side of Hindu religion, which has absolutely no connection with the problem at issue, so much so that some of the passages have become irrelevant and off the point. We would have been very pleased if you had confined your address to that portion given to me, or if an addition was necessary, it would have been limited to what you had written on

---

2013, 147). The conference was attended by ten thousand people, a conglomeration of Mahar panchayats and delegates from Hyderabad and the Central Provinces. "The conference included an instruction to stop temple entry movements and an exhortation to cease fruitless attempts to gain status on Hindu terms" (Zelliot 2013, 148). Sant Ram (1963/2008, 137) writes, "One of the reasons for my inviting Dr Ambedkar was that in matters we can't convince him with logic, we would convince him in love by appealing to his heart." Ambedkar's insistence on including in his address a detailed section on the destruction of the Hindu religion signalled the likelihood of failure if the Mandal insisted on trying to win him over to the cause of religious reform. At the same time, members of the Mandal's welcome committee were threatened with a black-flag protest if Ambedkar were to preside over the meeting, and this made Sant Ram unsure of endearing Ambedkar to the cause. Ambedkar's address at the Sikh Prachar Conference, Amritsar, in April 1936 would have further disoriented the Jat-Pat Todak Mandal, a point Ambedkar makes in his final letter to the Mandal (203).

Brahminism, etc. The last portion which deals with the complete annihilation of the Hindu religion and doubts the morality of the sacred books of the Hindus as well as a hint about your intention to leave the Hindu fold does not seem to me to be relevant.

I would therefore most humbly request you on behalf of the people responsible for the conference to leave out the passages referred to above, and close the address with what was given to me or add a few paragraphs on Brahminism. We doubt the wisdom of making the address unnecessarily provocative and pinching. There are several of us who subscribe to your feelings and would very much want to be under your banner for remodelling the Hindu religion. If you had decided to get together persons of your cult, I can assure you a large number would have joined your army of reformers from the Punjab.

In fact, we thought you would give us a lead in the destruction of the evil of [the] caste system, especially when you have studied the subject so thoroughly, and strengthen our hands by bringing about a revolution and making yourself as a nucleus in the gigantic effort, but [a] declaration of the nature made by you, when repeated, loses its power, and becomes a hackneyed term. Under the circumstances, I would request you to consider the whole matter and make your address more effective by saying that you would be glad to take a leading part in the destruction of the caste system if the Hindus are willing to work in right earnest towards that end, even if they had to forsake their kith and kin and the religious notions. In case you do so, I am sanguine that you would find a ready response from the Punjab in such an endeavour.

I shall be grateful if you will help us at this juncture as we have already undergone much expenditure and have been put to suspense, and let us know by the return of post that you have condescended to limit your address as above.

In case you still insist upon the printing of the address *in toto*, we very much regret it would not be possible—rather advisable—for us to hold the conference, and would prefer to postpone it *sine die*, although by doing so we shall be losing the goodwill of the people because of the repeated postponements. We should, however, like to point out that you have carved a niche in our hearts by writing such a wonderful treatise on the caste system, which excels all other treatises so far written and will prove to be a valuable heritage, so to say. We shall be ever indebted to you for the pains taken by you in its preparation.

Thanking you very much for your kindness and with best wishes.

I am yours sincerely,
Har Bhagwan

To this letter I sent the following reply:

27 April 1936
Dear Mr Har Bhagwan,
I am in receipt of your letter of the 22nd April. I note with regret that the reception committee of the Jat-Pat Todak Mandal "would prefer to postpone the conference *sine die*" if I insisted upon printing the address *in toto*. In reply I have to inform you that I also would prefer to have the conference cancelled—I do not like to use vague terms—if the Mandal insisted upon having my address pruned to suit its circumstances. You may not like my decision. But I cannot give up, for the sake of the honour of presiding over the conference,[16] the liberty

16 Sant Ram (1963/2008, 119), in his autobiography, lists the following past presidents of the Mandal's annual conferences in Lahore from a 1939 report of the Mandal: Swami Shraddhanand, Motilal Nehru, Raja Narendra Nath, Bhai Parmanand, Rameshwari Nehru, Swami Sarvadanand, Sir Hari Singh Gaur, Sri Satyananda Stokes, Sri Ramananda Chatterjee, Sri Harkishan Lal, Barrister Dr Gokul Chand, Barrister Dr N.B. Khare of Nagpur, Swami Satyanand and Dr Kalyandas Desai.

which every president must have in the preparation of the address. I cannot give up, for the sake of pleasing the Mandal, the duty which every president owes to the conference over which he presides, to give it a lead which he thinks right and proper. The issue is one of principle, and I feel I must do nothing to compromise it in any way.

I would not have entered into any controversy as regards the propriety of the decision taken by the reception committee. But as you have given certain reasons which appear to throw the blame on me, I am bound to answer them. In the first place, I must dispel the notion that the views contained in that part of the address to which objection has been taken by the committee have come to the Mandal as a surprise. Mr Sant Ram, I am sure, will bear me out when I say that in reply to one of his letters I had said that the real method of breaking up the caste system was not to bring about inter-caste dinners and inter-caste marriages but to destroy the religious notions on which caste was founded, and that Mr Sant Ram in return asked me to explain what he said was a novel point of view. It was in response to this invitation from Mr Sant Ram that I thought I ought to elaborate in my address what I had stated in a sentence in my letter to him. You cannot, therefore, say that the views expressed are new. At any rate, they are not new to Mr Sant Ram, who is the moving spirit and the leading light of your Mandal. But I go further and say that I wrote this part of my address not merely because I felt it desirable to do so. I wrote it because I thought that it was absolutely necessary to complete the argument. I am amazed to read that you characterise the portion of the speech to which your committee objects as "irrelevant and off the point". You will allow me to say that I am a lawyer and I know the rules of relevancy as well as any member of your committee. I most emphatically maintain that the portion objected to is not only most relevant but is also most important. It is in that part of the address that I have discussed the ways and means of breaking up the caste system. It may be that the conclusion I have arrived at as to the best method of destroying caste is startling and painful. You are entitled to say that my analysis is wrong. But you cannot say that in an address which deals with the problem of caste it is not open to me to discuss how caste can be destroyed.

Your other complaint relates to the length of the address. I have pleaded guilty to the charge in the address itself. But who is really responsible for this? I fear you have come rather late on the scene. Otherwise you would have known that originally I had planned to write a short address, for my own convenience, as I had neither the time nor the energy to engage myself in the preparation of an elaborate thesis. It was the Mandal which asked me to deal with the subject exhaustively, and it was the Mandal which sent down to me a list of questions relating to the caste system and asked me to answer them in the body of my address, as they were questions which were often raised in the controversy between the Mandal and its opponents, and which the Mandal found difficult to answer satisfactorily. It was in trying to meet the wishes of the Mandal in this respect that the address has grown to the length to which it has. In view of what I have said, I am sure you will agree that the fault respecting the length of the address is not mine.

I did not expect that your Mandal would be so upset because I have spoken of the destruction of the Hindu religion. I thought it was only fools who were afraid of words. But lest there should be any misapprehension in the minds of the people, I have taken great pains to explain what I mean by religion and destruction of religion. I am sure that nobody, on reading my address, could possibly misunderstand me. That your Mandal should have taken a fright at mere words as "destruction of religion, etc.", notwithstanding the explanation that accompanies them, does not raise the Mandal in my estimation. One cannot have any respect or regard for men who take the position of the reformer and then refuse even to see the logical consequences of that position, let alone following them out in action.

You will agree that I have never accepted to be limited in any way in the preparation of my address, and the question as to what the address should or should not contain was never even discussed between myself and the Mandal. I had always taken for granted that I was free to express in the address such views as I held on the subject. Indeed, until you came to Bombay on the 9th April, the Mandal did not know what sort of an address I was preparing. It was when you came to Bombay that I voluntarily told you that I had no desire to use your platform from which to advocate my views regarding change of religion by the Depressed Classes. I think I have scrupulously kept that promise in the preparation of the address. Beyond a passing reference of an indirect character where I say that "I am sorry I will not be here, etc.", I have said nothing about the subject in my address. When I see you object even to such a passing and so indirect a reference, I feel bound to ask, did you think that in agreeing to preside over your conference I would be agreeing to suspend or to give up my views regarding change of faith by the Depressed Classes? If you did think so, I must tell you that I am in no way responsible for such a mistake on your part. If any of you had even hinted to me that in exchange for the honour you were doing me by electing [me] as president, I was to abjure my faith in my programme of conversion, I would have told you in quite plain terms that I cared more for my faith than for any honour from you.

After your letter of the 14th, this letter of yours comes as a surprise to me. I am sure that anyone who reads them both will feel the same. I cannot account for this sudden volte-face on the part of the reception committee. There is no difference in substance between the rough draft which was before the committee when you wrote your letter of the 14th, and the final draft on which the decision of the committee communicated to me in your letter under reply was taken. You cannot point out a single new idea in the final draft which is not contained in the earlier draft. The ideas are the same. The only difference is that they have been worked out in greater detail in the final draft. If there was anything to object to in the address, you could have said so on the 14th. But you did not. On the contrary, you asked me to print off 1,000 copies, leaving me the liberty to accept or not the verbal changes which you suggested. Accordingly I got 1,000 copies printed, which are now lying with me. Eight days later you write to say that you object to the address and that if it is not amended the conference will be cancelled. You ought to have known that there was no hope of any alteration being made in the address. I told you when you were in Bombay that I would not alter a comma, that I would not allow any censorship over my address, and that you would have to accept the address as it came from me. I also told you that the responsibility for the views expressed in the address was entirely mine, and if they were not liked by the conference I would not mind at all if the conference passed a resolution condemning them. So anxious was I to relieve your Mandal from having to assume responsibility for my views—and also with the object of not getting myself entangled by too intimate an association with your conference—I suggested to you that I desired to have my address treated as a sort of an inaugural address and not as a presidential address, and that the Mandal should find someone else to preside over the conference and deal with the resolutions. Nobody could have been better placed to take a decision on the 14th than your committee. The committee failed to do that, and in the meantime cost of printing has been incurred which, I am sure, with a little more firmness on the part of your committee, could have been saved.

I feel sure that the views expressed in my address have little to do with the decision of your committee. I have reason to believe that my presence at the Sikh Prachar Conference held at Amritsar has had a good deal to do with the decision of the committee. Nothing else can satisfactorily explain the sudden volte face shown by the committee between the 14th and the 22nd April. I must not, however, prolong this controversy, and must request you to announce immediately that the session of the conference which was to meet under my presidentship is cancelled. All the grace has by now run out, and I shall not consent to preside, even if your committee agreed to accept my address as it is, *in toto*. I thank you for your appreciation of the pains I have taken in the preparation of the address. I certainly have profited by the labour, if no one else does. My only regret is that I was put to such hard labour at a time when my health was not equal to the strain it has caused.

Yours sincerely,
B.R. Ambedkar

▼

This correspondence will disclose the reasons which have led to the cancellation by the Mandal of my appointment as president, and the reader will be in a position to lay the blame where it ought properly to belong. This is I believe the first time when the appointment of a president is cancelled by the reception committee because it does not approve of the views of the president. But whether that is so or not, this is certainly the first time in my life to have been invited to preside over a conference of caste Hindus. I am sorry that it has ended in a tragedy. But what can anyone expect from a relationship so tragic as the relationship between the reforming sect of caste Hindus and the self-respecting sect of Untouchables, where the former have no desire to alienate their orthodox fellows, and the latter have no alternative but to insist upon reform being carried out?

B.R. Ambedkar
Rajgriha, Dadar
Bombay–14
15 May 1936

Annihilation of Caste

An Undelivered Speech, 1936

1

1.1

Friends, I am really sorry for the members of the Jat-Pat Todak Mandal who have so very kindly invited me to preside over this conference. I am sure they will be asked many questions for having selected me as the president. The Mandal will be asked to explain as to why it has imported a man from Bombay to preside over a function which is held in Lahore. I believe the Mandal could easily have found someone better qualified than myself to preside on the occasion. I have criticised the Hindus. I have questioned the authority of the Mahatma whom they revere. They hate me. To them I am a snake in their garden. The Mandal will no doubt be asked by the politically minded Hindus to explain why it has called me to fill this place of honour. It is an act of great daring. I shall not be surprised if some political Hindus regard it as an insult. This selection of mine certainly cannot please the ordinary religiously minded Hindus.

1.2

The Mandal may be asked to explain why it has disobeyed the shastric injunction in selecting the president. According to the shastras, the Brahmin is appointed to be the guru for the three varnas. वर्णानाम ब्राह्मणो गुरु:[1] is a direction of the shastras.

---

1 "*Varnanam Brahmano Guru.*" This is *Manusmriti* 10.3. Bibek Debroy's translation: "Among varnas, the Brahman is the teacher/preceptor." There is no standardised

The Mandal therefore knows from whom a Hindu should take his lessons and from whom he should not. The shastras do not permit a Hindu to accept anyone as his guru merely because he is well versed. This is made very clear by Ramdas,[2] a Brahmin saint from Maharashtra, who is alleged to have inspired Shivaji to establish a Hindu Raj. In his *Dasbodh*, a

---

text of the *Manusmriti*; in some versions, the text mentions *prabhu* (lord) instead of *guru* (teacher). George Bühler renders the entire couplet at 10.3 as follows: "On account of his pre-eminence, on account of the superiority of his origin, on account of his observance of (particular) restrictive rules, and on account of his particular sanctification the Brahmana is the lord of (all) castes (varna)" (1886/2004, 276). Chapter 10 of the *Manusmriti* discusses varnas and their duties at length and lists out dos and don'ts.

2 Ramdas (1608–81) was a seventeenth-century coeval of the Maratha king Shivaji (1627/30–80), and is said to have been his Brahmin guru. Bhakti poet Tukaram, Shudra by birth and trader by profession, was also his contemporary. Bhakti is devotional love for a personal god experienced without the mediation of the priest or ritual. The progenitors of the Bhakti movement, the Alvars (sixth to ninth centuries) and Nayanmars (twelfth century) of the Tamil country, were fiercely monotheistic in their expression of love for Vishnu and Siva or their forms, and this happened at the expense and persecution of Jains and Buddhists (see Monius 2011). What was crucial, however, was that anyone from any strata of society—men and women—could aspire to reach god. The twelfth-century Basava-led Veerashaiva movement in the Kannada-speaking South, that launched the literary *vachana* tradition, repudiated the caste system and the primacy of the Brahmin. Between the fourteenth and eighteenth centuries, sometimes fusing with elements of Islam and Sufism, the Bhakti movement manifested itself variously in the western, northern and eastern parts of the subcontinent through the work of sants, or teachers, who were largely from working-caste backgrounds but also included Brahmins (like Dnyaneshwar in western India or Chaitanya in Bengal) who embraced Bhakti's egalitarian credo. According to the scholar Veena Naregal (2001, 12), Ramdas's "religious and political pragmatism were quite at variance with the inspiration of the Bhakti poets". *Dasbodh*, composed of 70,000 *ovi*s over twenty sections, offers an interpretation of vedantic philosophy. Ramdas talked of the need for the return of Brahmin supremacy and viewed the crisis in Maratha society as a breakdown in the social order due to 'Muslim oppression', Hindu conversions to Islam, and the usurpation of Brahmin spiritual leadership by the non-Brahmin Varkari saints and gurus (Ranade 1983). Ramdas today is a hero for Hindu nationalists, especially the Chitpavan Brahmins of Maharashtra. See also Note 32 on the Varkari tradition. Also see Gail Omvedt's account (1976) of the differences between Mahanubhav Bhakti and Ramdas's version of it, which she argues blunted the radical potential of Mahanubhav.

socio-politico-religious treatise in Marathi verse, Ramdas asks, addressing the Hindus, can we accept an *antyaja*[3] to be our guru because he is a pandit (i.e., learned)? He gives an answer in the negative.

1.3

What replies to give to these questions is a matter which I must leave to the Mandal. The Mandal knows best the reasons which led it to travel to Bombay to select a president, to fix upon a man so repugnant to the Hindus, and to descend so low in the scale as to select an antyaja—an Untouchable—to address an audience of the savarnas.[4] As for myself, you will allow me to say that I have accepted the invitation much against my will, and also against the will of many of my fellow Untouchables. I know that the Hindus are sick of me. I know that I am not a *persona grata* with them. Knowing all this, I have deliberately kept myself away from them. I have no desire to inflict myself upon them. I have been giving expression to my views from my own platform. This has already caused a great deal of heartburn[5] and irritation.

1.4

I have no desire to ascend the platform of the Hindus, to do within their sight what I have been doing within their hearing. If I am here it is because of your choice and not because of my wish. Yours is a cause of social reform. That

3 Antyaja: last-born; a term used for those outside the pale of the fourfold varna system which comprises Brahmin (priests), Kshatriya (warriors), Vaishya (merchants and farmers) and Shudra (menials). Of these, the first three groups are considered dwija, twice-born. The Shudra are the servile class meant to serve the top three varnas. The antyaja are outside the pale—Untouchables meant to live outside the village.

4 Savarna: those with varna, a caste Hindu; a term used for those within the fourfold varna system. A Shudra is also a savarna; the opposite of savarna is avarna, the Untouchable.

5 "Heart-burning" in AoC 1936 and subsequent editions.

cause has always made an appeal to me, and it is because of this that I felt I ought not to refuse an opportunity of helping the cause—especially when you think that I can help it. Whether what I am going to say today will help you in any way to solve the problem you are grappling with, is for you to judge. All I hope to do is to place before you my views on the problem.

2

2.1

The path of social reform, like the path to heaven (at any rate, in India), is strewn with many difficulties. Social reform in India has few friends and many critics. The critics fall into two distinct classes. One class consists of political reformers, and the other of the socialists.

2.2

It was at one time recognised that without social efficiency,[6] no permanent progress in the other fields of activity was

6 Ambedkar is borrowing this term from John Dewey (1859–1952), the prominent American pragmatist philosopher, radical democrat and educational theorist who taught Ambedkar at Columbia University and influenced him deeply. Dewey, author of about forty books, helped create some of the most prominent political and educational organisations of his time: the American Civil Liberties Union, the National Association for the Advancement of Colored People (NAACP), the League for Industrial Democracy, the New York Teachers Union, the American Association of University Professors, and the New School for Social Research. "Social efficiency" was a term that began its career in 1884 when it was introduced by British sociologist Benjamin Kidd (known for his work *Social Evolution*, 1884) who used it in a social Darwinist sense, but Dewey and others sought to rescue the term from a narrow, utilitarian approach and imbue it with humanitarian value. In the field of education, the term acquired currency in the 1920s. Arun P. Mukherjee (2009), who offers a fine analysis of Ambedkar's refashioning of Deweyan thought into a tool for his own investigations of Indian society, argues that for Dewey and Ambedkar social efficiency lies in the individual being able to choose and develop his/her competencies to the fullest and thus mindfully contribute to the functioning of society. For a system that predetermines a person's occupation on the basis of caste or class affiliations cannot but result in inefficiency. The term has its origins in early-twentieth-century attempts at reorganising society, politics and the economy for 'efficiency' based on 'scientific principles'. For more on this, see Knoll (2009) and Holt (1994).

possible; that owing to mischief wrought by evil customs, Hindu society was not in a state of efficiency; and that ceaseless efforts must be made to eradicate these evils. It was due to the recognition of this fact that the birth of the National Congress was accompanied by the foundation of the Social Conference.[7] While the Congress was concerned with defining the weak points in the political organisation of the country, the Social Conference was engaged in removing the weak points in the social organisation of Hindu society. For some time the Congress and the Conference worked as two wings of one common activity, and they held their annual sessions in the same pandal.

2.3

But soon the two wings developed into two parties, a 'political reform party' and a 'social reform party', between whom there raged a fierce controversy. The 'political reform party' supported the National Congress, and the 'social reform party' supported the Social Conference. The two bodies thus became two hostile camps. The point at issue was whether social reform should precede political reform. For a decade the forces were evenly balanced, and the battle was fought without victory to either side.

2.4

It was, however, evident that the fortunes of the Social Conference were ebbing fast. The gentlemen who presided over the sessions of the Social Conference lamented that the majority of the educated Hindus were for political advancement and indifferent to social reform; and that

7 The (Indian National) Social Conference was founded by Mahadev Govind Ranade (1842–1901) in 1887, two years after the founding of the Indian National Congress. It was meant to serve as the social arm of the Congress, and it focused mainly on women's uplift. Conservative leaders like B.G. Tilak were staunchly opposed to even the mild reforms suggested by votaries of the Social Conference.

while the number of those who attended the Congress was very large, and the number who did not attend but who sympathised with it was even larger, the number of those who attended the Social Conference was very much smaller.

2.5

This indifference—this thinning of its ranks—was soon followed by active hostility from the politicians. Under the leadership of the late Mr Tilak,[8] the courtesy with which the Congress allowed the Social Conference the use of its pandal was withdrawn, and the spirit of enmity went to such a pitch that when the Social Conference desired to erect its own pandal, a threat to burn the pandal was held out by its opponents.[9] Thus in the course of time the party in favour of political reform won, and the Social Conference vanished and was forgotten.

2.6

The speech delivered by Mr W.C. Bonnerjee[10] in 1892 at

---

8 Bal Gangadhar 'Lokmanya' Tilak (1865–1920) was a Chitpavan Brahmin and a social conservative who sought to imbue Congress nationalism with a distinct right-wing hue. He published two newspapers, the Marathi-language *Kesari* and *Mahratta* in English. Jaffrelot (2005, 44) calls him "the Congress leader from Poona who tended *not to put in practice* the social reforms he articulated" (emphasis added). Tilak saw even the education of women and non-Brahmins as "a loss of nationality" and consistently opposed the establishment of girls' schools at a time when his coeval Jotiba Phule launched a full-scale attack on Brahminism, educated his wife Savitri, and established a school for girls which also admitted Untouchable children. See Rao (n.d.). For an account of the Phule-led non-Brahmin movement, see O'Hanlon (2002).

9 For a chronicle of the tussles between the Social Conference and conservative forces within the Congress, see John R. McLane (1988, 47–61). McLane writes: "In Maharashtra, Tilak demonstrated the potent political appeal of Hindu symbolism with the Ganapati and Shivaji festivals. In 1895, when the Congress met in Poona, the rowdyism of Tilak's anti-reformer allies forced the Social Conference to abandon the use of the Congress enclosure for its meeting" (55).

10 Womesh Chunder Bonnerjee was amongst the founders of the Indian National Congress and became its first president. As a lawyer, he divided his life between England and Calcutta, and on retirement settled in Croydon, England. See the account of his daughter Janaki Agnes Penelope Majumdar (2003). While studying

Allahabad, as president of the eighth session of the Congress, sounds like a funeral oration on the death of the Social Conference, and is so typical of the Congress attitude that I venture to quote from it the following extract. Mr Bonnerjee said:

> I for one have no patience with those who say we shall not be fit for political reform until we reform our social system. I fail to see any connection between the two... Are we not fit (for political reform) because our widows remain unmarried and our girls are given in marriage earlier than in other countries?... because our wives and daughters do not drive about with us visiting our friends?... because we do not send our daughters to Oxford and Cambridge? (Cheers from the audience)

2.7

I have stated the case for political reform as put by Mr Bonnerjee. There were many who were happy that the victory went to the Congress. But those who believe in the importance of social reform may ask, is an argument such as that of Mr Bonnerjee final? Does it prove that the victory went to those who were in the right? Does it prove conclusively that social reform has no bearing on political reform? It will help us to understand the matter if I state the other side of the case. I will draw upon the treatment of the Untouchables for my facts.

2.8

Under the rule of the Peshwas in the Maratha country,[11] the

---

in England, in 1865, Bonnerjee wrote in a letter to his uncle: "I have discarded all ideas of caste, I have come to hate all the demoralising practices of our countrymen and I write this letter an entirely altered man" (Kumar 1989, 48). Since he had 'lost caste' by crossing the seas, Bonnerjee was regarded an outcaste by his family. He set up a separate household refusing to undergo penance, and renounced Hindu customs. He brought his wife out of purdah, made her eat beef and wear English clothes, and sent his children to England for education (Majumdar 2003).

11 The Peshwas were initially ministers under Shivaji who founded the Maratha

Untouchable was not allowed to use the public streets if a Hindu was coming along, lest he should pollute the Hindu by his shadow. The Untouchable was required to have a black thread either on his wrist or around his neck, as a sign or a mark to prevent the Hindus from getting themselves polluted by his touch by mistake. In Poona, the capital of the Peshwa, the Untouchable was required to carry, strung from his waist, a broom to sweep away from behind himself the dust he trod on, lest a Hindu walking on the same dust should be polluted. In Poona, the Untouchable was required to carry an earthen pot hung around his neck wherever he went—for holding his spit, lest his spit falling on the earth should pollute a Hindu who might unknowingly happen to tread on it.

2.9

Let me take more recent facts. The tyranny practised by the Hindus upon the Balais, an Untouchable community in Central India, will serve my purpose. You will find a report of this in the *Times of India* of 4th January 1928. The correspondent of the *Times of India* reported that high-caste Hindus—viz., Kalotas, Rajputs and Brahmins, including the Patels and Patwaris of the villages of Kanaria, Bicholi-Hapsi, Bicholi-Mardana, and about fifteen other villages in Indore district (of Indore State)—informed the Balais of their respective villages that if they wished to live among them, they must conform to the following rules:

---

empire in seventeenth-century western India. After the death of Shivaji in 1680, the Peshwas, who were Chitpavan Brahmins, turned into a military-bureaucratic elite, and, in one of those rare instances, both ritual and secular power were vested with Brahmins. The reign of the Peshwas witnessed what feminist scholar Uma Chakravarti (1995, 3–21) terms "the consolidation of Brahmanya-raj". In 1818, the 30,000-strong army of the last Peshwa, Bajirao II (1795–1818), was defeated by the 500-member regiment of 'Untouchable' Mahar soldiers led by Capt F.F. Staunton. This is known as the Battle of Koregaon, along the river Bhima, northwest of Poona. For an account of the rise of the Brahmins in western India, see Eaton (2005).

1. Balais must not wear gold-lace–bordered pugrees.
2. They must not wear dhotis with coloured or fancy borders.
3. They must convey intimation of the death of any Hindu to relatives of the deceased—no matter how far away these relatives may be living.
4. In all Hindu marriages, Balais must play music before the processions and during the marriage.
5. Balai women must not wear gold or silver ornaments; they must not wear fancy gowns or jackets.
6. Balai women must attend all cases of confinement of Hindu women.[12]
7. Balais must render services without demanding remuneration, and must accept whatever a Hindu is pleased to give.
8. If the Balais do not agree to abide by these terms, they must clear out of the villages.

2.10

The Balais refused to comply; and the Hindu element proceeded against them. Balais were not allowed to get water from the village wells; they were not allowed to let their cattle graze. Balais were prohibited from passing through land owned by a Hindu, so that if the field of a Balai was surrounded by fields owned by Hindus, the Balai could have no access to his own field. The Hindus also let their cattle graze down the fields of Balais. The Balais submitted petitions to the Darbar[13] against these persecutions; but as they could get no timely relief, and the oppression continued, hundreds of Balais with their wives and children were obliged to abandon their homes—in which their ancestors had lived

12 In large parts of India, Dalit women act as *dais* (midwives) and are expected to help with childbirth in privileged-caste households.

13 Ambedkar is referring here to the court of Indore. This can be inferred from a citation of the same *Times of India* article in the posthumously published *Untouchables or the Children of India's Ghetto* (BAWS 5, 48–9).

for generations—and to migrate to adjoining states: that is, to villages in Dhar, Dewas, Bagli, Bhopal, Gwalior and other states. What happened to them in their new homes may for the present be left out of our consideration.

2.11

The incident at Kavitha[14] in Gujarat happened only last year. The Hindus of Kavitha ordered the Untouchables not to insist upon sending their children to the common village school maintained by the government. What sufferings the Untouchables of Kavitha had to undergo, for daring to exercise a civic right against the wishes of the Hindus, is too well known to need detailed description. Another instance occurred in the village of Zanu, in the Ahmedabad district of Gujarat. In November 1935 some Untouchable women of well-to-do families started fetching water in metal pots. The Hindus looked upon the use of metal pots by Untouchables as an affront to their dignity, and assaulted the Untouchable women for their impudence.

---

14 Following a Bombay government ruling, in August 1935, that Untouchable students should be admitted to schools, the Untouchables of Kavitha village enrolled four children in the local school. This invoked both physical assaults and social boycott, and the Untouchables turned to the Harijan Sevak Sangh, an organisation founded by M.K. Gandhi, for help. Gandhi and 'Sardar' Vallabhbhai Patel opposed the Untouchables' efforts at taking recourse to law, and forced them to withdraw their complaint. Ambedkar, while recounting this incident, does not mince words (BAWS 5, 43): "With all the knowledge of tyranny and oppression practised by the caste Hindus of Kavitha against the Untouchables all that Mr Gandhi felt like doing was to advise the Untouchables to leave the village. He did not even suggest that the miscreants should be hauled up before a court of law. His henchman, Mr Vallabhbhai Patel, played a part which was still more strange. He had gone to Kavitha to persuade the caste Hindus not to molest the Untouchables. But they did not even give him a hearing. Yet this very man was opposed to the Untouchables hauling them up in a court of law and getting them punished. The Untouchables filed the complaint notwithstanding his opposition. But he ultimately forced them to withdraw the complaint on the caste Hindus making some kind of a show of an understanding not to molest, an undertaking, which the Untouchables can never enforce. The result was that the Untouchables suffered and their tyrants escaped with the aid of Mr Gandhi's friend, Mr Vallabhbhai Patel."

2.12

A most recent event is reported from the village of Chakwara in Jaipur state. It seems from the reports that have appeared in the newspapers that an Untouchable of Chakwara who had returned from a pilgrimage had arranged to give a dinner to his fellow Untouchables of the village, as an act of religious piety. The host desired to treat the guests to a sumptuous meal, and the items served included ghee (butter) also. But while the assembly of Untouchables was engaged in partaking of the food, the Hindus in their hundreds, armed with lathis, rushed to the scene, despoiled the food, and belaboured the Untouchables who left the food, and ran[15] for their lives. And why was this murderous assault committed on defenceless Untouchables? The reason given is that the Untouchable host was impudent enough to serve ghee, and his Untouchable guests were foolish enough to taste it. Ghee is undoubtedly a luxury for the rich. But no one would think that consumption of ghee was a mark of high social status. The Hindus of Chakwara thought otherwise, and in righteous indignation avenged themselves for the wrong done to them by the Untouchables, who insulted them by treating ghee as an item of their food—which they ought to have known could not be theirs—consistently with the dignity of the Hindus. This means that an Untouchable must not use ghee, even if he can afford to buy it, since it is an act of arrogance towards the Hindus. This happened on or about the 1st of April 1936![16]

15 "Ran away" in AoC 1936 and subsequent editions.

16 The state of affairs in Chakwara has far from improved. Dalits in this village, denied access to the local pond, have been waging a struggle since 1980. In 2001, two Dalits were fined Rs 50,000 by the Jat- and Brahmin-dominated village panchayat for using water from the Chakwara pond (Usmani, 2008).

2.13

Having stated the facts let me now state the case for social reform. In doing this, I will follow Mr Bonnerjee as nearly as I can, and ask the political minded Hindus, "Are you fit for political power even though you do not allow a large class of your own countrymen like the Untouchables to use public schools? Are you fit for political power even though you do not allow them the use of public wells? Are you fit for political power even though you do not allow them the use of public streets? Are you fit for political power even though you do not allow them to wear what apparel or ornaments they like? Are you fit for political power even though you do not allow them to eat any food they like?" I can ask a string of such questions. But these will suffice.

2.14

I wonder what would have been the reply of Mr Bonnerjee. I am sure no sensible man will have the courage to give an affirmative answer. Every Congressman who repeats the dogma of Mill[17] that one country is not fit to rule another country, must admit that one class is not fit to rule another class. How is it then that the 'social reform party' lost the battle? To understand this correctly it is necessary to take

---

17 John Stuart Mill (1806–73) in the last chapter of *Considerations on Representative Government* (1861/2004) poses a critique of the colonial administration of the British empire. However, Mill's criticism has to be seen in the context of his advocating "representative government" for the Americas and Australia for they are "composed of people of similar civilisation to the ruling country", and "whose population", he says, "is in a sufficiently advanced state", compared to which "others, like India, are still at a great distance from that state". Here, Mill argues, the coloniser must rule to introduce a higher form of civilisation. Ambedkar is alluding here to his contemporaries' reverence for a complex figure who on the one hand championed the cause of individual freedom and liberty, and on the other, defended British imperialism by justifying the right of 'civilised' nations to rule over 'barbarians'. In his essay "A Few Words on Non-Intervention" (1859/1984), Mill outlines the circumstances under which states should be allowed to intervene in the sovereign affairs of another country.

note of the kind of social reform which the reformers were agitating for. In this connection it is necessary to make a distinction between social reform in the sense of the reform of the Hindu family, and social reform in the sense of the reorganisation and reconstruction of Hindu society. The former has a relation to widow remarriage, child marriage, etc., while the latter relates to the abolition of the caste system.

2.15

The Social Conference was a body which mainly concerned itself with the reform of the high-caste[18] Hindu family. It consisted mostly of enlightened high-caste Hindus who did not feel the necessity for agitating for the abolition of caste, or had not the courage to agitate for it. They felt quite naturally a greater urge to remove such evils as enforced widowhood, child marriages, etc.—evils which prevailed among them and which were personally felt by them. They did not stand up for the reform of Hindu society. The battle that was fought centred round the question of the reform of the family. It did not relate to social reform in the sense of the break-up of the caste system. It was never put in issue by the reformers. That is the reason why the 'social reform party' lost.

2.16

I am aware that this argument cannot alter the fact that political reform did in fact gain precedence over social reform. But the argument has this much value, if not more: it explains why social reformers lost the battle. It also helps us to understand how limited was the victory which the 'political reform party' obtained over the 'social reform party', and to understand that the view that social reform need not precede political reform is a view which may stand only when by social reform is meant the reform of the family. That political

18 Term added in 1937.

reform cannot with impunity take precedence over social reform in the sense of the reconstruction of society, is a thesis which I am sure cannot be controverted.

2.17

That the makers of political constitutions must take account of social forces is a fact which is recognised by no less a person than Ferdinand Lassalle,[19] the friend and co-worker of Karl Marx. In addressing a Prussian audience in 1862, Lassalle said:

> The constitutional questions are in the first instance not questions of right but questions of might. The actual constitution of a country has its existence only in the actual condition of force which exists in the country: hence political constitutions have value and permanence only when they accurately express those conditions of forces which exist in practice within a society.[20]

2.18

But it is not necessary to go to Prussia.[21] There is evidence at home. What is the significance of the Communal Award,[22]

---

19 Ferdinand Lassalle (1825–64) was a philologist, legal expert and social agitator, the first to organise a socialist party in Germany and rally the workers to assert their rights. He came to prominence as an interpreter of Marxism for the workers. However, from a letter written by Marx to Ludwig Kugelmann on 23 February 1865 it is clear that Marx considered Lassalle's interpretation plagiarism. In the same letter he also expresses his condemnation of Lassalle's attempt at striking a deal with Bismarck urging him to introduce universal adult suffrage in exchange of working-class support for the government.

20 Ambedkar is quoting from "On the Essence of Constitutions", the famous speech Lassalle delivered on 16 April 1862 in Berlin.

21 Rendered as "Lasalle" in AoC 1936.

22 The Communal Award, also known as the Ramsay Macdonald Award after the British Prime Minister, issued on 16 August 1932, was the result of the Second Round Table Conference (September–December 1931) that granted separate electorates to minorities in the dominion of India. Besides Muslims and Sikhs, the Depressed Classes were also granted a separate electorate for twenty years. The award granted a double vote to Untouchables that allowed them to choose their own representatives from special constituencies, as well as to cast their vote in general constituencies. The Congress and Gandhi opposed this, and Gandhi went

with its allocation of political power in defined proportions to diverse classes and communities? In my view, its significance lies in this: that political constitution must take note of social organisation. It shows that the politicians who denied that the social problem in India had any bearing on the political problem were forced to reckon with the social problem in devising the constitution. The Communal Award is, so to say, the nemesis following upon the indifference to and neglect of social reform. It is a victory for the 'social reform party', which shows that, though defeated, they were in the right in insisting upon the importance of social reform. Many, I know, will not accept this finding. The view is current—and it is pleasant to believe in it—that the Communal Award is unnatural and that it is the result of an unholy alliance between the minorities and the bureaucracy.[23] I do not wish to rely on the Communal Award as a piece of evidence to support my contention, if it is said that it is not good evidence.

2.19

Let us turn to Ireland. What does the history of Irish Home Rule show? It is well known that in the course of the negotiations between the representatives of Ulster and Southern Ireland, Mr Redmond, the representative of Southern Ireland, in order to bring Ulster into a Home Rule constitution common to the whole of Ireland, said to the representatives of Ulster: "Ask any political safeguards you like and you shall have them." What was the reply that Ulstermen

---

on indefinite hunger strike in Poona jail. A compromise was reached with the signing of the Poona Pact on 24 September 1932, under which the Untouchables were allotted reserved constituencies but not separate electorates. See the text of the Communal Award in B.R. Ambedkar (BAWS 9, 81). For a further delineation of the Communal Award and the Poona Pact and their implications, see "A Note on the Poona Pact" in this book (357–76).

23 For an analysis and discussion of the Communal Award and the Poona Pact, see Zelliot (2013, 128–42); Jaffrelot (2005, 52–73); Kumar (1985).

gave? Their reply was, "Damn your safeguards, we don't want to be ruled by you on any terms."[24] People who blame the minorities in India ought to consider what would have happened to the political aspirations of the majority, if the minorities had taken the attitude which Ulster took. Judged by the attitude of Ulster to Irish Home Rule, is it nothing that the minorities agreed to be ruled by the majority (which has not shown much sense of statesmanship), provided some safeguards were devised for them? But this is only incidental. The main question is, why did Ulster take this attitude? The only answer I can give is that there was a social problem between Ulster and Southern Ireland: the problem between Catholics and Protestants, which is essentially a problem of caste. That Home Rule in Ireland would be Rome Rule was the way in which the Ulstermen had framed their answer. But that is only another way of stating that it was the social problem of caste between the Catholics and Protestants, which prevented the solution of the political problem. This evidence again is sure to be challenged. It will be urged that here too the hand of the Imperialist was at work.

2.20

But my resources are not exhausted. I will give evidence from the history of Rome. Here no one can say that any evil genius was at work. Anyone who has studied the history of Rome

24 The Irish Home Rule movement was launched in the second half of the nineteenth century to recover legislative independence from the British after Ireland had become part of the Union. See more in Alan O'Day (1998) and Alvin Jackson (2003). Howard Brasted (1980) argues that the precedent of the Irish Home Rule movement awoke the nationalist spirit amongst the educated Indian elite and provided a model for the Congress. Home Rule could never be implemented in Ireland due to the strong oppostion by the Protestant Unionists of Northern Ireland (Ulstermen). Here, it is not clear if Ambedkar is referring to John Edward Redmond (1856–1918), Member of Parliament and leader of the Irish Parliamentary Party and the National League, or his brother, William (Willie) Redmond (1861–1917), also an MP and nationalist politician.

will know that the republican constitution of Rome bore marks having strong resemblance to the Communal Award. When the kingship in Rome was abolished, the kingly power or the Imperium was divided between the consuls and the Pontifex Maximus.[25] In the consuls was vested the secular authority of the king, while the latter took over the religious authority of the king. This republican constitution had provided that of the two consuls, one was to be patrician and the other plebeian.[26] The same constitution had also provided that of the priests under the Pontifex Maximus half were to be plebeians and the other half patricians. Why is it that the republican constitution of Rome had these provisions—which, as I said, resemble so strongly the provisions of the Communal Award? The only answer one can get is that the constitution of republican Rome had to take account of the social division between the patricians and the plebeians, who formed two distinct castes.[27] To sum up, let political reformers

25 Pontifex Maximus was the highest priest of the college of pontiffs in ancient Rome.

26 Patricians (derived from the root *patre*, meaning 'father') were the upper class in ancient Rome. Their ancestry was traced back by Roman historians such as Livy to the legend of Romulus, the mythical founder of Rome, who is said to have appointed one hundred men as senators. Patricians claimed to be descendants of these first senators and the Sabine women kidnapped and raped for procreation. Plebeians were the general body of lower-class, free citizens. There were other lower classes like the *peregrini* and slaves. Most historians agree that the distinction between patricians, plebeians and other classes was based purely on birth. The most readily available tool to distinguish between the classes was *gentes*, family names. See Livy (2006).

27 In his speech during the second leg of the Mahad Satyagraha on 25 December 1927, Ambedkar refers to the patrician–plebeian struggle, or 'the Conflict of the Orders' as it is more commonly known, in greater detail. The Conflict of the Orders, in which the plebeians sought political equality with the patricians, lasted between 494 and 287 BCE. In this protracted conflict, the patricians were occasionally forced to give some concession to the plebeians, but always sought to retain the final authority. Thus the provisions for economic reform in laws like Lex Licinia Sextia (367 BCE) and Leges Genuciae (342 BCE)—ceiling on the ownership of land by a single person, ban on lending that carried interest, etc.—were largely ignored by the patricians. In his Mahad speech, Ambedkar gives a very interesting

turn in any direction they like, they will find that in the making of a constitution, they cannot ignore the problem arising out of the prevailing social order.

2.21

The illustrations which I have taken in support of the proposition that social and religious problems have a bearing on political constitutions seem to be too particular. Perhaps they are. But it should not be supposed that the bearing of the one on the other is limited. On the other hand, one can say that generally speaking, history bears out the proposition that political revolutions have always been preceded by social and religious revolutions. The religious reformation started by Luther[28] was the precursor of the political emancipation of the European people. In England, Puritanism led to the establishment of political liberty. Puritanism founded the new world. It was Puritanism which won the war of American independence, and Puritanism was a religious movement.[29]

---

account of how the positions of 'tribunes', constituted to protect the rights of the plebeians, were held exclusively by patricians in the beginning. Even when later laws stipulated that one of the two tribunes must be a plebeian, the patricians retained the power to reject an elected plebeian tribune through the authority of the oracle at Delphi (always a patrician). For excerpts of this speech, see Satyanarayana and Tharu (2013, 25–6). Ambedkar's worst fears on the question of representation and final authority became a reality five years after the Mahad events when Gandhi's suicide threat forced him to sign the Poona Pact of 1932. Therefore, in *Annihilation of Caste*, he returns to the theme of the Conflict of Orders with the bitterness of experience. See also Note 10 on Bodh Gaya in Ambedkar's "A Reply to the Mahatma".

28 Martin Luther (1483–1546), German monk who held the chair of Theology at the University of Wittenberg, was a key figure (along with John Calvin, John Wycliffe and Jan Hus) in the sixteenth-century Reformation movement. He sought to shift the religious leadership's focus away from fees and payments as part of a renewal of the medieval Church. The reformers hoped to restore and clarify the core tenets of the faith, which they would then make accessible to all Christians. For a history of European Reformation, see Peter G. Wallace (2004).

29 The English Civil War (1642–51), which questioned the prerogative of the king and challenged the theory of divine right, owed much to the spirit of European Reformation. The Puritans—who espoused a militant, biblically based Calvinistic

2.22

The same is true of the Muslim empire. Before the Arabs became a political power, they had undergone a thorough religious revolution started by the Prophet Muhammad.[30] Even Indian history supports the same conclusion. The political revolution led by Chandragupta was preceded by the religious and social revolution of Buddha.[31] The political revolution led by Shivaji was preceded by the religious and social reform brought about by the saints of Maharashtra.[32] The political

---

Protestantism—sought to 'purify' the Church of England of remnants of the Catholic popery, and argued that the Anglican Church established by Queen Elizabeth was far too close to Roman Catholicism. ('Puritan' means that the followers had a pure soul and lived a good life.) Alexis de Tocqueville (1805–59), the French political thinker best known for his two-volume *Democracy in America* (1835, 1840), argued that the tradition of political liberty in the United States of America began with the settling of New England by the Puritans from England. For an in-depth study of debates around puritanism and liberty in England, see *Puritanism and Liberty, being the Army Debates (1647–9) from the Clarke Manuscripts with Supplementary Documents* in A.S.P. Woodhouse (1951). This contains the Putney Debates, the Whitehall Debates, and numerous other documents about Puritan religious and political views during the English Revolution.

30 Prophet Muhammad (570–632 CE) unified scores of warring Arab tribes into a single religious polity (*ummah*, community) under *Islam* (which means to submit, surrender). For a concise history of Islam, see Karen Armstrong (2000), who writes: "Muhammad had become the head of a collection of tribal groups that were not bound together by blood but by a shared ideology, an astonishing innovation in Arabian society" (14). Nobody was forced to convert, but all Muslims belonged to one ummah, they could not attack one another, and they vowed to give one another protection.

31 Chandragupta Maurya (340–298 BCE), founder of the Mauryan dynasty, is credited with being the first emperor to rule large parts of the Indian subcontinent as one state. Gautama Buddha (c. 563–483 BCE), on whose teachings Buddhism was founded, preceded him. Chandragupta's grandson was the emperor Ashoka (304–232 BCE), who turned from a warmonger to an advocate of Buddhism and pacifism (though he continued to give the death penalty till the end of his reign).

32 The allusion here is to the Varkari tradition that was established in western India with the Brahmin Dnyandev or Dnyaneswar, and the Untouchable Cokhamela in the fourteenth century, and was followed by saint-poets from the subaltern castes like Namdeo, Bahinabai and Tukaram into the seventeenth century. While Ambedkar disregarded the piety of Cokhamela, he quite often quoted the radical Tukaram who was Shivaji's contemporary. For a discussion of the political aspects of Tukaram, who was of the Kunabi peasant caste, and his influence on Shivaji,

revolution of the Sikhs was preceded by the religious and social revolution led by Guru Nanak.[33] It is unnecessary to add more illustrations. These will suffice to show that the emancipation of the mind and the soul is a necessary preliminary for the political expansion of the people.

3

3.1

Let me now turn to the socialists. Can the socialists ignore the problem arising out of the social order? The socialists of India,[34] following their fellows in Europe, are seeking to apply the economic interpretation of history to the facts of

---

see Gail Omvedt (2008, 109–32). A *varkar* is a pilgrim, and the Varkari tradition revolves around the god Vithoba or Vitthala in Pandharpur (in Maharashtra's Solapur district). In popular lore Vitthala has come to be regarded as a form of Krishna and this tradition is seen as Vaishnavite. The Varkari cult is seven hundred years old, and with it begins the Marathi literary tradition, according to Omvedt (85). She discusses how scholars believe Vitthala could have had origins in Saivism, Buddhism or even among pastoral nomadic tribes. Omvedt discusses the Sanskritisation and Vishnu-isation of Vitthala and believes the god could have been originally female ("wide hips, narrow waist, busty, long hair, straight though harsh face") and that contemporary Dalit Buddhists point to "the god's blackness as evidence of indigenous origins" based on iconography (see 85–90). For an overview of the Bhakti tradition and sants in Maharashtra, see Zelliot and Berntsen (1998). Also see the volume edited by Lele (1981).

33 Guru Nanak (1469–1539) was the first of the ten gurus and founder of the Sikh religion. He started a strand of *nirguni* (without attributes) Bhakti tradition that advocated spending one's life immersed in *nam simran* (remembrance of the divine name). Guru Nanak and the gurus that followed him preached spiritual equality against varnashrama dharma and imparted their teaching to devotees from all castes. Puri (2003, 2694) writes that while the Sikh holy book, *Guru Granth Sahib*, includes compositions by Kabir, a weaver, and Ravidas, a tanner (Chamar), the ten gurus of Sikhism came from Khatri families—the highest caste among Sikhs—and married their children within their caste. Despite the preaching of spiritual equality in the eyes of god, there was no expectation on the part of the gurus or their devotees to give up caste identity and thus the doctrine was not translated into social equality.

34 Ambedkar is referring here to the socialists within the Congress who in 1934 formed a faction called the Congress Socialist Party (CSP). Jawaharlal Nehru, at this juncture, was also actively advocating socialist ideas but did join the CSP.

India. They propound that man is an economic creature, that his activities and aspirations are bound by economic facts, that property is the only source of power. They therefore preach that political and social reforms are but gigantic illusions, and that economic reform by equalisation of property must have precedence over every other kind of reform. One may join issue with every one of these premises—on which rests the socialists' case for economic reform as having priority over every other kind of reform. One may contend that the economic motive is not the only motive by which man is actuated. That economic power is the only kind of power, no student of human society can accept.

3.2

That the social status of an individual by itself often becomes a source of power and authority is made clear by the sway which the Mahatmas have held over the common man. Why do millionaires in India obey penniless sadhus and fakirs? Why do millions of paupers in India sell their trifling trinkets which constitute their only wealth, and go to Benares and Mecca? That religion is the source of power is illustrated by the history of India, where the priest holds sway over the common man often greater than that of the magistrate, and where everything, even such things as strikes and elections, so easily takes a religious turn and can so easily be given a religious twist.

3.3

Take the case of the plebeians of Rome as a further illustration of the power of religion over man. It throws great light on this point. The plebeians had fought for a share in the supreme executive under the Roman Republic, and had secured the appointment of a plebeian consul elected by a separate electorate constituted by the Comitia Centuriata,[35] which was an assembly of plebeians. They wanted a consul of their own because they felt that the patrician consuls used to discriminate against the plebeians in carrying on the administration. They had apparently obtained a great gain, because under the republican constitution of Rome one consul had the power of vetoing an act of the other consul.

3.4

But did they in fact gain anything? The answer to this question must be in the negative. The plebeians never could get a plebeian consul who could be said to be a strong man, and who could act independently of the patrician consul. In the ordinary course of things the plebeians should have got a strong plebeian consul, in view of the fact that his election was to be by a separate electorate of plebeians. The question is, why did they fail in getting a strong plebeian to officiate as their consul?

3.5

The answer to this question reveals the dominion which religion exercises over the minds of men. It was an accepted creed of the whole Roman populus that no official could enter upon the duties of his office unless the Oracle of

35 Comitia Centuriata, or the Century Assembly, was originally an assembly of the Roman military, but soon turned into a political assembly, and became one of the three public assemblies of the Republic of Rome where citizens, grouped into 'centuries', voted on legislative, electoral and judicial matters. In the early days, entry to the Senate was only by birth and rank—so the patricians called the shots. Even in the Comitia Centuriata, instituted in about 450 BCE, entry was restricted initially to the patricians and the plebeians were kept at bay. Even after the Comitia Centuriata came to include plebeians, its organisation and voting system nevertheless gave greater influence to the rich than to the poor, which as Ambedkar points out, resembled the Communal Award. Ambedkar understands, in the caste context, the plight of plebeians with voting rights as being similar to that of Untouchables who were denied a separate electorate—the mere right to vote does not necessarily empower them. For more on the evolution of the Roman republic, see Olga Tellegen-Couperus (1993).

Delphi[36] declared that he was acceptable to the goddess. The priests who were in charge of the temple of the goddess of Delphi were all patricians. Whenever therefore the plebeians elected a consul who was known to be a strong party man and opposed to the patricians—or 'communal', to use the term that is current in India—the Oracle invariably declared that he was not acceptable to the goddess. This is how the plebeians were cheated out of their rights.

3.6

But what is worthy of note is that the plebeians permitted themselves to be thus cheated because they too, like the patricians, held firmly the belief that the approval of the goddess was a condition precedent to the taking charge by an official of his duties, and that election by the people was not enough. If the plebeians had contended that election was enough and that the approval by the goddess was not necessary, they would have derived the fullest benefit from the political right which they had obtained. But they did not. They agreed to elect another, less suitable to themselves but more suitable to the goddess—which in fact meant more amenable to the patricians. Rather than give up religion, the plebeians gave up the material gain for which they had fought so hard. Does this not show that religion can be a source of power as great as money, if not greater?

3.7

The fallacy of the socialists[37] lies in supposing that because in

---

36 While Delphi, associated with the Greek god Apollo, was an important site in Hellenic political life, the Romans did not seem to consult the Oracle regularly owing to its considerable distance from Rome. They, however, tended to refer to the Sibylline Books, kept at the Capitolium. See Fontenrose (1978). For an account of the hold of religion on the Romans, see Rüpke (2007).

37 Ambedkar's ire here is likely directed at the socialist turn within the Congress. Following the 1936 Congress session in Lucknow, where Nehru took over as party president at Gandhi's behest, the Agrarian Resolution declared that "the

the present stage of European society property as a source of power is predominant, the same is true of India, or the same was true of Europe in the past. Religion, social status, and property are all sources of power and authority which one man has to control the liberty of another. One is predominant at one stage; the other is predominant at another stage. That is the only difference. If liberty is the ideal, and if liberty means the destruction of the dominion which one man holds over another, then obviously it cannot be insisted upon that economic reform must be the one kind of reform worthy of pursuit. If the source of power and dominion is, at any given time or in any given society, social and religious, then social reform and religious reform must be accepted as the necessary sort of reform.

3.8

One can thus attack the doctrine of economic interpretation of history adopted by the socialists of India. But I recognise that the economic interpretation of history is not necessary for the validity of the socialist contention that equalisation of property is the only real reform and that it must precede everything else. However, what I would like to ask the

---

most important and urgent problem of the country is the appalling poverty, unemployment and indebtedness of the peasantry, fundamentally due to the antiquated and repressive land revenue system". Nehru and the few socialists he managed to sneak into the thirteen-member Congress Working Committee (CWC)—Acharya Narayan Dev, Jayaprakash Narayan and Achyut Patwardhan—sought to end the 'middle class domination' of the Congress and sought direct representation for peasants and workers in the party. But tacitly backed by Gandhi, the right wing within the Congress opposed Nehru's socialist tendencies. On 29 June 1936, CWC members Babu Rajendra Prasad, Jairamdas Daulatram, Jamnalal Bajaj, Acharya Kripalani and S.D. Dev submitted their resignations from the CWC in a joint letter, contending that Nehru's preaching of socialism in his election speeches was "prejudicial to the interests of the country and to the success of the national struggle for freedom". Gandhi backed the conservatives, as did the business classes. Subsequently Nehru recanted. For a detailed account of Nehru and socialism, see R.C. Dutt (1980, 30–90).

socialists is this: Can you have economic reform without first bringing about a reform of the social order? The socialists of India do not seem to have considered this question.[38] I do not wish to do them an injustice. I give below a quotation from a letter which a prominent socialist wrote a few days ago to a friend of mine, in which he said, "I do not believe that we can build up a free society in India so long as there is a trace of this ill-treatment and suppression of one class by another. Believing as I do in a socialist ideal, inevitably I believe in perfect equality in the treatment of various classes and groups. I think that socialism offers the only true remedy for this as well as other problems."

3.9

Now the question that I would like to ask is: Is it enough for a socialist to say, "I believe in perfect equality in the treatment of the various classes?" To say that such a belief is enough is to disclose a complete lack of understanding of what is involved in socialism. If socialism is a practical programme and is not merely an ideal, distant and far off, the question for a socialist is not whether he believes in equality. The question for him is whether he minds one class ill-treating and suppressing another class as a matter of system, as a matter of principle—and thus allow tyranny and oppression to continue to divide one class from another.

3.10

Let me analyse the factors that are involved in the realisation of

38 Ambedkar (in Das, 2010b, 49–68) mounts a more direct attack on the socialists in the presidential address delivered on 12 and 13 February 1938 to the GIP (Great Indian Peninsular) Railway Depressed Classes Workmen's Conference held in Nashik, Manmad district. In this speech he offers a trenchant critique of capitalism and Brahminism, and examines the problems with Indian socialists at greater length. Ambedkar was addressing the GIP conference in his capacity as president of the Independent Labour Party, the first political party founded by him in August 1936, a few months after the publication of *Annihilation of Caste*.

socialism, in order to explain fully my point. Now it is obvious that the economic reform contemplated by the socialists cannot come about unless there is a revolution resulting in the seizure of power. That seizure of power must be by a proletariat. The first question I ask is: Will the proletariat of India combine to bring about this revolution? What will move men to such an action? It seems to me that, other things being equal, the only thing that will move one man to take such an action is the feeling that other men with whom he is acting are actuated by feelings of equality and fraternity and—above all—of justice. Men will not join in a revolution for the equalisation of property unless they know that after the revolution is achieved they will be treated equally, and that there will be no discrimination of caste and creed.

3.11

The assurance of a socialist leading the revolution that he does not believe in caste, I am sure, will not suffice. The assurance must be the assurance proceeding from a much deeper foundation—namely, the mental attitude of the compatriots towards one another in their spirit of personal equality and fraternity. Can it be said that the proletariat of India, poor as it is, recognises no distinctions except that of the rich and the poor? Can it be said that the poor in India recognise no such distinctions of caste or creed, high or low? If the fact is that they do, what unity of front can be expected from such a proletariat in its action against the rich? How can there be a revolution if the proletariat cannot present a united front?

3.12

Suppose for the sake of argument that by some freak of fortune a revolution does take place and the socialists come into power, will they not have to deal with the problems created by the particular social order prevalent in India? I can't see how a socialist state in India can function for a second without having to grapple with the problems created by the prejudices which make Indian people observe the distinctions of high and low, clean and unclean. If socialists are not to be content with the mouthing of fine phrases, if the socialists wish to make socialism a definite reality, then they must recognise that the problem of social reform is fundamental, and that for them there is no escape from it.

3.13

That the social order prevalent in India is a matter which a socialist must deal with; that unless he does so he cannot achieve his revolution; and that if he does achieve it as a result of good fortune, he will have to grapple with the social order if he wishes to realise his ideal—is a proposition which in my opinion is incontrovertible. He will be compelled to take account of caste after the revolution, if he does not take account of it before the revolution. This is only another way of saying that, turn in any direction you like, caste is the monster that crosses your path. You cannot have political reform, you cannot have economic reform, unless you kill this monster.

4

4.1

It is a pity that caste even today has its defenders. The defences are many. It is defended on the ground that the caste system is but another name for division of labour; and if division of labour is a necessary feature of every civilised society, then it is argued that there is nothing wrong in the caste system. Now the first thing that is to be urged against this view is that the caste system is not merely a division of labour. *It is also a division of labourers.*[39] Civilised society undoubtedly needs division of labour. But in no civilised society is division of

39 Emphasis in original.

labour accompanied by this unnatural division of labourers into watertight compartments. The caste system is not merely a division of labourers—which is quite different from division of labour—it is a hierarchy in which the divisions of labourers are graded one above the other. In no other country is the division of labour accompanied by this gradation of labourers.

4.2

There is also a third point of criticism against this view of the caste system. This division of labour is not spontaneous; it is not based on natural aptitudes. Social and individual efficiency requires us to develop the capacity of an individual to the point of competency to choose and to make his own career. This principle is violated in the caste system, in so far as it involves an attempt to appoint tasks to individuals in advance—selected not on the basis of trained original capacities, but on that of the social status of the parents.[40]

4.3

Looked at from another point of view, this stratification of occupations which is the result of the caste system is positively pernicious. Industry is never static.[41] It undergoes rapid and

---

40 Ambedkar is echoing the words of Dewey. According to Mukherjee (2009, 347): "So deeply embedded is Dewey's thought in Ambedkar's consciousness that quite often his words flow through Ambedkar's discourse without quotation marks." She also notes "how Ambedkar culled sentences from *Democracy and Education* to describe his version of the ideal society" (351). Ambedkar expresses his debt to Dewey in section 25.4 of AoC. The relevant paragraph from Dewey's *Democracy and Education*, quoted by Mukherjee, reads: "A democratic criterion requires us to develop capacity to the point of competency to choose and make its own career. This principle is violated when the attempt is made to fit individuals in advance for definite industrial callings, selected not on the basis of trained original capacities, but on that of the wealth or social status of parents" (364). See Dewey (1916). All further citations from *Democracy and Education* are from the online edition.

41 John Dewey was an advocate of industrial democracy, which, in Noam Chomsky's (2003) words "means democratising production, commerce, and so on, which means eliminating the whole structure of capitalist hierarchy". Chomsky terms Dewey a "radical" in this interview. In another essay, Chomsky (2013) says: "Dewey called for workers to be 'masters of their own industrial fate' and for all institutions

abrupt changes. With such changes, an individual must be free to change his occupation. Without such freedom to adjust himself to changing circumstances, it would be impossible for him to gain his livelihood. Now the caste system will not allow Hindus to take to occupations where they are wanted, if they do not belong to them by heredity. If a Hindu is seen to starve rather than take to new occupations not assigned to his caste, the reason is to be found in the caste system. By not permitting readjustment of occupations, caste becomes a direct cause of much of the unemployment we see in the country.

4.4

As a form of division of labour, the caste system suffers from another serious defect. The division of labour brought about by the caste system is not a division based on choice. Individual sentiment, individual preference, has no place in it. It is based on the dogma of predestination. Considerations of social efficiency would compel us to recognise that the greatest evil in the industrial system is not so much poverty and the suffering that it involves, as the fact that so many persons have callings which make no appeal to those who are engaged in them. Such callings constantly provoke one to aversion, ill will and the desire to evade.[42]

4.5

There are many occupations in India which, on account of

---

to be brought under public control, including the means of production, exchange, publicity, transportation and communication. Short of this, Dewey argued, politics will remain 'the shadow cast on society by big business.'"

42 This latter sentence also echoes Dewey (1916): "Sentimentally, it may seem harsh to say that the greatest evil of the present régime is not found in poverty and in the suffering which it entails, but in the fact that so many persons have callings which make no appeal to them, which are pursued simply for the money reward that accrues. For such callings constantly provoke one to aversion, ill will, and a desire to slight and evade" (cited in Mukherjee 2009, 364).

the fact that they are regarded as degraded by the Hindus, provoke those who are engaged in them to aversion. There is a constant desire to evade and escape from such occupations, which arises solely because of the blighting effect which they produce upon those who follow them, owing to the slight and stigma cast upon them by the Hindu religion. What efficiency can there be in a system under which neither men's hearts nor their minds are in their work? As an economic organisation caste is therefore a harmful institution, inasmuch as it involves the subordination of man's natural powers and inclinations to the exigencies of social rules.

5

5.1

Some have dug a biological trench in defence of the caste system. It is said that the object of caste was to preserve purity of race and purity of blood. Now ethnologists[43] are of the opinion that men of pure race exist nowhere and that there has been a mixture of all races in all parts of the world. Especially is this the case with the people of India. Mr D.R. Bhandarkar in his paper on "Foreign Elements in the Hindu Population" has stated that "There is hardly a class or caste in India which has not a foreign strain in it. There is an admixture of alien blood not only among the warrior classes—the Rajputs and the Marathas—but also among the

43 Ethnology draws upon ethnographic material to compare and contrast different cultures. Ethnography is the study of single groups through direct contact with their cultures. In the nineteenth century, ethnologists and ethnographers studied caste mainly as a subsidiary exercise in the supposedly higher and grander task of uncovering the evolutionary heritage of all humanity. In doing so they contributed to the 'Orientalist' exercise of the census and gazetteers and to the racial understanding of caste. Caste was thus subsumed into theories of biologically determined race essences. Ambedkar, in fact, begins his 1916 essay, "Castes in India", with a reference to ethnology. Further, on caste and ethnology, see Bayly (1999, 11–19); and Dirks (2001, 126–38). See also Ketkar (1909/1998, 165–70).

Brahmins who are under the happy delusion that they are free from all foreign elements."[44] The caste system cannot be said to have grown as a means of preventing the admixture of races, or as a means of maintaining purity of blood.

5.2

As a matter of fact the caste system came into being long after the different races of India had commingled in blood and culture.[45] To hold that distinctions of castes are really distinctions of race, and to treat different castes as though they were so many different races, is a gross perversion of

44 Devadatta Ramakrishna Bhandarkar (1875–1950) was an epigraphist and archaeologist who worked for the Archaeological Survey of India. Ambedkar is citing from p.37 of this 1911 essay. Based on epigraphic research, Bhandarkar uses evidence from the Vedas and the epics of the Hindu tradition, such as the *Rig Veda* and the Mahabharata, to disprove the 'purity of blood' myth attributed to Brahmins. "It may be said that after all the Mahabharata … is a conglomeration of legends, which are not of much historical importance, though they cannot be objected to by an orthodox Brahmana and consequently may be adduced to silence his pretensions to purity of origin and the consequent highest place in Hindu society" (1911, 10).

45 In his understanding of the caste system and its evolution, Ambedkar here differs strongly from Brahminic appropriations (such as by B.G. Tilak who authored *The Arctic Home in the Vedas*, 1903) of the racial theory of Aryans and Dravidians propounded by European Indologists. In fact, as seen in Roy's introduction to this edition, even Gandhi, in his South Africa years, strongly believed in the British and India's ruling classes both being 'Aryan'. Ambedkar, however, also differs on this front from his predecessor and radical thinker Jotiba Phule and his contemporary fellow traveller 'Periyar' E.V. Ramasamy Naicker (1879–1973) who turned the racial theory inside out, postulated a pre-Aryan golden age, and regarded the Brahmins as Aryans, and hence foreigners, who imposed the caste system upon the non-Brahmins who were seen as an indigenous race. For Phule's writings, especially *Gulamgiri* (Slavery, 1873), see G.P. Deshpande (2002, 23–101). Periyar, on the eve of independence, quite radically called upon the Dravidian people of South India to "guard against the transfer of power from the British to the Aryans" (*The Hindu*, 11 February 1946). As sociologist T.K. Oommen (2005, 99) argues, "According to Periyar, Brahmins had tried to foist their language and social system on Dravidians to erase their race consciousness and, therefore, he constantly reminded the Dravidians to uphold their 'race consciousness'. However, Periyar did not advocate the superiority of one race over the other but insisted on [the] equality of all races. Thus the fundamental difference between Aryan Hinduism and Dravidian Hinduism is crucial: the former [is] hegemonic, but the latter is emancipatory."

facts. What racial affinity is there between the Brahmin of the Punjab and the Brahmin of Madras? What racial affinity is there between the Untouchable of Bengal and the Untouchable of Madras? What racial difference is there between the Brahmin of the Punjab and the Chamar of the Punjab? What racial difference is there between the Brahmin of Madras and the Pariah of Madras? The Brahmin of the Punjab is racially of the same stock as the Chamar of the Punjab, and the Brahmin of Madras is of the same race as the Pariah of Madras.

5.3

The caste system does not demarcate racial division. The caste system is a social division of people of the same race. Assuming it, however, to be a case of racial divisions, one may ask: What harm could there be if a mixture of races and of blood was permitted to take place in India by intermarriages between different castes? Men are no doubt divided from animals by so deep a distinction that science recognises men and animals as two distinct species. But even scientists who believe in purity of races do not assert that the different races constitute different species of men. They are only varieties of one and the same species. As such they can interbreed and produce an offspring which is capable of breeding and which is not sterile.

5.4

An immense lot of nonsense is talked about heredity and eugenics[46] in defence of the caste system. Few would object

46 Eugenics is the 'science' of predicting and controlling heredity that was popular at the turn of the twentieth century, in that it was perceived to be an effort at the 'improvement' of the human species. The term was coined by Francis Galton inspired by Darwin's theory of natural selection as well as the rediscovery of Mendel's work on heredity (see also Note 47). Galton advocated that only the best and most meritorious should be encouraged to breed; a more disastrous strand of his theory led to Hitler's 'final solution'. According to Mark Singleton (2007, 125–46), the popularity of eugenics in India can be understood by the place it

to the caste system if it was in accord with the basic principle of eugenics, because few can object to the improvement of the race by judicious mating. But one fails to understand how the caste system secures judicious mating. The caste system is a negative thing. It merely prohibits persons belonging to different castes from intermarrying. It is not a positive method of selecting which two among a given caste should marry.

5.5

If caste is eugenic in origin, then the origin of sub-castes must also be eugenic. But can anyone seriously maintain that the origin of sub-castes is eugenic? I think it would be absurd to contend for such a proposition, and for a very obvious reason. If caste means race, then differences of sub-castes cannot mean differences of race, because sub-castes become *ex hypothesi* sub-divisions of one and the same race. Consequently the bar against intermarrying and inter-dining between sub-castes cannot be for the purpose of maintaining purity of race or of blood. If sub-castes cannot be eugenic in origin, there cannot be any substance in the contention that caste is eugenic in origin.

5.6

Again, if caste is eugenic in origin[47] one can understand the

---

occupied as a 'scientific explanation' for the 'degeneration' of Hindu society and colonial subjugation by the British. Another reason for the popularity of eugenics was its valorisation of the endogamy of the caste system as a mechanism of racial purity.

47 For a good example of the use of eugenics to defend caste, see T.N. Roy (1927, 67–72), who begins with this assertion: "The greatest eugenic movement that the world has as yet witnessed originated in India. It was the institution of the caste system." Arguing that "the earliest eugenic movement began with the institution of what is known as Gotra", Roy blames the "downfall of Hinduism" on not observing caste distinctions well enough. "The Brahmin was originally created by eugenic selection," he argues, and gives the finest examples of intellect in Bengal as being all Brahmin men—Raja Ram Mohan Roy, Ishwar Chandra Vidyasagar and Bankim Chandra Chatterjee.

bar against intermarriage. But what is the purpose of the interdict placed on inter-dining between castes and sub-castes alike? Inter-dining cannot infect blood, and therefore cannot be the cause either of the improvement or of the deterioration of the race.

5.7

This shows that caste has no scientific origin, and that those who are attempting to give it a eugenic basis are trying to support by science what is grossly unscientific. Even today, eugenics cannot become a practical possibility unless we have definite knowledge regarding the laws of heredity. Prof Bateson in his *Mendel's Principles of Heredity* says, "There is nothing in the descent of the higher mental qualities to suggest that they follow any single system of transmission. It is likely that both they and the more marked developments of physical powers result rather from the coincidence of numerous factors than from the possession of any one genetic element."[48] To argue that the caste system was eugenic in its conception is to attribute to the forefathers of present-day Hindus a knowledge of heredity which even the modern scientists do not possess.

5.8

A tree should be judged by the fruits it yields. If caste is eugenic, what sort of a race of men should it have produced? Physically speaking the Hindus are a C3 people.[49] They are

48 William Bateson (1861–1926) was a British scientist and is considered the founder of genetics. He wrote *Mendel's Principles of Heredity* (1909) after the discovery of Gregor Mendel's article written in 1866. Ambedkar is citing from p.205 of Bateson's book. Bateson elaborated his own research findings following the investigation of Mendel's theories. This discovery laid down the basis for not only genetics but also eugenics. However, early into his research Bateson had recognised the dangers of the application of genetics to social engineering and warned against the uniformising tendencies of eugenic thinking. See Harvey (1995).

49 Ambedkar here slips into an essentialist understanding of caste, race and morphology. He is drawing upon a British military categorisation of working class soldiers during the First World War. Then British Prime Minister David Lloyd

a race of pygmies and dwarfs, stunted in stature and wanting in stamina. It is a nation nine-tenths of which is declared to be unfit for military service. This shows that the caste system does not embody the eugenics of modern scientists. It is a social system which embodies the arrogance and selfishness of a perverse section of the Hindus who were superior enough in social status to set it in fashion, and who had the authority to force it on their inferiors.

6

6.1

Caste does not result in economic efficiency. Caste cannot improve, and has not improved, race.[50] Caste has, however, done one thing. It has completely disorganised and demoralised the Hindus.

6.2

The first and foremost thing that must be recognised is that Hindu society is a myth. The name Hindu is itself a foreign name.[51] It was given by the Mahomedans to the natives for

---

George lamented: "How can Britain run an A1 empire with a C3 population?" Ina Zweiniger-Bargielowska (2006) argues that though the obsession with a deteriorating national health and physical fitness echoed fascist narratives, these eugenic categories were used as metaphors across the political spectrum in Britain. Ambedkar is using this premise to dismiss the 'biological' defence of the caste system. See also the work of Heather Streets (2004), who discusses how the British, from 1857 to 1914, identified and taxonomised 'martial races' that are believed to possess a biological or cultural disposition to the racial and masculine qualities necessary for the arts of war.

50 In AoC 1936 and subsequent editions, this reads as: "Caste cannot and has not improved race."

51 Derived from Sindhu, the native name for the Indus river, the term Hind was first used in Persian and came to be established after the eleventh-century polymath Al-Biruni (973–1048), commissioned by the king Mahmud of Ghazni (in present-day Afghanistan), travelled to the Indian subcontinent in 1017 and wrote the famous encyclopedic account of India called *Tarikh al-Hind*. The word 'Hindu', derived thus, did not indicate a religious group but was used as a geographical demarcator for the inhabitants of the land near and east of the Indus. Later, the

the purpose of distinguishing themselves. It does not occur in any Sanskrit work prior to the Mahomedan invasion. They did not feel the necessity of a common name, because they had no conception of their having constituted a community. Hindu society as such does not exist. It is only a collection of castes. Each caste is conscious of its existence. Its survival is the be-all and end-all of its existence. Castes do not even form a federation. A caste has no feeling that it is affiliated to other castes, except when there is a Hindu–Moslem riot. On all other occasions each caste endeavours to segregate itself and to distinguish itself from other castes.

6.3

Each caste not only dines among itself and marries among itself, but each caste prescribes its own distinctive dress. What other explanation can there be of the innumerable styles of dress worn by the men and women of India, which so amuse the tourists? Indeed the ideal Hindu must be like a rat living in his own hole, refusing to have any contact with others. There is an utter lack among the Hindus of what the sociologists call 'consciousness of kind'.[52] There is no Hindu

---

word may have been adopted by those inhabitants to distinguish themselves from the Muslims who came to initially rule the northern parts of India. The ancient texts that so-called Hindus today claim their roots from—the Vedas, Ramayana, Mahabharata, *Bhagvad Gita*, Upanishads—do not ever use the terms Hindu or Hindusim. Recent research argues that the terms came into vogue with Orientalist and colonial scholarship. For an overview of the debates around 'Hindu' and 'Hinduism' and a nuanced counter-argument see D.N. Lorenzen (2006, 7–10). See also Romila Thapar's essay, "Syndicated Hinduism" (1989/2001, 54) where she says, "The term Hinduism as we understand it today to describe a particular religion is modern." Ambedkar, for his times, was far-sighted in jettisoning a term around which Indian nationalism and anticolonialism came to be constructed.

52 The phrase 'consciousness of kind' was coined by the American sociologist Franklin Henry Giddings (1855–1931), and was first elaborated in *The Principles of Sociology* (1896). Giddings sought to define the fundamental underlying law that defined human society. He defined 'consciousness of kind' as "a state of consciousness in which any being, whether low or high in the scale of life, recognises another conscious being as of like kind with itself." See Giddings (1896/2004, 17).

consciousness of kind. In every Hindu the consciousness that exists is the consciousness of his caste. That is the reason why the Hindus cannot be said to form a society or a nation.

6.4

There are, however, many Indians whose patriotism does not permit them to admit that Indians are not a nation, that they are only an amorphous mass of people. They have insisted that underlying the apparent diversity there is a fundamental unity which marks the life of the Hindus, inasmuch as there is a similarity of those habits and customs, beliefs and thoughts, which obtain all over the continent of India. Similarity in habits and customs, beliefs and thoughts, there is. But one cannot accept the conclusion that therefore, the Hindus constitute a society. To do so is to misunderstand the essentials which go to make up a society. Men do not become a society by living in physical proximity, any more than a man ceases to be a member of his society by living so many miles away from other men.

6.5

Secondly, similarity in habits and customs, beliefs and thoughts, is not enough to constitute men into society. Things may be passed physically from one to another like bricks. In the same way habits and customs, beliefs and thoughts of one group may be taken over by another group, and there may thus appear a similarity between the two. Culture spreads by diffusion, and that is why one finds similarity between various primitive tribes in the matter of their habits and customs, beliefs and thoughts, although they do not live in proximity. But no one could say that because there was this similarity, the primitive tribes constituted one society. This is because similarity in certain things is not enough to constitute a society.

6.6

Men constitute a society because they have things which they possess in common. To have similar things is totally different from possessing things in common. And the only way by which men can come to possess things in common with one another is by being in communication[53] with one another. This is merely another way of saying that society continues to exist by communication—indeed, in communication.[54] To make it concrete, it is not enough if men act in a way which agrees with the acts of others. Parallel activity, even if similar, is not sufficient to bind men into a society.

6.7

This is proved by the fact that the festivals observed by the different castes amongst the Hindus are the same. Yet these parallel performances of similar festivals by the different castes have not bound them into one integral whole. For that purpose what is necessary is for a man to share and participate in a common activity, so that the same emotions are aroused in him that animate the others. Making the individual a sharer or partner in the associated activity, so that he feels its success as his success, its failure as his failure, is the real thing that binds men and makes a society of them. The caste system prevents common activity; and by preventing common activity, it has prevented the Hindus from becoming a society with a unified life and a consciousness of its own being.

7

7.1

The Hindus often complain of the isolation and exclusiveness of a gang or a clique and blame them for anti-social spirit.

---

53 Rendered as "communion" in AoC 1936 and subsequent editions.

54 This echoes Dewey's words in *Democracy and Education* (1916): "Society exists not only by transmission, by communication, but it may fairly be said to exist in transmission, in communication."

But they conveniently forget that this anti-social spirit is the worst feature of their own caste system. One caste enjoys singing a hymn of hate against another caste as much as the Germans enjoyed singing their hymn of hate against the English during the last war. The literature of the Hindus is full of caste genealogies in which an attempt is made to give a noble origin to one caste and an ignoble origin to other castes. The Sahyadrikhand is a notorious instance of this class of literature.[55]

7.2

This anti-social spirit is not confined to caste alone. It has gone deeper and has poisoned the mutual relations of the sub-castes as well. In my province the Golak Brahmins, Deorukha Brahmins, Karada Brahmins, Palshe Brahmins,[56] and Chitpavan Brahmins[57] all claim to be sub-divisions of

55 The Sahyadrikhand is a latter-day addition to the *Skanda Purana*, the most volatile of Sanskrit texts, continuously expanding and incorporating new traditions. Wendy Doniger (1993, 60) terms it "surely the shiftiest, or sandiest, of all" puranas (collections of stories revolving around divinities and myths that allude to history though they cannot be accused of historicity). The Sahyadrikhand recounts the genealogy of several Maharashtrian Brahmin sub-castes to incorporate them into caste hierarchy. See also Rao (2009, 55). Ambedkar (BAWS 3, 48) elsewhere writes of the Sahyadrikhand: "It assigns noble origin to other castes while it assigns to the Brahmin caste the filthiest origin. It was a revenge on Manu. It was the worst lampoon on the Brahmins as a caste. The Peshwas very naturally ordered its destruction. Some survived the general destruction."

56 Golak or Govardhan Brahmins are a sub-caste in western India (largely Maharashtra) considered of inferior birth by other Brahmin communities of the region. See Hassan (1920). Deorukha (Devrukhe) Brahmins and Karada (Karhade) are sub-castes of the Panchadravid (living south of the Vindhya mountains) Maharashtrian Brahmins. Palshe is another Maharashtrian Brahmin sub-caste considered inferior by Chitpavan Brahmins. In *Anandrav Bhikaji Phadke* vs. *Shankar Daji Charye* (1883 ILR 7 Bom 323) the Bombay Court upheld the right of Chitpavan Brahmins to exclude Palshe Brahmins from worshipping at a temple, on the ground that such an exclusive right is one which the courts must guard, as otherwise all 'high-caste Hindus' would hold their sanctuaries and perform their worship only so far as those of the 'lower castes' chose to allow them (Naval 2004, 14).

57 The origin of the Chitpavan Brahmins is traced to the myth of Parashurama, believed to be an 'immortal' Brahmin incarnation of Vishnu. Parashurama is said to

the Brahmin caste. But the anti-social spirit that prevails between them is quite as marked and quite as virulent as the anti-social spirit that prevails between them and other non-Brahmin castes. There is nothing strange in this. An anti-social spirit is found wherever one group has 'interests of its own' which shut it out from full interaction with other groups, so that its prevailing purpose is protection of what it has got.

7.3

This anti-social spirit, this spirit of protecting their own interests, is as much a marked feature of the different castes in their isolation from one another as it is of nations in their isolation. The Brahmin's primary concern is to protect 'his interests' against those of the non-Brahmins; and the non-Brahmins' primary concern is to protect their interests against those of the Brahmins. The Hindus, therefore, are not merely an assortment of castes, but are so many warring groups, each living for itself and for its selfish ideal.

7.4

There is another feature of caste which is deplorable. The ancestors of the present-day English fought on one side or the other in the Wars of the Roses and the Cromwellian War.[58]

---

have burned the bodies of fourteen people who were washed ashore on a funeral pyre, purifying them, and then restored them to life—thus the name *chita* (pyre) *pavan* (purified). These fourteen people are said to be of Jewish, Persian or, in some versions, Berber descent. Another version gives the etymology of their name as "pure of the mind" (Figueira 2002, 121–33). Their recorded history, however, begins in the eighteenth century, when Chattrapati Shahu, grandson of Shivaji, appointed Balaji Vishwanath Bhat, a Chitpavan Brahmin, as Peshwa (Johnson 2005, 58). M.G. Ranade, founder-member of the Indian National Congress; G.K. Gokhale, 'moderate' Congress leader and mentor to M.K. Gandhi; Pandita Ramabai, a pioneer of education and women's rights; B.G. Tilak, Hindu nationalist leader; Vinoba Bhave, 'spiritual successor' to Gandhi; V.D. Savarkar, who coined the term Hindutva, and who was one of the co-accused in Gandhi's assassination; and Nathuram Godse, who assassinated Gandhi, were all Chitpavan Brahmins.

58 The Wars of the Roses were fought between 1455 and 1485 between Lancaster

But the descendants of those who fought on the one side do not bear any animosity—any grudge—against the descendants of those who fought on the other side. The feud is forgotten. But the present-day non-Brahmins cannot forgive the present-day Brahmins for the insult their ancestors gave to Shivaji.[59] The present-day Kayasthas will not forgive the present-day Brahmins for the infamy cast upon their forefathers by the forefathers of the latter.[60] To what is this difference due?

---

and York, two houses of the royal line Plantagenet. Ambedkar most probably is referring to the Second English Civil War as the Cromwellian war which was fought between the parliamentarians and the royalists in 1648–59, in which Cromwell and his parliamentarian forces defeated the royalists and established the precedent that the king can only rule with the Parliament's consent.

59 In 1674, the Deccan Brahmins refused to allow the coronation of Shivaji, the Maratha king (1627/30–80), according to Vedic rites. They doubted his Kshatriya origins and saw him as a Shudra claimant. As Rao (2009, 42) says: "A Brahmin from Benares, Gaga Bhatta, supported Shivaji's claim to Kshatriya status after much persuasion and traced the Bhosle lineage to the Sisodia Rajputs of Udaipur." Gaga Bhatta is also said to have charged a hefty fee for legitimising Shivaji's claim. On Shivaji's coronation story, see V.S. Bendrey (1960); see also Laine (2003), a book that was banned in Maharashtra in 2004. (The ban was lifted in 2007 by the Bombay High Court and this was upheld by the Supreme Court of India in 2010.) A recent paper by Rosalind O'Hanlon (2010a) throws light on the migration of several Maratha Brahmins to Benares in the sixteenth century and the story behind Gaga Bhatta's return to the Konkan region in the mid-seventeenth century.

60 Kayasthas are a caste of scribes whose varna status has been the subject of a raging debate. While they trace their origin to Chitragupta, the scribe of god Yama, and claim a status equal to Brahmins, or to Kshatriyas, many Brahmin texts position them as Shudras. The poet (and Kayastha) Harivansh Rai Bachchan (1998, 7) writes that Brahmins "have sought to degrade the Kayasthas in many a Sanskrit verse such as the following: That the foetal Kayastha eats not his mother's flesh/speaks not of tenderness, but of toothlessness."The Peshwa Brahmins of the Deccan had resented the Kayasthas' right to learning and becoming scribes and record-keepers in the seventeenth century. "The head of the state, though a Brahman, was despised by his other Brahman servants, because the first Peshwa's great-grandfather's great-grandfather had once been lower in society than the Desh Brahmans' great-grandfathers' great-grandfathers. While the Chitpavan Brahmans were waging social war with the Deshastha Brahmans, a bitter jealousy raged between the Brahman ministers and governors and the Kayastha secretaries" (Sarkar 1948, 357). See also Sections 9.1–3 of AoC. Further, see O'Hanlon (2010b) who says from the mid-fifteenth century, periodic but intense disputes developed over Kayastha entitlement to the rituals of the twice-born. "Often migrants

Obviously to the caste system. The existence of caste and caste consciousness has served to keep the memory of past feuds between castes green, and has prevented solidarity.

8

8.1

The recent discussion about the excluded and partially excluded[61] areas has served to draw attention to the position of what are called the aboriginal tribes in India.[62] They number about thirteen million, if not more. Apart from the question of whether their exclusion from the new Constitution[63] is proper or improper, the fact still remains that these aborigines have remained in their primitive uncivilised state[64] in a land

---

who had come into the Maratha regions as servants of the Bahmani kings and to Deccan Sultanate states, Kayasthas were intruders into local societies whose Brahmin communities had hitherto commanded more exclusive possession of scribal skills" (566). See also Note 108 at 18.1.

61 In AoC 1936 and 1937, Ambedkar uses "excluded and partially excluded areas"; whereas the 1944 edition uses "excluded and partially included areas". Since the latter is incorrect, the former has been retained.

62 Ambedkar is referring to the constitutional discussions culminating in the Government of India Act of 1935 in which areas inhabited by tribals were classified as "excluded" and "partially excluded areas" for the purpose of administration. Laws were only applicable in these areas when the governor approved it, purportedly not to harm these "backward" societies with the implementation of laws instituted for the more "developed" parts of India. See also Chandra (2013).

63 Ambedkar is referring to the Government of India Act of 1935 as the new Constitution.

64 Ambedkar's views on Adivasis—officially classified as Scheduled Tribes—are problematic. Even as he appears well intentioned and protectionist, he argues for "civilising the savages" and looks at them as leading the life of "hereditary animals", and even warns "the Hindus" that the "aborigines are a source of potential danger". Later, in his address to the All-India Scheduled Castes Federation held in Bombay on 6 May 1945, ("The Communal Deadlock and a Way to Solve It"), while discussing the issue of proportionate representation, he says: "My proposals do not cover the Aboriginal Tribes although they are larger in number than the Sikhs, Anglo-Indians, Indian Christians and Parsees… [T]he Aboriginal Tribes *have not as yet developed any political sense to make the best use of their political opportunities and they may easily become mere instruments in the hands either of*

which boasts of a civilisation thousands of years old. Not only are they not civilised, but some of them follow pursuits which have led to their being classified as criminals.[65]

8.2

Thirteen million people living in the midst of civilisation are still in a savage state, and are leading the life of hereditary

---

a majority or a minority and thereby disturb the balance without doing any good to themselves ... the proper thing to do for these backward communities is to establish a Statutory Commission to administer what are now called the 'excluded areas' on the same basis as was done in the case of the South African Constitution. Every Province in which these excluded areas are situated should be compelled to make an annual contribution of a prescribed amount for the administration of these areas" (BAWS 1, 375, emphasis added). Ironically, Gandhi used a similar logic to argue that the Untouchables had not yet developed the political sense to use the vote, let alone make use of separate electorates that Ambedkar had championed and won for the Untouchables in the 1931 Round Table Conferences. Shashank Kela (2012, 297–8) says, "Racism and prejudice marked the Constituent Assembly's 'adivasi' debates. Members referred to their subhuman existence, primitiveness and propensity for summary justice; invoked the threat of separatism; and adduced arguments of the greatest good of the greatest numbers." Uday Chandra (2013) has argued how both Ambedkar and Jawaharlal Nehru partook of a liberalist-colonial understanding, and fear, of the 'primitive' during the making of the Constitution of independent India, almost retaining the colonialist approach to so-called tribals. In contrast, the Adivasi leader from Jharkhand and member of the Constitutent Assembly (CA), Jaipal Singh, had argued on 19 December 1946: "What my people require, Sir, is not adequate safeguards... We do not ask for any special protection. We want to be treated like every other Indian." As Chandra points out, this was a perception shared by Vallabhbhai Patel, Chairman of the Tribal and Excluded Areas Committee and future Home Minister. However, later, during the CA debates on the Sixth Schedule, the Ambedkar-led proposal to allow Scheduled Tribes to function from excluded areas found favour with Adivasi spokespersons such as Rev. J.J.M. Nichols-Roy, who said on 19 November 1949: "The Sixth Schedule concerns the hill-districts of Assam in which the hill men in Assam live by themselves in their own territories, who have their own language and their culture and the Constituent Assembly has rightly agreed ... that there should be councils for these different districts in order to enable the people who live in those areas to develop themselves according to their genius and culture." For the workings of autonomous district councils established under the Sixth Schedule in the Northeastern states, see Bengt G. Karlsson (2011) and Sanjib Baruah (2007).

65 By the beginning of the twentieth century, huge sections of the population, mostly itinerant, were labelled criminal under the Criminal Tribes Acts of 1871 and 1911. Seeing criminality as hereditary was a logical outcome of the caste system. If people could be born scholars, weavers and cobblers they could also be born thieves and thugs. See D'Souza (2001) and Radhakrishna (2001).

criminals! But the Hindus have never felt ashamed of it. This is a phenomenon which in my view is quite unparalleled. What is the cause of this shameful state of affairs? Why has no attempt been made to civilise these aborigines and to lead them to take to a more honourable way of making a living?

8.3

The Hindus will probably seek to account for this savage state of the aborigines by attributing to them congenital stupidity. They will probably not admit that the aborigines have remained savages because they had made no effort to civilise them, to give them medical aid, to reform them, to make them good citizens. But supposing a Hindu wished to do what the Christian missionary is doing for these aborigines, could he have done it? I submit not. Civilising the aborigines means adopting them as your own, living in their midst, and cultivating fellow-feeling—in short, loving them. How is it possible for a Hindu to do this? His whole life is one anxious effort to preserve his caste. Caste is his precious possession which he must save at any cost. He cannot consent to lose it by establishing contact with the aborigines, the remnants of the hateful *anaryas*[66] of the Vedic days.

8.4

Not that a Hindu could not be taught the sense of duty to fallen humanity, but the trouble is that no amount of sense of duty can enable him to overcome his duty to preserve his caste. Caste is, therefore, the real explanation as to why the Hindu has let the savage remain a savage in the midst of his civilisation without blushing, or without feeling any sense of remorse or repentance. The Hindu has not realised that these

66 Anaryas: Sanskrit for non-Aryans. *Anasa* (literally those without a nose, figuratively those without an aquiline nose) is another term frequently used in the Vedas to refer to the local, indigenous populations, whom the Aryas regarded as different from them and therefore to be stigmatised.

aborigines are a source of potential danger. If these savages remain savages, they may not do any harm to the Hindus. But if they are reclaimed by non-Hindus and converted to their faiths, they will swell the ranks of the enemies of the Hindus. If this happens, the Hindu will have to thank himself and his caste system.

9

9.1

Not only has the Hindu made no effort for the humanitarian cause of civilising the savages, but the higher-caste Hindus have deliberately prevented the lower castes who are within the pale of Hinduism from rising to the cultural level of the higher castes. I will give two instances, one of the Sonars and the other of the Pathare Prabhus.[67] Both are communities quite well known in Maharashtra. Like the rest of the communities desiring to raise their status, these two communities were at one time endeavouring to adopt some of the ways and habits of the Brahmins.

9.2

---

67 *Pathare* means stone and *prabhu* means lord. This caste claims to have descended from the Kshatriyas. The mythological claim around origins goes thus: "The first of them was Ashvapati (700 BCE), a lineal descendant of Rama and Prithu, who, as is stated in the local chronology, governed India in the Dvapara and Treta Yugas, which is a good while ago! The Patarah Prabhus are the only caste within which Brahmans have to perform certain purely Vedic rites known under the name of the 'Kshatriya rites'" (Blavatsky, 1892/2010, 145–6). Veena Naregal (2001, 168–9) says: "In western India it was mainly brahmins and some sub-brahmin groups like the *prabhus* and *shenvis* who were among the first to perceive the benefits of the new literate order and respond to the opportunities it created. The *prabhus* and the *shenvis* were traditionally trained scribes who had a long and successful history of employment as *karkuns* in different parts of the Peshwa kingdom and in the offices of the colonial trading houses of Bombay. The possession of uncommon literate skills had also allowed the *prabhus* to be closely associated with pre-modern book production." See also Uma Chakravarti (2000) for a discussion of the Peshwa intervention on norms for widows and enforced widowhood claims of upwardly mobile middle caste groups.

The Sonars were styling themselves Daivadnya Brahmins[68] and were wearing their dhotis with folds in them, and using the word 'namaskar' for salutation. Both the folded way of wearing the dhoti and the namaskar were special to the Brahmins. The Brahmins did not like this imitation and this attempt by Sonars to pass off as Brahmins. Under the authority of the Peshwas, the Brahmins successfully put down this attempt on the part of the Sonars to adopt the ways of the Brahmins. They even got the president of the councils of the East India Company's settlement in Bombay to issue a prohibitory order against the Sonars residing in Bombay.

9.3

At one time the Pathare Prabhus had widow remarriage as a custom of their caste. This custom of widow remarriage was later on looked upon as a mark of social inferiority by some members of the caste, especially because it was contrary to the custom prevalent among the Brahmins. With the object of raising the status of their community, some Pathare Prabhus sought to stop this practice of widow remarriage that was prevalent in their caste. The community was divided into two camps, one for and the other against the innovation. The Peshwas took the side of those in favour of widow remarriage, and thus virtually prohibited the Pathare Prabhus from following the ways of the Brahmins.

9.4

The Hindus criticise the Mahomedans for having spread their religion by the use of the sword. They also ridicule Christianity on the score of the Inquisition.[69] But really

68 On Daivadnya (also Daivajna) Brahmins, the *Census of India* (1961, 14) says: "They are locally known as 'Sonars' and 'Sonagars' and are the traditional goldsmiths. They are found in almost all the towns and big villages of North Kanara District. They are said to have migrated from Goa."

69 Here Ambedkar is referring to the polemics used by the Vedic missionaries of

speaking, who is better and more worthy of our respect—the Mahomedans and Christians who attempted to thrust down the throats of unwilling persons what they regarded as necessary for their salvation, or the Hindu who would not spread the light, who would endeavour to keep others in darkness, who would not consent to share his intellectual and social inheritance with those who are ready and willing to make it a part of their own make-up? I have no hesitation in saying that if the Mahomedan has been cruel, the Hindu has been mean; and meanness is worse than cruelty.

10

10.1

Whether the Hindu religion was or was not a missionary religion has been a controversial issue.[70] Some hold the view that it was never a missionary religion. Others hold that it was. That the Hindu religion was once a missionary religion must be admitted. It could not have spread over the face of India, if it was not a missionary religion. That today it is not a

---

the Arya Samaj to counter the influence of Muslim and Christian preachers and missionaries—adopting their established practices of preaching at religious fairs, challenging missionaries in pamphlets and on the streets. The rise of the Arya Samaj owed much to the demographic shifts that characterised the history of the Punjab due to its proximity to Central Asia and the predominance of Sikh and Muslim rulers. In the nineteenth century, British rule added to this list, and the conversions of the oppressed castes in large numbers to Islam and Christianity exacerbated the situation. See Jones (2006, 139–45). According to Gopal Krishan (2004, 77–89), in 1881, the Hindus constituted 43.8 per cent of the population, the Sikhs 8.2 per cent and Christians 0.1 per cent. The Muslims, at 47.6 per cent, were well short of an absolute majority. But by 1941, the Muslims were in absolute majority in the Punjab accounting for 53.2 per cent of the total population. The Hindus made 29.1 per cent of the total, the Sikhs 14.9 per cent, Christians 1.9 per cent and others 1.3 per cent. The erosion in the percentage share of the Hindus was caused by the conversion of many Hindus—especially the 'lower castes', such as Chuhras, Chamars, Jhiwars and Malis—to Islam, Sikhism and Christianity.

70 Reads in AoC 1936 as: "Whether the Hindu religion is a missionary religion is a question which was once a subject of controversy." Amended in 1937.

missionary religion is also a fact which must be accepted. The question therefore is not whether or not the Hindu religion was a missionary religion. The real question is, why did the Hindu religion cease to be a missionary religion?[71]

10.2

My answer is this: the Hindu religion ceased to be a missionary religion when the caste system grew up among the Hindus. Caste is inconsistent with conversion. Inculcation of beliefs and dogmas is not the only problem that is involved in conversion. To find a place for the convert in the social life of the community is another, and a much more important, problem that arises in connection with conversion. That problem is where to place the convert, in what caste? It is a problem which must baffle every Hindu wishing to make aliens convert to his religion.

10.3

Unlike a club, the membership of a caste is not open to all and sundry.[72] The law of caste confines its membership to persons born in the caste. Castes are autonomous, and there is no authority anywhere to compel a caste to admit a newcomer to its social life. Hindu society being a collection of castes, and each caste being a closed corporation, there is no place for a convert. Thus it is caste which has prevented the Hindus from expanding and from absorbing other religious communities. So long as caste remains, Hindu religion cannot be made a

---

71 For a discussion of conversion during the colonial period, see Gauri Viswanathan (1998), especially the chapter "Conversion to Equality" (211–40) that discusses Ambedkar's quest for equality through conversion. Also see Chakravarti (2000), where she alludes to the problems of the convert, Pandita Ramabai, in terms of cultural and 'nationalist' positions vis-à-vis the colonial structure which bear out Ambedkar's point.

72 Phrase added in AoC 1937.

missionary religion, and *shuddhi*[73] will be both a folly and a futility.

11

11.1

The reasons which have made shuddhi impossible for Hindus are also responsible for making *sangathan*[74] impossible. The idea underlying sangathan is to remove from the mind of the Hindu that timidity and cowardice which so painfully mark him off from the Mahomedan and the Sikh, and which have led him to adopt the low ways of treachery and cunning for protecting himself. The question naturally arises: From where does the Sikh or the Mahomedan derive his strength, which makes him brave and fearless? I am sure it is not due to relative superiority of physical strength, diet or drill. It is due to the strength arising out of the feeling that all Sikhs will come to the rescue of a Sikh when he is in danger, and that all Mahomedans will rush to save a Muslim if he is attacked.

11.2

---

73 Shuddhi or *shuddhikaran*—a movement for 'reconversion' to Hinduism—was initiated by Dayananda Saraswati, founder of the Arya Samaj. In 1877, two years after founding the Arya Samaj, Dayananda is said to have performed the first ever shuddhi of a Muslim man (Parel 2000, 122). Swami Shraddhananda (1856–1926) carried on this legacy more militantly in the early twentieth century in the Punjab and the United Provinces. For an account, see Jaffrelot (1995). However, as Ambedkar points out, shuddhi created many problems since the privileged castes were not willing to mingle with newly 'purified' lower caste members. See also Jones (2006, 129–35, 202–14).

74 The Hindu Mahasabha launched the sangathan movement in the early 1920s in response to the Khilafat Movement (1918–24), which had Gandhi's support, aimed at a pan-Islamic mobilisation to save the Ottoman Empire from dismemberment and to secure political reforms for India. The underlying logic of sangathan was to defend the Hindu community from so-called foreign forces through organisation and unification. It aimed to integrate the different sections of the Hindu community, including the Untouchables. The main proponents of sangathan were Bhai Parmanand (see Note 11 in Prologue) and V.D. Savarkar. See Jaffrelot (1999a, 19–24) and also Bapu (2013, 47–60).

The Hindu can derive no such strength. He cannot feel assured that his fellows will come to his help. Being one and fated to be alone, he remains powerless, develops timidity and cowardice, and in a fight surrenders or runs away. The Sikh as well as the Muslim stands fearless and gives battle, because he knows that though one he will not be alone. The presence of this belief in the one helps him to hold out, and the absence of it in the other makes him to give way.

11.3

If you pursue this matter further and ask what is it that enables the Sikh and the Mahomedan to feel so assured, and why is the Hindu filled with such despair in the matter of help and assistance, you will find that the reasons for this difference lie in the difference in their associated mode of living.[75] The associated mode of life practised by the Sikhs and the Mahomedans produces fellow-feeling. The associated mode of life of the Hindus does not. Among Sikhs and Muslims there is a social cement which makes them *bhais*.[76] Among Hindus there is no such cement, and one Hindu does not regard another Hindu as his bhai. This explains why a Sikh says and feels that one Sikh, or one Khalsa, is equal to *sava lakh* men.[77] This explains why one Mahomedan is equal to a crowd of Hindus. This difference is undoubtedly a difference

75 Ambedkar is invoking the Deweyan concept of "associated life", which he picks up and develops further into a political tool. Both Dewey and Ambedkar believed that democracy should not be restricted to the political realm, but should also manifest itself in other areas, such as education, industry and the public sphere. See Mukherjee (2009, 356).

76 A feeling of brotherhood (*ikhwaan*) among Muslims across the world (*ummat*) is an important conceptual category in Islam. Sikhs are also enjoined by their religion to practise universal brotherhood and often address each other as *bhai* (brother).

77 *Sava lakh*: 125,000. The complete phrase, "*Sava lakh se ek laraun*" (My one follower will take on 125,000), is attributed to Govind Singh, the tenth Sikh Guru, who is said to have given this battle cry at Chamkaur in 1704.

due to caste. So long as caste remains, there will be no sangathan; and so long as there is no sangathan the Hindu will remain weak and meek.

11.4

The Hindus claim to be a very tolerant people. In my opinion this is a mistake. On many occasions they can be intolerant, and if on some occasions they are tolerant, that is because they are too weak to oppose or too indifferent to oppose. This indifference of the Hindus has become so much a part of their nature that a Hindu will quite meekly tolerate an insult as well as a wrong. You see amongst them, to use the words of Morris, "The great treading down the little, the strong beating down the weak, cruel men fearing not, kind men daring not and wise men caring not."[78] With the Hindu gods all-forbearing, it is not difficult to imagine the pitiable condition of the wronged and the oppressed among the Hindus. Indifferentism is the worst kind of disease that can infect a people. Why is the Hindu so indifferent? In my opinion this indifferentism is the result of the caste system, which has made sangathan and cooperation even for a good cause impossible.

12

12.1

The assertion by the individual of his own opinions and beliefs, his own independence and interest—over and against group standards, group authority, and group interests—is the beginning of all reform. But whether the reform will

---

78 William Morris (1834–96) was a poet, author, leader of the early British socialist movement, and the founder of the Arts and Crafts Movement in Britain. The quote is from *A Dream of John Ball* (1888), a dream travel in time to the Peasants' Revolt of 1381 (also known as Wat Tyler's Rebellion or the Great Rising). Ambedkar here is quoting from the speech given by the character of John Ball, a radical travelling priest excommunicated for his preaching of equality to the Kentish rebels.

continue depends upon what scope the group affords for such individual assertion. If the group is tolerant and fair-minded in dealing with such individuals, they will continue to assert, and in the end will succeed in converting their fellows. On the other hand if the group is intolerant, and does not bother about the means it adopts to stifle such individuals, they will perish and the reform will die out.

12.2

Now a caste has an unquestioned right to excommunicate any man who is guilty of breaking the rules of the caste; and when it is realised that excommunication involves a complete cesser of social intercourse, it will be agreed that as a form of punishment there is really little to choose between excommunication and death. No wonder individual Hindus have not had the courage to assert their independence by breaking the barriers of caste.

12.3

It is true that man cannot get on with his fellows. But it is also true that he cannot do without them. He would like to have the society of his fellows on his terms. If he cannot get it on his terms, then he will be ready to have it on any terms, even amounting to complete surrender. This is because he cannot do without society. A caste is ever ready to take advantage of the helplessness of a man, and to insist upon complete conformity to its code in letter and in spirit.

12.4

A caste can easily organise itself into a conspiracy to make the life of a reformer hell; and if a conspiracy is a crime, I do not understand why such a nefarious act as an attempt to excommunicate a person for daring to act contrary to the rules of caste should not be made an offence punishable by law. But as it is, even law gives each caste autonomy to regulate its membership and punish dissenters with excommunication. Caste in the hands of the orthodox has been a powerful weapon for persecuting the reformers and for killing all reform.

13

13.1

The effect of caste on the ethics of the Hindus is simply deplorable. Caste has killed public spirit. Caste has destroyed the sense of public charity. Caste has made public opinion impossible. A Hindu's public is his caste. His responsibility is only to his caste. His loyalty is restricted only to his caste. Virtue has become caste-ridden, and morality has become caste-bound. There is no sympathy for the deserving. There is no appreciation of the meritorious. There is no charity to the needy. Suffering as such calls for no response. There is charity, but it begins with caste and ends with caste. There is sympathy, but not for men of other castes.

13.2

Would a Hindu acknowledge and follow the leadership of a great and good man? The case of a Mahatma apart, the answer must be that he will follow a leader if he is a man of his caste. A Brahmin will follow a leader only if he is a Brahmin, a Kayastha if he is a Kayastha, and so on. The capacity to appreciate merits in a man, apart from his caste, does not exist in a Hindu. There is appreciation of virtue, but only when the man is a fellow caste-man. The whole morality is as bad as tribal morality. My caste-man, right or wrong; my caste-man, good or bad. It is not a case of standing by virtue or not standing by vice. It is a case of standing by, or not standing by, caste. Have not Hindus committed treason against their country in the interests of their castes?

14

14.1

I would not be surprised if some of you have grown weary

listening to this tiresome tale of the sad effects which caste has produced. There is nothing new in it. I will therefore turn to the constructive side of the problem. What is your ideal society if you do not want caste, is a question that is bound to be asked of you. If you ask me, my ideal would be a society based on liberty, equality, and fraternity. And why not?

14.2

What objection can there be to fraternity? I cannot imagine any. An ideal society should be mobile, should be full of channels for conveying a change taking place in one part to other parts. In an ideal society there should be many interests consciously communicated and shared. There should be varied and free points of contact with other modes of association. In other words there must be social endosmosis.[79] This is fraternity, which is only another name for democracy. Democracy is not merely a form of government. It is primarily a mode of associated living, of conjoint communicated experience.[80] It is essentially an attitude of respect and reverence towards fellow men.

14.3

Any objection to liberty? Few object to liberty in the sense

---

79 Endosmosis was another Deweyan term that Ambedkar deployed and developed. It is derived from a biological term which means the passage of a fluid through a permeable membrane from a region of lower to a region of higher concentration. Mukherjee points out that the term was used originally by the French philosopher Henri Louis Bergson (1859–1941) and, after him, by American philosopher and psychologist William James (1842–1910), who was, like Dewey, a leading exponent of pragmatism, "to describe the interaction of the mind with nature". Dewey appropriated it as a descriptor for interaction between social groups. In Ambedkar and Dewey's work the term came to be a metaphor of the fluidity of communications between social groups, in which, according to Mukherjee (2009, 352), they managed to reconcile the two extremes and give a sense of being both separate and connected.

80 These lines appear almost exactly in Dewey's *Democracy and Education*, chapter 7: "A democracy is more than a form of government; it is primarily a mode of associated living, of conjoint communicated experience."

of a right to free movement, in the sense of a right to life and limb. There is no objection to liberty in the sense of a right to property, tools and materials, as being necessary for earning a living, to keep the body in a due state of health. Why not allow a person the liberty to benefit from an effective and competent use of a person's powers? The supporters of caste who would allow liberty in the sense of a right to life, limb, and property, would not readily consent to liberty in this sense, inasmuch as it involves liberty to choose one's profession.

14.4

But to object to this kind of liberty is to perpetuate slavery. For slavery does not merely mean a legalised form of subjection. It means a state of society in which some men are forced to accept from others the purposes which control their conduct. This condition obtains even where there is no slavery in the legal sense. It is found where, as in the caste system, some persons are compelled to carry on certain prescribed callings which are not of their choice.

14.5

Any objection to equality? This has obviously been the most contentious part of the slogan of the French Revolution. The objections to equality may be sound, and one may have to admit that all men are not equal. But what of that? Equality may be a fiction, but nonetheless one must accept it as the governing principle. A man's power is dependent upon (1) physical heredity; (2) social inheritance or endowment in the form of parental care, education, accumulation of scientific knowledge, everything which enables him to be more efficient than the savage; and finally, (3) on his own efforts. In all these three respects men are undoubtedly unequal. But the question is, shall we treat them as unequal because they are unequal? This is a question which the opponents of equality must answer.

14.6

From the standpoint of the individualist, it may be just to treat men unequally so far as their efforts are unequal. It may be desirable to give as much incentive as possible to the full development of everyone's powers. But what would happen if men were treated as unequally as they are unequal in the first two respects?[81] It is obvious that those individuals also in whose favour there is birth, education, family name, business connections, and inherited wealth, would be selected in the race. But selection under such circumstances would not be a selection of the able. It would be the selection of the privileged. The reason, therefore, which forces that in the third respect we should treat men unequally, demands that in the first two respects we should treat men as equally as possible.

14.7

On the other hand, it can be urged that if it is good for the social body to get the most out of its members, it can get the most out of them only by making them equal as far as possible at the very start of the race. That is one reason why we cannot escape equality. But there is another reason why we must accept equality. A statesman is concerned with vast numbers of people. He has neither the time nor the knowledge to draw fine distinctions and to treat each one equitably, i.e., according to need or according to capacity. However desirable or reasonable an equitable treatment of men may be, humanity is not capable of assortment and classification. The statesman, therefore, must follow some rough and ready rule, and that rough and ready rule is to treat all men alike,

81 In AoC 1936 this part reads as: "men were treated unequally unequally as they are"; in 1937 as: "men were treated unequally as they are". The 1945 version is retained here.

not because they are alike but because classification and assortment is impossible. The doctrine of equality is glaringly fallacious but, taking all in all, it is the only way a statesman can proceed in politics—which is a severely practical affair and which demands a severely practical test.

15

15.1

But there is a set of reformers who hold out a different ideal. They go by the name of the Arya Samajists,[82] and their ideal of social organisation is what is called *chaturvarnya*, or the division of society into four classes instead of the four thousand castes that we have in India. To make it more attractive and to disarm opposition, the protagonists of chaturvarnya take great care to point out that their chaturvarnya is based not on birth but on *guna* (worth).[83] At the outset, I must confess that notwithstanding the worth-basis of this chaturvarnya, it is an ideal to which I cannot reconcile myself.

15.2

In the first place, if under the chaturvarnya of the Arya Samajists an individual is to take his place in Hindu society according to his worth, I do not understand why the Arya Samajists insist upon labelling men as Brahmin, Kshatriya, Vaishya and Shudra. A learned man would be honoured without his being labelled a Brahmin. A soldier would be respected without his

82 It must be remembered that the Jat-Pat Todak Mandal, which invited Ambedkar for its annual conference, for which this address was prepared, was originally affiliated to the Arya Samaj and continued to have several important Arya Samaj leaders of the Punjab influencing it. Ambedkar chooses to take them on in this section of his speech, and this would likely have made them most uncomfortable, and caused them to withdraw their invitation to him. For a summary of the Arya Samaj's views on varnashrama (also known as chaturvarnya and *varnavyavastha*), based on Dayananda Saraswati's 'Vedic' approach, see Jones (2006).

83 Refer to Note 161 at 24.3 on the guna–karma theory.

being designated a Kshatriya. If European society honours its soldiers and its servants[84] without giving them permanent labels, why should Hindu society find it difficult to do so, is a question which Arya Samajists have not cared to consider.

15.3

There is another objection to the continuance of these labels. **All reform consists in a change in the notions, sentiments and mental attitudes of the people towards men and things.**[85] It is common experience that certain names become associated with certain notions and sentiments which determine a person's attitude towards men and things. The names Brahmin, Kshatriya, Vaishya and Shudra are names which are associated with a definite and fixed notion in the mind of every Hindu. That notion is that of a hierarchy based on birth.

15.4[86]

So long as these names continue, Hindus will continue to think of the Brahmin, Kshatriya, Vaishya and Shudra as hierarchical divisions of high and low, based on birth, and to act accordingly. The Hindu must be made to unlearn all this. But how can this happen if the old labels remain and continue to recall to his mind old notions? If new notions are to be inculcated in the minds of people, it is necessary to give them new names.

---

84 "Savants" in 1936 and 1937; amended in 1944.

85 Text in semibold in this paragraph does not appear in AoC 1936. In the first edition, the lines after the highlighted text appear thus: "It is human experience that notions and sentiments associated with certain names become part of ourselves, stiffening into attitudes that which hold even trained minds in bondage. Intellectual servitude to old associations is very common and is more difficult to break than is generally thought. Facts may change, but if names remain the same, then the notions associated with those names linger not only in sentiments but also in practice. These labels have had all along in Indian history the *de facto* connotation of designating a hierarchy of castes based on birth. They were understood to be marks of superiority and inferiority." These lines were amended in the 1937 edition used here.

86 All of this paragraph, except its last sentence, does not appear in AoC 1936.

To continue the old names is to make the reform futile. To allow this chaturvarnya based on worth to be designated by such stinking labels as Brahmin, Kshatriya, Vaishya, Shudra, indicative of social divisions based on birth, is a snare.

16

16.1

To me this chaturvarnya with its old labels is utterly repellent, and my whole being rebels against it. But I do not wish to rest my objection to chaturvarnya on mere grounds of sentiments. There are more solid grounds on which I rely for my opposition to it. A close examination of this ideal has convinced me that as a system of social organisation, chaturvarnya is impracticable, is harmful, and has turned out to be a miserable failure.[87] From a practical point of view, the system of chaturvarnya raises several difficulties which its protagonists do not seem to have taken into account. The principle underlying caste is fundamentally different from the principle underlying chaturvarnya.[88] Not only are they fundamentally different, but they are also fundamentally opposed.

16.2

The former, chaturvarnya, is based on worth. How are you going to compel people who have acquired a higher status based on birth, without reference to their worth, to vacate that status? How are you going to compel people to recognise the status due to a man, in accordance with his worth, who is occupying a lower status based on his birth? For this, you

---

87 The lines at the beginning of 16.1 till "... a miserable failure" figure under Section XV of AoC 1936. The lines that follow from here (beginning, "From a practical...") till the first sentence of 16.3 (ending, "... chaturvarnya a success.") have been added in the 1937 edition.

88 This is given as "varna" in AoC 1936 and 1937; Ambedkar changes it to "chaturvarnya" in 1944.

must first break up the caste system, in order to be able to establish the chaturvarnya system. How are you going to reduce the four thousand castes, based on birth, to the four varnas, based on worth? This is the first difficulty which the protagonists of chaturvarnya must grapple with.

16.3

There is a second difficulty which the protagonists of chaturvarnya must grapple with, if they wish to make the establishment of chaturvarnya a success.[89] Chaturvarnya presupposes that you can classify people into four definite classes. Is this possible?[90] In this respect, the ideal of chaturvarnya has, as you will see, a close affinity to the Platonic ideal. To Plato, men fell by nature into three classes. In some individuals, he believed,[91] mere appetites dominated. He assigned them to the labouring and trading classes. Others revealed to him that over and above appetites, they had a courageous disposition. He classed them as defenders in war and guardians of internal peace. Others showed a capacity to grasp the universal—the reason underlying things. He made them the law-givers of the people.

16.4

The criticism to which Plato's *Republic* is subject is also the criticism which must apply to the system of chaturvarnya, in so far as it proceeds upon the possibility of an accurate classification of men into four distinct classes.[92] The chief

89 In AoC 1936, Section 16 begins here, with the sentence: "The practicability of the chaturvarnya presupposes two things. It presupposes…"

90 This question does not appear in AoC 1936.

91 Phrase added in 1937.

92 Plato's *The Republic*, addressing the question of justice, deduces that the human soul has three parts: the "logical", thinking part; the "spirited" part, by which we develop anger and get into a temper; and the "appetitive" part, by which we experience hunger, thirst, eroticism, love for moneymaking and other such desires. The book also categorises men into three classes based on which part of their soul

criticism against Plato is that his idea of lumping individuals into a few sharply marked-off classes is a very superficial view of man and his powers. Plato had no perception of the uniqueness of every individual, of his incommensurability with others, of each individual as forming a class of his own. He had no recognition of the infinite diversity of active tendencies, and the combination of tendencies of which an individual is capable. To him, there were types of faculties or powers in the individual constitution.

16.5

All this is demonstrably wrong. Modern science has shown that the lumping together of individuals into a few sharply marked-off classes is a superficial view of man, not worthy of serious consideration. Consequently, the utilisation of the qualities of individuals is incompatible with their stratification by classes, since the qualities of individuals are so variable. Chaturvarnya must fail for the very reason for which Plato's Republic must fail—namely, that it is not possible to pigeon men into holes according to class.[93] That it is impossible to

---

masks the others: the 'guardians' are persons in whom the logical part dominates, in the 'auxiliaries' spirit dominates, and the 'producers' are people who have let their appetite dominate. The guardians must rule, the auxiliaries must help in running the guardians' writ, and the producers must work. (See also Note 161 on the guna–karma theory.) Ambedkar disagrees with Plato on many levels. He is not convinced that there are only three qualities on the basis of which a soul can be divided. He believes that the multitude of human characteristics is so complex that it is impossible to identify and categorise them. He also points out that different characteristics become more or less important in the same person at different times. His criticism is also what was later popularised as the problem of the 'one-dimensional man' by Herbert Marcuse (1964/1991). From his experience of caste, Ambedkar's critique is that in such an arrangement where most of the power is vested with the guardians and the remaining with the auxiliaries (the 'twice-born' Brahmins, Kshatriyas and Vaishyas in the caste context), there is no mechanism to ensure that they will not oppress the producers (Shudras and Untouchables).

93 In AoC 1936, this merely reads as "not possible to pigeon men into holes". In 1937, Ambedkar amends this to "not possible to pigeon men into holes according as he belongs to one class or the other". The subsequent lines, beginning "That it is

accurately classify people into four definite classes is proved by the fact that the original four classes have now become four thousand castes.

16.6

There is a third difficulty in the way of the establishment of the system of chaturvarnya. How are you going to maintain the system of chaturvarnya, supposing it was established? One[94] important requirement for the successful working of chaturvarnya is the maintenance[95] of the penal system which could maintain it by its sanction. The system of chaturvarnya must perpetually face the problem of the transgressor. Unless there is a penalty attached to the act of transgression, men will not keep to their respective classes. The whole system will break down, being contrary to human nature. Chaturvarnya cannot subsist by its own inherent goodness. It must be enforced by law.

16.7

That without penal sanction the ideal of chaturvarnya cannot be realised is proved by the story in the Ramayana of Rama killing Shambuka.[96] Some people seem to blame

---

impossible…" till "… it was established?" in 16.6 are absent in AoC 1936.

94 This sentence begins with "Another" in AoC 1936; perhaps changed in the light of new sentences added in 1937.

95 The word used is "existence" in AoC 1936.

96 The story of Shambuka is told in the seventh book, Uttarakanda, of the Valmiki Ramayana. Shambuka wants to achieve a higher status than the *suras* (*devtas*, gods) through meditation and austerities. On discovering that Shambuka, a Shudra, was indeed meditating, Rama promptly beheads him to restore varnasharma dharma. The story has been used by the Dravidian movement and in anticaste literature to ridicule the idea of Rama as the embodiment of perfection. Kuvempu (Kuppalli Venkatappa Puttappa) (1904–94), a Jnanpith-winning Kannada author wrote *Sudra Tapasvi* (1944), a novel based on Shambuka's life. Sikhamani, a contemporary Telugu Dalit poet, writes: "The sword that severed/ Shambuka's head could remain/ sharp and safe for centuries./ It has just changed hands/ and no longer recognises you./ No Manu to save you now!" See "Steel Nibs are Sprouting…" in Satyanarayana and Tharu (2013, 554).

Rama because he wantonly and without reason killed Shambuka. But to blame Rama for killing Shambuka is to misunderstand the whole situation. Ram Raj was a raj based on chaturvarnya. As a king, Rama was bound to maintain chaturvarnya. It was his duty therefore to kill Shambuka, the Shudra who had transgressed his class and wanted to be a Brahmin. This is the reason why Rama killed Shambuka. But this also shows that penal sanction is necessary for the maintenance of chaturvarnya. Not only penal sanction is necessary, but the penalty of death is necessary. That is why Rama did not inflict on Shambuka a lesser punishment. That is why the *Manusmriti*[97] prescribes such heavy sentences

97 The *Manusmriti* represents itself as the dharma that Brahma declares to Manu, 'the first Man', and is passed on by him to Bhrigu, one of the ten 'great sages'. The text is believed to have attained its present form around the second century CE. Ambedkar writes in another, posthumously published work, *Revolution and Counter-Revolution in Ancient India* (BAWS 5, 273): "Pushyamitra Sunga and his successors could not have tolerated these exaggerated claims of the Brahmins unless they themselves were Brahmins interested in the establishment of Brahmanism. Indeed it is quite possible that the *Manusmriti* was composed at the command of Pushyamitra Brahman king (185–149 BC) himself, and forms the book of the philosophy of Brahmanism." In another work, *The Untouchables: Who Were They and Why they Became Untouchable*, Ambedkar (BAWS 9, 373) says: "After taking all facts into consideration Prof Bühler has fixed a date which appears to strike the truth. According to Bühler, the *Manusmriti*, in the shape in which it exists now, came into existence in the Second Century AD." A contemporary scholar, J.L. Brockington (1996, 92) arrives at a similar conclusion. Many editions of the *Manusmriti* have been published in Sanskrit since its first edition in 1813. The first translation was *Institutes of Hindu law, or, The ordinances of Menu* [sic], *according to the gloss of Cullúca: comprising the Indian system of duties, religious and civil: verbally translated from the original Sanscrit: with a preface*, by Sir William Jones (1796). One of the best-known translations is George Bühler's *Laws of Manu* (1886/2004), which contains an exhaustive introduction and extracts from seven commentaries. In her modern translation, Wendy Doniger states that no work in the tradition of Western scholarship compares with the fame and sustained authority exercised across centuries by the *Manusmriti*. See Doniger and Smith (1991, xviii–xix). As C.J. Fuller (2003, 484) notes, British administrators depended on Dharmashastras such as the *Manusmriti* to develop a legal system for India, thus subjecting the Hindu population as a whole to a Brahminical legal code. For the most authoritative, exhaustively annotated edition (1,131 pages) of the *Manusmriti*, see Patrick Olivelle (2005).

as cutting off the tongue, or pouring of molten lead in the ears, of the Shudra who recites or hears the Veda.[98] The supporters of chaturvarnya must give an assurance that they could successfully classify men, and that they could induce modern society in the twentieth century to re-forge the penal sanctions of the *Manusmriti*.

16.8[99]

The protagonists of chaturvarnya do not seem to have considered what is to happen to women in their system. Are they also to be divided into four classes, Brahmin, Kshatriya, Vaishya and Shudra? Or are they to be allowed to take the status of their husbands? If the status of the woman is to be the consequence of marriage, what becomes of the underlying principle of chaturvarnya—namely, that the status of a person should be based upon the worth of that person? If they are to be classified according to their worth, is their classification to be nominal or real?

---

98 Such verses do not figure in the *Manusmriti*. Bühler's edition, which Ambedkar may have possibly accessed, offers two verses that come close to the import. "A once-born man (a Shudra), who insults a twice-born man with gross invective, shall have his tongue cut out; for he is of low origin" (8.270; 1886/2004, 211). And: "If he arrogantly teaches Brahmins their duty, the king shall cause hot oil to be poured into his mouth and into his ears" (8.272; 2004, 211). For Ambedkar's extended discussion of the *Manusmriti*, see the annotated edition of "Castes in India" in Rege (2013, 77–108). Ambedkar seems to be citing these punishments from chapter 12 of *Gautama Dharma Sutra* (600 BCE to 300 BCE, predating the *Manusmriti*) which he also cites in his posthumous work, *Philosophy of Hinduism* (BAWS 3). Bühler's translation (1898, 239) of *Gautama Dharma Sutra* talks of similar punishments for the Shudra: "4. Now if a Shudra listens intentionally to (a recitation of) the Veda, his ears shall be filled with (molten) tin or lac. 5. If he recites (Vedic texts), his tongue shall be cut out. 6. If he remembers them, his body shall be split in twain. 7. If he assumes a position equal (to that of twice-born men) in sitting, in lying down, in conversation or on the road, he shall undergo (corporal) punishment."

99 Paragraphs 16.8 and 16.9 were added in 1937. The sentence with which 16.9 ends—"Given these *difficulties* ... chaturvarnya."—figures in 1936 as the last sentence of AoC 1936; the word "conditions" is used in the place of "difficulties".

16.9

If it is to be nominal, then it is useless; and then the protagonists of chaturvarnya must admit that their system does not apply to women. If it is real, are the protagonists of chaturvarnya prepared to follow the logical consequences of applying it to women? They must be prepared to have women priests and women soldiers. Hindu society has grown accustomed to women teachers and women barristers. It may grow accustomed to women brewers and women butchers. But he would be a bold person who would say that it will allow women priests and women soldiers. But that will be the logical outcome of applying chaturvarnya to women. Given these difficulties, I think no one except a congenital idiot could hope for and believe in a successful regeneration of chaturvarnya.

17

17.1

Assuming that chaturvarnya is practicable, I contend that it is the most vicious system. That the Brahmins should cultivate knowledge, that the Kshatriya should bear arms, that the Vaishya should trade, and that the Shudra should serve,[100] sounds as though it was a system of division of

100 In AoC 1936, after "serve", it reads "—all this sounds very simple and appears to be perfect. But what does it all come to in practice? It means the pauperisation of the many for the sake of the few. It means the disarming of the many for the sake of the few. It means the deadening and darkening of the lives of the many in order that the few may have life and light. As has been observed, there is no country in the world which has suffered so much as a result of social evils of its own creation as India." Ambedkar drops this passage in AoC 1937, and in its place offers an extended reflection—of 650 words—on the exploitative and illogical nature of the chaturvarnya system. This appears to be triggered by Gandhi's response to this speech-essay in *Harijan*, where he upholds the fourfold varnashrama dharma but denounces the proliferation of castes. In this edition, this new material appears from this point in 17.1 till the close of 17.4.

labour. Whether the theory was intended to state that the Shudra need not, or whether it was intended to lay down that he must not, is an interesting question. The defenders of chaturvarnya give it the first meaning. They say, why need the Shudra trouble to acquire wealth, when the three higher varnas are there to support him? Why need the Shudra bother to take to education, when there is the Brahmin to whom he can go when the occasion for reading or writing arises? Why need the Shudra worry to arm himself, when there is the Kshatriya to protect him? The theory of chaturvarnya, understood in this sense, may be said to look upon the Shudra as the ward and the three higher varnas as his guardians. Thus interpreted, it is a simple, elevating, and alluring theory.

17.2

Assuming this to be the correct view of the underlying conception of chaturvarnya, it seems to me that the system is neither foolproof nor knave-proof. What is to happen if the Brahmins, Vaishyas, and Kshatriyas fail to pursue knowledge, to engage in economic enterprise, and to be efficient soldiers, which are their respective functions? Contrary-wise, suppose that they discharge their functions, but flout their duty to the Shudra or to one another; what is to happen to the Shudra if the three classes refuse to support him on fair terms, or combine to keep him down? Who is to safeguard the interests of the Shudra—or for that matter, those of the Vaishya and Kshatriya—when the person who is trying to take advantage of his ignorance is the Brahmin? Who is to defend the liberty of the Shudra—and for that matter, of the Brahmin and the Vaishya—when the person who is robbing him of it is the Kshatriya?

17.3

Interdependence of one class on another class is inevitable. Even dependence of one class upon another may sometimes become allowable. But why make one person depend upon another in the matter of his vital needs? Education, everyone must have. Means of defence, everyone must have. These are the paramount requirements of every man for his self-preservation. How can the fact that his neighbour is educated and armed help a man who is uneducated and disarmed? The whole theory is absurd. These are the questions which the defenders of chaturvarnya do not seem to be troubled about. But they are very pertinent questions. Assuming that in their conception of chaturvarnya the relationship between the different classes is that of ward and guardian, and that this is the real conception underlying chaturvarnya, it must be admitted that it makes no provision to safeguard the interests of the ward from the misdeeds of the guardian.

17.4

Whether or not the relationship of guardian and ward was the real underlying conception on which chaturvarnya was based, there is no doubt that in practice the relation was that of master and servants. The three classes, Brahmins, Kshatriyas and Vaishyas, although not very happy in their mutual relationship, managed to work by compromise. The Brahmin flattered the Kshatriya, and both let the Vaishya live in order to be able to live upon him. But the three agreed to beat down the Shudra. He was not allowed to acquire wealth, lest he should be independent of the three varnas. He was prohibited from acquiring knowledge, lest he should keep a steady vigil regarding his interests. He was prohibited from bearing arms, lest he should have the means to rebel against their authority. That this is how the Shudras were treated by the *tryavarnikas*[101] is evidenced by the laws of Manu. There is no code of laws more infamous regarding social rights than

101 Tryavarnikas: Sanskrit for 'three varnas'; refers to the dwija, 'twice-born', varnas.

the laws of Manu. Any instance from anywhere of social injustice must pale before it.

17.5

Why have the mass of people tolerated the social evils to which they have been subjected? There have been social revolutions in other countries of the world. Why have there not been social revolutions in India, is a question which has incessantly troubled me. There is only one answer which I can give, and it is that the lower classes of Hindus[102] have been completely disabled for direct action[103] on account of this wretched

102 Highlighted words read in AoC 1936 as "similar" (for *social*), "occurred to" (*troubled*), "have been able to" (*can*), and "masses" (*lower classes*) respectively.

103 'Direct action' is a method Ambedkar (BASWS 5, 375) advocated for the assertion of the civil rights of Untouchables. When Ambedkar was at Columbia University (1913–16), he was likely exposed to the views of American feminist anarchist Voltairine de Cleyre (1866–1912), whom the anarchist Emma Goldman called the "most gifted and brilliant anarchist woman America ever produced". In 1912, de Cleyre wrote a famous essay called "Direct Action", which she defined as collective action against and mass resistance to state and capitalist oppression. "Every person who ever had a plan to do anything, and went and did it, or who laid his plan before others, and won their cooperation to do it with him, without going to external authorities to please do the thing for them, was a direct actionist... Every person who ever in his life had a difference with anyone to settle, and went straight to the other persons involved to settle it, either by a peaceable plan or otherwise, was a direct actionist." The term was also popularised by the Industrial Workers of the World founded in 1905 in Chicago; its mouthpiece was called *Direct Action*. On his part, Ambedkar called for "open revolt in the form of direct action against the Hindu Established Order". He lists the Chavadar Tank satyagraha in Mahad and the Kalaram temple satyagraha as instances of direct action which created a 'crisis' among Hindus. Ambedkar contrasts this method with that of Gandhi's Harijan Sevak Sangh that believed caste Hindus must feel remorse and guilt (for practising untouchability) and thus voluntarily ask the Untouchables to participate in the general village life, that is, accessing waterbodies, roads or temples. Ambedkar here cites his letter to A.V. Thakkar, general secretary of the Harijan Sevak Sangh: "The salvation of the Depressed Classes will come only when the Caste Hindu is made to think and is forced to feel that he must alter his ways. For that you must create a crisis by direct action against his customary code of conduct. The crisis will compel him to think and once he begins to think he will be more ready to change than he is otherwise likely to be. The great defect in the policy of least resistance and silent infiltration of rational ideas lies in that they do not 'compel', for they do not produce a crisis. The direct action in respect of the Chavadar Tank in Mahad 1927, the Kalaram temple in Nasik 1930 and the Guruvayur temple in Malabar

caste system.[104] They could not bear arms, and without arms they could not rebel. They were all ploughmen—or rather, condemned to be ploughmen—and they never were allowed to convert their ploughshares into swords. They had no bayonets, and therefore everyone who chose, could and did sit upon them. On account of the caste system, they could receive no education. They could not think out or know the way to their salvation. They were condemned to be lowly; and not knowing the way of escape, and not having the means of escape, they became reconciled to eternal servitude,[105] which they accepted as their inescapable fate.

17.6[106]

It is true that even in Europe the strong have not shrunk from the exploitation—nay, the spoliation—of the weak. But in Europe, the strong have never contrived to make the weak helpless against exploitation so shamelessly as was the case in India among the Hindus. Social war has been raging between the strong and the weak far more violently in Europe than it has ever been in India. Yet the weak in Europe has had in his freedom of military service, his physical weapon; in suffering, his political weapon; and in education, his moral weapon. These three weapons for emancipation were never withheld by

---

1931–32 have done in a few days what million days of preaching by reformers would never have done." In the 1920s, Ambedkar did invest a little faith in the Gandhian satyagraha method; as noted in Roy's introduction (p.107), Gandhi's portrait was displayed during the December leg of the Mahad satyagraha in 1927. Muhammad Ali Jinnah, founder of the All-India Muslim League, also called for 'direct action' in 1946 if the Muslims were not granted Pakistan. For a discussion of Jinnah's lack of clarity on what he meant by direct action, see Ayesha Jalal (1985, 211–3).

104 In AoC 1936, it is the "wretched system of chaturvarnya". Ambedkar in the next few passages of Section 17 consistently replaces references to chaturvarnya with "caste system"—all these instances are highlighted with semibold text.

105 In AoC 1936, this sentence ends with "the fate of eternal servitude".

106 This paragraph does not appear in AoC 1936.

the strong from the weak in Europe. All these weapons were, however, denied to the masses in India by the caste system.

17.7

There cannot be a more degrading system of social organisation than the caste system. It is the system which deadens, paralyses, and cripples the people, from helpful activity. This is no exaggeration. History bears ample evidence. There is only one period in Indian history which is a period of freedom, greatness and glory. That is the period of the Maurya empire.[107] At all other times the country suffered from defeat and darkness. But the Maurya period was a period when the caste system was completely annihilated—when the Shudras, who constituted the mass of the people, came into their own and became the rulers of the country. The period of defeat and darkness is the period when the caste system flourished, to the damnation of the greater part of the people of the country.

18

18.1

Chaturvarnya is not new. It is as old as the Vedas. That is one of the reasons why we are asked by the Arya Samajists

---

107 The Mauryan empire lasted from 322 BCE to 185 BCE and reached its zenith under Ashoka, who, after securing the empire and extending its borders, embraced Buddhism and spread it through the territories under his control. He even sent ambassadors across Asia to spread the faith. Ambedkar (BAWS 3, 268) considered this Buddhist phase a 'revolution' in ancient India, and termed the re-emergence of Brahminism under the Brahmin king Pushyamitra Sunga (185–149 BCE) the 'counter-revolution': "The Brahmins had not only lost state patronage but they lost their occupation which mainly consisted of performing sacrifices for a fee which oftentimes was very substantial and which constituted their chief source of living. The Brahmins therefore lived as the suppressed and Depressed Classes for nearly 140 years during which the Maurya Empire lasted. A rebellion against the Buddhist state was the only way of escape left to the suffering Brahmins and there is special reason why Pushyamitra should raise the banner of revolt against the rule of the Mauryas."

to consider its claims. Judging from the past, as a system of social organisation it has been tried, and it has failed. How many times have the Brahmins annihilated the seed of the Kshatriyas! How many times have the Kshatriyas annihilated the Brahmins! The Mahabharata and the Puranas are full of incidents of the strife between the Brahmins and the Kshatriyas. They even quarrelled over such petty questions as to who should salute first, as to who should give way first, the Brahmins or the Kshatriyas, when the two met in the street.[108]

18.2

Not only was the Brahmin an eyesore to the Kshatriya and the Kshatriya an eyesore to the Brahmin, it seems that the Kshatriyas had become tyrannical, and the masses, disarmed as they were under the system of chaturvarnya, were praying to almighty god for relief from their tyranny. The Bhagwat[109] tells us very definitely that Krishna had taken avatar for one sacred purpose: and that was, to annihilate the Kshatriyas. With these instances of rivalry and enmity between the different varnas before us, I do not understand how anyone

---

108 Ambedkar discusses the many conflicts between Brahmins and Kshatriyas at length elsewhere (BAWS 3, 392–415). Here, he is alluding to the mythical Brahmin warrior Parashurama's twenty-one wars of extermination against the Kshatriyas after Parashurama's father is killed by a Kshatriya and he sees his mother beating her chest twenty-one times. Mythical and legendary narratives asserting the authority of the Brahmins were in conflict with each other as Brahmin sub-castes tried to establish superiority over one another through competitive myth-making. See Figueira (2002). For a typical example of a legalistic inter-Brahmin conflict in modern India, see Notes 56–7 at 7.2. See Johnson (2005) for an account of how many of these factors played out in Bombay province in the formative years of Indian nationalism. The reference to "who should salute first, as to who should give way first" pertains to the Brahmin–Kayastha conflict (see Note 60 to 7.4).

109 The Bhagwat is the *Bhagvad Gita*. For a detailed discussion of the *Bhagvad Gita* by Ambedkar, see "Krishna and His Gita" (BAWS 3). On how, for Ambedkar, the *Bhagvad Gita* is neither a book of religion nor a treatise on philosophy, see Pandit (1992). See also Kumar (2010) on "Ambedkar's attempt to retrieve a counterhistory of Indian antiquity".

can hold out chaturvarnya as an ideal to be aimed at,[110] or as a pattern on which Hindu society should be remodelled.

19

19.1

I have dealt with those who are without you and whose hostility to your ideal is quite open. There appear to be others who are neither without you nor with you. I was hesitating whether I should deal with their point of view. But on further consideration I have come to the conclusion that I must, and that for two reasons. Firstly, their attitude to the problem of caste is not merely an attitude of neutrality, but is an attitude of armed neutrality.[111] Secondly, they probably represent a considerable body of people. Of these, there is one set which finds nothing peculiar or odious in the caste system of the Hindus. Such Hindus cite the case of Muslims, Sikhs and Christians, and find comfort in the fact that they too have castes amongst them.

19.2

In considering this question, you must at the outset bear in mind that nowhere is human society one single whole. It is always plural. In the world of action, the individual is one limit and society the other. Between them lie all sorts of associative arrangements of lesser and larger scope—families, friendships, cooperative associations, business combines, political parties, bands of thieves and robbers. These small groups are usually firmly welded together, and are often as exclusive as castes. They have a narrow and intensive code, which is often anti-social. This is true of every society, in Europe as well as

110 "To be copied" in AoC 1936.

111 This is a war and diplomacy term. "One speaks of an armed neutrality when a neutral State takes military measures for the purpose of defending its neutrality against possible or probable attempts of either belligerent [sic] to make use of the neutral territory" (Oppenheim 1905, 353).

in Asia. The question to be asked in determining whether a given society is an ideal society is not whether there are groups in it, because groups exist in all societies.

19.3

The questions to be asked in determining what is an ideal society are: How numerous and varied are the interests which are consciously shared by the groups? How full and free is the interplay with other forms of associations? Are the forces that separate groups and classes more numerous than the forces that unite them? What social significance is attached to this group life? Is its exclusiveness a matter of custom and convenience, or is it a matter of religion? It is in the light of these questions that one must decide whether caste among non-Hindus is the same as caste among Hindus.[112]

19.4

If we apply these considerations to castes among Mahomedans, Sikhs and Christians on the one hand, and to castes among Hindus on the other, you will find that caste among non-Hindus is fundamentally different from caste among Hindus. First, the ties which consciously make the Hindus hold together are non-existent, while among non-Hindus there are many that hold them together. The strength of a society depends upon the presence of points of contact, possibilities

112 Ambedkar, once again, is drawing on his mentor John Dewey whom he mentions and acknowledges later in the essay. Discussing the "need of a measure for the worth of any given mode of social life", Dewey writes (1916, ch. 7): "How numerous and varied are the interests which are consciously shared? How full and free is the interplay with other forms of association? If we apply these considerations to, say, a criminal band, we find that the ties which consciously hold the members together are few in number, reducible almost to a common interest in plunder; and that they are of such a nature as to isolate the group from other groups with respect to give and take of the values of life." See also Lenart Škof (2011) who maps the influence of Dewey's pragmatism on Ambedkar's political philosophy, tracks his debt to not just Dewey but also to British idealist and liberal T.H. Green (1836–82), and connects this to the work of contemporary Brazilian philosopher and social theorist Roberto Mangabeira Unger, who taught Barack Obama at Harvard.

of interaction, between different groups which exist in it. These are what Carlyle calls "organic filaments"—i.e., the elastic threads which help to bring the disintegrating elements together and to reunite them.[113] There is no integrating force among the Hindus to counteract the disintegration caused by caste. While among the non-Hindus there are plenty of these "organic filaments" which bind them together.

19.5

Again it must be borne in mind that although there are castes among non-Hindus, as there are among Hindus, caste has not the same social significance for non-Hindus as it has for Hindus. Ask a Mahomedan or a Sikh who he is. He tells you that he is a Mahomedan or a Sikh, as the case may be. He does not tell you his caste although he has one, and you are satisfied with his answer. When he tells you that he is a Muslim, you do not proceed to ask him whether he is a Shia or a Sunni; Sheikh or Saiyad; Khatik or Pinjari.[114] When he tells you he is a Sikh, you do not ask him whether he is Jat or Roda; Mazbi or

113 Thomas Carlyle (1795–1881) was a pre-eminent figure in Victorian letters. In *History of the French Revolution* (1837), he sympathised with the revolutionaries to an extent but despised anarchy, and appeared to fear the rule of the people. The concept of 'organic filaments' here is borrowed from *Sartor Resartus* (1833–4), a well-disguised autobiography and a critique of utilitarianism and British society, presenting fragments of Carlyle's philosophy in the form of a satire featuring a loose collection of papers written by a fictional German philosopher Diogenes Teufelsdröckh. In the seventh chapter of Book 3, Carlyle describes the world as a phoenix that begins to resurrect itself while dying. The 'organic filaments' are the processes of creation that hold together a world while it is destroying itself.

114 There has been a lot of recent research on caste among Muslims in India. Besides Imtiaz Ahmad (1978), see Ali Anwar's *Masawat ki Jung* [Battle for equality] (2005) and Masood Alam Falahi's *Hindustan mein zaat-paat aur Musalman* [Casteism in India and Muslims] (2007). For a quick overview, see Khalid Anis Ansari (2013) who chronicles the contemporary pasmanda movement: "'Pasmanda', a Persian term meaning 'those who have fallen behind', refers to Muslims belonging to the Shudra (backward) and Ati-Shudra (Dalit) castes. It was adopted as an oppositional identity to that of the dominant ashraf Muslims (forward castes) in 1998 by the Pasmanda Muslim Mahaz, a group which mainly worked in Bihar. Since then, however, the pasmanda discourse has found resonance elsewhere too."

Ramdasi.[115] But you are not satisfied if a person tells you that he is a Hindu. You feel bound to inquire into his caste. Why? Because so essential is caste in the case of a Hindu that without knowing it you do not feel sure what sort of a being he is.

19.6

That caste has not the same social significance among non-Hindus as it has among Hindus is clear, if you take into consideration the consequences which follow breach of caste. There may be castes among Sikhs and Mahomedans, but the Sikhs and the Mahomedans will not outcast a Sikh or a Mahomedan if he broke his caste. Indeed, the very idea of excommunication is foreign to the Sikhs and the Mahomedans. But with the Hindus the case is entirely different. A Hindu is sure to be outcasted if he broke caste. This shows the difference in the social significance of caste to Hindus and non-Hindus. This is the second point of difference.

19.7

But there is also a third and a more important one. Caste among the non-Hindus has no religious consecration; but among the Hindus most decidedly it has. Among the non-Hindus, caste is only a practice, not a sacred institution. They did not originate it. With them it is only a survival mechanism.[116] They do not regard caste as a religious dogma. Religion compels the Hindus to treat isolation and segregation of castes as a virtue. Religion does not compel the non-Hindus to take the same attitude towards caste. If Hindus wish to break caste, their religion will come in their way. But it will not be so in the case of non-Hindus. It is, therefore, a dangerous delusion to take comfort in the mere existence of caste among non-Hindus, without caring

115 On the practice of caste in Sikhism, see Notes 33 and 168 at 2.22 and 26.3.

116 This word does not figure in prior editions, and has been introduced for clarity.

to know what place caste occupies in their life and whether there are other "organic filaments" which subordinate the feeling of caste to the feeling of community. The sooner the Hindus are cured of this delusion, the better.

19.8

The other set denies that caste presents any problem at all for the Hindus to consider. Such Hindus seek comfort in the view that the Hindus have survived, and take this as a proof of their fitness to survive. This point of view is well expressed by Prof S. Radhakrishnan in his *Hindu View of Life*.[117] Referring to Hinduism, he says:

> The civilisation itself has not been a short-lived one. Its historic records date back to over four thousand years and even then it had reached a stage of civilisation which has continued its unbroken, though at times slow and static, course until the present day. It has stood the stress and strain of more than four or five millenniums of spiritual thought and experience. Though peoples of different races and cultures have been pouring into India from the dawn of history, Hinduism has been able to maintain its supremacy and even the proselytising creeds backed by political power have not been able to coerce the large majority of Hindus to their views. The Hindu culture possesses some vitality which seems to be denied to some other more

117 S. Radhakrishnan (1888–1975) was a prolific writer, an apologist of Hinduism, and the second president of independent India. Ambedkar is citing from the book *The Hindu Way of Life* (1927, 12–13), a compilation of the lectures delivered at Oxford in 1926. Later in the work, Radhakrishnan says: "In dealing with the problem of the conflict of the different racial groups, Hinduism adopted the only safe course of democracy, viz., that each racial group should be allowed to develop the best in it without impeding the progress of others. Every historical group is unique and specific and has an ultimate value, and the highest morality requires that we should respect its individuality. Caste, on its racial side, is the affirmation of the infinite diversity of human groups" (97). Furthermore, "Caste was the answer of Hinduism to the forces pressing on it from outside. It was the instrument by which Hinduism civilised the different tribes it took in. Any group of people appearing exclusive in any sense is a caste. Whenever a group represents a type a caste arises" (104). Tellingly, his birth anniversary, 5 September, is celebrated as Teacher's Day in India.

> forceful currents. It is no more necessary to dissect Hinduism than to open a tree to see whether the sap still runs.

The name of Prof Radhakrishnan is big enough to invest with profundity whatever he says, and impress the minds of his readers.[118] But I must not hesitate to speak out my mind. For I fear that his statement may become the basis of a vicious argument that the fact of survival is proof of fitness to survive.

19.9

It seems to me that the question is not whether a community lives or dies; the question is on what plane does it live. There are different modes of survival. But not all are equally honourable. For an individual as well as for a society, there is a gulf between merely living, and living worthily. To fight in a battle and to live in glory is one mode. To beat a retreat, to surrender, and to live the life of a captive is also a mode of survival. It is useless for a Hindu to take comfort in the fact that he and his people have survived. What he must consider is, what is the quality of their survival. If he does that, I am sure he will cease to take pride in the mere fact of survival. A Hindu's life has been a life of continuous defeat, and what appears to him to be life everlasting is not living everlastingly, but is really a life which is perishing everlastingly. It is a mode of survival of which every right-minded Hindu who is not afraid to own up to the truth will feel ashamed.

20

20.1

There is no doubt, in my opinion, that unless you change your social order you can achieve little by way of progress. You cannot mobilise the community either for defence or for offence. You cannot build anything on the foundations of

118 AoC 1936: "impress the minds of many with the profundity of whatever he says."

caste. You cannot build up a nation, you cannot build up a morality. Anything that you will build on the foundations of caste will crack, and will never be a whole.

20.2

The only question that remains to be considered is—How to bring about the reform of the Hindu social order? How to abolish caste?[119] This is a question of supreme importance. There is a view that in the reform of caste, the first step to take is to abolish sub-castes. This view is based upon the supposition that there is a greater similarity in manners and status between sub-castes than there is between castes. I think this is an erroneous supposition. The Brahmins of northern and central India are socially of lower grade, as compared with the Brahmins of the Deccan and southern India. The former are only cooks and water-carriers, while the latter occupy a high social position. On the other hand, in northern India, the Vaishyas and Kayasthas are intellectually and socially on a par with the Brahmins of the Deccan and southern India.

20.3

Again, in the matter of food there is no similarity between the Brahmins of the Deccan and southern India, who are vegetarians, and the Brahmins of Kashmere and Bengal, who are non-vegetarians. On the other hand, the Brahmins of the Deccan and southern India have more in common so far as food is concerned with such non-Brahmins as the Gujaratis, Marwaris, Banias and Jains.

20.4

There is no doubt that from the standpoint of making the transition[120] from one caste to another easy, the fusion of the Kayasthas of northern India and the other non-Brahmins of

---

119 These questions are given in bold in AoC 1936.

120 "Transit" in AoC 1936 and subsequent editions.

southern India with the non-Brahmins of the Deccan and the Dravidian[121] country is more practicable than the fusion of the Brahmins of the south with the Brahmins of the north. But assuming that the fusion of sub-castes is possible, what guarantee is there that the abolition of sub-castes will necessarily lead to the abolition of castes? On the contrary, it may happen that the process may stop with the abolition of sub-castes. In that case, the abolition of sub-castes will only help to strengthen the castes, and make them more powerful and therefore more mischievous. This remedy is therefore neither practicable nor effective, and may easily prove to be a wrong remedy.

20.5

Another plan of action for the abolition of caste is to begin with inter-caste dinners. This also, in my opinion, is an inadequate remedy. There are many castes which allow inter-dining. But it is a common experience that inter-dining has not succeeded in killing the spirit of caste and the consciousness of caste. I am convinced that the real remedy is intermarriage. Fusion of blood can alone create the feeling of being kith and kin, and unless this feeling of kinship, of being kindred, becomes paramount, the separatist feeling—the feeling of being aliens—created by caste will not vanish. Among the Hindus, intermarriage must necessarily be a factor of greater force in social life than it need be in the life of the non-Hindus. Where society is already well knit by other ties, marriage is an ordinary incident of life. But where society is cut asunder, marriage as a binding force becomes a matter of urgent necessity. The real remedy for breaking caste is intermarriage. Nothing else will serve as the solvent of caste.

20.6

Your Jat-Pat Todak Mandal has adopted this line of attack.

121 "Dravid" in all previous editions.

It is a direct and frontal attack, and I congratulate you upon a correct diagnosis, and more upon your having shown the courage to tell the Hindus what is really wrong with them. Political tyranny is nothing compared to social tyranny, and a reformer who defies society is a much more courageous man than a politician who defies the government. You are right in holding that caste will cease to be an operative force only when inter-dining and intermarriage have become matters of common course. You have located the source of the disease.

20.7

But is your prescription the right prescription for the disease? Ask yourselves this question: Why is it that a large majority of Hindus do not inter-dine and do not intermarry? Why is it that your cause is not popular?

20.8

There can be only one answer to this question, and it is that inter-dining and intermarriage are repugnant to the beliefs and dogmas which the Hindus regard as sacred. Caste is not a physical object like a wall of bricks or a line of barbed wire which prevents the Hindus from commingling and which has, therefore, to be pulled down. Caste is a notion; it is a state of mind. The destruction of caste does not therefore mean the destruction of a physical barrier. It means a notional change.

20.9

Caste may be bad. Caste may lead to conduct so gross as to be called man's inhumanity to man. All the same, it must be recognised that the Hindus observe caste not because they are inhuman or wrong-headed. They observe caste because they are deeply religious. People are not wrong in observing caste. In my view, what is wrong is their religion, which has inculcated this notion of caste. If this is correct, then obviously the enemy you must grapple with is not the people who observe caste, but the shastras which teach them this religion of caste. Criticising and ridiculing people for not inter-dining or intermarrying, or occasionally holding inter-caste dinners and celebrating inter-caste marriages, is a futile method of achieving the desired end. The real remedy is to destroy the belief in the sanctity of the shastras.

20.10

How do you expect to succeed if you allow the shastras to continue to mould the beliefs and opinions of the people? Not to question the authority of the shastras—to permit the people to believe in their sanctity and their sanctions, and then to blame the people and to criticise them for their acts as being irrational and inhuman—is an incongruous way of carrying on social reform. Reformers working for the removal of untouchability, including Mahatma Gandhi, do not seem to realise that the acts of the people are merely the results of their beliefs inculcated in their minds by the shastras, and that people will not change their conduct until they cease to believe in the sanctity of the shastras on which their conduct is founded.

20.11

No wonder that such efforts have not produced any results. You also seem to be erring in the same way as the reformers working in the cause of removing untouchability. To agitate for and to organise inter-caste dinners and inter-caste marriages is like forced feeding brought about by artificial means. Make every man and woman free from the thraldom of the shastras, cleanse their minds of the pernicious notions founded on the shastras, and he or she will inter-dine and intermarry, without your telling him or her to do so.

20.12

It is no use seeking refuge in quibbles. It is no use telling people that the shastras do not say what they are believed to say, if they are grammatically read or logically interpreted.

What matters is how the shastras have been understood by the people. You must take the stand that Buddha took. You must take the stand which Guru Nanak took. You must not only discard the shastras, you must deny their authority, as did Buddha and Nanak. You must have courage to tell the Hindus that what is wrong with them is their religion—the religion which has produced in them this notion of the sacredness of caste. Will you show that courage?

21

21.1

What are your chances of success?[122] Social reforms fall into different species. There is a species of reform which does not relate to the religious notions of a people, but is purely secular in character. There is also a species of reform which relates to the religious notions of a people. Of such a species of reform, there are two varieties. In one, the reform accords with the principles of the religion, and merely invites people who have departed from it, to revert to them and to follow them.

21.2

The second is a reform which not only touches the religious principles but is diametrically opposed to those principles, and invites people to depart from and to discard their authority, and to act contrary to those principles. Caste is the natural outcome of certain religious beliefs which have the sanction of the shastras, which are believed to contain the command of divinely inspired sages who were endowed with a supernatural wisdom and whose commands, therefore, cannot be disobeyed without committing a sin.

21.3

The destruction of caste is a reform which falls under the

---

122 This is in bold in AoC 1936.

third category. To ask people to give up caste is to ask them to go contrary to their fundamental religious notions. It is obvious that the first and second species of reform are easy. But the third is a stupendous task, well-nigh impossible. The Hindus hold to the sacredness of the social order. Caste has a divine basis. You must therefore destroy the sacredness and divinity with which caste has become invested. In the last analysis, this means you must destroy the authority of the shastras and the Vedas.

21.4

I have emphasised this question of the ways and means of destroying caste, because I think that knowing the proper ways and means is more important than knowing the ideal. If you do not know the real ways and means, all your shots are sure to be misfired. If my analysis is correct, then your task is Herculean. You alone can say whether you are capable of achieving it.

21.5

Speaking for myself, I see the task to be well-nigh impossible. Perhaps you would like to know why I think so. Out of the many reasons which have led me to take this view, I will mention some which I regard as most important. One of these reasons is the attitude of hostility which the Brahmins have shown towards this question. The Brahmins form the vanguard of the movement for political reform, and in some cases also of economic reform. But they are not to be found even as camp-followers in the army raised to break down the barricades of caste. Is there any hope of the Brahmins ever taking up a lead in the future in this matter? I say no.

21.6

You may ask why. You may argue that there is no reason why Brahmins should continue to shun social reform. You may argue that the Brahmins know that the bane of Hindu society is caste, and as an enlightened class they could not be expected to be indifferent to its consequences. You may argue that there are secular Brahmins and priestly Brahmins,[123] and if the latter do not take up the cudgels on behalf of those who want to break caste, the former will.

21.7

All this of course sounds very plausible. But in all this it is forgotten that the break-up of the caste system is bound to adversely affect the Brahmin caste. Having regard to this, is it reasonable to expect that the Brahmins will ever consent to lead a movement, the ultimate result of which is to destroy the power and prestige of the Brahmin caste? Is it reasonable to expect the secular Brahmins to take part in a movement directed against the priestly Brahmins? In my judgement, it is useless to make a distinction between the secular Brahmins and priestly Brahmins. Both are kith and kin. They are two arms of the same body, and one is bound to fight for the existence of the other.

123 There has been a conventionally regarded division of labour between the *laukika* Brahmin, the so-called secular Brahmin, and the *shrotriya* or *vaidika* Brahmin, the Brahmin well versed in the Vedas (the *shruti* tradition; from *sru*, to hear, *sro-triya*; the oral tradition). The anthropologist M.N. Srinivas (1972, 8) uses these terms in this sense. The laukika—literally those who concern themselves with this-worldly, temporal (*loka*) matters—is not secular in the Western Enlightenment sense of the term, as in those who disavow belief or are free from religious rules and teachings. The laukika Brahmin—the Brahmin as minister, bureaucrat, civil servant, writer—whom Ambedkar goes on to refer as the intellectual class of the Hindus, pursues a non-priestly career; priestly work is the preserve of the vaidika/shrotriya Brahmins (again, priests who perform only Vedic rites are to be distinguished from priests who officiate in temples, attending to post-Bhakti, post-Vedic gods). However, the laukika Brahmin does not undermine the significance or role of the shrotriya Brahmin. In fact, he deploys and legitimises the services of the shrotriya Brahmin. The laukika Brahmin wields power over this-worldly matters, the shrotriya's domain is other-worldly. All the same, the laukika would even look down upon the shrotriya as lower in the pecking order; someone whose services can be easily bought, for a price. In effect, they are two flanks of Brahminism. For a discussion on the etymology of laukika and vaidika in Sanskrit grammarian Panini's *Ashtadhyayi* (c. 400 BCE), see Patrick Olivelle (2008, 161–3).

21.8

In this connection, I am reminded of some very pregnant remarks made by Prof Dicey in his *English Constitution.*[124] Speaking of the actual limitation on the legislative supremacy of parliament, Dicey says:

> The actual exercise of authority by any sovereign whatever, and notably by Parliament, is bounded or controlled by two limitations. Of these the one is an external, the other is an internal limitation. The external limit to the real power of a sovereign consists in the possibility or certainty that his subjects, or a large number of them, will disobey or resist his laws...
>
> The internal limit to the exercise of sovereignty arises from the nature of the sovereign power itself. Even a despot exercises his powers in accordance with his character, which is itself moulded by the circumstances under which he lives, including under that head the moral feelings of the time and the society to which he belongs. The Sultan could not, if he would, change the religion of the Mahommedan world, but even if he could do so, it is in the very highest degree improbable that the head of Mahommedanism should wish to overthrow the religion of Mahomet; the internal check on the exercise of the Sultan's power is at least as strong as the external limitation. People sometimes ask the idle question, why the Pope does not introduce this or that reform? The true answer is that a revolutionist is not the kind of man who becomes a Pope, and that the man who becomes a Pope has no wish to be a revolutionist.

21.9

I think these remarks apply equally to the Brahmins of India,

124 Albert Venn Dicey (1835–1922) was a British jurist and constitutional theorist who expounded the theory of the 'rule of law' and popularised the term. The quote that follows is from *Introduction to the Study of the Law of the Constitution* (1885, 75–6) which forms a part of the unwritten British Constitution and is therefore also referred to as *English Constitution.*

and one can say with equal truth that if a man who becomes a Pope has no wish to become a revolutionary, a man who is born a Brahmin has much less desire to become a revolutionary. Indeed, to expect a Brahmin to be a revolutionary in matters of social reform is as idle as to expect the British Parliament, as was said by Leslie Stephen,[125] to pass an Act requiring all blue-eyed babies to be murdered.

21.10

Some of you will say that it is a matter of small concern whether the Brahmins come forward to lead the movement against caste or whether they do not. To take this view is, in my judgement, to ignore the part played by the intellectual class in the community. Whether you accept the theory of the great man as the maker of history[126] or whether you do not, this much you will have to concede: that in every country the intellectual class is the most influential class, if not the governing class. The intellectual class is the class which can foresee, it is the class which can advise and give the lead. In no country does the mass of the people live the life of intelligent thought and action. It is largely imitative, and follows the intellectual class.

21.11

There is no exaggeration in saying that the entire destiny of a country depends upon its intellectual class. If the intellectual

125 Leslie Stephen (1832–1904) was a British philosopher, and literary and social critic. A reference to his comments on the prohibition of blue-eyed babies can be found in Dicey (1885, 78) cited above. Dicey is quoting Stephen from the *Science of Ethics* (1882), a work that sums up the ethical consequences of the theory of evolution.

126 Ambedkar is referring to the concept popularised by Carlyle in the nineteenth century: the great man theory. Carlyle's *On Heroes, Hero-Worship and the Heroic in History* (1840) points out the essential role of great men in history, such as Muhammad, Luther, Rousseau, Cromwell and Napoleon among others, as the moving force of history. The main criticism of the great man theory was formulated by Herbert Spencer in *The Study of Sociology* (1873), but Carlyle's theory has occupied the mind of many an influential thinker, for example Leo Tolstoy.

class is honest, independent and disinterested, it can be trusted to take the initiative and give a proper lead when a crisis arises. It is true that intellect by itself is no virtue. It is only a means, and the use of means depends upon the ends which an intellectual person pursues. An intellectual man can be a good man, but he can easily be a rogue. Similarly an intellectual class may be a band of high-souled persons, ready to help, ready to emancipate erring humanity—or it may easily be a gang of crooks, or a body of advocates for a narrow clique from which it draws its support.

21.12

You may think it a pity that the intellectual class in India is simply another name for the Brahmin caste. You may regret that the two are one; that the existence of the intellectual class should be bound up with one single caste; that this intellectual class should share the interest and the aspirations of that Brahmin caste, which has regarded itself as the custodian of the interest of that caste rather than of the interests of the country. All this may be very regrettable. But the fact remains that the Brahmins form the intellectual class of the Hindus. It is not only an intellectual class, but it is a class which is held in great reverence by the rest of the Hindus.

21.13

The Hindus are taught that the Brahmins are *Bhu-devas* (gods on earth). वर्णानाम ब्राह्मणो गुरु:[127] The Hindus are taught that Brahmins alone can be their teachers. Manu says:

> If it be asked how it should be with respect to points of the Dharma which have not been specially mentioned, the answer is, that which Brahmins who are *shishthas*

127 This is the injunction from the *Manusmriti* that Ambedkar cites at the opening of AoC. See Note 1 at 1.2.

propound shall doubtless have legal force.[128]

अनाम्नातेषु धर्मेषु कथं स्यादिति चेद्भवेत् ।
यं शिष्टा ब्राह्मणा ब्रूयुः स धर्मः स्यादशङ्कितः ।। [129]

21.14

When such an intellectual class, which holds the rest of the community in its grip, is opposed to the reform of caste, the chances of success in a movement for the break-up of the caste system appear to me very, very remote.

21.15

The second reason why I say the task is impossible will be clear, if you will bear in mind that the caste system has two aspects. In one of its aspects, it divides men into separate communities. In its second aspect, it places these communities in a graded order one above the other in social status. Each caste takes its pride and its consolation in the fact that in the scale of castes it is above some other caste. As an outward mark of this gradation, there is also a gradation of social and religious rights, technically spoken of as *ashtadhikaras*[130] and

128 Shishthas: Brahmins educated in religious matters.

129 (*Anaamnaateshu dharmeshu katham syaaditi chedbhavet/ yam shishtaa braahmanaa bruuyuh sa dharmah syaadashadgkitah.*) Ambedkar first cites the translation of *Manusmriti* 12.108 from Bühler (1886/2004, 337) and then gives the Sanskrit verse. Bibek Debroy's translation: "If asked about parts of Dharma that have not been stated, without a doubt, what learned/good Brahmins state is Dharma."

130 It is not clear what Ambedkar is referring to as the ashtadhikaras. *Adhikara*, in both Vedic Hinduism and tantra, refers to the religious qualification and eligibility to perform certain rituals. According to James Lochtefeld (2002, 6), "This refers partly to knowing how to perform the ritual, and thus being 'qualified'... More importantly, it refers to having gained the ritual status that entitles one to perform the ritual. This status is usually conferred by some sort of formal initiation ... by one's teacher." Thus we may say Shambuka, the pivotal Shudra in the Ramayana, does not have the adhikara to perform a Vedic rite, and is hence punished. For further discussion of the idea of adhikara, see Wilhelm Halbfass (1990, 67), where he says "*adhikara* assumes such meanings as 'authority,' 'competence,' 'vocation,' but also 'obligation,' and 'responsibility.' It refers to 'governing' functions and

sanskaras.[131] The higher the grade of a caste, the greater the number of these rights; and the lower the grade, the lesser their number.

21.16

Now this gradation, this scaling of castes, makes it impossible to organise a common front against the caste system. If a caste claims the right to inter-dine and intermarry with another caste placed above it, it is frozen the instant it is told[132] by mischief-mongers—and there are many Brahmins amongst such mischief-mongers—that it will have to concede inter-dining and intermarriage with castes below it! All are slaves of the caste system. But all the slaves are not equal in status.[133]

21.17

To excite the proletariat to bring about an economic revolution, Karl Marx told them: "You have nothing to lose except your chains."[134] But the artful way in which the social and religious rights are distributed among the different castes, whereby some have more and some have less, makes the slogan of Karl Marx quite useless[135] to excite the Hindus against the caste system. Castes form a graded system of sovereignties, high and

---

elements not only in nature or society, but also in texts and teachings, where it may indicate a governing rule or dominant theme."

131 *Sanskaras* (also samskaras) is the collective name given to various life-cycle sacrifices and rituals marking the different stages of human life; they are the rites that make people (or things) fit for a purpose (of performing rituals, taking one's rightful place in society), by removing taints and generating good qualities (Michaels, 2005, 74). Hindu Dharmashastras differ on the total number of sanskaras (twelve to eighteen) but sixteen sanskaras are generally agreed upon.

132 The word used in AoC 1936 is "silenced"; amended in 1937 and 1944 to "frozen instantly it is told". Edited here for clarity

133 In AoC 1936, this reads as "do not suffer equally"; amended in 1937.

134 This is the popularised version of one of the sentences from *The Communist Manifesto* (1848): "The proletarians have nothing to lose but their chains. They have a world to win. Working Men of All Countries, Unite!"

135 In AoC 1936: "you cannot use the slogan which Karl Marx used".

low, which are jealous of their status and which know that if a general dissolution came, some of them stand to lose more of their prestige and power than others do.[136] You cannot, therefore, have a general mobilisation of the Hindus (to use a military expression) for an attack on the caste system.

22

22.1

Can you appeal to reason, and ask the Hindus to discard caste as being contrary to reason? That raises the question: Is a Hindu free to follow his reason? Manu has laid down three sanctions to which every Hindu must conform in the matter of his behaviour:

वेदः स्म्रितिः सदाचारः स्वस्य च प्रियमात्मनः ।[137]

22.2

Here there is no place for reason to play its part. A Hindu must follow either Veda, smriti or *sadachar.*[138] He cannot follow anything else.

22.3

In the first place, how are the texts of the Vedas and smritis

---

136 In AoC 1936, this sentence reads: "The Caste System is an *imperium in imperio* and in the general dissolution of Caste, some castes stand to lose more of their prestige and power than other castes." *Imperium in imperio* means a state, power or sovereignty within a state, power or sovereignty.

137 (*Vedah smritih sadachara svasya cha priyamaatmanah.*) Debroy: "For his own self and for those who are loved by him, the Vedas, the Smritis and good conduct…" This is a half of the shloka couplet. The complete shloka, from *Manusmriti* 2.12, is rendered by Bühler as: "The Veda, the sacred tradition, the customs of virtuous men, and one's own pleasure, they declare to be visibly the fourfold means of defining the sacred law" (1886/2004, 19). The second line in Sanskrit reads as: एतज्ञचतुर्विधं प्राहुः साक्षाद्धर्मस्य लक्षणाम् II (*Etajna-chaturvidham praahu saakshadharmasya lakshanaam.*)

138 Sadachar: Sanskrit for ethics or right behaviour, what Doniger and Smith render as "the conduct of good people". Ambedkar gives his explication in 22.14–15 of AoC.

to be interpreted whenever any doubt arises regarding their meaning? On this important question the view of Manu is quite definite. He says:

योऽवमन्येत ते मूले हेतुशास्त्राश्रयाद्द्विजः ।
स साधुभिर्बहिष्कार्यो नास्तिको वेदनिन्दकः ।।[139]

22.4[140]

According to this rule, rationalism as a canon of interpreting the Vedas and smritis is absolutely condemned. It is regarded to be as wicked as atheism, and the punishment provided for it is excommunication. Thus, where a matter is covered by the Veda or the smriti, a Hindu cannot resort to rational thinking.

22.5

Even when there is a conflict between Vedas and smritis on matters on which they have given a positive injunction, the solution is not left to reason. When there is a conflict between two shrutis, both are to be regarded as of equal authority. Either of them may be followed. No attempt[141] is to be made to find out which of the two accords with reason. This is made clear by Manu:

---

139 (*Yo-avamanyeta tey muule hetushaastraashrayaatdvijah/ sa saadhubhirbahish-kaaryo naastiko vedanindakah.*) *Manusmriti* 2.11. Debroy's translation: "Every dwija [it can be rendered as either Brahmin or belonging to the first three varnas] who depends on texts of logic and ignores these two sources [the earlier shloka mentions] must be banished by virtuous people, as a person who is a non-believer and as one who criticises the Vedas." Bühler's edition renders this as: "Every twice-born man, who, relying on the Institutes of dialectics, treats with contempt those two sources (of the law), must be cast out by the virtuous, as an atheist and a scorner of the Veda" (1886/2004, 19).

140 At this point, in both AoC 1936 and 1937, Ambedkar introduces a verse from the Mahabharata, which in the 1944 edition he places later; see 22.7 in this edition: "The same rule is laid down in the Mahabharata:

पुराणं मानवो धर्मः सांगो वेदश्चिकित्सितं ।
आज्ञासिद्धानि चत्वारि न हन्तव्यानि हेतुभिः ।।"

141 In AoC 1936, the two sentences are conjoined with a "but", to read: "Either of them may be followed but no attempt…" In 1937 and 1944, the "but" is removed.

श्रुतिद्वैधं तु यत्र स्यात्तत्र धर्मावुभौ स्मृतौ ।[142]

When there is a conflict between shruti and smriti, the shruti must prevail. But here too no attempt must be made to find out which of the two accords with reason. This is laid down by Manu in the following shloka:

या वेदवावाह्याः स्मृतयो याश्च काश्च कुद्दष्टयः ।
सर्वास्ता निष्फलाः प्रेत्य तमोनिष्ठा हि ताः स्मृताः ।।[143]

22.6

Again, when there is a conflict between two smritis, the *Manusmriti* must prevail, but no attempt is to be made to find out which of the two accords with reason. This is the ruling given by Brihaspati:[144]

वेद।र्थत्वोपनिबंधूत्बात प्रामाण्यं हि मनोः स्म्रितं ।
मन्वर्थविपरीता तु या स्मृतिः सा न शस्यते ।।[145]

---

142 (*Shrutidvaidham tu yatra syaattatra dharmaavubhau smritau.*) This is the first line of *Manusmriti* 2.14. Debroy's translation: "When there are two shruti texts that conflict, both are said to be Dharma." Bühler: "But when two sacred texts (shruti) are conflicting, both are held to be law; for both are pronounced by the wise (to be) valid law" (1886/2004, 20). Ambedkar paraphrases the verse after citing it.

143 (*Yaa vedavaahyaah smrutayo yaashcha kaashcha kudrishtayah/ Smritisarvaastaa nishphalaah pretya tamonishthaa hi tah smritaah.*) *Manusmriti* 12.95. Debroy: "All the smriti and other texts which are based on wicked doctrines and are outside the Vedas, lead to no fruits after death. It is said that they are based on darkness." Bühler renders this as: "All those traditions (smriti) and those despicable systems of philosophy, which are not based on the Veda, produce no reward after death; for they are declared to be founded on Darkness" (1886/2004, 335).

144 Brihaspati was a Brahmin law-giver of the sixth or seventh century CE. Brihaspati's major work, the *Brihaspati Smriti*, survives only in fragments. It has been published in *The Minor Lawbooks* (1889), translated by Julius Jolly. Brihaspati is considered the first Hindu law-giver to separate civil law from criminal law, and his views concerning women's rights are considered liberal. Nonetheless, he confers the death sentence on a man who has a sexual relationship with a 'high'-caste woman, while merely assigning fines for men who have a sexual relationship with a woman of equal or of 'lower' caste. Consent (or the absence of it) on the woman's part does not alter the severity of the punishment. See G.S. Ghurye (1969, 245).

145 (*Vedaarthatvopanibandhutbaat praamaanyam hi manoh smritam/ Manvartha-vipareeta tu yaa smrutih saa na shasyatey.*) Debroy: "In the first line of this verse there seems to be a typographic error. The first line should actually read

22.7

It is therefore clear that in any matter on which the shrutis and smritis have given a positive direction, a Hindu is not free to use his reasoning faculty. The same rule is laid down in the Mahabharata:

पुराणं मानवो धर्मः सांगो वेदश्चिकित्सितं ।
आज्ञासिद्धानि चत्वारि न हन्तव्यानि हेतुभिः ।।[146]

22.8

He must abide by their directions. Caste and varna are matters which are dealt with by the Vedas and the smritis, and consequently, appeal to reason can have no effect on a Hindu.

22.9

So far as caste and varna are concerned, not only the shastras do not permit the Hindu to use his reason in the decision of the question, but they have taken care to see that no occasion is left to examine in a rational way the foundations of his belief in caste and varna. It must be a source of silent amusement to many a non-Hindu to find hundreds and thousands of Hindus

---

वेदार्थोपनिबद्धत्वात् प्राधान्यं तु मनोः स्मृतं। (*Vedaarthopanibaddhatvaat praadhaanyam tu manoh smrutam.*) This is from the Vyavahara-kanda of *Brihaspati Smriti*. However, it is not from the main text; it is tagged on at the end of Vyavahara-kanda, chapter 1. The shloka therefore does not have a number." Debroy's translation: "But, for determining the boundaries of the meaning of the Vedas, Manu's smriti is pre-eminent. Any smriti that is contrary to Manu should not be taught/praised."

146 (*Puraanam maanavo dharmah saango vedashchikitsitam/ Aajnaasiddhaani chatvaari na hantavyaani hetubhih.*) Debroy: "This verse does not exist in the complete Critical Edition of the Mahabharata (Bhandarkar Oriental Research Institute, launched in 1966, ten years after Ambedkar's demise). Bhandarkar has it listed as 14.98–72 in the rejected texts, but there it occurs as the following, with a minor variation in the first word. That is, it is in Ashvamedhika parva, which does not figure in the Critical Edition:

भारतं मानवो धर्मो वेदाः साङ्गाश्चिकित्सितम्।
आज्ञासिद्धानि चत्वारि न हन्तव्यानि हेतुभिः।।

(*Bhaaratam maanavo dharmo vedaah saadgaashchikitsitam/ Aajnaasiddhaani chatvaari na hantavyaani hetubhih.*) A translation of the version Ambedkar uses: 'The Puranas, Manu's dharma, the Vedas and their limbs, and medicine—these four are in the nature of commandments. Under no circumstances must they be killed/destroyed.'"

breaking caste on certain occasions, such as railway journeys and foreign travel, and yet endeavouring to maintain caste for the rest of their lives!

22.10

The explanation of this phenomenon discloses another fetter on the reasoning faculties of the Hindus. Man's life is generally habitual and unreflective. Reflective thought—in the sense of active, persistent, and careful consideration of any belief or supposed form of knowledge, in the light of the grounds that support it and the further conclusions to which it tends—is quite rare, and arises only in a situation which presents a dilemma or a crisis. Railway journeys and foreign travels are really occasions of crisis in the life of a Hindu, and it is natural to expect a Hindu to ask himself why he should maintain caste at all, if he cannot maintain it at all times. But he does not. He breaks caste at one step, and proceeds to observe it at the next, without raising any question.[147]

22.11

The reason for this astonishing conduct is to be found in the rule of the shastras, which directs him to maintain caste as far as possible and to undergo *prayaschitta*[148] when he cannot. By this theory of prayaschitta, the shastras, by following a spirit of compromise, have given caste a perpetual lease on life, and have smothered the reflective thought which would have otherwise led to the destruction of the notion of caste.[149]

---

147 Refer to the experiences of W.C. Bonnerjee discussed in Note 10 to AoC 2.6 as illustrative of Ambedkar's point.

148 Prayaschitta: Sanskrit for the purification rituals undertaken in penance after breaking caste taboos. It has also been variously understood as a combination of atonement, expiation and repentance. The Dharmashastras discuss prayaschitta (expiation) along with *achara* (ritual) and *vyavahara* (jurisprudence) as aspects of Hindu law.

149 The Slovenian Marxist philosopher Slavoj Žižek says of the *Manusmriti* and the caste system that such a system can be sustained "only by a complex panoply of tricks,

22.12

There have been many who have worked in the cause of the abolition of caste and untouchability. Of those who can be mentioned, Ramanuja,[150] Kabir,[151] and others stand out prominently. Can you appeal to the acts of these reformers and exhort the Hindus to follow them?

22.13

It is true that Manu has included सदाचार (sadachar) as one of the sanctions along with shruti and smriti. Indeed, sadachar

---

displacements and compromises whose basic formula is that of universality with exceptions: in principle yes, but … *The Laws of Manu* demonstrates a breath-taking ingenuity in accomplishing this task." Žižek believes that the true regulating power of the law does not reside in its "direct prohibitions, in the division of our acts into permitted and prohibited, but in regulating the very violations of prohibitions: the law silently accepts that the basic prohibitions are violated (or even discreetly solicits us to violate them), and then, it tells us how to reconcile the violation with the law by way of violating the prohibition in a regulated way." Cited in S. Anand (2010). Ambedkar deals with this aspect later in his discussion of *Annihilation of Caste* with Gandhi featured in "A Reply to the Mahatma" (11.5), where he talks of how a Brahmin can remain a Brahmin irrespective of what he does: "The number of Brahmins who sell shoes is far greater than those who practise priesthood. Not only have the Brahmins given up their ancestral calling of priesthood for trading, but they have entered trades which are prohibited to them by the shastras. Yet how many Brahmins who break caste every day will preach against caste and against the shastras?" Wendy Doniger, in the introduction to her translation of the *Manusmriti* (Doniger and Smith, 1991, liv), talks of how it was "law in extremity", where every stringent rule has an exception that almost contradicts the rule; an emergency—*apad*—escape clause. "The concept of apad recognises human fallibility: don't do this, says Manu, but if you do, this is what to do to fix it."

150 Ramanuja, or Ramanujacharya, was a twelfth-century Brahmin philosopher, a proponent of the Vishishtadvaita, or qualified monism, school of thought. Coming as he did after the monotheistic Tamil Bhakti movements of the Saivite Nayanmars and Vaishnavite Alwars (sixth to eighth centuries), Ramanuja gave primacy to Bhakti or worship of a personal god. In his commentary of the *Brahma Sutra* he declares the Shudra to be equally fit for studying the Vedas as the Brahmin and is said to have adopted a non-Brahmin as a guru. See Bartley (2002).

151 Kabir was a fifteenth-century radical saint-poet who was born a weaver; the thousands of songs/poems attributed to him question the caste system, declare equality in the eyes of god and promote Bhakti. See Hess and Singh (2002), and Hess (2009) for translations of Kabir. See www.kabirproject.org, curated by Shabnam Virmani, for an audio and video documentation of various Kabir traditions across the subcontinent.

has been given a higher place than shastras:

यद्यदाचर्यते येन धर्म्यं वा ऽधर्म्यमेव वा ।
देशस्याचरणं नित्यं चरित्रं तद्धिकीर्तितम् ॥[152]

22.14

According to this, sadachar, whether it is धर्म्य or अधर्म्य,[153] in accordance with shastras or contrary to shastras, must be followed. But what is the meaning of sadachar? If anyone were to suppose that sadachar means right or good acts—i.e., acts of good and righteous men—he would find himself greatly mistaken. Sadachar does not mean good acts or acts of good men. It means ancient custom, good or bad. The following verse makes this clear:

यस्मिन देशे य आचारः पारंपर्यक्रमागत ।
वर्णानां किल सर्वेषां स सदाचार उच्यते ॥[154]

22.15

As though to warn people against the view that sadachar means good acts or acts of good men, and fearing that people

---

152 (*Yadhyaddaacharyate yena dharmyam vaa-adharmyameva vaa/ Deshasyaacharanam nityam charitram taddhikiirtitam.*) Debroy says this verse has not been traceable since it does not say anything important enough for it to be cited or reproduced. Translation: "Whatever is followed in a country, be it dharma or be it adharma, that must always be observed and applauded."

153 *Dharmya* or *adharmya*. These terms broadly mean lawful/sacred and unlawful. According to the Kautilya's *Arthashastra*, there are eight types of marriage, of which four are accorded dharmya status and the other four adharmya (1992, 394–5). For Ambedkar's discussion of these marriages, see "Riddle No. 19: The Change from Paternity to Maternity—What did the Brahmins Wish to Gain by it?" in Sharmila Rege (2013, 169–76).

154 (*Yasmin deshe ya acharah paramparya-kramaagata / Varnanaam kila sarveshaam sa sadaachara uchyatey.*) This almost echoes the previous verse Ambedkar cites. Debroy: "Whatever has been practised in whichever country, deriving from tradition, for all the varnas, is certainly said to be good conduct." This corresponds to Bühler's *Manusmriti* 2:18: "The custom handed down in regular succession (since time immemorial) among the (four chief) castes (varna) and the mixed (races) of that country, is called the conduct of virtuous men" (1886/2004, 20). However, the Sanskrit original does not use वर्णानां किल सर्वेषां (*Varnanam kila sarvesham*) but वर्णानां सान्तरालानाम् (*Varnanam saantaraalaanaam*).

might understand it that way and follow the acts of good men, the smritis have commanded the Hindus in unmistakable terms not to follow even gods in their good deeds, if they are contrary to shruti, smriti and sadachar. This may sound to be most extraordinary, most perverse, but the fact remains that न देवचरितमं चरेत्[155] is an injunction issued to the Hindus by their shastras.

22.16

Reason and morality are the two most powerful weapons in the armoury of a reformer. To deprive him of the use of these weapons is to disable him for action. How are you going to break up caste, if people are not free to consider whether it accords with reason? How are you going to break up caste, if people are not free to consider whether it accords with morality? The wall built around caste is impregnable, and the material of which it is built contains none of the combustible stuff of reason and morality. Add to this the fact that inside this wall stands the army of Brahmins who form the intellectual class, Brahmins who are the natural leaders of the Hindus, Brahmins who are there not as mere mercenary soldiers but as an army fighting for its homeland, and you will get an idea why I think that the breaking up of caste among the Hindus is well-nigh impossible. At any rate, it would take ages before a breach is made.

22.17

But whether the doing of the deed takes time or whether it can be done quickly, you must not forget that if you wish to bring about a breach in the system, then you have got to apply the dynamite to the Vedas and the shastras, which deny any part to reason; to the Vedas and shastras, which deny

155 (*Na deva charitamam charet.*) Debroy: "One should not follow the conduct of the gods."

any part to morality. You must destroy the religion of the shrutis and the smritis. Nothing else will avail. This is my considered view of the matter.

23

23.1

Some may not understand what I mean by destruction of religion, some may find the idea revolting to them, and some may find it revolutionary. Let me therefore explain my position. I do not know whether you draw a distinction between principles and rules. But I do. Not only do I make a distinction, but I say that this distinction is real and important. Rules are practical; they are habitual ways of doing things according to prescription. But principles are intellectual; they are useful methods of judging things. Rules seek to tell an agent just what course of action to pursue. Principles do not prescribe a specific course of action. Rules, like cooking recipes, do tell just what to do and how to do it. A principle, such as that of justice, supplies a main heading by reference to which he is to consider the bearings of his desires and purposes; it guides him in his thinking by suggesting to him the important consideration which he should bear in mind.

23.2

This difference between rules and principles makes the acts done in pursuit of them different in quality and in content.[156]

156 Once again, Ambedkar seems to be alluding to his mentor Dewey (1922, 239), who writes: "As habits set in grooves dominate activity and swerve it from conditions instead of increasing its adaptability, so principles treated as fixed rules instead of as helpful methods take men away from experience. The more complicated the situation, and the less we really know about it, the more insistent is the orthodox type of moral theory upon the prior existence of some fixed and universal principle or law which is to be directly applied and followed." There is a certain tension here between Dewey's words—who seems critical of rigid application of principles—and those of Ambedkar, who advocates sound principles as the only possible foundation for morality.

Doing what is said to be good by virtue of a rule and doing good in the light of a principle are two different things. The principle may be wrong, but the act is conscious and responsible. The rule may be right, but the act is mechanical. A religious act may not be a correct act, but must at least be a responsible act. To permit of this responsibility, religion must mainly be a matter of principles only. It cannot be a matter of rules. The moment it degenerates into rules it ceases to be religion, as it kills the responsibility which is the essence of a truly religious act.

23.3

What is this Hindu religion? Is it a set of principles, or is it a code of rules? Now the Hindu religion, as contained in the Vedas and the smritis, is nothing but a mass of sacrificial, social, political, and sanitary rules and regulations, all mixed up. What is called religion by the Hindus is nothing but a multitude of commands and prohibitions. Religion, in the sense of spiritual principles, truly universal, applicable to all races, to all countries, to all times, is not to be found in them; and if it is, it does not form the governing part of a Hindu's life. That for a Hindu dharma means commands and prohibitions is clear from the way the word dharma is used in the Vedas and the smritis and understood by the commentators. The word dharma as used in the Vedas in most cases means religious ordinances or rites. Even Jaimini in his *Purva Mimamsa*[157] defines dharma as "a desirable goal or

157 Jaimini's *Purva Mimamsa Sutras*, dated sometime between the second century BCE and second century CE, is the first text in the Mimamsa school of philosophy, a school of exegesis concerned with the understanding of Vedic ritual injunctions. (Orthodox Hinduism has six schools of philosophy: Nyaya, Vaiseshika, Samkhya, Yoga, Mimamsa and Vedanta.) The *Purva Mimamsa Sutras* consists of a systematically ordered collection of approximately 2,745 short statements, also referred to individually as sutra. Ambedkar here is referring to sutra 1.1.2. For an account of the various explanations which have been offered for the terms 'Purva

result that is indicated by injunctive (Vedic) passages".

23.4

To put it in plain language, what the Hindus call religion is really law, or at best legalised class-ethics. Frankly, I refuse to call this code of ordinances as religion. The first evil of such a code of ordinances, misrepresented to the people as religion, is that it tends to deprive moral life of freedom and spontaneity, and to reduce it (for the conscientious, at any rate) to a more or less anxious and servile conformity to externally imposed rules. Under it, there is no loyalty to ideals; there is only conformity to commands.

23.5

But the worst evil of this code of ordinances is that the laws it contains must be the same yesterday, today and forever. They are iniquitous in that they are not the same for one class as for another. But this iniquity is made perpetual in that they are prescribed to be the same for all generations. The objectionable part of such a scheme is not that they are made by certain persons called prophets or law-givers. The objectionable part is that this code has been invested with the character of finality and fixity. Happiness notoriously varies with the conditions and circumstances of a person, as well as with the conditions of different people and epochs. That being the case, how can humanity endure this code of eternal laws, without being cramped and without being crippled?

23.6

I have, therefore, no hesitation in saying that such a religion must be destroyed, and I say there is nothing irreligious in working for the destruction of such a religion. Indeed I hold

---

Mimamsa' and 'Uttara Mimamsa', see Parpola (1981). For a full translation of *Purva Mimamsa Sutras* with commentary, see Jha (1942); see also Benson (2010) and Clooney, S.J. (1990).

that it is your bounden duty to tear off the mask, to remove the misrepresentation that is caused by misnaming this law as religion. This is an essential step for you. Once you clear the minds of the people of this misconception and enable them to realise that what they are told is religion is not religion, but that it is really law, you will be in a position to urge its amendment or abolition.

23.7

So long as people look upon it as religion they will not be ready for a change, because the idea of religion is generally speaking not associated with the idea of change. But the idea of law is associated with the idea of change, and when people come to know that what is called religion is really law, old and archaic, they will be ready for a change, for people know and accept that law can be changed.

24

24.1

While I condemn a religion of rules, I must not be understood to hold the opinion that there is no necessity for a religion. On the contrary, I agree with Burke when he says that "True religion is the foundation of society, the basis on which all true Civil Government rests, and both their sanction."[158] Consequently, when I urge that these ancient rules of life be annulled, I am anxious that their place shall be taken by a

158 Edmund Burke (1729–97) was a British statesman, orator and political thinker of Irish origin. A staunch supporter of the American Revolution, he opposed the French Revolution in his work *Reflections on the Revolution in France* (1790). Ambedkar cites him often, especially during his interventions at the Round Table Conference (see Das 2010b). Though the source of this quotation has been difficult to trace, a fuller version of it has been widely cited. See O'Brien (1947, 191): "True religion is the foundation of society, the basis on which all true Civil Government rests and from which power derives its authority, laws their efficacy, and both their sanction. If it is once shaken by contempt, the whole fabric cannot be stable or lasting."

religion of principles, which alone can lay claim to being a true religion. Indeed, I am so convinced of the necessity of religion that I feel I ought to tell you in outline what I regard as necessary items in this religious reform. The following, in my opinion, should be the cardinal items in this reform:

1. There should be one and only one standard book of Hindu religion, acceptable to all Hindus and recognised by all Hindus. This of course means that all other books of Hindu religion such as Vedas, shastras, and puranas, which are treated as sacred and authoritative, must by law cease to be so, and the preaching of any doctrine, religious or social, contained in these books should be penalised.
2. It would be better if priesthood among Hindus were abolished. But as this seems to be impossible, the priesthood must at least cease to be hereditary. Every person who professes to be a Hindu must be eligible for being a priest. It should be provided by law that no Hindu shall be entitled to be a priest unless he has passed an examination prescribed by the state, and holds a *sanad*[159] from the state permitting him to practise.
3. No ceremony performed by a priest who does not hold a sanad shall be deemed to be valid in law, and it should be made

159 Sanad: Hindi for certificate or diploma. The Merriam-Webster dictionary gives the meaning of sanad as "an Indian government charter, warrant, diploma, patent or deed". Ambedkar's thoughts here on reform, and on giving a semblance of meritocracy to the institution of priesthood, gesture towards an alternate meaning of sanad as well. *Isnaad* (from Arabic *sanad*, 'support') in Islam is a list of authorities who have transmitted a report (*hadith*, also *hadees*) of a statement, action or approbation of Muhammad, one of his companions (*sahaabah*), or of a later authority (*tabee*); its reliability determines the validity of a hadith. The isnaad precedes the actual text (*matn*) and takes the form, "It has been related to me by A on the authority of B on the authority of C on the authority of D (usually a Companion of the Prophet) that Muhammad said…" A careful scrutiny of the isnaads, rating each hadith according to the completeness of its chain of transmitters, and the reliability and orthodoxy of its authorities, was done in the second century AH (after 720 CE) to avoid confusion and multiple narrations, and to assist in giving precedence to the *ahadith* (the total body of hadith) over whatever local customs might have developed in Muslim communities (Scott 2004).

penal for a person who has no sanad to officiate as a priest.

4. A priest should be the servant of the state,[160] and should be subject to the disciplinary action of the state in the matter of his morals, beliefs, and worship, in addition to his being subject along with other citizens to the ordinary law of the land.

5. The number of priests should be limited by law according to the requirements of the state, as is done in the case of the ICS [Indian Civil Service].

24.2

To some, this may sound radical. But to my mind there is nothing revolutionary in this. Every profession in India is regulated. Engineers must show proficiency, doctors must show proficiency, lawyers must show proficiency, before they are allowed to practise their professions. During the whole of their career, they must not only obey the law of the land, civil as well as criminal, but they must also obey the special code of morals prescribed by their respective professions. The priest's is the only profession where proficiency is not required. The profession of a Hindu priest is the only profession which is not subject to any code.

24.3

Mentally a priest may be an idiot, physically a priest may be suffering from a foul disease such as syphilis or gonorrhoea, morally he may be a wreck. But he is fit to officiate at solemn ceremonies, to enter the *sanctum sanctorum* of a Hindu temple, and to worship the Hindu god. All this becomes possible among the Hindus because for a priest it is enough to be born in a priestly caste. The whole thing is abominable, and is due to the fact that the priestly class among Hindus is subject neither to law nor to morality. It recognises no duties. It

160 In AoC 1936 and 1937, this reads: "A priest should be the servant of the state like any civil servant *and should be paid by the state.*" The italicised words are edited out in 1944.

knows only of rights and privileges. It is a pest which divinity seems to have let loose on the masses for their mental and moral degradation.

24.4

The priestly class must be brought under control by some such legislation as I have outlined above. This will prevent it from doing mischief and from misguiding people. It will democratise it by throwing it open to everyone. It will certainly help to kill Brahminism and will also help to kill caste, which is nothing but Brahminism incarnate. Brahminism is the poison which has spoiled Hinduism. You will succeed in saving Hinduism if you will kill Brahminism. There should be no opposition to this reform from any quarter. It should be welcomed even by the Arya Samajists, because this is merely an application of their own doctrine of guna–karma.[161]

---

161 It was the *Bhagvad Gita*—which Marxist historian D.D. Kosambi (1962, 16) says was added to the epic Mahabharata "somewhere between 150 and 350 AD"—that made the first popular case for the guna–karma theory. Here, guna means intrinsic qualities or attributes, and karma is actions. Much before the *Gita*, around the second century BCE, the Samkhya school of upanishadic philosophy propounded the tri-guna theory, the three gunas being *sattva* (corresponding to clarity of thought and purity of mind, associated with the Brahmin), *rajas* (passionate, excitable state of mind, associated with the Kshatriya) and *tamas* (darkness, a state of confusion, associated with the Shudra). Drawing on this Samkhya core, the *Gita* says in 4.13:

चातुर्वण्यां मयाः स्त्रुष्टं गुणकर्मविभागशः |
तस्य कर्तारम अपि मां विद्धिय अकर्तारमव्ययम् ||

(*Chaaturvanyaam mayaah srushtam gunakarmavibhaagasha: / Tasya kartaarama api maam viddhiya akartaaramavyayam.*) Debroy (2005: 65) renders this as: "In accordance with gunas and action, the four varnas were created by me. But despite being the creator of these, know me to be constant and not the agent." This shloka makes the case that the varna attribute is determined by worth (guna) and action (karma) and not by birth as purported by the *Rig Veda* (hymns 11–12, Sukta 90, Book 10) and subsequently by Manu and other smritis. The Arya Samaj, and figures like Gandhi and Aurobindo, who sought to defend varnashrama but denounce jati, cited the guna–karma theory to say that caste need not be birth-based. Contrast this with how Ambedkar examines the origin and genesis of caste, and what he terms the System of Castes in his 1916 essay "Castes in India" (in Rege 2013). See also 16.4 and Note 92 on Plato's *Republic*.

24.5

Whether you do that or you do not, you must give a new doctrinal basis to your religion—a basis that will be in consonance with liberty, equality and fraternity; in short, with democracy. I am no authority on the subject. But I am told that for such religious principles as will be in consonance with liberty, equality and fraternity, it may not be necessary for you to borrow from foreign sources, and that you could draw for such principles on the Upanishads. Whether you could do so without a complete remoulding, a considerable scraping and chipping off from the ore they contain, is more than I can say. This means a complete change in the fundamental notions of life. It means a complete change in the values of life. It means a complete change in outlook and in attitude towards men and things.

24.6

It means conversion; but if you do not like the word, I will say it means new life. But a new life cannot enter a body that is dead. New life can enter only into a new body. The old body must die before a new body can come into existence and a new life can enter into it. To put it simply: the old must cease to be operative before the new can begin to enliven and to pulsate. This is what I meant when I said you must discard the authority of the shastras, and destroy the religion of the shastras.

25

25.1

I have kept you too long. It is time I brought this address to a close. This would have been a convenient point for me to have stopped. But this would probably be my last address to a Hindu audience, on a subject vitally concerning the Hindus. I would therefore like, before I close, to place before the

Hindus, if they will allow me, some questions which I regard as vital, and invite them seriously to consider the same.

25.2

In the first place, the Hindus must consider whether it is sufficient to take the placid view of the anthropologist that there is nothing to be said about the beliefs, habits, morals and outlooks on life which obtain among the different peoples of the world, except that they often differ; or whether it is not necessary to make an attempt to find out what kind of morality, beliefs, habits, and outlook have worked best and have enabled those who possessed them to flourish, to grow strong, to people the earth and to have dominion over it. As is observed by Professor Carver:

> [M]orality and religion, as the organised expression of moral approval and disapproval, must be regarded as factors in the struggle for existence as truly as are weapons for offence and defence, teeth and claws, horns and hoofs, fur and feathers, plumage, beards, and antlers. The social group, community, tribe or nation which develops an unworkable scheme of morality, or within which those social acts which weaken it and unfit it for survival habitually create the sentiment of approval, while those which would strengthen it and enable it to expand habitually create the sentiment of disapproval, will eventually be eliminated. Its habits of approval and disapproval handicap it as really as the possession of two wings on one side with none on the other would handicap a colony of flies. It would be as futile in one case as in the other to argue that one system was just as good as another.[162]

162 This excerpt is from the first chapter, "What is Justice?", of Thomas Nixon Carver's *Essays in Social Justice* (1915, 20). Carver (1865–1961) was a neoclassical American economist who wrote on a wide array of topics such as rural economics, the problems of distribution of wealth, social justice, the place of religion in society, and social evolution. He was professor of economics and sociology at Harvard University from 1900 to 1932. Minor errors in Ambedkar's quotation of Carver—

25.3

Morality and religion, therefore, are not mere matters of likes and dislikes. You may dislike exceedingly a scheme of morality which, if universally practised within a nation, would make that nation the strongest nation on the face of the earth. Yet in spite of your dislike, such a nation will become strong. You may like exceedingly a scheme of morality and an ideal of justice which, if universally practised within a nation, would make it unable to hold its own in the struggle with other nations. Yet in spite of your admiration, this nation will eventually disappear. The Hindus must, therefore, examine their religion and their morality in terms of their survival value.

25.4

Secondly, the Hindus must consider whether they should conserve the whole of their social heritage, or select what is helpful and transmit to future generations only that much and no more. Prof John Dewey, who was my teacher and to whom I owe so much, has said:

> Every society gets encumbered with what is trivial, with dead wood from the past, and with what is positively perverse… As a society becomes more enlightened, it realises that it is responsible not to conserve and transmit the whole of its existing achievements, but only such as make for a better future society.[163]

Even Burke, in spite of the vehemence with which he opposed the principle of change embodied in the French Revolution, was compelled to admit that

---

that perist in the 1936, 1937 and 1944 editions—have been corrected.

163 Towards the close of his address, Ambedkar records his debt to John Dewey from whose work, as has been shown, he draws extensively. This being a presidential address at a conference it is understandable that Ambedkar does not always cite references—not just from Dewey but for various other materials he marshals to make his case. This quote is from the second chapter of *Democracy and Education: An Introduction to the Philosophy of Education* (1916), concerning the role of the school in implementing social change.

> a State without the means of some change is without the means of its conservation. Without such means it might even risk the loss of that part of the constitution which it wished the most religiously to preserve.[164]

What Burke said of a state applies equally to society.

25.5

Thirdly, the Hindus must consider whether they must not cease to worship the past as supplying their ideals. The baneful effects of this worship of the past are best summed up by Prof Dewey when he says:

> An individual can live only in the present. The present is not just something which comes after the past; much less something produced by it. It is what life is in leaving the past behind it. The study of past products will not help us to understand the present. A knowledge of the past and its heritage is of great significance when it enters into the present, but not otherwise. And the mistake of making the records and remains of the past the main material of education is that it tends to make the past a rival of the present and the present a more or less futile imitation of the past. [165]

The principle, which makes little of the present act of living and growing, naturally looks upon the present as empty and upon the future as remote. Such a principle is inimical to progress and is a hindrance to a strong and a steady current of life.

25.6

Fourthly, the Hindus must consider whether the time has not come for them to recognise that there is nothing fixed,

164 Quote from Burke's *Reflections on the Revolution in France* (1790), in which he launched a bitter attack on the French Revolution.

165 Dewey, *Democracy and Education*, chapter 7.

nothing eternal, nothing sanatan;[166] that everything is changing, that change is the law of life for individuals as well as for society. In a changing society, there must be a constant revolution of old values; and the Hindus must realise that if there must be standards to measure the acts of men, there must also be a readiness to revise those standards.

26

26.1

I have to confess that this address has become too lengthy. Whether this fault is compensated to any extent by breadth or depth is a matter for you to judge. All I claim is to have told you candidly my views. I have little to recommend them but some study and a deep concern in your destiny. If you will allow me to say it, these views are the views of a man who has been no tool of power, no flatterer of greatness. They come from one, almost the whole of whose public exertion has been one continuous struggle for liberty for the poor and for the oppressed, and whose only reward has been a continuous shower of calumny and abuse from national journals and national leaders,[167] for no other reason except that I refuse

166 Sanatan literally means eternal, everlasting; sanatan dharm (also rendered as sanatana dharma) is the religion that is said to have no beginning nor end. An orthodox person in the nationalist period would prefer to describe himself as someone who belonged to the 'sanatan dharm', the everlasting religion. The Anglicised terms 'Hindu' and 'Hinduism' do not capture the conservative fundamentalism inherent in sanatan dharm. While the Arya Samaj or Brahmo Samaj advocated reforms, the sanatani Hindus (the orthodoxy) believed in an eternal/sanatan Hinduism without any need for reforms. Ambedkar discusses Gandhi's sanatani tendencies in Appendix 9.30.

167 Much before right-wing Hindutva ideologue Arun Shourie (1997) suggested that Ambedkar was a 'stooge' of the British and cast aspersions on his 'nationalist' credentials, the newspapers of Ambedkar's time constantly doubted his credentials. In *What Congress and Gandhi Have Done to the Untouchables* (BAWS 9, 200), Ambedkar writes: "[The Untouchables] have no Press and the Congress Press is closed to them. It is determined not to give them the slightest publicity.

to join with them in performing the miracle—I will not say trick—of liberating the oppressed with the gold of the tyrant, and raising the poor with the cash of the rich.

26.2

All this may not be enough to commend my views. I think they are not likely to alter yours. But whether they do or do not, the responsibility is entirely yours. You must make your efforts to uproot caste, if not in my way, then in your way.

26.3

I am sorry, I will not be with you. I have decided to change. This is not the place for giving reasons. But even when I am gone out of your fold, I will watch your movement with active sympathy, and you will have my assistance for what it may be worth. Yours is a national cause. Caste is no doubt primarily the breath of the Hindus. But the Hindus have fouled the air all over, and everybody is infected—Sikh, Muslim and Christian.[168] You, therefore, deserve the support of all those who are suffering from this infection—Sikh, Muslim and Christian.

26.4

Yours is more difficult than the other national cause, namely,

---

They cannot have their own Press. It is obvious that no paper can survive without advertisement revenue.... The staff of the Associated Press in India, which is the main news distributing agency in India, is entirely drawn from Madras Brahmins—indeed the whole of the Press in India is in their hands and who for well-known reasons are entirely pro-Congress and will not allow any news hostile to the Congress to get publicity. These are reasons beyond the control of the Untouchables." For a documentation of the insensitive way in which the so-called nationalist press reported on Ambedkar, see Ramnarayan Rawat (2001, 128–9).

168 The import here is that caste has contaminated even the new faiths that emerged from within India (such as Sikhism) as it did religions that came to India (Islam and Christianity). For an account of how caste affects Sikhism, see Mark Juergensmeyer (2009); on caste among Muslims in India, see Imtiaz Ahmad (1978); and among Christians, see Kenneth Ballhatchet (1998), and the more recent study focused on Tamil Nadu by David Mosse (2012).

swaraj.[169] In the fight for swaraj you fight with the whole nation on your side. In this, you have to fight against the whole nation—and that too, your own.[170] But it is more important than swaraj. There is no use having swaraj, if you cannot defend it. More important than the question of defending swaraj is the question of defending the Hindus under the swaraj. In my opinion, it is only when Hindu society becomes a casteless society that it can hope to have strength enough to defend itself. Without such internal strength, swaraj for Hindus may turn out to be only a step towards slavery. Goodbye, and good wishes for your success.

169 Swaraj, literally 'self-rule', was the term used by the Congress party and other nationalist leaders to refer to the struggle for independence from British rule. The conservative leader Bal Gangadhar Tilak famously declared in 1899: "Swaraj is my birthright, and I shall have it!" However, it was Gandhi who popularised the term, especially with his manifesto-like *Hind Swaraj or Indian Home Rule* (1909). According to Gandhi, "It is swaraj when we learn to rule ourselves." For an annotated edition of *Hind Swaraj*, see Parel (1997). According to Lelyveld (2011, xiv), swaraj for Gandhi was bigger than the struggle for mere independence from British rule. "As used by Gandhi, poorna [complete] swaraj put the goal on yet a higher plane. At his most utopian, it was a goal not just for India but for each individual Indian; only then could it be poorna, or complete. It meant a sloughing not only of British rule but of British ways, a rejection of modern industrial society in favor of a bottom-up renewal of India, starting in its villages…"

170 Echoing a similar sentiment in 1927, when he led the civil rights struggle for Untouchables' access to the Chavadar Tank in Mahad, Ambedkar said: "The satyagraha movement started by Gandhi was backed by the people as it was against foreign domination. Our struggle is against the mass of caste Hindus and naturally we have little support from outside." Excerpts of Ambedkar's speech in Mahad, where he compares the event to the storming of the Bastille, can be found in Arjun Dangle (1992, 223–33) and in Satyanarayana and Tharu (2013, 22–31). For an account of the Mahad struggle, see Zelliot (2013, 78–82) and Rao (2009, 83–8).

The Ambedkar–Gandhi debate

A Vindication of Caste by Mahatma Gandhi

Dr Ambedkar's Indictment—1

1

1.1[1]

The readers will recall the fact that Dr Ambedkar was to have presided last May at the annual conference of the Jat-Pat Todak Mandal of Lahore. But the conference itself was cancelled because Dr Ambedkar's address was found by the reception committee to be unacceptable. How far a reception committee is justified in rejecting a president of its choice because of his address that may be objectionable to it is open to question. The committee knew Dr Ambedkar's views on caste and the Hindu scriptures. They knew also that he had in unequivocal terms decided to give up Hinduism. Nothing less than the address that Dr Ambedkar had prepared was to be expected from him. The committee appears to have deprived the public of an opportunity of listening to the original views of a man who has carved out for himself a unique position in

---

1 The title given by Gandhi to his two-part response to AoC, published first in *Harijan*, was "Dr Ambedkar's Indictment". Ambedkar includes Gandhi's response in the revised 1937 edition of AoC and gives it his own title "A Vindication of Caste by Mahatma Gandhi". While Sant Ram's rejoinder to Gandhi was published in *Harijan*, Ambedkar chose to publish his own exhaustive reply to Gandhi in the 1937 edition. All these are sequentially arranged here as they appear in AoC 1937.

society. Whatever label he wears in future, Dr Ambedkar is not the man to allow himself to be forgotten.

1.2

Dr Ambedkar was not going to be beaten by the reception committee. He has answered their rejection of him by publishing the address at his own expense. He has priced it at 8 annas, I would suggest a reduction to 2 annas or at least 4 annas.[2]

1.3

No reformer can ignore the address. The orthodox will gain by reading it. This is not to say that the address is not open to objection. It has to be read only because it is open to serious objection. Dr Ambedkar is a challenge to Hinduism. Brought up as a Hindu,[3] educated by a Hindu potentate,[4] he has become so disgusted with the so-called savarna Hindus or the treatment that he and his people have received at their hands that he proposes to leave not only them but the very religion that is his and their common heritage. He has transferred to that religion his disgust against a part of its professors.

1.4

But this is not to be wondered at. After all, one can only judge

2 Primary membership to the Congress party cost four annas.

3 Gandhi 'moved from truth to truth' on Ambedkar's identity and the motives for his commitment to the anticaste struggle. Shortly before the Round Table Conference, when they first met in Bombay, Gandhi took Ambedkar to be a radical Brahmin fighting untouchability. As his grandson Rajmohan Gandhi notes in his biography of Gandhi (2007, 334), Gandhi did not, however, say this to Ambedkar, and quickly realised his mistake.

4 The reference is to the Maharaja of Baroda, Sayajirao Gaekwad (1863–1939), who pioneered social reform by opening eighteen special schools for Untouchables in his state, and supported Ambedkar's education—both in India (with a stipend of twenty-five rupees for Ambedkar's B.A. at Elphinstone College, Bombay) and abroad (his M.A. and Ph.D. at Columbia University, on a scholarship of 11.5 British pounds per month for three years, in 1913–16). See Fatehsinhrao Gaekwad's (1989) biography of Maharaja Sayajirao III.

a system or an institution by the conduct of its representatives. What is more, Dr Ambedkar found that the vast majority of savarna Hindus had not only conducted themselves inhumanly against those of their fellow religionists whom they classed as Untouchables, but they had based their conduct on the authority of their scriptures, and when he began to search them he had found ample warrant for their beliefs in untouchability and all its implications. The author of the address has quoted chapter and verse in proof of his three-fold indictment—inhuman conduct itself, the unabashed justification for it on the part of the perpetrators, and the subsequent discovery that the justification was warranted by their scriptures.

1.5

No Hindu who prizes his faith above life itself can afford to underrate the importance of this indictment. Dr Ambedkar is not alone in his disgust. He is its most uncompromising exponent and one of the ablest among them. He is certainly the most irreconcilable among them. Thank god, in the front rank of the leaders he is singularly alone, and as yet but a representative of a very small minority. But what he says is voiced with more or less vehemence by many leaders belonging to the Depressed Classes. Only the latter, for instance Rao Bahadur M.C. Rajah and Dewan Bahadur Srinivasan,[5] not only do not threaten to give up Hinduism,

5 Rao Bahadur M.C. Rajah (1883–1943) and Rettamalai Srinivasan (1860–1945, conferred the title Dewan Bahadur) were Untouchable leaders from Madras Presidency. Rajah—author of *The Oppressed Hindus* (1925), the first ever book in English by an Untouchable in India—was the chief political rival of Ambedkar to the position of the representative of the Depressed Classes on the national scene. Like Ambedkar, his grandfather served the British army. In 1922, Rajah was conferred the British honorary title, Rao Bahadur, after his entrance to the Madras Legislative Council as the first Adi Dravida (as Untouchables were known in Tamil-speaking areas) member. In 1927, he became the first Depressed Classes member to be nominated to the Central Legislative Council. Rajah was piqued

but find enough warmth in it to compensate for the shameful persecution to which the vast mass of Harijans are exposed.

1.6

But the fact of many leaders remaining in the Hindu fold is no warrant for disregarding what Dr Ambedkar has to say. The savarnas have to correct their belief and their conduct. Above all, those who are, by their learning and influence, among the savarnas have to give an authoritative interpretation of the scriptures. The questions that Dr Ambedkar's indictment suggests are:

---

that Ambedkar chose Srinivasan, also a member of the Madras Legislative Council, over him as a delegate to the Round Table Conference. Srinivasan accompanied Ambedkar to the two Round Table Conferences, in 1930 and 1931. He testified alongside Ambedkar to the Simon Commission, and followed him in the demand for separate electorates. In 1932, during the negotiations after the 1931 Round Table Conference, Rajah aligned himself with B.S. Moonje of the Hindu Mahasabha and came up with the Rajah–Moonje Pact guaranteeing reserved seats for Depressed Classes in a joint electorate with Hindus; this was vehemently rejected by the All-India Depressed Classes Conference held at Nagpur. Depressed Class groups across India threw in their lot with Ambedkar. Rajah came to regret his position much later. When Ambedkar was browbeaten into signing the Poona Pact in September 1932, the arrangement was in fact not so different from the Rajah–Moonje Pact. As Jaffrelot (2005, 67) notes: "This scheme was in fact close to that advocated by the Rajah–Moonje pact. For Gandhi, the Poona Pact was much more than an exercise in political engineering: it had wider implications for society as a whole, as evident from his comment to Ambedkar in 1933: 'In accepting the Poona Pact you accept the position that you are Hindus.'" Three years later, goaded by Gandhians and the Mahasabha, Rajah even denounced Ambedkar's announcement that he would not die a Hindu. For an account of how Rajah was manipulated by Gandhi in this, see Keer (1954/1990, 266–84). See also Zelliot (2013, 124–39). However, as Jaffrelot notes: "Rajah was to join Ambedkar six years later, in 1938, after having been dismayed by the conservatism of the government formed by Congress in his province of Madras. He complained about it to Gandhi, who advised him to be patient and reaffirmed his confidence in the leader of the Madras government, a Brahmin, Rajagopalachari. Rajah, demoralised, thus came to regret the Poona Pact, and opposed, like Ambedkar, the Quit India Movement of 1942" (2005, 181–2 n48). Further, the proposals made by the Cripps Mission in 1942 caused "M.C. Rajah to become still closer to Ambedkar. Like him, he regretted the absence, in this set of proposals, of a provision granting a separate electorate to Untouchables... During his tour in the south, in 1944, Ambedkar was invited by M.C. Rajah to Madras" (184 n31).

1. What are the scriptures?
2. Are all the printed texts to be regarded as an integral part of them, or is any part of them to be rejected as unauthorised interpolation?
3. What is the answer of such accepted and expurgated scriptures on the question of untouchability, caste, equality of status, inter-dining and intermarriages? (These have been all examined by Dr Ambedkar in his address.)

I must reserve for the next issue my own answer to these questions and a statement of the (at least some) manifest flaws in Dr Ambedkar's thesis.

Harijan, 11 July 1936

Dr Ambedkar's Indictment—2

2

2.1

The Vedas, Upanishads, smritis and puranas, including the Ramayana and the Mahabharata, are the Hindu scriptures. Nor is this a finite list. Every age or even generation has added to the list. It follows, therefore, that everything printed or even found handwritten is not scripture. The smritis, for instance, contain much that can never be accepted as the word of God. Thus many of the texts that Dr Ambedkar quotes from the smritis cannot be accepted as authentic. The scriptures, properly so called, can only be concerned with eternal verities and must appeal to any conscience, i.e., any heart whose eyes of understanding are opened. Nothing can be accepted as the word of God which cannot be tested by reason or be capable of being spiritually experienced. And even when you have an expurgated edition of the scriptures, you will need their interpretation. Who is the best interpreter? Not learned men surely. Learning there must be. But religion does not live by it. It lives in the experiences of its saints and seers, in their lives and sayings. When all the most learned commentators of the scriptures are utterly forgotten, the accumulated experience of the sages and saints will abide and be an inspiration for ages to come.

2.2

Caste has nothing to do with religion. It is a custom whose origin I do not know, and do not need to know for the satisfaction of my spiritual hunger. But I do know that it is harmful both to spiritual and national growth. Varna and ashrama[6] are institutions which have nothing to do with castes. The law of varna teaches us that we have each one of us to earn our bread by following the ancestral calling. It defines not our rights but our duties. It necessarily has reference to callings that are conducive to the welfare of humanity and to no other. It also follows that there is no calling too low and none too high. All are good, lawful and absolutely equal in status. The callings of a Brahmin—spiritual teacher—and a scavenger are equal, and their due performance carries equal merit before God, and at one time seems to have carried identical reward before man. Both were entitled to their livelihood and no more. Indeed one traces even now in the

6 Just like human beings are divided into four varnas, a 'twice-born' savarna Hindu male's life has four stages (ashramas), ascending from the status of *brahmacharya* (unmarried, where man devotes his time to education), *grihastha* (householder), and *vanaprastha* (he dwells in the forest as a hermit but without severing ties with his family) to *sannyasa* (total renunciation of the world). The *Manusmriti*, among other Hindu scriptures, discusses the ashramas at length.

villages the faint lines of this healthy operation of the law.[7]

2.3

Living in Segaon[8] with its population of six hundred, I do not find a great disparity between the earnings of different tradesmen, including Brahmins. I find too that real Brahmins are to be found, even in these degenerate days, who are living on alms freely given to them and are giving freely of what they have of spiritual treasures. It would be wrong and improper to judge the law of varna by its caricature in the lives of men who profess to belong to a varna, whilst they openly commit a breach of its only operative rule. Arrogation of a superior status by and of a varna over another is a denial of the law. And there is nothing in the law of varna to warrant a belief in untouchability. (The essence of Hinduism is contained in its enunciation of one and only God as truth and its bold acceptance of ahimsa as the law of the human family.)

2.4

I am aware that my interpretation of Hinduism will be disputed by many besides Dr Ambedkar. That does not affect my position. It is an interpretation by which I have lived for nearly half a century, and according to which I have endeavoured to the best of my ability to regulate my life.

---

7 Gandhi here is restating his views on the benefits of varnashrama explicated by him in one of his earlier writings (*Young India*, 13 August 1925; CWMG 32, 286), in which he says: "Varnashrama, in my opinion, was not conceived in any narrow spirit. On the contrary, it gave the labourer, the Shudra, the same status as the thinker, the Brahmin." Even earlier, he wrote (*Young India*, 25 February 1920; CWMG 19, 417): "I am one of those who do not consider caste to be a harmful institution. In its origin, caste was a wholesome custom and promoted national well-being. In my opinion, the idea that inter-dining or intermarrying is necessary for national growth, is a superstition borrowed from the West." While later coming around to criticising caste/jati as a corruption, throughout his life Gandhi steadfastly defended an 'idealised' *varnavyavastha* (varna system). Nauriya (2006) believes that Gandhi came to recant his views on varnashrama.

8 Segaon: later called Sevagram, the ashram established by Gandhi, near Wardha (in today's Maharashtra).

2.5

In my opinion the profound mistake that Dr Ambedkar has made in his address is to pick out the texts of doubtful authenticity and value, and the state of degraded Hindus who are no fit specimens of the faith they so woefully misrepresent. Judged by the standard applied by Dr Ambedkar every known living faith will probably fail.

2.6

In his able address, the learned doctor has over-proved his case. Can a religion that was professed by Chaitanya, Jnyandeo, Tukaram, Tiruvalluvar, Ramakrishna Paramahansa, Raja Ram Mohan Roy, Maharshi Devendranath Tagore, Vivekananda,[9] and a host of others who might be easily mentioned, be so utterly devoid of merit as is made out in Dr Ambedkar's address? A religion has to be judged not by its worst specimens but by the best it might have produced. For that and that alone can be used as the standard to aspire to, if not to improve upon.

Harijan, 18 July 1936

9 Chaitanya was a Vaishnava saint from sixteenth-century Bengal, a proponent of Bhakti yoga. Jnyandeo, or Gyandev (also Dnyandev), was a thirteenth-century Bhakti poet-saint from western India; he wrote a commentary on the *Bhagvad Gita*. Tukaram was a seventeenth-century sant of the Varkari tradition; Cokhamela was a fourteenth0century Mahar sant of the same tradition (not mentioned by Gandhi). Tiruvalluvar was a Tamil poet and philosopher, the author of the *Thirukkural*, from sometime between the second and eighth centuries CE. Ramakrishna Paramahansa was a nineteenth-century Kali worshipping mystic from Bengal. Raja Ram Mohan Roy and Maharshi Devendranath Tagore together founded the Brahmo Samaj, a social and religious reform movement in nineteenth-century Bengal (Kopf 1979). Vivekananda was a self-styled Hindu monk. A disciple of Ramakrishna Paramahansa, he founded the Ramakrishna Mission (see Sharma 2012).

Sant Ram responds to Gandhi

Varna versus Caste

3

3.1

Shri Sant Ramji of the Jat-Pat Todak Mandal of Lahore wants me to publish the following:[10]

3.2

"I have read your remarks about Dr Ambedkar and the Jat-Pat Todak Mandal, Lahore. In that connection I beg to submit as follows:

"We did not invite Dr Ambedkar to preside over our conference because he belonged to the Depressed Classes, for we do not distinguish between a Touchable and an Untouchable Hindu. On the contrary our choice fell on him simply because his diagnosis of the fatal disease of the Hindu community was the same as ours, i.e., he too was of the opinion that the caste system was the root cause of the disruption and downfall of the Hindus. The subject of the doctor's thesis for his doctorate being the caste system,[11]

10 Gandhi published Sant Ram's letter in *Harijan* and appended his own response to it.

11 While Ambedkar did write a paper called "Castes in India" in 1916 during his years in Columbia University, the subject of his doctoral dissertation was *not* the caste

he has studied the subject thoroughly. Now the object of our conference was to persuade the Hindus to annihilate caste, but the advice of a non-Hindu in social and religious matters can have no effect on them. The doctor in the supplementary portion of his address insisted on saying that that was his last speech as a Hindu,[12] which was irrelevant as well as pernicious to the interests of the conference. So we requested him to expunge that sentence, for he could easily say the same thing on any other occasion. But he refused, and we saw no utility in making merely a show of our function. In spite of all this, I cannot help praising his address, which is, as far as I know, the most learned thesis on the subject and worth translating into every vernacular of India.

3.3

"Moreover, I want to bring to your notice that your philosophical difference between caste and varna is too subtle to be grasped by people in general, because for all practical purposes in Hindu society, caste and varna are one and the same thing, for the function of both of them is one and the same, i.e. to restrict inter-caste marriages and inter-dining. Your theory of varnavyavastha is impracticable in this age, and there is no hope of its revival in the near future. But Hindus are slaves of caste, and do not want to destroy it. So

---

system. His doctoral work was on *The Evolution of Provincial Finance in British India: A Study in the Provincial Decentralisation of Imperial Finance*, and it was later published by P.S. King and Co., London, in 1925, with a foreword by Edwin Seligman who taught Ambedkar at Columbia.

12 This seems to be a deliberate misreading of what Ambedkar actually says in his speech, made not only by Sant Ram but also Har Bhagwan (see his letter to Ambedkar in the Prologue to AoC). While Ambedkar did denounce Hinduism and declared he would walk out of the Hindu fold in 1935 (see Note 15 to Prologue of AoC), the exact words of Ambedkar in AoC 25.1 are "this would probably be my last *address to* a Hindu audience, on a subject vitally concerning the Hindus" (emphasis added).

when you advocate your ideal of imaginary varnavyavastha, they find justification for clinging to caste. Thus you are doing a great disservice to social reform by advocating your imaginary utility of the division of varnas, for it creates a hindrance in our way. To try to remove untouchability without striking at the root of varnavyavastha is simply to treat the outward symptoms of a disease, or to draw a line on the surface of water. As in the heart of their hearts dwijas do not want to give social equality to the so-called Touchable and Untouchable Shudras, so they refuse to break caste—and give liberal donations for the removal of untouchability simply to evade the issue. To seek the help of the shastras for the removal of untouchability and caste is simply to wash mud with mud."

3.4

The last paragraph of the letter surely cancels the first. If the Mandal rejects the help of the shastras, they do exactly what Dr Ambedkar does, i.e., cease to be Hindus. How then can they object to Dr Ambedkar's address merely because he said that that was his last speech as a Hindu? The position appears to be wholly untenable, especially when the Mandal, for which Shri Sant Ram claims to speak, applauds the whole argument of Dr Ambedkar's address.

3.5

But it is pertinent to ask what the Mandal believes in, if it rejects the shastras. How can a Muslim remain one if he rejects the Quran, or a Christian remain Christian if he rejects the Bible? If caste and varna are convertible terms, and if varna is an integral part of the shastras which define Hinduism, I do not know how a person who rejects caste, i.e., varna, can call himself a Hindu.

3.6

Shri Sant Ram likens the shastras to mud. Dr Ambedkar

has not, so far as I remember, given any such picturesque name to the shastras. I have certainly meant when I have said: that if shastras support the existing untouchability I should cease to call myself a Hindu. Similarly, if the shastras support caste, as we know it today in all its hideousness, I may not call myself or remain a Hindu, since I have no scruples about inter-dining or intermarriage. I need not repeat my position regarding shastras and their interpretation. I venture to suggest to Shri Sant Ram that it is the only rational and correct and morally defensible position, and it has ample warrant in Hindu tradition.

Harijan, 15 August 1936

A Reply to the Mahatma

B.R. Ambedkar

1

1.1

I appreciate greatly the honour done me by the Mahatma in taking notice in his *Harijan* of the speech on caste which I had prepared for the Jat-Pat Todak Mandal. From a perusal of his review of my speech, it is clear that the Mahatma completely dissents from the views I have expressed on the subject of caste. I am not in the habit of entering into controversy with my opponents unless there are special reasons which compel me to act otherwise. Had my opponent been some mean and obscure person I would not have pursued him. But my opponent being the Mahatma himself, I feel I must attempt to meet the case to the contrary which he has sought to put forth.

1.2

While I appreciate the honour he has done me, I must confess to a sense of surprise on finding that of all people the Mahatma should accuse me of a desire to seek publicity, as he seems to do when he suggests that in publishing the undelivered speech my object was to see that I was not 'forgotten'. Whatever the Mahatma may choose to say, my object in publishing the speech was to provoke the Hindus to think, and to take stock of their position. I have never hankered for publicity, and if I may say so, I have more of it than I wish or need. But supposing it was out of the motive of gaining publicity that I printed the speech, who could cast a stone at me? Surely not those who, like the Mahatma, live in glass houses.

2

2.1

Motive apart, what has the Mahatma to say on the question raised by me in the speech? First of all, anyone who reads my speech will realise that the Mahatma has entirely missed the issues raised by me, and that the issues he has raised are not the issues that arise out of what he is pleased to call my indictment of the Hindus. The principal points which I have tried to make out in my speech may be catalogued as follows:

2.2

(1) That caste has ruined the Hindus; (2) that the reorganisation of Hindu society on the basis of chaturvarnya is impossible because the varnavyavastha is like a leaky pot or like a man running at the nose.[1] It is incapable of sustaining itself by its own virtue and has an inherent tendency to degenerate into a caste system unless there is a legal sanction behind it which can be enforced against everyone transgressing his varna; (3) that the reorganisation of Hindu society on the basis of chaturvarnya would be harmful, because the effect of the varnavyavastha would be to degrade the masses by denying them opportunity to acquire knowledge and to emasculate them by denying them the right to be armed; (4) that Hindu society must be reorganised on a religious basis which would recognise the principles of liberty, equality and

---

1 Same as 'runny nose'. The expression here means snivelling, "pitiful, whining" according to Samuel Johnson's *A Dictionary of the English Language*.

fraternity; (5) that in order to achieve this object the sense of religious sanctity behind caste and varna must be destroyed; (6) that the sanctity of caste and varna can be destroyed only by discarding the divine authority of the shastras.

2.3

It will be noticed that the questions raised by the Mahatma are absolutely besides the point, and show that the main argument of the speech was lost upon him.

3

3.1

Let me examine the substance of the points made by the Mahatma. The first point made by the Mahatma is that the texts cited by me are not authentic. I confess I am no authority on this matter. But I should like to state that the texts cited by me are all taken from the writings of the late Mr Tilak,[2] who was a recognised authority on the Sanskrit language and on the Hindu shastras. His second point is that these shastras should be interpreted not by the learned but by the saints; and that as the saints have understood them the shastras do not support caste and untouchability.

3.2

As regards the first point, what I would like to ask the Mahatma is, what does it avail to anyone if the texts are interpolations,

2 Ambedkar is likely referring to Tilak's two-volume opus, *Srimad Bhagavad Gita Rahasya*, known in short as *Gita Rahasya* and translated as *The Esoteric Import of the Gita*, in his own words. It was written when Tilak was imprisoned for six years on charges of sedition in Mandalay (Burma) from 1907 and first published in Marathi in June 1915. An English version translated by B.S. Sukthankar, which Ambedkar likely accessed, was published in 1935 by Tilak Bros in Poona. By then *Gita Rahasya* had been published in many Indian languages. This English edition features several pages of endorsements from a phalanx of leaders: Swami Vivekananda, Annie Besant, Madan Mohan Malaviya, Gopal Krishna Gokhale, Aurobindo Ghose and also Gandhi, who says Tilak's "masterwork commentary on the Gita is unsurpassed and will remain so for a long time to come" (xvi).

and if they have been differently interpreted by the saints? The masses do not make any distinction between texts which are genuine and texts which are interpolations. The masses do not know what the texts are. They are too illiterate to know the contents of the shastras. They have believed what they have been told, and what they have been told is that the shastras do enjoin as a religious duty the observance of caste and untouchability.

3.3

With regard to the saints, one must admit that howsoever different and elevating their teachings may have been as compared to those of the merely learned, they have been lamentably ineffective. They have been ineffective for two reasons. Firstly, none of the saints ever attacked the caste system. On the contrary—they were staunch believers in the system of castes. Most of them lived and died as members of the castes to which they respectively belonged. So passionately attached was Jnyandeo to his status as a Brahmin that when the Brahmins of Paithan would not admit him to their fold, he moved heaven and earth to get his status as a Brahmin recognised by the Brahmin fraternity.

3.4

And even the saint Eknath,[3] who now figures in the film *Dharmatma*[4] as a hero for having shown the courage to touch the Untouchables and dine with them, did so not because he was opposed to caste and untouchability, but because he felt

---

3 Eknath (1533–99) was a sixteenth-century Marathi sant of the Varkari tradition founded by Jnyandeo (see Note 32 to AoC 2.22). *Eknathi Bhagavat* is a commentary on the eleventh canto of the Sanskrit *Bhagavata Purana* (a circa tenth-century puranic text—though scholars disagree on the dating—focused on Krishna and the *Bhagvad Gita*), in the form of *abhangas*, a Marathi verse form meaning unbroken, written in the *ovi* metre.

4 V. Shantaram made this film in 1935 on Eknath's life. The famous actor Bal Gandharv starred in the role of Eknath.

that the pollution caused thereby could be washed away by a bath in the sacred waters of the river Ganges.[5] The saints have never, according to my study, carried on a campaign against caste and untouchability. They were not concerned with the struggle between men. They were concerned with the relation between man and god. They did not preach that all men were equal. They preached that all men were equal in the eyes of god—a very different and a very innocuous proposition, which nobody can find difficult to preach or dangerous to believe in.[6]

3.5

The second reason why the teachings of the saints proved ineffective was because the masses have been taught that a saint might break caste, but the common man must not. A saint therefore never became an example to follow. He always

---

5 अन्त्यजाचा विटाळ ज्यासि । गंगास्नाने शुद्धत्व त्यासि ॥ एक्राथि भागवत्, अ.२८, ओ.१९१. (*Antyajancha vital jyasi/ Gangasnane shuddhatva tyasi—Eknathi Bhagavat*, a.28, o.191). This verse with reference to the source figures in the 1937 edition of AoC as a footnote at this point. This Marathi verse has been transcribed and translated by Debroy as: "Those among outcastes who are impure/ can be purified by bathing in the Ganga."

6 Despite his scepticism and rejection of the Bhakti movement and Bhakti saints, Ambedkar did recognise the agentive role of the 'Untouchable' Bhakti saints and dedicated *The Untouchables: Who Were They and Why They Became Untouchable* (1948/1990) thus: "Inscribed to the memory of Nandanar, Ravidas, Chokhamela—three renowned saints who were born among the Untouchables, and who by their piety and virtue won the esteem of all." Nandanar, however, was not a historical figure unlike Ravidas and Cokhamela. In the twelfth-century Tamil work *Periya Puranam* by Sekkilar, a hagiographical account of the sixty-three Tamil Saiva saints (Nayanmars) of whom only a handful were historical figures, the Paraiyar-born Nandanar is referred to as Thirunaali Povar. As Anushiya Ramaswamy (2010, 76) points out, Sekkilar shows Nandanar as "unquestioningly accepting the edicts of a caste-defined order, going so far as to willingly die in a ritualistic immolation at the gates of Chidambaram [Nataraja temple]". During the colonial-nationalist movement, the figure of Nandanar was resurrected. Gopalakrishna Bharathi, a Saivite poet-composer had published the *Nandanar Charitram* (The story of Nandanar) in 1861–2 which, during the early twentieth century, was adapted for stage as dance dramas. Later, five Tamil feature films were made on Nandanar—two silent films, in 1923 and 1930; and three talkies, in 1933, 1935 and 1942.

remained a pious man to be honoured. That the masses have remained staunch believers in caste and untouchability shows that the pious lives and noble sermons of the saints have had no effect on their life and conduct, as against the teachings of the shastras. Thus it can be a matter of no consolation that there were saints, or that there is a Mahatma who understands the shastras differently from the learned few or ignorant many.[7]

3.6

That the masses hold a different view of the shastras is a fact which should and must be reckoned with. How that is to be dealt with, except by denouncing the authority of the shastras which continue to govern their conduct, is a question which the Mahatma has not considered. But whatever the plan the Mahatma puts forth as an effective means to free the masses from the teachings of the shastras, he must accept that the pious life led by one good Samaritan may be very elevating to himself, but in India, with the attitude the common man has to saints and to Mahatmas—to honour but not to follow—one cannot make much out of it.

4

4.1

The third point made by the Mahatma is that a religion professed by Chaitanya, Jnyandeo, Tukaram, Tiruvalluvar, Ramakrishna Paramahansa, etc., cannot be devoid of merit as is made out by me, and that a religion has to be judged not

7 Ambedkar is also perhaps alluding to the fact that Gandhi often compared himself to the 'Bhangi'—the caste among Untouchables forced into sweeping and scavenging work—and often announced that he cleaned the toilets in his ashrams. As far as Ambedkar is concerned, a saint or a Mahatma indulging in such performative gestures does not alter the beliefs of people as such. For an account of Gandhi's writings on manual scavengers, see Ramaswamy (2005, 86–95); for a critique of Gandhi's approach to issues concerning sweepers and scavengers, see Prashad (1996, 2001).

by its worst specimens but by the best it might have produced. I agree with every word of this statement. But I do not quite understand what the Mahatma wishes to prove thereby. That religion should be judged not by its worst specimens but by its best is true enough, but does it dispose of the matter? I say it does not.

4.2

The question still remains, why the worst number so many and the best so few. To my mind there are two conceivable answers to this question: (1) that the worst by reason of some original perversity of theirs are morally uneducable, and are therefore incapable of making the remotest approach to the religious ideal. Or: (2) that the religious ideal is a wholly wrong ideal which has given a wrong moral twist to the lives of the many, and that the best have become best in spite of the wrong ideal—in fact, by giving to the wrong twist a turn in the right direction.

4.3

Of these two explanations I am not prepared to accept the first, and I am sure that even the Mahatma will not insist upon the contrary. To my mind the second is the only logical and reasonable explanation, unless the Mahatma has a third alternative to explain why the worst are so many and the best so few. If the second is the only explanation, then obviously the argument of the Mahatma that a religion should be judged by its best followers carries us nowhere—except to pity the lot of the many who have gone wrong because they have been made to worship wrong ideals.

5

5.1

The argument of the Mahatma that Hinduism would be tolerable if only many were to follow the example of the saints is fallacious for another reason. (In this connection, see the illuminating article on "Morality and the Social Structure" by H.N. Brailsford in the *Aryan Path* for April 1936.[8]) By citing the names of such illustrious persons as Chaitanya, etc., what the Mahatma seems to me to suggest in its broadest and simplest form is that Hindu society can be made tolerable and even happy without any fundamental change in its structure, if all the high-caste Hindus can be persuaded to follow a high standard of morality in their dealings with the low-caste Hindus. I am totally opposed to this kind of ideology.

5.2

I can respect those of the caste Hindus who try to realise a high social ideal in their life. Without such men, India would be an uglier and a less happy place to live in than it is. But nonetheless, anyone who relies on an attempt to turn the members of the caste Hindus into better men by improving their personal character is, in my judgement, wasting his energy and hugging an illusion. Can personal character make

8 The sentence in parenthesis is given as a footnote in AoC 1937. Ambedkar is referring to Brailsford's essay in the *Aryan Path* (April 1936, 166–9). *Aryan Path* was a journal published from Bombay by the Theosophical Society since 1930. Henry Noel Brailsford (1873–1958) was a British left-wing journalist and writer who started his career as a foreign correspondent during the war in Crete. He continued to report from Paris and then Macedonia after the First World War. He supported the women's suffrage movement. He was made editor of *The New Leader*, the British Independent Labour Party newspaper, in 1922. After a seven-week tour of India he became a member of the India League, a British organisation spreading awareness about the ills of colonialism, and wrote *Rebel India* (1931), a treatise against colonial rule. In the essay Ambedkar is referring to, Brailsford offers a thesis "that our existing society can be made tolerable and even happy, without any fundamental change in its structure, if all of us, but more especially the privileged classes, can be induced to follow a high standard of morality in our dealings with our fellows. This was always the teaching of the Roman Catholic Church, though it used to forbid usury, and is still critical of high finance. Mr Gandhi has preached impressive sermons on these lines to landlords (especially in the United Provinces) and to industrial capitalists." Here, Brailsford comes to echo Gandhi's doctrine of trusteeship; for a critical analysis of this doctrine, see Roy's introduction to this volume.

the maker of armaments a good man, i.e., a man who will sell shells that will not burst and gas that will not poison? If it cannot, how can you accept personal character to make a man loaded with the consciousness of caste a good man, i.e., a man who would treat his fellow men as his friends and equals? To be true to himself he must deal with his fellow man either as a superior or inferior, according as the case may be; at any rate, differently from his own caste-fellows. He can never be expected to deal with his fellow men as his kinsmen and equals.

5.3

As a matter of fact, a Hindu does treat all those who are not of his caste as though they were aliens, who could be discriminated against with impunity, and against whom any fraud or trick may be practised without shame. This is to say that there can be a better or a worse Hindu. But a good Hindu there cannot be. This is so not because there is anything wrong with his personal character. In fact, what is wrong is the entire basis of his relationship to his fellows. The best of men cannot be moral if the basis of relationship between them and their fellows is fundamentally a wrong relationship. To a slave, his master may be better or worse. But there cannot be a good master. A good man cannot be a master, and a master cannot be a good man.

5.4

The same applies to the relationship between high caste and low caste. To a low-caste man, a high-caste man can be better or worse as compared to other high-caste men. A high-caste man cannot be a good man, in so far as he must have a low caste man to distinguish him as a high-caste man. It cannot be good to a low-caste man to be conscious that there is a high-caste man above him. I have argued in my speech that a society based on varna or caste is a society which is based on a wrong relationship. I had hoped that the Mahatma would attempt to demolish my argument. But instead of doing that, he has merely reiterated his belief in chaturvarnya without disclosing the ground on which it is based.

6

6.1

Does the Mahatma practise what he preaches? One does not like to make personal reference in an argument which is general in its application. But when one preaches a doctrine and holds it as a dogma there is a curiosity to know how far he practises what he preaches. It may be that his failure to practise is due to the ideal being too high to be attainable; it may be that his failure to practise is due to the innate hypocrisy of the man. In any case he exposes his conduct to examination, and I must not be blamed if I ask how far has the Mahatma attempted to realise his ideal in his own case?

6.2

The Mahatma is a Bania trader by birth. His ancestors had abandoned trading in favour of ministership, which is a calling of the Brahmins. In his own life, before he became a Mahatma, when the occasion came for him to choose his career he preferred law to scales. On abandoning law, he became half saint and half politician. He has never touched trading, which is his ancestral calling.

6.3

His youngest son—I take the one who is a faithful follower of his father—was born a Vaishya, has married a Brahmin's daughter, and has chosen to serve a newspaper magnate.[9]

---

9 When Ambedkar refers to "the one who is a faithful follower of his father", he is alluding to Gandhi's third son, Devdas Gandhi, who, in 1937, was appointed managing editor of *Hindustan Times*, the newspaper owned by G.D. Birla, a Marwari Bania industrialist who was a close associate and financier of Gandhi.

The Mahatma is not known to have condemned him for not following his ancestral calling. It may be wrong and uncharitable to judge an ideal by its worst specimens. But surely the Mahatma as a specimen is no better, and if he even fails to realise the ideal then the ideal must be an impossible ideal, quite opposed to the practical instincts of man.

6.4

Students of Carlyle know that he often spoke on a subject before he thought about it. I wonder whether such has not been the case with the Mahatma in regard to the subject matter of caste. Otherwise, certain questions which occur to me would not have escaped him. When can a calling be deemed to have become an ancestral calling, so as to make it binding on a man? Must a man follow his ancestral calling even if it does not suit his capacities, even when it has ceased to be profitable? Must a man live by his ancestral calling even if he finds it to be immoral? If everyone must pursue his ancestral calling, then it must follow that a man must continue to be a pimp because his grandfather was a pimp, and a woman must continue to be a prostitute because her grandmother was a prostitute. Is the Mahatma prepared to accept the logical conclusion of his doctrine? To me his ideal of following one's ancestral calling is not only an impossible and impractical ideal, but it is also morally an indefensible ideal.

In Delhi, Gandhi made the palatial Birla House his residence for over twenty-five years. (The Birla House was renamed Gandhi Smriti in 1971.) Gandhi's swarajist economic policies resulted in his colluding with the conservative industrialists of his time. For an analysis of Gandhi's relationship with G.D. Birla and other Swadeshi business houses, see Leah Renold (1994, 16–38). Gandhi's first son Harilal Gandhi was estranged from Gandhi and was not a 'faithful follower' of his since he embraced Islam on 29 May 1936, the same month and year in which AoC was first published. Harilal's conversion happened within a year after Ambedkar declared on 13 October 1935 in Yeola that he shall not die a Hindu and exhorted Untouchables to seek relief in a new religion. For an account of Harilal's life, see Chandulal Bhagubhai Dalal (2007).

7

7.1

The Mahatma sees great virtue in a Brahmin remaining a Brahmin all his life. Leaving aside the fact that there are many Brahmins who do not like to remain Brahmins all their lives, what can we say about those Brahmins who have clung to their ancestral calling of priesthood? Do they do so from any faith in the virtue of the principle of ancestral calling, or do they do so from motives of filthy lucre? The Mahatma does not seem to concern himself with such queries. He is satisfied that these are "real Brahmins who are living on alms freely given to them, and giving freely what they have of spiritual treasures". This is how a hereditary Brahmin priest appears to the Mahatma—a carrier of spiritual treasures.

7.2

But another portrait of the hereditary Brahmin can also be drawn. A Brahmin can be a priest to Vishnu—the god of love. He can be a priest to Shankar—the god of destruction. He can be a priest at Buddha Gaya[10] worshipping Buddha—the greatest teacher of mankind, who taught the noblest doctrine of love. He also can be a priest to Kali, the goddess who must have a daily sacrifice of an animal to satisfy her

10 Buddha Gaya or Bodh Gaya is the most sacred site in Buddhism, revered as the place where Buddha attained enlightenment. The temple complex has for long been controlled by Brahmin *mahants* (priests). The Bodhgaya Temple Act, passed two years after India's independence, provides for a chairman and a committee of eight members, four Buddhist and four Hindu, "to manage and control the temple land and the properties appertaining thereto". Section 3(3) of the Act provides that "the District Magistrate of Gaya shall be the ex-officio Chairman of the Committee: provided that the State Government shall nominate a Hindu as Chairman of the Committee for the period during which the district Magistrate of Gaya is non-Hindu". For the uncanny resemblance this state of affairs has with the Conflict of Orders in ancient Rome, especially with the history of the process of appointment of consuls and tribunes, and the role of the Oracle at Delphi, see Note 27 at 2.20 and Note 36 at 3.5 of AoC. An amendment to allow non-Hindu chairmen in the committee was passed only in August 2013 by the Bihar Assembly.

thirst for blood. He will be a priest of the temple of Rama—the Kshatriya god! He will also be a priest of the temple of Parshuram, the god who took on an avatar to destroy the Kshatriyas! He can be a priest to Brahma, the creator of the world. He can be a priest to a pir,[11] whose god Allah will not brook the claim of Brahma to share his spiritual dominion over the world! No one can say that this is a picture which is not true to life.

7.3

If this is a true picture, one does not know what to say of this capacity to bear loyalties to gods and goddesses whose attributes are so antagonistic that no honest man can be a devotee to all of them. The Hindus rely upon this extraordinary phenomenon as evidence of the greatest virtue of their religion—namely, its catholicity, its spirit of toleration. As against this facile view, it can be urged that what is toleration and catholicity may be really nothing more creditable than indifference or flaccid latitudinarianism. These two attitudes are hard to distinguish in their outer seeming. But they are so vitally unlike in their real quality

---

11 A *pir*, meaning elder or saint, is the spiritual guide to the followers of Sufism, the mystic branch of Islam. Sufis are organised into orders around a master who helps his disciples along the path of surrendering the ego in the worship of god. When Ambedkar says a Brahmin can be a priest to a pir, he is referring to the adaptability of the Brahmin which helps him survive any challenge. Elaborating on this in a sharper way in his critique of the Congress and Gandhi, he says (BAWS 9, 195): "I am quite aware that there are some protagonists of Hinduism who say that Hinduism is a very adaptable religion, that it can adjust itself to everything and absorb anything. I do not think many people would regard such a capacity in a religion as a virtue to be proud of just as no one would think highly of a child because it has developed the capacity to eat dung, and digest it. But that is another matter. It is quite true that Hinduism can adjust itself. The best example of its adjustability is the literary production called *Allahupanishad* which the Brahmins of the time of Akbar produced to give a place to his *Din-e-Ilahi* within Hinduism and to recognise it as the Seventh system of Hindu philosophy." For an understanding of Sufism, see the classic work of Annemarie Schimmel (1975) and the more recent work of Tanvir Anjum (2011).

that no one who examines them closely can mistake one for the other.

7.4

That a man is ready to render homage to many gods and goddesses may be cited as evidence of his tolerant spirit. But can it not also be evidence of an insincerity born of a desire to serve the times? I am sure that this toleration is merely insincerity. If this view is well founded, one may ask, what spiritual treasure can there be within a person who is ready to be a priest and a devotee to any deity which it serves his purpose to worship and to adore? Not only must such a person be deemed to be bankrupt of all spiritual treasures, but for him to practise so elevating a profession as that of a priest simply because it is ancestral—without faith, without belief, merely as a mechanical process handed down from father to son—is not a conservation of virtue; it is really the prostitution of a noble profession which is no other than the service of religion.

8

8.1

Why does the Mahatma cling to the theory of everyone following his or her ancestral calling? He gives his reasons nowhere. But there must be some reason, although he does not care to avow it. Years ago, writing on "Caste versus Class" in his *Young India*,[12] he argued that the caste system

---

12 *Young India*, a weekly in English, was founded and published from Bombay since 1915 by Indulal Yagnik, along with Jamnadas Dwarkadas and Shankerlal Banker. Yagnik also brought out *Navajivan*, a monthly in Gujarati. In 1919, Yagnik requested Gandhi, who had returned from South Africa, to take over as editor of *Young India* and *Navajivan*. Under Gandhi's editorship, *Young India* appeared since 7 May 1919 as a biweekly and from 7 September 1919 as a weekly from Sabarmati Ashram, Ahmedabad (Rajmohan Gandhi, 2007, 211). Gandhi published *Young India* till he founded the *Harijan* in 1932. Ambedkar here is referring to Gandhi's piece dated

was better than a class system on the ground that caste was the best possible adjustment for social stability. If that be the reason why the Mahatma clings to the theory of everyone following his or her ancestral calling, then he is clinging to a false view of social life.

8.2

Everybody wants social stability, and some adjustment must be made in the relationship between individuals and classes in order that stability may be had. But two things, I am sure, nobody wants. One thing nobody wants is a static relationship, something that is unalterable, something that is fixed for all times. Stability is wanted, but not at the cost of change when change is imperative. The second thing nobody wants is mere adjustment. Adjustment is wanted, but not at the sacrifice of social justice.

8.3

Can it be said that the adjustment of social relationships on the basis of caste—i.e., on the basis of each to his hereditary calling—avoids these two evils? I am convinced that it does not. Far from being the best possible adjustment, I have no doubt that it is of the worst possible kind, inasmuch as it offends against both the canons of social adjustment—namely, fluidity and equity.

29 December 1920, where he argues why caste is better than class: "The beauty of the caste system is that it does not base itself upon distinctions of wealth-possessions. Money, as history has proved, is the greatest disruptive force in the world. Even the sacredness of family ties is not safe against the pollution of wealth, says Shankaracharya. Caste is but an extension of the principle of the family. Both are governed by blood and heredity… Caste does not connote superiority or inferiority. It simply recognises different outlooks and corresponding modes of life. But it is no use denying the fact that a sort of hierarchy has been evolved in the caste system, but it cannot be called the creation of the Brahmins" (CWMG 22, 154–5).

9

9.1

Some might think that the Mahatma has made much progress, inasmuch as he now only believes in varna and does not believe in caste. It is true that there was a time when the Mahatma was a full-blooded and a blue-blooded sanatani Hindu.[13] He believed in the Vedas, the Upanishads, the puranas, and all that goes by the name of Hindu scriptures; and therefore, in avatars and rebirth. He believed in caste and defended it with the vigour of the orthodox.[14] He condemned the cry for inter-dining, inter-drinking, and intermarrying, and argued that restraints about inter-dining to a great extent

---

13 Gandhi on his being a sanatani: "The friend next asked me for a definition of a sanatani Hindu and said: 'Could a sanatani Hindu Brahmin interdine with a Hindu non-Brahmin although the latter may be a non-vegetarian?' My definition of a sanatani Brahmin is: He who believes in the fundamental principles of Hinduism is a sanatani Hindu. And the fundamental principles of Hinduism are absolute belief in truth (satya) and ahimsa (non-violence)." Reported in *The Hindu*, 23 March 1925, from a speech in Madras at the height of the Non-Brahmin Movement in the Madras Presidency. In another speech in Calcutta, around the same time, Gandhi says: "Let the sanatani Hindus understand from me who claims to be a sanatani Hindu. I do not ask you to interdine with anybody; I do not ask you to exchange your daughters with the Untouchables or with anybody, but I do ask you to remove this curse [of untouchability] so that you may not put him beyond the pale of service." From *Amrita Bazar Patrika*, 2 May 1925. Anil Nauriya, however, makes the case (2006, 1835) that Gandhi's views on varna changed in the mid-1940s and that he came to denounce varnashrama: "Gandhi incrementally unfurled a critique of the fourfold varna order, taking the concept of such an order in the end, by the mid-1940s, to vanishing point." On such exercises in 'cherry picking', see Roy's introduction to this volume.

14 David Hardiman writes (2004, 126) that during the South African years, Gandhi "had appeared to have little time for the caste system. He had been expelled from his own Baniya sub-caste for travelling overseas—considered a 'polluting' act at that time—and had never sought to gain readmission to the caste. In 1909, he condemned the caste system and caste tyranny. On his return to India he adopted a much softer line on the question. He denied that the caste system had harmed India, arguing that it was no more than a form of labour division, similar to occupational divisions all over the world. It was in fact superior to class divisions, 'which were based on wealth primarily'. He also believed that reform could be brought about through caste organisations."

"helped the cultivation of will-power and the conservation of a certain social virtue".[15]

9.2

It is good that he has repudiated this sanctimonious nonsense and admitted that caste "is harmful both to spiritual and national growth", and maybe his son's marriage outside his caste has had something to do with this change of view. But has the Mahatma really progressed? What is the nature of the varna for which the Mahatma stands? Is it the Vedic conception as commonly understood and preached by Swami Dayanand Saraswati and his followers, the Arya Samajists? The essence of the Vedic conception of varna is the pursuit of a calling which is appropriate to one's natural aptitude. The essence of the Mahatma's conception of varna is the pursuit of one's ancestral calling, irrespective of natural aptitude.

9.3

What is the difference between caste and varna, as understood by the Mahatma? I find none. As defined by the Mahatma varna becomes merely a different name for caste, for the simple reason that it is the same in essence—namely, pursuit of one's ancestral calling. Far from making progress, the Mahatma has suffered retrogression. By putting this interpretation upon the Vedic conception of varna, he has really made ridiculous what was sublime. While I reject the Vedic varnavyavastha for reasons given in the speech, I must admit that the Vedic theory of varna as interpreted by Swami Dayanand and some others is a sensible and an inoffensive thing. It did not admit birth as a determining factor in fixing

15 Ambedkar is once again citing Gandhi from his *Young India* piece of 29 December 1920: "Inter-dining has never been known to promote brotherhood in any special sense. But the restraints about interdining have to a great extent helped the cultivation of will-power and the conservation of certain social virtues" (CWMG 22, 156).

the place of an individual in society. It only recognised worth.

9.4

The Mahatma's view of varna not only makes nonsense of the Vedic varna, but it makes it an abominable thing. Varna and caste are two very different concepts. Varna is based on the principle of each according to his worth, while caste is based on the principle of each according to his birth. The two are as distinct as chalk is from cheese. In fact, there is an antithesis between the two. If the Mahatma believes, as he does, in everyone following his or her ancestral calling, then most certainly he is advocating the caste system, and in calling it the varna system he is not only guilty of terminological inexactitude, but he is causing confusion worse confounded.

9.5

I am sure that all his confusion is due to the fact that the Mahatma has no definite and clear conception as to what is varna and what is caste, and as to the necessity of either for the conservation of Hinduism. He has said—and one hopes that he will not find some mystic reason to change his view—that caste is not the essence of Hinduism. Does he regard varna as the essence of Hinduism? One cannot as yet give any categorical answer.

9.6

Readers of his article on "Dr Ambedkar's Indictment" will answer "No." In that article he does not say that the dogma of varna is an essential part of the creed of Hinduism. Far from making varna the essence of Hinduism, he says "the essence of Hinduism is contained in its enunciation of one and only God as truth and its bold acceptance of ahimsa as the law of the human family".

9.7

But readers of his article in reply to Mr Sant Ram will say "Yes." In that article he says "How can a Muslim remain one if he rejects the Quran, or a Christian remain Christian if he rejects the Bible? If caste and varna are convertible terms, and if varna is an integral part of the shastras which define Hinduism, I do not know how a person who rejects caste, i.e., varna, can call himself a Hindu." Why this prevarication? Why does the Mahatma hedge? Whom does he want to please? Has the saint failed to sense the truth? Or does the politician stand in the way of the saint?

9.8

The real reason why the Mahatma is suffering from this confusion is probably to be traced to two sources. The first is the temperament of the Mahatma. He has in almost everything the simplicity of the child, with the child's capacity for self-deception. Like a child, he can believe in anything he wants to believe in. We must therefore wait till such time as it pleases the Mahatma to abandon his faith in varna, as it has pleased him to abandon his faith in caste.

9.9

The second source of confusion is the double role which the Mahatma wants to play—of a Mahatma and a politician. As a Mahatma, he may be trying to spiritualise politics. Whether he has succeeded in it or not, politics have certainly commercialised him. A politician must know that society cannot bear the whole truth, and that he must not speak the whole truth; if he is speaking the whole truth it is bad for his politics. The reason why the Mahatma is always supporting caste and varna is because he is afraid that if he opposed them he would lose his place in politics. Whatever may be the source of this confusion the Mahatma must be told that he is deceiving himself, and also deceiving the people, by preaching caste under the name of varna.

10

10.1

The Mahatma says that the standards I have applied to test Hindus and Hinduism are too severe, and that judged by those standards every known living faith will probably fail. The complaint that my standards are high may be true. But the question is not whether they are high or whether they are low. The question is whether they are the right standards to apply. A people and their religion must be judged by social standards based on social ethics. No other standard would have any meaning, if religion is held to be a necessary good for the well-being of the people.

10.2

Now, I maintain that the standards I have applied to test Hindus and Hinduism are the most appropriate standards, and that I know of none that are better. The conclusion that every known religion would fail if tested by my standards may be true. But this fact should not give the Mahatma as the champion of Hindus and Hinduism a ground for comfort, any more than the existence of one madman should give comfort to another madman, or the existence of one criminal should give comfort to another criminal.

10.3

I would like to assure the Mahatma that it is not the mere failure of the Hindus and Hinduism which has produced in me the feelings of disgust and contempt with which I am charged. I realise that the world is a very imperfect world, and anyone who wants to live in it must bear with its imperfections.

10.4

But while I am prepared to bear with the imperfections and shortcomings of the society in which I may be destined to labour, I feel I should not consent to live in a society which cherishes wrong ideals, or a society which, having right ideals, will not consent to bring its social life into conformity with those ideals. If I am disgusted with Hindus and Hinduism, it is because I am convinced that they cherish wrong ideals and live a wrong social life. My quarrel with Hindus and Hinduism is not over the imperfections of their social conduct. It is much more fundamental. It is over their ideals.

11

11.1

Hindu society seems to me to stand in need of a moral regeneration which it is dangerous to postpone. And the question is, who can determine and control this moral regeneration? Obviously, only those who have undergone an intellectual regeneration and those who are honest enough to have the courage of their convictions born of intellectual emancipation. Judged by this standard, the Hindu leaders who count are, in my opinion, quite unfit for the task. It is impossible to say that they have undergone the preliminary intellectual regeneration. If they had undergone an intellectual regeneration, they would neither delude themselves in the simple way of the untaught multitude, nor would they take advantage of the primitive ignorance of others as one sees them doing.

11.2

Notwithstanding the crumbling state of Hindu society, these leaders will nevertheless unblushingly appeal to ideals of the past which have in every way ceased to have any connection with the present—ideals which, however suitable they might have been in the days of their origin, have now become a warning rather than a guide. They still have a mystic respect for the earlier forms which makes them disinclined—nay, opposed—to any examination of the foundations of their society. The Hindu masses are of course incredibly heedless in the formation of their beliefs. But so are the Hindu leaders. And what is worse is that these Hindu leaders become filled with an illicit passion for their beliefs when anyone proposes to rob them of their companionship.

11.3

The Mahatma is no exception. The Mahatma appears not to believe in thinking. He prefers to follow the saints. Like a conservative with his reverence for consecrated notions, he is afraid that if he once starts thinking, many ideals and institutions to which he clings will be doomed. One must sympathise with him. For every act of independent thinking puts some portion of an apparently stable world in peril.

11.4

But it is equally true that dependence on saints cannot lead us to know the truth. The saints are after all only human beings, and as Lord Balfour said, "the human mind is no more a truth-finding apparatus than the snout of a pig".[16] In so far as he does think, to me he really appears to be prostituting his intelligence to find reasons for supporting this archaic social structure of the Hindus. He is the most influential apologist of it and therefore the worst enemy of the Hindus.

11.5

Unlike the Mahatma, there are Hindu leaders who are not content merely to believe and follow. They dare to think, and act in accordance with the result of their thinking. But

---

16 Lord (Arthur James) Balfour was a British conservative politician who served as Prime Minister between 1902 and 1905 and as Foreign Secretary between 1916 and 1919. It is not clear where Lord Balfour spoke these words, but there are other citations of this from the same period, each slightly differing in detail. *The World Review* (1936, 67) cites Balfour thus: "Lord Balfour has wisely said that 'The human brain is as much an organ for seeking food as the pig's snout.' After all, the human brain is only an enlarged piece of the spinal column, whose first function is to sense danger and preserve life."

unfortunately they are either a dishonest lot, or an indifferent lot when it comes to the question of giving right guidance to the mass of the people. Almost every Brahmin has transgressed the rule of caste. The number of Brahmins who sell shoes is far greater than those who practise priesthood. Not only have the Brahmins given up their ancestral calling of priesthood for trading, but they have entered trades which are prohibited to them by the shastras. Yet how many Brahmins who break caste every day will preach against caste and against the shastras?

11.6

For one honest Brahmin preaching against caste and shastras because his practical instinct and moral conscience cannot support a conviction in them, there are hundreds who break caste and trample upon the shastras every day, but who are the most fanatic upholders of the theory of caste and the sanctity of the shastras. Why this duplicity? Because they feel that if the masses are emancipated from the yoke of caste, they would be a menace to the power and prestige of the Brahmins as a class. The dishonesty of this intellectual class, who would deny the masses the fruits of their thinking, is a most disgraceful phenomenon.

11.7

The Hindus, in the words of Matthew Arnold, are "wandering between two worlds, one dead, the other powerless to be born".[17] What are they to do? The Mahatma to whom they

17 These lines are from the poem "Stanzas from the Grande Chartreuse" by Matthew Arnold (1822–88), English poet and literary critic, reflecting the inner conflict of the Victorian era between scientific progress on the one hand, and religion, identity and values on the other. Ambedkar cites Arnold in "Castes in India" (1916) as well, written during his years at Columbia University. It is possible that Ambedkar often turned to Arnold thanks to his mentor Dewey, who was fond of quoting him.According to S. Morris Eames (1969, xxxvii), Dewey's essay "Poetry and Philosophy" (1890) begins with a long epigraph from Arnold. Eames

appeal for guidance does not believe in thinking, and can therefore give no guidance which can be said to stand the test of experience. The intellectual classes to whom the masses look for guidance are either too dishonest or too indifferent to educate them in the right direction. We are indeed witnesses to a great tragedy. In the face of this tragedy all one can do is to lament and say—such are thy leaders, O Hindus!

---

says: "Dewey is appreciative of many of the insights of Matthew Arnold, and in later years he turns again and again to ideas he attributed to this poet and critic. Arnold once wrote that 'poetry is a criticism of life', and while Dewey thinks that poetry is more than this, he was influenced by Arnold's view in transferring it into philosophy, for he later writes that philosophy 'is inherently criticism', and in his own method makes philosophy 'a criticism of criticisms'." This idea is also echoed by the Italian political thinker Antonio Gramsci (1891–1937), a contemporary of Ambedkar: "The crisis consists precisely in the fact that the old is dying and the new cannot be born; in this interregnum a great variety of morbid symptoms appear" (1971, 276).

A Note on the Poona Pact

A Note on the Poona Pact

S. Anand

If the Communal Award of 16 August 1932 was a victory of sorts for those who sought to take social difference seriously in India, the Poona Pact of 24 September 1932 was a defeat. At a time of urgent political and ideological contestation over the future of India, the pact abruptly came in the way of more ambitious ways of fashioning a democracy that would suit a subcontinent made up essentially of caste, religious, regional and linguistic minorities, what B.R. Ambedkar termed a "congeries of communities".[1] This was a time when Ambedkar, with radical foresight, was trying to stymie the adoption of a first-past-the-post system, which he feared in the Indian context would result in a Hindu communal majority parading as a political majority. M.K. Gandhi, on the other hand, opposed special representation to every other community except the Muslims and the Sikhs. He argued that separate electorates "would simply vivisect and disrupt" Hinduism, and suggested that the Communal Award "will create a division in Hinduism which I cannot possibly look forward to with any satisfaction whatsoever".[2] It was to oppose the political rights granted to the Untouchables by the Communal Award that Gandhi took a dramatic and coercive step—a fast unto death on 20 September 1932 that culminated in the Poona Pact only four days later.

Indian academia, its intelligentsia and the political establishment have remained, for the most part, indifferent to the complex workings of both the Communal Award and the Poona

Pact. (The few exceptions have mostly been followers of the Dalit movement.[3]) In nationalist histories, the Communal Award, which granted separate electorates not just to Untouchables but to Muslims, Sikhs, Christians, Anglo-Indians, Europeans, landlords, labourers and traders, continues to be depicted as unambiguously divisive. Since *Annihilation of Caste* is in part a response to the disappointment Ambedkar felt over the Poona Pact, it is important to understand what it practically meant. What led to the Communal Award? What was the thrust of Gandhi's opposition to it? What were the terms of the Poona Pact? Did the Congress honour these terms? The answers to these questions also hold the key to understanding Ambedkar's vehement attack on not just the caste system, but on Hinduism itself and its founding texts, in *Annihilation of Caste*.[4] Indeed Ambedkar was so devastated that he also went on to write—thirteen years after the Poona Pact—the strongest indictment of the pact, Gandhi and the Congress in *What Congress and Gandhi Have Done to the Untouchables.*

The first Round Table Conference (RTC) was convened in London by the Labour government of Ramsay MacDonald from 12 November 1930 to 19 January 1931 to discuss the future constitution of India. Since Gandhi had initiated the Civil Disobedience Movement in 1930, the Congress abstained from the first round, which was eventually attended by Ambedkar and Rettamalai Srinivasan representing the Untouchables, M.A. Jinnah (among others) representing the Muslims, and representatives of various minority communities as well as of the princely states. However, by the time of the second RTC, Lord Irwin came to an agreement with the Congress, and it decided to attend the conference (from 7 September 1931 to 1 December 1931), with Gandhi as its representative.

At the conference, Gandhi impugned the leaders of the Muslim, Sikh, Untouchable and Christian communities, ridiculing their claims to self-representation. While he eventually came around to accepting the communal scheme of representation for Sikhs and Muslims, Gandhi was particularly opposed to Ambedkar, who made a case for "separate electorates" for the Depressed Classes. What for Ambedkar was a matter of securing the political rights of the Untouchables was for Gandhi a matter of religion. In a letter to Sir Samuel Hoare, then Secretary of State for India, on 11 March 1932, he said: "For me the question of these classes is predominantly moral and religious. The political aspect, important though it is, dwindles into insignificance compared to the moral and religious issue."[5]

Ambedkar's report on the seriousness with which Gandhi attended the conference is worth quoting at length:

> I am sure I am not exaggerating or misrepresenting facts when I say that the Congress point of view at the Round Table Conference was that the Congress was the only party in India and that nobody else counted and that the British should settle with the Congress only. This was the burden of Mr Gandhi's song at the Round Table Conference. He was so busy in establishing his own claim to recognition by the British as the dictator of India that he forgot altogether that the important question was not with whom the settlement should be made but what were to be the terms of that settlement. As to the terms of the settlement, Mr Gandhi was quite unequal to the task. When he went to London he had forgotten that he would have before him not those who go to him to obtain his advice and return with his blessings but persons who would treat him as a lawyer treats a witness in the box. Mr Gandhi also forgot that he was going to a political conference. He went there as though he was going to a Vaishnava Shrine singing Narsi Mehta's songs. When I think of the whole affair I am wondering if any nation had ever sent a representative to negotiate the terms of a national settlement who was more unfit than Mr Gandhi.[6]

Gandhi held on to the view that the Congress was the

sole representative of all Indians. In an article in *Harijan* on 21 October 1939, tellingly captioned "The Fiction of Majority", he wrote with the conviction that only a Mahatma can summon:

> I know that many have been angry with me for claiming an exclusive right for the Congress to speak for the people of India as a whole. It is not an arrogant pretension. It is explicit in the first article of the Congress. It wants and works for independence for the whole of India. It speaks neither for majority nor minority. It seeks to represent all Indians without any distinction. Therefore those who oppose it should not count, if the claim for independence is admitted. Those who support the claim simply give added strength to the Congress claim... In other words and in reality, so far as India is concerned, there can only be political parties and no majority or minority communities. The cry of the tyranny of the majority is a fictitious cry.[7]

In this piece, Gandhi goes on to mock all claims to minority rights, saying Brahmins and zamindars (landlords) too could claim the minority tag.

Notwithstanding Gandhi's opposition, the Communal Award of 16 August 1932 allotted, among other things, separate electorates and two votes to the Depressed Classes/Untouchables for twenty years, though Ambedkar had sought them only for ten years. Clause 9 of the Award read:

> Members of the 'Depressed Classes' qualified to vote will vote in a general constituency. In view of the fact that for a considerable period these classes would be unlikely, by this means alone, to secure any adequate representation in the Legislature, a number of special seats will be assigned to them... These seats will be filled by election from special constituencies in which only members of the 'Depressed Classes' electorally qualified will be entitled to vote. Any person voting in such a special constituency will, as stated above, be also entitled to vote in a general constituency. It is intended that these constituencies should be formed in selected

areas where the Depressed Classes are most numerous, and that, except in Madras, they should not cover the whole area of the Province.[8]

In these double-member constituencies (DMCs), one member was to be selected from among Untouchables (or Adivasis/Scheduled Tribes as the case may be), and one from among the Hindus.[9] This meant, first, that Untouchables, and only Untouchables, would choose their representatives to legislatures. Second, they would be able to cast a second ballot to have a say in who among the caste Hindus was best suited—or least inimical—to represent Untouchable interests in a legislative body. Such safeguards were necessary, argued Ambedkar, since not only were Untouchables outnumbered by savarnas (caste Hindus), sometimes to the tune of "one to ten", they were also physically vulnerable to attacks by caste Hindus during elections—the kind of violence that continues to take place in most parts of India even today. Since the Untouchables did not enjoy civil, economic or religious rights on a par with the caste Hindus, and they were widely and routinely stigmatised, Ambedkar believed that a mere right to vote would do them no good, and that they would be subject to the manipulations and machinations of Hindus. The double vote, with the right to exclusively elect their own representatives, would ensure that the savarnas and the rest of society came to regard Untouchables as worthy of respect and dignity. Indeed, Untouchables would become politically consequential citizens—Dalits.

Gandhi's response to the Communal Award was to deploy the most powerful weapon in his arsenal. He announced that he would fast—unto death—until the Award was revoked. The nation flew into panic. Gandhi's lieutenant, C. Rajagopalachari, suggested that the "20th of September should be observed as a day of fasting and prayer all over India".[10]

The British government said it would revoke the Award only if Ambedkar agreed. At first, Ambedkar asked Gandhi to weigh in the truth: "If the Mahatma chooses to ask the Depressed Classes to make a choice between Hindu faith and possession of political power, I am quite sure that the Depressed Classes will choose political power and save the Mahatma from self-immolation."[11] Ambedkar was making a point he had always made—about his unease with being told that the Untouchables belong to the 'Hindu' fold. "I'm not a part of the whole. I am a part apart," he was to say as a member of the Bombay Legislative Assembly in 1939.[12]

As Ambedkar stood his ground, the British Prime Minister Ramsay MacDonald tried to reassure Gandhi that the provisions of the Communal Award did not in any way divide the Depressed Classes and the Hindus. In a letter dated 8 September 1932, he explained to Gandhi that "the Depressed Classes will remain part of the Hindu community and will vote with the Hindu electorate on an equal footing". MacDonald pointed out that in the "limited number of special constituencies" meant to safeguard the "rights and interests" of the Untouchables, "the Depressed Classes will not be deprived of their votes in the general Hindu constituencies, but will have two votes in order that their membership of the Hindu community should remain unimpaired". He further argued that such safeguards were not applicable to Muslims who "cannot vote or be a candidate in a general constituency, whereas any electorally qualified member of the Depressed Classes can vote in and stand for the general constituency".[13]

On 19 September, one day before the commencement of Gandhi's fast, Ambedkar said, "I can never consent to deliver my people bound hand and foot to the Caste Hindus for generations to come." He described Gandhi's epic fast as an "extreme form of coercion", a "foul and filthy act", and a "vow of self-immolation".[14]

Gandhi nevertheless went ahead with his religious "vow". Almost all the leaders of the national movement rallied behind him, and by implication, against Ambedkar. Gandhi's son Devdas publicly begged Ambedkar to save his father's life. Pleading with the Mahatma to relent, Ambedkar pointed out that should Gandhi die, it would "result in nothing but terrorism by his followers against the Depressed Classes all over the country".[15] Vulnerable and hated and living on the margins of a society that routinely resorted to collective punishment against them, this was not a chance Ambedkar could, in good conscience, afford to take on behalf of the Untouchables. He had been placed in an impossible position, and forced into a decision that would haunt him for the rest of his life. On 24 September 1932, Ambedkar gave in and signed the Poona Pact as the principal signatory on behalf of the Depressed Classes, while the right-wing Hindu Mahasabha leader, Pandit Madan Mohan Malaviya, represented Gandhi and the Hindus. Gandhi did not sign the pact.

Under the Poona Pact, Untouchables had to give up their separate electorate and be part of joint electorates with Hindus. They also had to give up the unique political weapon Ambedkar had won for them—the second vote that would give them a say in the election of caste-Hindu candidates in their constituency. All that remained for Scheduled Castes was a reserved seat whose holder would be selected by the general population. The Scheduled Caste representative would, in effect, be selected by the very caste-Hindu majority that had already proved its hostility to Scheduled Caste political aspirations.

What was the immediate fallout of the 1932 arrangement? Once the provisions of the Poona Pact were incorporated into the Government of India Act of 1935—the Constitution of British India—elections to the provincial legislatures took place in February 1937. This was to be the first test of the efficacy of the Poona Pact, whose key provision lay in Clause 2:

> Election to these seats shall be by joint electorates subject, however, to the following procedure:
>
> All the members of the Depressed Classes, registered in the general electoral roll in a constituency, will form an electoral college, which will elect a panel of four candidates belonging to the Depressed Classes for each of such reserved seats by the method of the single vote; the four persons getting the highest number of votes in such primary election shall be candidates for election by the general electorate.[16]

While the novel concept of 'primaries' was thus introduced for the first time in India, the vague wording left a lot to interpretation. The seemingly innocuous "panel of four", Ambedkar felt, could be misused and abused. Should the panel have a minimum of four members or a maximum of four candidates? And what would be the method of voting in the final election? To address such questions a committee, headed by Sir Laurie Hammond, was constituted. According to Ambedkar, the Hindus maintained that the panel of four was intended to be a minimum. This meant that if four candidates were not forthcoming or available, there could be no primary election, and thus there would be no election for the reserved seat. In his deposition before the Hammond Committee, Ambedkar asserted that four in the Poona Pact meant "not more than four", and not "not less than four". Ambedkar believed that a baggy panel of four meant the Hindus would be at an advantage "to capture the seat for an election of such a representative of the Untouchable candidate who would be their nominee and who would be most willing to be the tool of the Hindus".[17] That is, the Hindus would ensure a weak and pliable Untouchable candidate in the panel, and further on elect such a person. Suppose there was no panel, and only Untouchables got to decide who would represent them, such a candidate, according to Ambedkar, "would be the staunchest representative of the Untouchables and worst from the standpoint of the Hindus".[18]

Furthermore, the representative of the Hindus deposing to the Hammond Committee claimed that the "compulsory distributive" vote was the most appropriate, while Ambedkar argued for the "cumulative" system of voting. Under compulsory distributive vote, "the elector has also as many votes as there are seats, but he can give only one vote to any one candidate". This means the Untouchable voter cannot cast all four votes to one favoured candidate. This could happen under the cumulative system, where "the elector has as many votes as there are seats" and "may give them all to one candidate or he may distribute them over two or more candidates as he may desire".[19] Ambedkar argued that under the distributive mechanism the possibilities of manipulation were higher:

> Their main object was to flood the election to the seat reserved for the Untouchables in the joint electorate by using the surplus votes of the Hindus in favour of the Untouchable candidate who happens to be their nominee. The object was to outnumber the Untouchable voters and prevent them from electing their own nominee. This cannot be done unless the surplus votes of the Hindu voters were diverted from the Hindu candidate towards the Untouchable candidates. There is a greater chance of the diversion of these surplus votes under the distributive system than there is under the cumulative system.[20]

In Ambedkar's reckoning, if the caste Hindus were given a clearer choice under the cumulative system, they would prefer to fight their battles with one another—a caste-Hindu voter could give all votes to his favourite caste-Hindu candidate as against rival caste-Hindu candidates, and leave the Untouchable candidates untouched. But if they were forced to give only one vote per candidate, in the distributive system, their hatred for a radical Untouchable candidate would outweigh, in their minds, the preference for a second, third or fourth caste-Hindu candidate.

After hearing out all views, the Hammond Committee ruled that the number four in the primaries panel is "neither a maximum nor a minimum, but an optimum". It further ruled that "if there is only one candidate as the result of the primary election, or on account of subsequent withdrawals, that candidate should be returned unopposed for the reserved seat at the final election".[21] Another crucial decision was that the "primary election should take place two months before the final election", thus providing ample scope for the caste Hindus to back their preferred Untouchable candidate.

The tug of war since the Round Table Conferences was about who would have the 'final say'. The caste Hindus wanted to have the final say in the lives of Untouchables even in the new paradigms of electoral democracy and representation. However, given that they were a persecuted minority, the Untouchables—represented by Ambedkar—wanted to reverse this historical logic and have a final say in the lives of caste Hindus, the majority community. For the Hindus, led by Gandhi, this radical idea was anathema. Ambedkar reflects on this conundrum in *Annihilation of Caste* by comparing the Communal Award with the republican constitution of Rome, where he argues that the patricians and the plebeians "formed two distinct castes". The plebeians "never could get a plebeian consul who could be said to be a strong man, and who could act independently of the patrician consul". Ambedkar likens the manner in which the plebeians lose their rights to how Untouchables lose out in the Poona Pact—the caste Hindus and patricians offer some concessions but retain a final say in the lives of Untouchables and plebeians respectively.[22]

Although Ambedkar conceded that the number of seats Untouchables got after the Poona Pact had almost doubled compared to what he had bargained for in the Communal Award,[23] he was alert to its true import. Ambedkar lamented the loss of the "priceless privilege" of the double vote whose "value as a political weapon was beyond reckoning":

> No caste-Hindu candidate could have dared to neglect the Untouchable in his constituency or be hostile to their interest if he was made dependent upon the votes of the Untouchables. Today the Untouchables have a few more seats than were given to them by the Communal Award. But this is all that they have. Every other member is indifferent, if not hostile. If the Communal Award with its system of double voting had remained the Untouchables would have had a few seats less but every other member would have been a member for the Untouchables. The increase in the number of seats for the Untouchables is no increase at all and was no recompense for the loss of separate electorates and the double vote.[24]

At the heart of Ambedkar's approach to democracy was the question of how to ensure that all minorities—especially, but not only, the Untouchables—could successfully bargain for adequate protections. Democracy, in theory, was premised on the idea of 'one person, one value' and hence 'one person, one vote'. But Untouchables, treated as lesser humans, were not accorded the same value as Touchables. To make democracy substantive in a caste-differentiated society, therefore, it required modification. In such a redesigned democracy, the value of a devalued Untouchable had to be deliberately raised through special provisions such as the double vote or the adoption of the principle of reservation, or both.

In the 1937 elections, there were 151 reserved seats[25] from which only Untouchables could be elected. The Congress won seventy-eight of these, and in Ambedkar's words, it "left only 73 seats to be filled by true and independent representatives of the Untouchables" (BAWS 9, 92). For, he argued, the majority of seventy-eight seats won by the Congress "were won with the help of Hindu votes and they do not therefore in any way represent the Scheduled Castes" (BAWS 9, iii). Significantly, the Congress, despite its financial muscle, lost out to non-Congress Untouchable candidates in Bombay and Bengal, where the Dalit movement was strong. Ambedkar formed the Independent Labour Party only five months before the February 1937 election, despite which the ILP "obtained an astonishing degree of success. Out of the 15 seats assigned to the Scheduled Castes in Bombay Presidency it captured 13 and in addition it won 2 general seats".[26]

More crucially, according to Ambedkar, the Congress provincial ministries across the country decided not to offer any cabinet posts to a single one of the seventy-eight Untouchable legislators. At the Round Table Conferences, Ambedkar had "pressed the claim of the Untouchables for the recognition of their right to representation in the Cabinet with the same emphasis" as he had done for "the recognition of their right to representation in the Legislature".[27] When Narayan Bhaskar Khare,[28] the Prime Minister of the Congress ministry in the Central Provinces, formed a Cabinet with R.G. Agnibhoj, an Untouchable, as one of his ministers, the Congress Working Committee met in Wardha and passed a resolution on 26 July 1938 condemning Khare. Ambedkar says:

> Dr Khare openly said that according to Mr Gandhi the act of indiscipline consisted in the inclusion of an Untouchable in the Ministry. Dr Khare also said that Mr Gandhi told him that it was wrong on his part to have raised such aspirations and ambitions in the Untouchables and it was such an act of bad judgement that he would never forgive him. This statement was repeatedly made by Dr Khare from platforms. Mr Gandhi has never contradicted it.[29]

In 1942, an Untouchable member of the Congress, having attended the All-India Scheduled Castes Conference, wrote a letter to Gandhi and signed it as "Five Questions by a Harijan M.L.A." He sought to know from Gandhi if in the future constitution of India he would ensure the representation of Untouchables by agreeing "to fix the five seats from a Panchayat Board upwards to the State Council on population basis"; if, "in view of the backwardness of the Harijans", Gandhi would advise the government to ensure that executive posts in the "Local Boards and Municipal Councils be held on communal rotation, so as to enable the Harijans to become Presidents and Chairmen"; if he would advise Congress ministries to ensure that Scheduled Caste legislators are made Cabinet ministers; and if he could "fix some percentage of seats for Harijans from District Congress Committee upwards to the Working Committee of the Congress". Gandhi's reply, given on 2 August 1942 in his mouthpiece *Harijan*, resorted to the logic of meritocracy used often by those opposed to any form of affirmative action:

> The principle is dangerous. Protection of its neglected classes should not be carried to an extent which will harm them and harm the country. A cabinet minister should be a topmost man commanding universal confidence. A person after he has secured a seat in an elected body should depend upon his intrinsic merit and popularity to secure coveted positions.[30]

Ambedkar also saw a pattern in the manner in which the Congress oversaw the selection of non-Brahmin and Untouchable candidates:

> From candidates who came from high caste Hindus, such as Brahmins and the allied communities, those with the highest qualifications were selected. In the case of the Non-Brahmins those with low qualifications were preferred to those with higher qualifications. And in the case of the Untouchables those with little or no qualifications were selected in preference to those who had.[31]

He came to the conclusion that "the Congress sucked the juice out of the Poona Pact and threw the rind in the face of the Untouchables".[32]

The ghost of the Poona Pact was to haunt the man who knew how the caste Hindus would use its logic to ensure the defeat of the best of Dalits.[33] Thus the man who from 1946 to 1950 piloted the drafting of the Indian Constitution was humiliated twice at the hustings in independent India, both times by less able candidates that the Congress fielded. In the first ever polls to the Lok Sabha in 1951, contesting on the ticket of his party, the Scheduled Castes Federation, from the reserved part of the double-member Bombay North constituency, Ambedkar was defeated by 14,374 votes by Narayan Sadoba Kajrolkar of the Congress. The Congress deliberately fielded a candidate who was a Chambhar, the largest Untouchable caste after the Mahars in the region. He was also a known opponent of Ambedkar, a Mahar.[34] Kajrolkar had opposed Ambedkar on the Communal Award as well as over his call for conversion, saying "we are shocked at the advice given to us, Harijans, by our veteran leader Dr Ambedkar, to abandon the Hindu religion… It breaks our hearts to see … [that] Dr Ambedkar who gave us a prominent lead in the past, should ask us to commit suicide by abandoning our religion."[35] When Ambedkar tried his luck in the 1954 by-election from Bhandara, Maharashtra, he lost again, this time to another Congress candidate, Bhaurao Borkar, someone who earlier used to organise workers for the Scheduled Castes Federation, the party founded and led by Ambedkar.

Today, India boasts of having a system of political reservations that ensures that Scheduled Castes and Scheduled Tribes are elected to all legislative bodies—from the panchayat upwards—in proportion to their share in the population. In the case of the Lok Sabha, the Lower House of Parliament, of its 543 seats, seventy-nine are reserved for Dalits, and forty-one for Adivasis.

However, Ambedkar, and Dalits today, would have been happier with more juice and less rind.

NOTES

1 BAWS 4, 13.

2 Cited in BAWS 9, 78.

3 The demand to restore the double vote to Dalits and separate electorates has been made by both fringe and frontline Dalit groups—to no effect. In Tamil Nadu, the initiatives led by Ravikumar in the mid-1990s, where eleven conferences were held demanding that the Communal Award be re-introduced, are documented in the film *One Weapon* (1997) by Sanjay Kak. The most vociferous attack on the Poona Pact in post-independence India was led by Kanshi Ram even before he founded the Bahujan Samaj Party (BSP) in 1984. On 24 September 1982, he catapulted onto the national stage by mourning the fiftieth anniversary of the signing of the Poona Pact. Less than a year before, Kanshi Ram—then relatively unknown—had founded the Dalit Shoshit Samaj Sangharsh Samiti (known as DS4) on the anniversary of Ambedkar's death, 6 December 1981. His frontal attack on the Poona Pact, through sixty simultaneous denunciation programmes from Poona to Jalandhar, made Prime Minister Indira Gandhi abandon her plans to commemorate the occasion. Kanshi Ram believed that it was the Poona Pact that had turned elected Dalit representatives into lackeys of the Congress party. He called them chamchas (stooges), and termed the post-Poona Pact era the 'Chamcha Age'. For Kanshi Ram, the best representative of Congress-reared chamchas was Jagjivan Ram—projected by Gandhi and the Congress as the 'Harijan face' of their party—who eventually rose to become Deputy Prime Minister. Till date, the BSP remains the only mainstream political party that speaks unambiguously against the Poona Pact and Gandhi.

4 Those keen on an exhaustive engagement with the Communal Award and the Poona Pact would benefit by reading Ambedkar's 1945 classic, *What Congress and Gandhi Have Done to the Untouchables* (BAWS 9). The essays of Ravinder Kumar (1985) and Upendra Baxi (1979, 1995) may also be consulted. For a Gandhian account of the Poona Pact, see his secretary Pyarelal's

volume (1932), which, Ambedkar says "bears the picturesque and flamboyant title of *The Epic Fast*. The curious may refer to it. I must, however, warn him that it is written by a Boswell and has all the faults of Boswelliana" (BAWS 9, 87).

5 Cited in BAWS 9, 78.

6 BAWS 1, 351–2.

7 CWMG 77, 5.

8 BAWS 9, 81.

9 Baxi explains the workings of a DMC: "On counting of votes, the leading Scheduled Caste or Tribe candidate got the reserved seat. Thereafter, all the other candidates, including the scheduled groups, were considered to be in competition for the general seat, which was awarded to the candidate who polled the largest number of votes. Thus, if the scheduled groups polled the largest number of votes in the second category the system will produce two of their representatives, instead of one as in the system of reserved constituency" (1979, 19). Even the Poona Pact worked on the basis of such double-member constituencies, and these continued to operate in India till 1961, when they were abolished after two Scheduled Tribe candidates "got higher votes than the two non-tribal candidates and were declared elected" (Baxi 1979, 19), resulting in the defeat of the Congress stalwart and future President of India V.V. Giri from the Parvatipuram constituency in Andhra Pradesh in 1959 to Dippala Suri Dora. Giri contested this 'injustice' in the Supreme Court, which saw nothing wrong with a tribal candidate winning the confidence of the general electorate. As Baxi puts it, "Giri's election petition, in which he even argued that [the] reservations policies infringe the fundamental right guaranteed under Article 14, was negatived by the Supreme Court in 1959." The Congress-dominated Parliament then decided to do away with DMCs through the Two-Member Constituencies (Abolition) Act, 1961, putting an end to ninety-one such Lok Sabha constituencies, which were subsequently delimited and converted to single-member constituencies.

10 Pyarelal 1932, 19.

11 BAWS 9, 326.

12 BAWS 10, 166.

13 BAWS 9, 85.
14 Ibid., 253. 259, 312.
15 Ibid., 316.
16 For the full text of the Poona Pact, see ibid., 88–9
17 Ibid., 92.
18 Ibid., 92.
19 Ibid., 92.
20 Ibid., 92.
21 Cited in Khan 1937, 319.
22 See AoC, 2.20, 3.3–3.6.
23 The Poona Pact gave the Untouchables 148 seats, while the Communal Award had given them seventy-eight.
24 Ibid., 90.
25 While 148 was the number agreed upon in the Poona Pact, three seats had to be added to make adjustments to accommodate Bihar and Orissa.
26 Ibid., iii.
27 Ibid., 95.
28 It is worth noting that Khare had been among those who delivered a presidential address to the Jat-Pat Todak Mandal. See Note 16 to AoC Preface.
29 BAWS 9, 98.
30 CWMG 83, 119.
31 BAWS 9, 101.
32 Ibid., 103.
33 The Poona Pact continues to haunt Dalits and Dalit-led political parties. While pliable candidates can contest and win with a ticket from any of the mainstream parties—Congress, Bharatiya Janata Party, Dravida Munnetra Kazhagam or the communist parties—it took many defeats before Bahujan Samaj Party stalwarts Kanshi Ram and Mayawati could win elections, even from reserved constituencies. Even today, it is rare for a Dalit candidate to win from a general, non-reserved constituency—irrespective of the party she represents. In fact, this has not been possible even at the height of the BSP's popularity in Uttar Pradesh. During the 2007 assembly elections in the state, the BSP fielded only four of its ninety-three Dalit candidates in general constituencies. The non-Dalit vote in a general constituency does not easily transfer

to a Dalit, it seems, as all four lost; meanwhile, sixty-two of the eighty-nine candidates fielded in reserved constituencies won. For an analysis of how the BSP managed to wrest power despite parliamentary democracy, see Anand (2008).

34 Zelliot in Kothari 1973, 53.

35 Burra 1986, 430.

BIBLIOGRAPHY

Ahmad, Imtiaz. 1978. *Caste and Social Stratification Among Muslims in India.* Delhi: Manohar.

Aloysius, G. 1997. *Nationalism Without a Nation in India.* New Delhi: Oxford University Press.

——. 2004. Introd. to *Swami Dharmateertha, No Freedom with Caste: The Menace of Hindu Imperialism.* New Delhi: Media House. (Orig. publ. Krishnanagar, Lahore: Happy Home Publication, 1941.)

Ambedkar, B.R. 1979. "Castes in India: Their Mechanism, Genesis and Development." *Indian Antiquary* 41:81–95. Repr. BAWS, vol. 1, 5–22. Mumbai: Education Department, Government of Maharashtra. (Orig. publ. 1917.)

——. 1987a. "Krishna and His Gita." In BAWS, vol. 3, 375–80. Bombay: Education Department, Government of Maharashtra.

——. 1987b. "Revolution and Counter-Revolution in Ancient India." In BAWS, vol. 3. Bombay: Education Department, Government of Maharashtra.

——. 1987c. "Philosophy of Hinduism." In BAWS, vol. 3, 1–92. Bombay: Education Department, Government of Maharashtra.

——. 1989a. "Essays on Untouchables and Untouchability." In BAWS, vol. 5, Bombay: Education Department, Government of Maharashtra.

——. 1989b. "Untouchables or the Children of India's Ghetto." In BAWS, vol. 5. Bombay: Education Department, Government of Maharashtra.

——. 1990. *The Untouchables: Who Were They and Why They Became Untouchable.* In BAWS, vol. 7. Bombay: Education Department, Government of Maharashtra. (Orig. publ. 1948.)

——. 1991. *What Congress and Gandhi Have Done to the Untouchables.* In BAWS, vol. 9. Bombay: Education Department, Government of Maharashtra. (Orig. publ. 1945.)

——. 1992. "Dr Ambedkar's Speech at Mahad [1927]." In *Poisoned Bread: Translations from Modern Marathi Dalit Literature.* Ed. Arjun Dangle, 223–33. Hyderabad: Orient Longman.

——. 2010. "Capitalism, Labour and Brahminism." Speech delivered 12–13 February 1938. In *Thus Spoke Ambedkar, Vol. 1: A Stake in the*

Nation. Ed. Bhagwan Das, 49–68. New Delhi: Navayana.

Anand, S. 2008. "Despite Parliamentary Democracy." *Himal*, August. http://www.himalmag.com/component/content/article/838-despite-parliamentary-democracy.html. Accessed 20 July 2013.

——. 2010. "Equalisation to Annihilation—and Beyond." *Himal*, April. http://www.himalmag.com/component/content/article/53/118-equalisation-to-annihilation-and-beyond.html. Accessed 10 March 2013.

Anjum, Tanvir. 2011. *From Restrained Indifference to Calculated Defiance: Chishti Sufis in the Sultanate of Delhi (1190–1400)*. New Delhi: Oxford University Press.

Ansari, Khalid Anis. 2013. "Muslims that 'Minority Politics' Left Behind." *The Hindu*, 17 June. http://www.thehindu.com/opinion/lead/muslims-that-minority-politics-left-behind/article4820565.ece. Accessed 20 April 2013.

Anwar, Ali. 2005. *Masawat ki Jung* [Battle for equality]. New Delhi: Indian Social Institute.

Armstrong, Karen. 2000. *Islam: A Short History*. New York: Random House.

Bachchan, Harivansh Rai. 1998. *In the Afternoon of Time: An Autobiography*. New Delhi: Penguin.

Ballhatchet, Kenneth. 1998. *Caste, Class and Catholicism in India: 1789–1914*. Cornwall: Curzon Press.

Bapu, Prabhu. 2013. *Hindu Mahasabha in Colonial North India, 1915–1930: Constructing Nation and History*. Oxon: Routledge.

Bartley, C.J. 2002. *The Theology of Ramanuja: Realism and Religion*. London: Routledge.

Baruah, Sanjib. 2007. *Durable Disorder: Understanding the Politics of Northeast India*. New Delhi: Oxford University Press.

Bateson, William. 1909. *Mendel's Principles of Heredity*. Cambridge: Cambridge University Press.

Baxi, Upendra. 1979. *Political Reservations for the Scheduled Castes: B.R. Ambedkar Memorial Lecture*. Madras: University of Madras.

——. 1995. "Emancipation as Justice: Babasaheb Ambedkar's Legacy and Vision." In *Crisis and Change in Contemporary India*. Ed. Upendra Baxi and Bhikhu Parekh, 122–49. New Delhi: Sage.

Bayly, Susan. 1999. *Caste, Society and Politics in India: From the Eighteenth Century to Modern India*. Cambridge: Cambridge University Press.

Bendrey, V.S. 1960. *Coronation of Sivaji the Great*. Bombay: PPH Bookstall.

Benson, James, ed. 2010. *Mahadeva Vedantin: Mimamsanyayasamgraha: A Compendium of the Principles of Mimamsa*. Wiesbaden: Harrassowitz Verlag.

Bhagwan, Har (Sethi). 1974. "Experiences of a Worker". *The Atheist* 6, March–April. Vijayawada: Atheist Centre.

Bhai Parmanand. 2003. *The Story of My Life*. Tr.N. Sundra Iyer and Lal Chand. Lahore: The Central Hindu Yuvak Sabha. Repr. New Delhi: Ocean Books. (Orig. publ. 1934.)

Bhandarkar, D.R. 1911. "Foreign Elements in the Hindu Population." *Indian Antiquary* 40: 7–37.

Blavatsky, H.P. 1892/2010. *From the Caves and Jungles of Hindostan*. Gloucester: Dodo Press.

Brailsford, Henry Noel. 1931. *Rebel India*. London: Leonard Stein and Victor Gollancz.

——. 1936. "Morality and the Social Structure". *Aryan Path*, April: 166–9.

Brasted, Howard. 1980. "Indian Nationalist Development and the Influence of Irish Home Rule, 1870–1886." *Modern Asian Studies* 14 (1): 37–63.

Brockington, J.L. 1996. *The Sacred Thread: A Short History of Hinduism*. Edinburgh: Edinburgh University Press.

Bühler, George. 1886. *The Laws of Manu*. Sacred Books of the East 25. Oxford: Clarendon Press. Repr. 2004. New Delhi: Cosmo.

——. 1898. *The Sacred Laws of the Aryas: As Taught in the Schools of Apastamba, Gautama, Vasishtha and Baudhayana*. New York: The Christian Literature Company. (Orig. publ. 1879.)

Burke, Edmund. 2001. *Reflections on the Revolution in France: A Critical Edition*. Ed. J.C.D. Clark. Stanford: Stanford University Press. (Orig. publ. 1790.)

Burra, Neera. 1986. "Was Ambedkar Just a Leader of the Mahars?" *Economic & Political Weekly*, 15 March: 429–31.

Carlyle, Thomas. 1831. *Sartor Resartus: The Life and Opinions of Herr Teufelsdrockh*. http://archive.org/details/sartor00-resartuslicarlrich.

Accessed 20 June 2013.

——. 1840. *On Heroes, Hero-Worship and the Heroic in History*. London: Chapman and Hall. http://www.gutenberg.org/files/1091/1091-h/1091-h.htm. Accessed 20 June 2013.

Carver, Thomas Nixon. 1915. *"What is Justice?" Essays in Social Justice*. Cambridge: Harvard University Press. http://archive.org/details/essaysinsocialju00carv. Accessed 12 May 2013.

Census of India. 1961. Volume 11, Part 6, Issue 14. New Delhi: Office of the Registrar General.

Chakravarti, Uma. 1995. "Wifehood, Widowhood, and Adultery: Female Sexuality, Surveillance, and the State in Eighteenth-Century Maharashtra." *Contributions to Indian Sociology*, n.s., 29 (1–2): 3–21.

——. 2000. *Rewriting History: Life and Times of Pandita Ramabai*. New Delhi: Kali for Women.

Chandra, Uday. 2013. "Liberalism and Its Other: The Politics of Primitivism in Colonial and Postcolonial Indian Law." *Law & Society Review* 47 (1): 135–68.

Charsley, Simon. 1996. "'Untouchable': What is in a Name?" *The Journal of the Royal Anthropological Institute* 2 (1): 1–23.

Chomsky, Noam. 2003. On Dewey. http://www.american-philosophy.org/Chomsky_on_Dewey_transcript_2003.html.

——. 2013. "Can Civilization Survive Capitalism?" AlterNet. http://www.alternet.org/noam-chomsky-can-civilization-survive-capitalism.

Clooney, Francis, S.J. 1990. *Thinking Ritually: Rediscovering the Purva Mimamsa of Jaimini*. Vienna: Publications of the de Nobili Research Library.

Dalal, Chandulal Bhagubhai. 2007. *Harilal Gandhi: A Life*. Ed. and tr. Tridip Suhrud. Hyderabad: Orient Blackswan.

Dangle, Arjun, ed. 1992. *Poisoned Bread: Translations from Modern Marathi Dalit Literature*. Hyderabad: Orient Longman.

Das, Bhagwan. 2010a. *In Pursuit of Ambedkar: A Memoir*. New Delhi: Navayana.

——., ed. 2010b. *Thus Spoke Ambedkar, Vol. 1: A Stake in the Nation*. New Delhi: Navayana.

Debroy, Bibek, tr. 2005. *The Bhagavad Gita*. New Delhi: Penguin.

Deshpande, G.P., ed. 2002 *Selected Writings of Jotirao Phule*. New Delhi: LeftWord.

Dewey, John. 1916. *Democracy and Education: An Introduction to the Philosophy of Education*. Repr. New York: Macmillan, 1958. Indian ed. Aakar Books. New Delhi: 2004. Available online: Electronic Text Center, University of Virginia Library: http://etext.lib.virginia.edu/toc/modeng/public/DewDemo.html. Accessed 15 March 2013.

——. 1922. "The Nature of Principles." In *Human Nature and Conduct: An Introduction to Social Psychology*, 238–47. New York: Modern Library.

Dharmateertha, Swami. 1941. *The Menace of Hindu Imperialism*. Krishnanagar, Lahore: Happy Home Publication. New edition: *No Freedom with Caste: The Menace of Hindu Imperialism*. Ed. and introd. by G. Aloysius. New Delhi: Media House, 2004.

Dicey, Albert Venn. 1885. *Introduction to the Study of the Law of the Constitution*. London: Macmillan.

Dirks, Nicholas B. 2001. *Castes of Mind: Colonialism and the Making of Modern India*. New Delhi: Permanent Black.

Doniger, Wendy, ed. 1993. *Purana Perennis: Reciprocity and Transformation in Hindu and Jaina Texts*. New York: SUNY Press.

—— and Brian K. Smith. Tr. 1991. *The Laws of Manu*. New Delhi: Penguin Books.

D'Souza, Dilip. 2001. *Branded by Law: Looking at India's Denotified Tribes*. New Delhi: Penguin.

Dutt, R.C. 1980. *Socialism of Jawaharlal Nehru*. New Delhi: Abhinav.

Eames, S. Morris. 1969. "Introduction." *The Early Works of John Dewey, 1882–1898: Essays and Outlines of a Critical Theory of Ethics, 1889–1892*, vol. 3. Carbondale: Southern Illinois University Press.

Eaton, Richard M. 2005. "Tarabai (1675–1761): The Rise of Brahmins in Politics." In *A Social History of the Deccan, 1300–1761: Eight Indian Lives*, 177–201. The New Cambridge History of India 8. Cambridge: Cambridge University Press.

Falahi, Masood Alam. 2007. *Hindustan mein zaat-paat aur Musalman* [Casteism in India and Muslims]. New Delhi: Al Qazi Publishers.

Figueira, Dorothy. 2002. *Aryans, Jews, Brahmins: Theorizing Authority through Myths of Identity*. New York: SUNY Press.

Fontenrose, Joseph. 1978. *The Delphic Oracle: Its Responses and Operations, with a Catalogue of Responses*. Berkeley: University of California Press.

Fuller, C.J. "Caste." 2003. In *The Oxford India Companion to Sociology and Social Anthropology*. Ed. Veena Das, 477–501. Oxford: Oxford University Press.

Fürer Haimendorf, Christoph von. 1982. *Tribes of India: The Struggle for Survival*. Berkley: University of California Press.

Gaekwad, Fatehsinhrao. 1989. *Sayajirao of Baroda: The Prince and the Man*. Bombay: Popular Prakashan.

Gandhi, M.K. 1925. "Varnashrama and Untouchability." *Young India*, 3 August.

——. 1920. "Caste versus Class." *Young India*, 29 December. Repr. CWMG, vol. 22, 154–5.

——. 1931. *Mahatma Gandhi: His Own Story*. Ed. C.F. Andrews. New York: Macmillan.

——. 1997. *Hind Swaraj and Other Writings of M.K. Gandhi*. Ed. and annotated by Anthony Parel. Cambridge: Cambridge University Press.

——. 1999. *The Collected Works of Mahatma Gandhi* (Electronic Book). 98 volumes. New Delhi: Publications Division, Government of India.

Gandhi, Rajmohan. 2007. *Gandhi: The Man, His People, and the Empire*. New Delhi: Penguin.

Ghurye, Govind Sadashiv. 1969. *Caste and Race in India*. New Delhi: Popular Prakashan.

Giddings, Franklin H. 2004. *The Principles of Sociology*. New Delhi: Cosmo. (Orig. publ. 1896.)

Gramsci, Antonio. 1971. *Selections from Prison Notebooks*. New York: International Publishers.

Halbfass, Wilhelm. 1990. *Tradition and Reflection: Explorations in Indian Thought*. New York: SUNY Press.

Hansen, Thomas Blom. 1999. *The Saffron Wave Democracy and Hindu Nationalism in Modern India*. New Jersey: Princeton University Press.

Hardiman, David. 2004. *Gandhi: In His Time and Ours: The Global Legacy of His Ideas*. New York: Columbia University Press.

Harvey, R.D. 1995. "Pioneers of Genetics: A Comparison of the Attitudes of William Bateson and Erwin Baur to Eugenics." *Notes and Records of the Royal Society of London* 49 (1): 105–17.

Hassan, Syed Sirajul. 1920. *The Castes and Tribes of H.E.H. the Nizam's Dominions: Vol. 1*. Bombay: The Times Press.

Hawley, John Stratton. 2005. *Three Bhakti Voices: Mirabai, Surdas, and Kabir in Their Time and Ours*. New Delhi: Oxford University Press.

Hess, Linda and Shukdeo Singh. 2002. *The Bijak of Kabir*. New Delhi: Oxford University Press.

——. 2009. *Singing Emptiness: Kumar Gandharva Performs the Poetry of Kabir.* Calcutta: Seagull Books.

Holt, Mara. 1994. "Dewey and the 'Cult of Efficiency': Competing Ideologies in Collaborative Pedagogies of the 1920s." *Journal of Advanced Composition* 14 (1): 73–92.

Jackson, Alvin. 2003. *Home Rule: An Irish History, 1800–2000*. Oxford: Oxford University Press.

Jaffrelot, Christophe. 1995. "The Genesis and Development of Hindu Nationalism in the Punjab: From the Arya Samaj to the Hindu Sabha (1875–1990)." *The Indo-British Review* 21 (1): 3–39.

——. 1999a. "Militant Hindus and the Conversion Issue (1885–1990): From Shuddhi to Dharm Parivartan: The Politicization and the Diffusion of an 'Invention of Tradition'." In *The Resources of History: Tradition and Narration in South Asia*. Ed. J. Assayag. 127–52. Paris: EFEO.

——. 1999b. *The Hindu Nationalist Movement and Indian Politics, 1925 to the 1990s: Strategies of Identity-building, Implantation and Mobilization*. New Delhi: Penguin.

——. 2005. *Dr Ambedkar and Untouchability: Analysing and Fighting Caste*. New Delhi: Permanent Black.

——. 2010. *Religion, Caste, and Politics in India*. New Delhi: Primus Books.

Jalal, Ayesha. 1985. *The Sole Spokesman: Jinnah, the Muslim League and the Demand for Pakistan*. Cambridge: Cambridge University Press.

Jha, Ganganatha. 1942. *The Purva-Mimamsa Sutras of Jaimini: With an Original Commentary in English*. Banaras: Banaras Hindu University.

Johnson, Gordon. 2005. *Provincial Politics and Indian Nationalism: Bombay and the Indian National Congress*. Cambridge: Cambridge University Press.

Jolly, Julius. 1889. *The Minor Lawbooks: Narada and Brihaspati*. Sacred Texts of the East, vol. 33. Oxford: Clarendon Press. http://www.sacred-texts.com/hin/sbe33/index.htm. Accessed 1 March 2013.

Jones, Kenneth W. 2006. *Arya Dharm: Hindu Consciousness in 19th Century Punjab*. Delhi: Manohar. (Orig. publ. 1976.)

Jones, William. 1796. *Institutes of Hindu law, or, The Ordinances of Menu*. Calcutta: Government; London: J. Sewell, Cornhill; and J. Debrett.

Juergensmeyer, Mark. 2009. *Religious Rebels in the Punjab: The Ad Dharm Challenge to Caste*. New Delhi: Navayana. (Orig. publ. 1982.)

Kak, Sanjay. 1997. *One Weapon*. DVD, documentary film.

Karlsson, Bengt G. 2011. *Unruly Hills: Nature and Nation in India's Northeast*. New Delhi: Social Sciences Press.

Keer, Dhananjay. 1990. *Dr Ambedkar: Life and Mission*. Bombay: Popular Prakashan. (Orig. publ. 1954.)

Kela, Shashank. 2012. *A Rogue and Peasant Slave: Adivasi Resistance 1800–2000*. New Delhi: Navayana.

Ketkar, S.V. 1998. *History of Caste in India*. New Delhi: Low Price Publications. (Orig. publ. 1909.)

Khan, Shafa'at Ahmad. 1937. *The Indian Federation: An Exposition and Critical Review*. London: Macmillan.

Klaus K. Klostermaier, 2007. *A Survey of Hinduism*. New York: SUNY Press.

Knoll, Michael. 2009. "From Kidd to Dewey: The Origin and Meaning of 'Social Efficiency'." *Journal of Curriculum Studies* 41 (3): 361–91.

Kopf, David. 1979. *The Brahmo Samaj and the Shaping of the Modern Indian Mind*. Princeton, N.J.: Princeton University Press.

Kosambi, D.D. 1962. *Myth and Reality: Studies in the Formation of Indian Culture*. Bombay: Popular Prakashan.

Krishan, Gopal. 2004. "Demography of the Punjab (1849–1947)." *Journal of Punjab Studies* 11(1): 77–89.

Kshirsagar, R.K. 1994. *Dalit Movement in India and its Leaders, 1857–1956*. New Delhi: MD Publications.

Kumar, Aishwary. 2010. "Ambedkar's Inheritances." *Modern Intellectual History* 7 (2): 391–415.

——. 2014 (forthcoming). *Equality at War: Ambedkar, Gandhi, and the Antinomies of Democracy*. Stanford: Stanford University Press.

Kumar, Krishna. 1989. "Colonial Citizen as an Educational Ideal."

Economic & Political Weekly, 28 January: 45–51.

Kumar, Ravinder. 1985. "Ambedkar, Gandhi and the Poona Pact." *South Asia: Journal of South Asian Studies* 8 (1–2): 87–101.

Laine, James. 2003. *Shivaji: Hindu King in Islamic India*. New Delhi: Oxford University Press.

Lassalle, Ferdinand. 1862 "On the Essence of Constitutions." Speech delivered on 16 April. Berlin. Repr. *Fourth International* 3 (1), January 1942: 25–31. http://www.marxists.org/history/etol/newspape/fi/vol03/no01/lassalle.htm. Accessed 16 February 2013.

Lele, Jayant, ed. 1981. *Tradition and Modernity in Bhakti Movements*. Leideon: E.J. Brill.

Lelyveld, Joseph. 2011. *Great Soul: Mahatma Gandhi and His Struggle With India*. New York: Alfred A. Knopf.

Livy. 2006. *The History of Rome: Books 1–5*. Tr. Valerie Warrior. Indianapolis: Hackett Publishing Company, Inc.

Lochtefeld, James. 2002. *The Illustrated Encyclopedia of Hinduism*, vol 1. New York: Rosen Publishing Group.

Lorenzen, David N. 2006. "Who Invented Hinduism?" In *Who Invented Hinduism: Essays on Religion in History*, 1–36. New Delhi: Yoda Press.

Louis, Prakash. 2003. *The Political Sociology of Dalit Assertion*. New Delhi: Gyan Publishing.

Lucas, Scott. 2004. *Constructive Critics, Hadith Literature, and the Articulation of Sunni Islam: The Legacy of the Generation of Ibn Seed, Ibn Main, and Ibn Hanbal*. Leiden: Brill. Majumdar, Janaki Agnes Penelope. 2003. *Family History*. Ed. Antoinette Burton. New Delhi: Oxford University Press.

Marcuse, Herbert. 1991. *One-Dimensional Man: Studies in the Ideology of Advanced Industrial Society*. Massachusetts: Beacon Press. (Orig. publ. 1964.)

Marx, Karl, 1865. "Letter to Ludwig Kugelman." 23 February. Marx & Engels Internet Archive. http://www.marxists.org/archive/marx/works/1865/letters/65_02_23.htm. Accessed 16 February 2013.

Marx, Karl, and Friedrich Engels. 2004. *The Communist Manifesto*. London: Penguin. (Orig. publ. 1848.)

McLane, John R. 1988. "The Early Congress, Hindu Populism, and the Wider Society." In *Congress and Indian Nationalism: The Pre-*

Independence Phase. Ed. Richard Sisson and Stanley A. Wolpert. California: University of Berkeley Press.

Michaels, Axel. 2005. *Hinduism: Past and Present*. New Delhi: Orient Longman.

Mill, John Stuart. 1984. "A Few Words on Non-Intervention." In *The Collected Works of John Stuart Mill*, vol. 21. Toronto: The University of Toronto Press. (Orig. publ. 1859.) http://oll.libertyfund.org/?option=com_staticxt&staticfile=show.php%3Ftitle=255&chapter=21666&layout=html&Itemid=27. Accessed 18 March 2013.

——. 2004. *Considerations on Representative Government*. Online publ. Pennsylvania: The Pennsylvania State University. (Orig. publ. 1861.) http://www2.hn.psu.edu/faculty/jmanis/jsmill/considerations.pdf. Accessed 20 March 2013.

Monius, Anne. 2009. *Imagining a Place for Buddhism. Literary Culture and Religious Community in Tamil-Speaking South India*. New Delhi: Navayana.

Morris, William. 1888. *A Dream of John Ball*. http://morrisedition.lib.uiowa.edu/dream1888text.html. Accessed 20 March 2013.

Mosse, David. 2012. *The Saint in the Banyan Tree: Christianity and Caste Society in India*. Berkeley: University of California Press.

Mukherjee, Arun P. 2009. "B.R. Ambedkar, John Dewey, and the Meaning of Democracy." *New Literary History* 40 (2): 345–70.

Naregal, Veena. 2001. *Language Politics, Elites, and the Public Sphere: Western India Under Colonialism*. New Delhi: Permanent Black.

Nauriya, Anil, 2006. "Gandhi's Little-Known Critique of Varna." *Economic & Political Weekly*, 13 May: 1835–8.

——. 2012. "Gandhi and Some Contemporary African Leaders from KwaZulu-Natal." *Natalia* 42: 45–64.

Naval, T.R. 2004. *Legally Combating Atrocities on Scheduled Castes and Scheduled Tribes*. New Delhi: Concept Publishing Company.

O'Brien, John A. 1947. *Truths Men Live By: A Philosophy of Religions and Life*. New York: Macmillan.

O'Day, Alan. 1998. *Irish Home Rule, 1867–1921*. Manchester: Manchester University Press.

O'Hanlon, Rosalind. 2002. *Caste, Conflict and Ideology: Mahatma Jotirao Phule and Low-Caste Protest in Nineteenth-Century Western India*.

Cambridge: Cambridge University Press.

——. 2010a. "Letters Home: Banaras Pandits and the Maratha Regions in Early Modern India". *Modern Asian Studies* 44 (2): 201–40.

——. 2010b. "The Social Worth of Scribes: Brahmins, Kayasthas and the Social Order in Early Modern India." *Indian Economic Social History Review* 47 (4): 563–96.

Olivelle, Patrick. 2005. *Manu's Code of Law: A Critical Edition and Translation of the Manava-Dharmasastra*. New York: Oxford University Press.

——. 2008. *Collected Essays 1—Language, Texts and Society: Explorations in Ancient Indian Culture and Religion*. Florence: University of Florence Press.

Omvedt, Gail. 1976. *Cultural Revolt in a Colonial Society: The Non-Brahman Movement in Western India, 1873–1930*. Bombay: Scientific Socialist Education Trust.

——. 1994. *Dalits and the Democratic Revolution: Dr Ambedkar and the Dalit Movement in Colonial India*. New Delhi: Sage.

——. 2003. *Buddhism in India: Challenging Brahmanism and Caste*. New Delhi: Sage.

——. 2004. *Ambedkar: Towards an Enlightened India*. New Delhi: Penguin.

——. 2008. *Seeking Begumpura: The Social Vision of Anticaste Intellectuals*. New Delhi: Navayana.

Oommen, T.K. 2005. *Crisis and Contention in Indian Society*. New Delhi: Sage.

Oppenheim, Lassa Francis. 1905. *International Law: A Treatise*, vol. 2. London: Longmans Green and Co.

Pandit, Nalini. 1992. "Ambedkar and the Bhagwat Gita." *Economic & Political Weekly*, 16 May: 1063–5.

Pappas, Gregory Fernando. 2008. *John Dewey's Ethics: Democracy as Experience*. Bloomington: Indiana University Press.

Parel, Anthony, ed. 2000. *Gandhi, Freedom, and Self-Rule*. Oxford: Lexington.

——. Parel, Anthony, ed. 1997. *'Hind Swaraj' and Other Writings*. Cambridge: Cambridge University Press.

Parpola, Asko. 1981. "On the Formation of the Mimamsa and the Problems concerning Jaimini, With Particular Reference to the

Teacher Quotations and the Vedic Schools, Part 1." *Wiener Zeitschrift für die Kunde Südasiens* 25: 145–9.

Prashad, Vijay. 1996. "The Untouchable Question." *Economic & Political Weekly*, 2 March: 551–9.

——. 2001. *Untouchable Freedom: A Social History of a Dalit Community*. New Delhi: Oxford University Press.

Puri, Harish K. 2003. "Scheduled Castes in Sikh Community: A Historical Perspective." *Economic & Political Weekly*, 4 July: 2693–701.

Pyarelal. 1932. *The Epic Fast*. Ahmedabad: Navajivan.

Radhakrishna, Meena. 2001. *Dishonoured by History: 'Criminal Tribes' and British Colonial Policy*. New Delhi: Orient Longman.

Radhakrishnan, S. 1927. *The Hindu Way of Life*. London: George Allen and Unwin Ltd.

Raghavan, T.C.A. 1983. "Origins and Development of Hindu Mahasabha Ideology: The Call of V.D. Savarkar and Bhai Parmanand." *Economic & Political Weekly* 9 April: 595–600.

Rajah, M.C. 1925. *The Oppressed Hindus.* Madras: The Huxley Press:

Ramasamy, Anushiya. 2010. "Where Reason is Dazzled and Magic Regins Supreme." In N.D. Rajkumar, *Give Us This Day a Feast of Flesh: Poems from Tamil*. New Delhi: Navayana.

Ramaswamy, Gita. 2005. "Mohandas Gandhi on Manual Scavenging." Appendix 4. In *India Stinking: Manual Scavengers in Andhra Pradesh and Their Work*, 86–95. Chennai: Navayana.

Rangarajan. L.N., tr. 1992. *Kautilya: The Arthashastra*. New Delhi: Penguin.

Rao, Anupama. 2009. *The Caste Question: Dalits and the Politics of Modern India*. Berkeley: University of California Press.

Rao, Parimala V. n.d. "Educating Women and Non-Brahmins as 'Loss of Nationality': Bal Gangadhar Tilak and the Nationalist Agenda in Maharashtra." CWDS Occasional Paper. http://www.cwds.ac.in/OCPaper/EducatingWomen-Parimala.pdf. Accessed 30 March 2013.

Rawat, Ramnarayan. 2001. "Partition Politics and Achhut Identity: A Study of the Scheduled Castes Federation and Dalit Politics in UP, 1946–48." In *The Partitions of Memory: The Afterlife of the Division of India*. Ed. Suvir Kaul, 111–39. New Delhi: Permanent Black.

Rege, Sharmila. 2013. *Against the Madness of Manu: B.R. Ambedkar's*

Writings on Brahmanical Patriarchy. New Delhi: Navayana.

Renold, Leah. 1994. "Gandhi: Patron Saint of the Industrialist." *Sagar: South Asia Graduate Research Journal* 1 (1): 16–38.

Roy, T.N. 1927. "Hindu Eugenics." *The Journal of Heredity* 18 (2): 67–72.

Rüpke, Jörg, ed. 2007. *A Companion to Roman Religion*. Oxford: Blackwell.

Sant Ram, B.A. 2008 *Mere jivan ke anubhav* [Experiences of my life]. Repr. New Delhi: Gautam Book Centre. (Orig. pub. 1963.)

Sarkar, Sir Jadunath. 1948. *Shivaji and His Times*. Calcutta: S.C. Sarkar and Sons.

Satyanarayana, K. and Susie Tharu, ed. 2013. *The Exercise of Freedom: An Introduction to Dalit Writing*. New Delhi: Navayana.

Schimmel, Annemarie. 1975. *Mystical Dimensions of Islam*. North Carolina: University of North Carolina Press.

Sharma, Jyotirmaya. 2012. *Cosmic Love and Human Apathy: Swami Vivekananda's Restatement of Religion*. New Delhi: HarperCollins.

Shourie, Arun. 1997. *Worshipping False Gods: Ambedkar and the Facts which have been Erased*. New Delhi: ASA Publishers.

Siim, Birte and Monika Mokre. 2013. *Negotiating Gender and Diversity in an Emergent European Public Sphere*. Hampshire: Palgrave Macmillan.

Singleton, Mark. 2007. "Yoga, Eugenics, and Spiritual Darwinism in the Early Twentieth Century." *International Journal of Hindu Studies* 11 (2): 125–46.

Škof, Lenart. 2011. "Pragmatism and Deepened Democracy: Ambedkar Between Dewey and Unger." In *Democratic Culture: Historical and Philosophical Essays*. Ed. Akeel Bilgrami, 122–42. New Delhi: Routledge.

Spencer, Herbert . 1873. *The Study of Sociology*. London: Henry S. King.

Srinivas, M.N. 1972. *Social Change in Modern India*. Hyderabad: Orient Longman. (Orig. publ. 1966.)

Streets, Heather. 2004. *Martial Races: The Military, Race and Masculinity in British Imperial Culture, 1857–1914*. Manchester: Manchester University Press.

Swaris, Nalin. 2011. *The Buddha's Way to Human Liberation: A Socio-Historical Approach*. New Delhi: Navayana.

Tejani, Shabnum. 2013. "The Necessary Conditions for Democracy: B.R. Ambedkar on Nationalism, Minorities and Pakistan." *Economic*

& Political Weekly, 14 December: 111–19.

Tellegen-Couperus, Olga. 1993. *A Short History of Roman Law*. London: Routledge.

Thapar, Romila. 1989. "Syndicated Hindusim." *Hinduism Reconsidered*. Ed. Günther-Dietz Sontheimer and Hermann Kulke, 54–81. Delhi: Manohar.

Tilak, B.G. 1903. *The Arctic Home in the Vedas: Being Also a New Key to the Interpretation of Many Vedic Texts and Legends*. Pune: Tilak Bros.

——. 1935. *The Esoteric Import of the Gita* (Srimad Bhagavad Gita Rahasya). Tr. B.S. Sukthankar. Pune: Tilak Bros.

Tocqueville, Alexis de. *Democracy in America*. Tr. Henry Reeve. Available online at http://www.gutenberg.org/files/815/815-h/815-h.htm. Accessed 10 September 2013.

Usmani, Salman. 2008. "Shackling Water." *Tehelka*, 26 January.

Viswanathan, Gauri. 1998. *Outside the Fold: Conversion, Modernity, and Belief*. Princeton: Princeton University Press.

Wallace, Peter G. 2004. *The Long European Reformation: Religion, Political Conflict, and the Search for Conformity, 1350–1750*. New York: Palgrave Macmillan.

Woodhouse, A.S.P., ed. 1951. *Puritanism and Liberty, being the Army Debates (1647–9) from the Clarke Manuscripts with Supplementary Documents*. Chicago: University of Chicago Press. http://oll.libertyfund.org/?option=com_staticxt&staticfile=show.php%3Ftitle=2183. Accessed 25 August 2013.

Yadav, Kripal Chandra and Krishan Singh Arya. 1988. *Arya Samaj and the Freedom Movement: 1875–1918*. Delhi: Manohar.

Zelliot, Eleanor. 2013. *Ambedkar's World: The Making of Babasaheb and the Dalit Movement*. New Delhi: Navayana.

—— and Maxine Berntsen, ed. 1998. *The Experience of Hinduism: Essays on Religion in Maharashtra*. New York: SUNY Press.

——. 1970. "Learning the Use of Political Means: The Mahars of Maharashtra." In *Caste in Indian Politics*. Ed. Rajni Kothari, 29–69. New Delhi: Allied.

Zweiniger-Bargielowska, Ina. 2006. "Building a British Superman: Physical Culture in Interwar Britain." *Journal of Contemporary History* 41 (4): 595–610.

ACKNOWLEDGEMENTS

Arundhati Roy

For the privilege of being invited to write this introduction, I am indebted to my publisher and dear friend, S. Anand. I could not have wished for a finer, more committed and knowledgeable editor.

I should especially like to thank Gail Omvedt, Sharmila Rege, Anand Teltumbde, Eleanor Zelliot, Leah Renold, Vijay Prashad, Kathryn Tidrick and Rupa Viswanath whose work has enhanced my understanding of Gandhi and Ambedkar, as well as the complex history of the debates around caste. A special thanks to G.B. Singh whose book, *Gandhi: Behind the Mask of Divinity*, provided me with a rare archive of Gandhi's writings during his years in South Africa.

Several people read "The Doctor and the Saint" and their comments have been invaluable. My thanks to Thomas Blom Hansen, Satish Deshpande, Anand Teltumbde, Uma Chakravarti, Tarun Bharatiya and Pankaj Mishra. Nate R's close reading of my text, and his comments and criticism have fortified it in important ways.

For our many journeys across South Africa, for responding with profound perceptiveness to early drafts, for his published work on indentured labour and his soon-to-be-published writing on Gandhi in South Africa, I thank my friend Ashwin Desai.

I'm deeply grateful to my oldest friend Golak Khandual whose portrait of Dr Ambedkar is on the cover of this book.

Thanks too, to John Cusack for an observation that he will recognise as his when he reads it; to Jawed Naqvi for getting me riled up and setting me down on a trail which has become an important theme in this essay (which he will chuckle at when he recognises it); to Ravikumar for his book *Venomous Touch*, for his erudition and his insights and for our travels through Cuddalore; to Shohini Ghosh who helped me formulate a somewhat complicated idea and to Mayank Austen Soofi for inchoate and delightful things.

My gratitude to Kancha Ilaiah and Dr Mondru Francis Gopinath for all that I learned from meeting and talking to them, to my friend Pravin Anand who steered this project through some ridiculous roadblocks and to Arif Ayaz Parrey and Shyama Haldar for copy-editing the manuscript.

I will always be indebted to my agents David Godwin and Anthony Arnove for their cool heads and their wise counsel.

Pradip Krishen my earliest, most elegant and always editor helped me to comb the anger out of my writing.

Sanjay Kak read every one of the innumerable drafts of the manuscript. I thank him for his calm precision, for his important structural suggestions, for his attention to the most minute of details, and for always looking out for me.

Finally, I thank Dr B.R. Ambedkar for writing *Annihilation of Caste*.

ACKNOWLEDGEMENTS

S. Anand

The journey of battling caste began for me at a personal level—making a new life with Sivapriya (always rightly sceptical about my writing, my finest editor). This happened around the same time as my encounter with Kancha Ilaiah and his early work, *Why I am Not a Hindu*. He led me to Ambedkar in 1996, as did the Dalit students of B Hostel in Central University of Hyderabad in 1994 when they won a small battle to put up a portrait of Ambedkar in the TV room where Gandhi ubiquitously smiled down at us in singular glory. In Chennai, the team at *Dalit Murasu* led by Punitha Pandian and Jemima Alice offered me space and nurtured my ideas, and allowed me to join them in experimenting with the short-lived journal *The Dalit*, which also led me to Meena Kandasamy (who knows what I owe her). Pandian and Alice were both amused and circumspect about my enthusiasm, for Ambedkar does warn in *Annihilation of Caste*: "To expect a Brahmin to be a revolutionary in matters of social reform is as idle as to expect the British Parliament … to pass an Act requiring all blue-eyed babies to be murdered."

Then, there's Ravikumar—to whom I owe a debt words can't express. He sought to harness my energies and suggested the idea of a publishing house. Together we spawned this bastard child called Navayana in November 2003, and our first book was *Ambedkar: Autobiographical Notes*, for Rs 40. This edition of *Annihilation of Caste* would not have been possible without him.

Moving to Delhi in 2007, I met Bhagwan Das in his Munirka flat in Delhi. Das, along with Lahori Ram Balley of Jalandhar, had pioneered the publication of Ambedkar's writings and speeches in his *Thus Spoke Ambedkar* series in 1963. His work and life inspired me to soldier on with the task of annotating *Annihilation of Caste*. This edition is in many ways a tribute to him and scores like him in the Dalit movement who have kept the anticaste flame burning, who kept the faith.

Prakash Vishwasrao of Lokvangmaya Griha, Mumbai, connected

me with Ramesh Shinde, a passionate collector of Ambedkriana. Shinde generously gave us access to the May 1936 first edition of *Annihilation of Caste* as well as the 1937 and 1944 editions. My salaams to both Vishwasrao and Shinde.

In this journey, I have had the fortune of finding unstinting help from a range of friends and colleagues. First on this list is Juli Perczel. I could not have asked for a more dedicated research assistant at a time when work on the annotations was peaking. Nate and Rupa are part of a circle of love forged by shared politics. The two have literally held my hand through the final and testing stages of this enterprise.

I would also like to thank Uday Chandra, Nicolas Jaoul, Joel Lee and Sarah Hodges for friendship and solidarity; Rajeev Kumar, who has made work at Navayana easier for the last six years; Shyama Haldar who, at short notice, was there to copy-edit when I told her I could turn to none but her; Rimli Borooah, for proofing; Sanjiv Palliwal, friend and production man, for everything he does; Arif Ayaz Parrey, who walked in late into the project, for his unusual ardour for annotating concepts and terms that had escaped many eyes; Sanjay Kak for his calm observations on the Poona Pact essay; David Godwin for his generosity; Golak Khandual for the cover image; Pravin Anand and his team for their counsel.

Thanks are due to the peer reviewers of this book who generously allowed us to use their feedback as blurbs.

I would like to thank every author and translator who has placed faith in Navayana and published with us. There are those who have helped keep Navayana going: Akila Seshasayee, Hoshang Merchant, Ranvir Shah, Rama Lakshmi, Nithila Baskaran, Tara Brace-John, Aruna Rathnam.

Finally, Arundhati Roy, for reading *Annihilation of Caste* at my behest, ten years ago, and then agreeing to write the introduction. Ambedkar laid the foundation for our friendship.

INDEX